W9-CHF-147

Secured Transactions

Problems and Materials on Secured Transactions

Douglas J. Whaley
Professor of Law
The Ohio State University

Little, Brown and Company
Boston and Toronto

LIBRARY OF CONGRESS CATALOG CARD NO. 81-86024

Second Printing

ISBN 0-316-93216-7

HAD

Published simultaneously in Canada
by Little, Brown & Company (Canada) Limited

PRINTED IN THE UNITED STATES OF AMERICA

For My Son:
Clayton Robert Whaley

Summary of Contents

CONTENTS

PREFACE

This book explores the law of secured transactions and bulk transfers primarily through a series of problems designed to encourage the student to concentrate on the exact statutory language in the Uniform Commercial Code and related federal statutes.

Unfortunately, students reared on the case method sometimes have trouble concentrating on problem after problem. Such an attitude here can be academically fatal. As a guide to the degree of concentration required, I have used a hierarchy of signals. When the problem states "Read §9-203," I mean "Put down this book, pick up the Uniform Commercial Code, and study §9-203 carefully." When the instruction is "See §9-203," the reader need look at the cited section only if unsure of the answer. "Cf. §9-203" or simply "§9-203" are lesser references, included as a guide for the curious.

I have edited the footnotes out of most cases; the ones that remain have been stripped of their original numbering and have been consecutively numbered with my own footnotes. Unless clearly indicated otherwise, all footnotes in the cases are the court's own. I have also taken the liberty to change all statutory citations in cases to their simple Uniform Commercial Code form.

Everyone writing in this area owes an enormous debt to Professor Grant Gilmore for his peerless two volume treatise Security Interests in Personal Property (1965). I am no exception (and in fact the work so impressed me that I once wrote Professor Gilmore an unabashed fan letter). If not nonexistent, this book would be a great deal shorter and considerably less interesting but for the Gilmore treatise.

I also want to express my deep gratitude to the army of The Ohio State University typists who, under the direction of Dottie Flynn, struggled to put this material into regular form.

Finally, I thank my students who not only put up with this book in early unstructured versions but who taught me as much about secured transactions as I taught them.

Douglas J. Whaley
Columbus, Ohio

October 1, 1981

Secured Transactions

CHAPTER 1

INTRODUCTION TO SECURED TRANSACTIONS

It is understandable that someone extending credit in a sale or loan transaction wants to be sure of repayment. Some debtors are so solvent and/or trustworthy that the creditor demands nothing more than the debtor's promise to pay; creditors doing this are said to be *unsecured.* In many transactions the creditor is less sanguine about the debtor's ability or desire to repay, and may demand either a surety (called by various names: *co-signor, guarantor,* or, in Article 3 of the Uniform Commercial Code, an *accommodation party*) or that the debtor *secure* the debt by nominating some of the debtor's current or future property as collateral. If the debtor defaults the collateral may be seized and sold and the proceeds of the sale used to pay the debt.

A basic problem with mastering the law of secured transactions has always been in understanding the terminology: *lien, pledge, perfection, purchase money security interest,* etc. The terminology is complex because historically what we now call *secured transactions* has its source in many separate business devices, each with an individual set of descriptive terms, and on top of which Article 9 of the Uniform Commerical Code places a new and different nomenclature. To understand the pre-Code cases and the Code commentators' references to these pre-Code devices, it is necessary to have some minimal appreciation of how creditors protected their interests prior to the adoption of the UCC.

The core problem is that when a debtor cannot pay the bills, creditors must look to the debtor's property for whatever satisfaction they will get. These creditors must compete with other claimants for the property: donees, buyers, and (if financial death has occurred) the debtor's bankruptcy trustee. Worse yet, the creditors must compete with each other, and the law must somehow provide rules to determine who among all these individuals is to receive the property. As fast as the lawmakers create one set of statutes, those in business and their advisors think up new contractual arrangements that the statutes do not cover, and the law is chaotic until a new group of statutes can be added to those already regulating similar practices. (And, as we shall see, a new statute creates its own legal problems.)

Although it is impossible to make a categorical statement about this, generally the prior statutes regulating these matters established a hierarchy of winners in the derby to divide up the debtor's assets. Assuming a claimant qualifies, a "bona fide purchaser [BFP] in the ordinary course of business" was (and still is under Article 9) a favorite in the race. Another current favorite is the bankruptcy trustee who represents all of the bankrupt's unsecured creditors, and to whom the federal bankruptcy statute gives an awesome arsenal of weapons with which to attack the supposed interests that secured creditors assert in the estate's property. As of the date of the filing of the bankruptcy petition the trustee (and all the claims the trustee represents) is conclusively presumed to occupy the legal position of a judicial lien creditor who has levied on all of the bankrupt's property. If a creditor's claim to the property will survive the attack of the bankruptcy trustee, the creditor's security interest (*lien*) is said to be *perfected*. Perfection of the security interest then becomes the ultimate goal of any creditor taking an interest in the debtor's collateral. And — again this is a generality — creditors with perfected security interests not only beat out the bankruptcy trustee, they win over non-BFPs, creditors without perfected security interests, creditors whose security interests were perfected later in time, and creditors with no security interests at all (called, in bankruptcy parlance, *general creditors:* typically the corner grocer, the family doctor, etc.).

How is a creditor's security interest perfected? The answer depends on the nature of the collateral, the technical steps required by the statutes (or the courts if the legislature has not yet acted), and the particular moment in history in which the question is asked. Before embarking on a description of the major pre-Code security devices, there follows a brief outline of the bankruptcy rules against which the validity of these devices (and Article 9) must be viewed.

A. *BANKRUPTCY*

The United States Constitution states that Congress shall pass laws pertaining to bankruptcy; the result is the Bankruptcy Reform Act of 1978, 11 U.S.C. §§101 et seq. (hereinafter referred to as the Bankruptcy Code). There are three primary types of bankruptcy: straight bankruptcy (the normal type), Chapter XI (an "arrangement" proceeding for businesses), and Chapter XIII (an "arrangement" proceeding for wage earners). The vast majority of bankruptcies are straight bankruptcies, and over 90 percent of those are filed by individuals, as opposed to businesses. Consequently the rest of this discussion is a sketch of the proceedings in straight bankruptcy.

To commence bankruptcy, the debtor (a *voluntary* bankruptcy) or the debtor's creditors (an *involuntary* bankruptcy) files a petition with the bankruptcy court. This is a federal court under the direction of the local federal district court. The date on which the petition is filed is important because it is the measuring moment for many of the Act's sections. Along with the petition the debtor will file lists (called *schedules*) showing assets and creditors. The creditors are then summoned to a meeting (called, not unaptly, the *first meeting of creditors*) at which they get together and elect someone (called the *trustee*) to gather up the debtor's property, sell it, and represent their interests in the distributing of the proceeds. If the debtor's property must be tended to *before* the first meeting of creditors (say, for instance, a circus goes bankrupt — someone must see to it that the menagerie doesn't run loose), the bankruptcy judge appoints a temporary custodian (called an *interim trustee*), who acts until the trustee can take over.

The trustee collects the debtor's property. This can be a more complicated task than it may sound like. If other people claim the property (creditors, a relative who was the recipient of a very generous birthday gift, or even the bankrupt should there be an argument over *exempt* assets), the trustee may have to litigate the issue either before the bankruptcy judge or in the state or federal courts. Property exempt from bankruptcy under federal or, in some jurisdictions, state law and worthless property (the bankrupt's cat, for example) are returned to the bankrupt. The bankrupt then petitions the bankruptcy judge for a *discharge* (read *forgiveness*) of all the scheduled debts so that life can be resumed financially unburdened. With certain exceptions, bankrupts usually receive a discharge from most debts.

When the trustee gathers the estate's property, creditors with perfected security interests get their debts paid *first* from the sale of collateral which secured the debts owed to those creditors. The rest of the assets of the estate are also sold and the proceeds are used to pay the expenses of the bankruptcy proceeding, wages of the bankrupt's employees, some tax claims, certain other priority claimants, and, finally, the general creditors (who get nothing until all the above are paid in full).

The trustee need not accept the creditor's statement that the creditor has a perfected security interest; the validity (*perfection*) of the security interest is a matter of state law and will be measured by state standards. If the security interest is finally determined to be *unperfected,* the interest is destroyed and the creditor becomes just another general (*unsecured*) creditor. Not only is the trustee armed (as has been mentioned) with the position of a perfect *lien* creditor coming into existence on the date of the petition filing (Bankruptcy Code §544(a)), but the trustee also occupies the same legal position as any actual existing creditor (Bankruptcy Code §544(b)). Further the Bankruptcy Code codifies the old common law maxim that a debtor must "be just before he is generous." Section 547 of the Bankruptcy Code condemns as a *preference* the following type of conduct:

> On January 1, Alice owed to Tom, Dick, and Harry $1000 each for past due loans. On May 1st she paid Tom $1000 and the next day she filed a voluntary petition in bankruptcy.

Section 547 provides that many payments made by an insolvent debtor to an existing creditor within 90 days of the date of the filing of the petition are void as *preferences.* The trustee can recover the payment from the preferred creditor. (The fairness of §547 to Dick and Harry should be obvious.)

A final practical note worth remembering: in most bankruptcies the unsecured creditors receive NOTHING. For this reason most creditors want security (collateral) for their debts and they want their lawyers to advise them how they can perfect that security against other creditors and the bankruptcy trustee.

B. *PRE-CODE SECURITY DEVICES*

Students who know nothing other than Article 9 (and, as to real property creditor conflicts, know only what they learned in their basic property course), may not appreciate the wide variety of devices the UCC replaced. Such a student may ask why all these devices, particularly those which were very similar, were needed. The answer is historical. Our legal ancestors (lawyers, judges, and legislators) had some rigid ideas about what was transferable property (a diamond ring) and what was not (a right to sue your customer if the bill wasn't paid) and about the propriety of certain business practices that now seem commonplace. We begin our study with a famous case.

Benedict v. Ratner

268 U.S. 353, 45 S. Ct. 566 (1925)

Mr. Justice BRANDEIS. The Hub Carpet Company was adjudicated bankrupt by the federal court for southern New York in involuntary proceedings commenced September 26, 1921. Benedict, who was appointed receiver and later trustee, collected the book accounts of the company. Ratner filed in that court a petition in equity praying that the amounts so collected be paid over to him. He claimed them under a writing given May 23, 1921 — four months and three days before the commencement of the bankruptcy proceedings. By it the company purported to assign to him, as collateral for certain loans, all accounts present and future. Those collected by the receiver were, so far as appears, all accounts which had arisen after the date of the assignment, and were enumerated in the monthly list of accounts outstanding which was delivered to Ratner September 23. Benedict resisted the petition on the ground that the original assignment was void under the law of New York as a fraudulent conveyance; that, for this reason, the delivery of the September list of accounts was inoperative to perfect a lien in Ratner; and that it was a preference under the Bankruptcy Act. He also filed a cross-petition in which he asked that Ratner be ordered to pay to the estate the proceeds of certain collections which had been made by the company after September 17 and turned over to Ratner pursuant to his request made on that day. The company was then insolvent and Ratner had reason to believe it to be so. These accounts also had apparently been acquired by the company after the date of the original assignment.

The District Judge decided both petitions in Ratner's favor. He ruled that the assignment executed in May was not fraudulent in law; that it created an equity in the future acquired accounts; that because of this equity, Ratner was entitled to retain, as against the bankrupt's estate, the proceeds of the accounts which had been collected by the company in September and turned over to him; that by delivery of the list of the accounts outstanding on September 23, this equity in them had ripened into a perfect title to the remaining accounts; and that the title so perfected was good as against the supervening bankruptcy. Accordingly, the District Court ordered that, to the extent of the balance remaining unpaid on his loans, there be paid Ratner all collections made from accounts enumerated in any of the lists delivered to Ratner; and that the cross-petition of Benedict be denied. There was no finding of fraud in fact. On appeal, the Circuit Court of Appeals affirmed the order. 282 Fed. 12. A writ of cetiorari was granted by this Court. 259 U.S. 579.

The rights of the parties depend primarily upon the law of New York. Hiscock v. Varick Bank of N.Y., 206 U.S. 28. It may be assumed that, unless the arrangement of May 23 was void because fraudulent in law, the original assignment of the future acquired accounts became operative under the state law, both as to those paid over to Ratner before the bankruptcy proceedings and as to those collected by the receiver; and that the assignment will be deemed to have taken effect as of May 23. Sexton v. Kessler, 225 U.S. 90, 99. That being so, it is clear that, if the original assignment was a valid one under the law of New York, the Bankruptcy Act did not invalidate the subsequent dealings of the parties. Thompson v. Fairbanks, 196 U.S. 516; Humphrey v. Tatman, 198 U.S. 91. The sole question for decision is, therefore, whether on the following undisputed facts the assignment of May 23 was in law fraudulent.

The Hub Carpet Company was, on May 23, a mercantile concern doing business in New York City and proposing to continue to do so. The assignment was made there to secure an existing loan of $15,000, and further advances not exceeding $15,000 which were in fact made July 1, 1921. It included all accounts receivable then outstanding and all which should thereafter accrue in the ordinary course of business. A list of the existing accounts was delivered at the time. Similar lists were to be delivered to Ratner on or about the 23rd day of each succeeding month containing the accounts outstanding at such future dates. Those enumerated in each of the lists delivered prior to September, aggregated between $100,000 and $120,000. The receivables were to be collected by the company. Ratner was given the right, at any time, to demand a full disclosure of the business and financial conditions; to require that all amounts collected be applied in payment of his loans; and to enforce the assignment although no loan had matured. But until he did so, the company was not required to apply any of the collections to the repayment of Ratner's loan. It was not required to replace accounts collected by other collateral of equal value. It was not required to account in any way to Ratner. It was at liberty to use the proceeds of all accounts collected as it might see fit. The existence of the assignment was to be kept secret. The business was to be conducted as theretofore. Indebtedness was to be incurred, as usual, for the purchase of merchandise and otherwise in the ordinary course of business. The amount of such indebtedness unpaid at the time of the commencement of the bankruptcy proceedings was large. Prior to September 17, the company collected from accounts so assigned about $150,000, all of which it applied to purposes other than the payment of Ratner's loan. The outstanding accounts enumerated in the list delivered September 23 aggregated $90,000.

Under the law of New York a transfer of property as security which reserves to the transferor the right to dispose of the same, or to apply the proceeds thereof, for his own uses is, as to creditors, fraudulent in law and void. This is true whether the right of disposition for the transferor's use be reserved in the instrument or by agreement in pais, oral or written; whether the right of disposition reserved be unlimited in time or be expressly terminable by the happening of an event; whether the transfer cover all the property of the debtor or only a part; whether the right of disposition extends to all the property transferred or only to a part thereof; and whether the instrument of transfer be recorded or not.

If this rule applies to the assignment of book accounts, the arrangement of May 23 was clearly void; and the equity in the future acquired accounts, which it would otherwise have created, did not arise. Whether the rule applies to accounts does not appear to have been passed upon by the Court of Appeals of New York. But it would seem clear that whether the collateral consist of chattels or of accounts, reservation of dominion inconsistent with the effective disposition of title must render the transaction void. Ratner asserts that the rule stated above rests upon ostensible ownership, and argues that the doctrine of ostensible ownership is not applicable to book accounts. That doctrine raises a presumption of fraud where chattels are mortgaged (or sold) and possession of the property is not delivered to the mortgagee (or vendee). The presumption may be avoided by recording the mortgage (or sale). It may be assumed, as Ratner contends, that the doctrine does not apply to the assignment of accounts. In their transfer there is nothing which corresponds to the delivery of possession of chattels. The statutes which embody the doctrine and provide for recording as a substitute for delivery do not include accounts. A title to an account good against creditors may be transferred without notice to the debtor or record of any kind. But it is not true that the rule stated above and invoked by the receiver is either based upon or delimited by the doctrine of ostensible ownership. It rests not upon seeming ownership because of possession retained, but upon a lack of ownership because of dominion reserved. It does not raise a presumption of fraud. It imputs fraud conclusively because of the reservation of dominion inconsistent with the effective disposition of title and creation of a lien.

The nature of the rule is made clear by its limitations. Where the mortgagor of chattels agrees to apply the proceeds of their sale to the payment of the mortgage debt or to the purchase of other chattels which shall become subject to the lien, the mortgage is good as against creditors, if recorded. The mortgage is sustained in such cases "upon the ground that such sale and application of proceeds is the normal and proper purpose of a chattel mortgage, and within the precise boundaries of its lawful operation and effect. It does no more than to substitute the mortgagor as the agent of the mortgagee to do exactly what the latter had the right to do, and what it was his privilege and his duty to accomplish. It devotes, as it should, the mortgaged property to the payment of the mortgage debt." The permission to use the proceeds to furnish substitute collateral "provides only for a shifting of the lien from one piece of property to another taken in exchange." Brackett v. Harvey, 91 N.Y. 214, 221, 223. On the other hand, if the agreement is that the mortgagor may sell and use the proceeds for his own benefit, the mortgage is of no effect although recorded. Seeming ownership exists in both classes of cases because the mortgagor is permitted to remain in possession of the stock in trade and to sell it freely. But it is only where the unrestricted dominion over the proceeds is reserved to the mortgagor that the mortgage is void. This dominion is the differentiating and deciding element. The distinction was recognized in Sexton v. Kessler, 225 U.S. 90, 98, 32 S. Ct. 657, where a transfer of securities was sustained. It was pointed out that a reservation of full control by the mortgagor might well prevent the effective creation of a lien in the mortgagee and that the New York cases holding such a mortgage void rest upon that doctrine.

The results which flow from reserving dominion inconsistent with the effective disposition of title must be the same whatever the nature of the property transferred. The doctrine which imputes fraud where full dominion is reserved must apply to assignments of accounts although the doctrine of ostensible ownership does not. There must also be the same distinction as to degrees of dominion. Thus, although an agreement that the assignor of accounts shall collect them and pay the proceeds to the assignee will not invalidate the assignment which it accompanies, the assignment must be deemed fraudulent in law if it is agreed that the assignor may use the proceeds as he sees fit.

In the case at bar, the arrangement for the unfettered use by the company of the proceeds of the accounts precluded the effective creation of a lien and rendered the original assignment fraudulent in law. Consequently the payments to Ratner and the delivery of the September list of accounts were inoperative to perfect a lien in him, and were unlawful preferences. On this ground, and also because the payment was fraudulent under the law of the State, the trustee was entitled to recover the amount.

Stackhouse v. Holden, 66 App. Div. 423, 73 N.Y.S. 203, is relied upon by Ratner to establish the proposition that reservation of dominion does not invalidate an assignment of accounts. The decision was by an intermediate appellate court, and, although decided in 1901, appears never to have been cited since in any court of that state. There was a strong dissenting opinion. Moreover, the case is perhaps distinguishable on its facts, p. 426. Greey

v. Dockendorff, 231 U.S. 513, 34 S. Ct. 166, upon which Ratner also relies, has no bearing on the case at bar. It involved assignment of accounts, but there was no retention of dominion by the bankrupt. The sole question was whether successive assignments of accounts by way of security, made in pursuance of a contract, were bad because the contract embraced all the accounts. The lien acquired before knowledge by either party of insolvency was held good against the trustee.

Reversed.

The evil under attack in Benedict v. Ratner is the *secret lien* that other creditors do not know about. If it is enforced by the courts the other creditors who were deceived by the debtor's apparently unencumbered prosperity are hurt. But although the Court in this case ruled against the creditor's security interest, creditors took comfort from the decision because the Court had indicated methods by which the lien *would* have survived the trustee's attack. By requiring the creditor to *police* the debtor's conduct (record the mortgage, pay over collections to the creditor, etc.) the Court paved the way for increased commercial financing. Once the creditors knew what the rules were they were more willing to extend the credit.

Did the rule of Benedict v. Ratner survive the enactment of Article 9? Read §9-205[1] and the Official Comment thereto. How does the Code police the debtor's use of the property? See §§9-302(1), 9-306(1), and 9-306(2). Note that in a sale of goods transaction it still is a bad idea for the seller to retain possession of the sold objects for a long period of time after the sale is over; read §2-402(2).

One way around the problems encountered in this famous case was to permit the creditor to have physical possession of the property (a *pledge*, see below), though this is a solution only where the collateral has tangible form, which accounts receivable of course do not. Other ways were suggested by the opinion itself. A very brief summary of the major devices follows.

1. *Pledge*

In a *pledge* the debtor (called a *pledgor*) gives physical possession of the collateral to the creditor (called the *pledgee*) until the debt

1. Throughout this book, all hyphenated section references are to the Uniform Commercial Code (UCC) unless otherwise indicated.

is paid. Possession then *perfects* the creditor's interest in the collateral (even against the bankruptcy trustee). Obviously when the creditor has possession of, say, a diamond ring the whole world is on notice that the creditor has some legal interest therein. Pledging is a superior way to perfect the creditor's security interest, but it has two drawbacks: (1) only tangible objects can be pledged, and a business debtor may want to borrow money against intangible collateral (such as accounts receivable due from existing customers), and (2) for some types of collateral the debtor needs to keep possession (the machines used in manufacturing, for example). It was necessary to create *non*-possessory security interests.

2. *Chattel Mortgage*

The debtor could always mortgage land, so why not have something similar for personal property (*chattels*)? And, as with real property, the mortgage given by the debtor (the *mortgagor*) to the creditor (the *mortgagee*) was recorded in a designated place and indexed under the name of the debtor so that other potential creditors could check and see whether the collateral was encumbered. Thus the debtor could have possession, but the secret lien problem so dreaded in Benedict v. Ratner was avoided since the mortgage was (through the recording system) witness to the creditor's very public interest in the property.

3. *Conditional Sale*

Here's a surprise. Without first reading the text that follows, form an opinion as to the answer of this legal problem:

PROBLEM 1

Honest John sold Nancy Debts a used car for $900, to be paid off in three payments of $300 each. The contract was oral. Nancy missed the second payment and Alfred "Hotstart" Smith (one of Honest John's employees) repossessed the car and returned it to the seller. Nancy sued Honest John for conversion. Who should win? After forming your initial opinion, read U.C.C. §2-702 and see if that has any bearing on the problem.

Most people assume that the unpaid seller always has a right to repossess. THIS IS UNTRUE. The unpaid seller may repossess in only three circumstances: (1) U.C.C. §2-702, which you have just read and about which more later, (2) when the buyer has specifically granted the seller a *security interest* in the object sold, or (3) when the seller sues, recovers judgment, and has the sheriff seize the property as part of the execution of the seller's judgment (when an unsecured creditor sues and acquires a judgment and then sends the sheriff out to levy on the defendant's property, the creditor is called, variously, a *judgment creditor*, a *judicial creditor*, or, simply a *lien creditor*). Of course, prior to the UCC, the seller could take a chattel mortgage in the property sold and file to record this interest, but that was a lot of trouble. Another way was to have a *conditional sale* whereby the buyer got possession of the property but the seller reserved full and complete title to it until the buyer paid in full (the *condition* in *conditional sale* was this payment before the buyer got any title). A conditional sale has the Benedict v. Ratner problem of the debtor-in-possession and a secret lien in the seller's favor, and the ficticious title retention theory had as short a life here as it did in the real property mortgage situation. The upshot was that in many states the seller's "title" was treated as nothing more than an unperfected security interest so that the seller lost to later judicial creditors, to creditors who perfected their security interests, and to the buyer's trustee in bankruptcy. In most states the seller's interest in a conditional sale had to be filed to be perfected.

Some sellers still use conditional sale terminology in their contracts. What effect does the seller's retention of title have under the UCC? Read §§2-401(1) and 1-201(37) (second sentence of each).

4. *Trust Receipt*

A strained use of trust law principles helped the retail automobile dealer finance (*floor plan*) purchases of vehicles from the manufacturer. In trust receipt financing, the car dealer would ask a bank to buy the cars from the manufacturer. The bank would then turn them over to the dealer after two things happened: (1) the bank filed a notice in the appropriate place announcing its intention to indulge in trust receipt financing with this particular dealer, and (2) the dealer signed a *trust receipt* (thereby becoming a *trustee;* the bank was called an *entruster*) acknowledging receipt of the vehicles and granting the bank a security interest therein.

As the cars[2] were sold the bank's interest was paid off, and when paid in full the trust receipt was cancelled. Trust receipt financing rules were codified into the Uniform Trust Receipts Act, a very difficult statute that was adopted in two-thirds of the states.

5. *Factor's Lien*

The word *factor* originally meant any selling agent (wholesaler or retailer) who helped finance the principal's business. As time went on, the factor's selling function died out, and the factor became a financing entity who loaned money against inventory the manufacturer put up as collateral. In return, the factor was granted a lien (a security interest) in the inventory, but this security interest had to be filed to be perfected under most states' factor lien statutes. Most of these statutes contained this drawback: the lien did not extend to new additions to the inventory (*after-acquired property*); that is, it was not a *floating lien* that attached to the changing objects in the inventory. If the after-acquired property in the inventory was to become collateral for the factor, a new security agreement and, typically, a filing of the same was a prerequisite to perfection.

6. *Field Warehousing*

In Benedict v. Ratner the primary evil was that the debtor was in possession of property that secretly belonged to the creditor. With a pledge, possession of the collateral is in the creditor and no deception problem arises. If the collateral is too big to be conveniently left in the creditor's possession (say, for instance, the collateral is an inventory of Christmas tree ornaments, waiting for the Christmas season), one way of pulling off a pledge was for the debtor to store the goods in a warehouse and have the warehouseman issue a negotiable warehouse receipt made out to *bearer*. Such a warehouse receipt (a *document of title*, now regulated by Article 7 of the UCC) has to be surrendered before the warehouseman will turn over the goods to anyone (§7-403(3)); in effect

2. Trust receipt financing was, of course, used in financing the acquisition of inventory other than automobiles, but was available only where the inventory consisted of easily identifiable separate items, for instance those having serial numbers.

this rule makes the warehouse receipt the same thing as the goods, and thus the receipt was pledged to the creditor in return for the loan of money. Possession of a negotiable document of title (a warehouse receipt or a bill of lading) perfected the creditor's security interest. A *field warehouse* is the same thing as a normal warehouse with one difference: the warehouse comes to the goods instead of vice versa. If the goods are too bulky to move easily, the field warehouseman goes to the goods, stakes them out in some way, issues a warehouse receipt therefore, and guards them (even the debtor, on whose premises they remain, is not supposed to be able to get to the goods). The receipt is then pledged to a financing agency; when the debt is repaid, the warehouse receipt is returned to the debtor, who presents it to the field warehouseman, who surrenders the goods and then packs up and leaves the debtor's property. (The field warehouseman is frequently a regular employee of the debtor who is temporarily employed as an agent of the field warehouse company. The resulting loyalty conflicts often gave rise to warehouseman misbehavior and, inevitably, lawsuits.)

Article 9 of the Code replaced all these devices (though some of the practices, such as field warehousing, live on) with new rules as to creation of the security interest, the collateral to which it can attach, and the steps necessary for perfection. It is meant to be all inclusive so as to cover all possible security interests in personal property and fixtures (see §9-104 for a list of transactions excluded from Article 9's dominion). Read §§9-101 and 9-102 and the Official Comments thereto. We shall go through Article 9 section by section. Should you wish to do outside reading, the following are helpful:

G. Gilmore, Security Interests in Personal Property (1965). Professor Gilmore was one of the original draftsmen of Article 9, and this splendid two volume work is a source authority for many of the basic assumptions underlying the Code.

P. Coogan, W. Hogan, D. Vagts, Secured Transactions Under the Uniform Commercial Code (1981), an often consulted work, originally written in 1963 but kept current by replacement pages.

J. White & R. Summers, Uniform Commercial Code (2d ed. 1980), a shorter, but very readable treatment of Article 9.

R. Henson, Secured Transactions Under the Uniform Commercial Code (2d ed. 1979), a recent work by one of the drafters of the 1972 version of Article 9.

B. Clark, The Law of Secured Transactions Under the Uniform Commercial Code (1980), a recent work by an experienced commentator.

CHAPTER 2

THE SCOPE OF ARTICLE 9

A. *SECURITY INTEREST DEFINED*

Read §1-201(37) (defining *security interest*) and §9-102 (Policy and Scope of Article).

PROBLEM 2

Assume that a state statute gives all repairmen a possessory artisan's lien on the property repaired. Mr. Baker took his car into Mack's Garage for repair, but, being strapped for funds, couldn't pay the full bill and Mack wouldn't let him have the car back. Is Mack's artisan's lien an Article 9 *security interest*? See §9-104(c). If, prior to the repair work, Mr. Baker signed a statement giving Mack's Garage a right to repossess the car if the bill wasn't paid, is this agreement a *security interest* under the Code?

PROBLEM 3

To raise money Farmer Brown's Fresh Vegetables Roadside Stand sold all of its accounts receivable to Nightflyer Finance Company, which notified the customers that henceforth all payments should be made directly to Nightflyer. (Note that this is not a loan from the finance company to the farmer with the accounts put up as collateral; it is an outright sale. If it were a loan, if the collectible accounts exceeded the amount of the loan, the excess would be returned to Farmer Brown; in an actual sale Nightflyer can keep the surplus; §9-502(2), last sentence.) Is this sale nonetheless an Article 9 *security interest*? If so, even though Farmer Brown has no further obligations to Nightflyer, he would of necessity be termed an Article 9 *debtor* (see §9-105(1)(d)), and Nightflyer would have to file an Article 9 financing statement to perfect its interest against later parties. Why would the Code drafters have brought an outright sale of accounts (and *chattel paper,* defined below) under the coverage of Article 9? Remember Benedict v. Ratner? See the second sentence in the Official Comment to §9-102; Major's Furniture Mart, Inc. v. Castle Credit Corp., 602 F.2d 538, 26 U.C.C. Rep. Serv. 1319 (3d Cir. 1979); and Coogan, Leases of Equipment and Some Other Unconventional Security Devices: An Analysis of UCC Section 1-201(37) and Article 9, 1973 Duke L.J. 909, 942-947.

For the practicing attorney the possibility that a business transaction with no apparent *loan* or *collateral* may still fall within Article 9 is a matter of great concern. If the transaction creates an Article 9 *security interest,* the attorney's client had better have taken whatever steps Article 9 requires for perfection or the client may lose the property to later creditors. If the attorney has not advised the client of this possibility, the client's thoughts may turn to malpractice actions.

A few of the obviously troublesome areas where Article 9 may or may not apply are discussed next.

B. CONSIGNMENTS

A true consignment is neither a *sale* nor a *security device,* it is a marketing procedure by which the owner of goods (the *consignor*) sends (*consigns*) them to a retailer (the *consignee*) for sale to the public. The retailer does not *buy* the goods (so no sale takes place when the consignor delivers the goods to the consignee), and if the retailer cannot sell them they are returned to the consignor. In effect the consignee is the selling agent for the consignor or, looked at another way, the consignee is a bailee with the ability to sell the bailor's goods. The advantages to the consignor of a true consignment over an outright sale (with reservation of a security interest so the goods could be reclaimed if the retailer did not pay for them) is that the consignor retains control over the terms of the retail sale (and thus can dictate the retail price), and, at least at common law, there is no requirement that the consignor file a notice anywhere announcing that a consignment is going on (why, the consignors argued, should they have to notify anyone that they claimed an interest in their own property?).

Nonetheless consignments have the Benedict v. Ratner problem: the retailer appears to be the unfettered owner of goods in inventory that actually belong to someone else (the consignor). The retailer's other creditors may wish to extend credit with the inventory as collateral but there is no place they can go to check whether some or all of the inventory is actually held on consignment.

Further, some consignments are not *true consignments* at all but are sales on credit (i.e., secured transactions) disguised as consignments in order to escape the filing requirements. The Code drafters could hardly ignore the reality of the transaction, and to solve the problem they created a test based on the intention of the parties. If the parties intended a *true consignment,* Article 9 (except for §9-114) does not apply but Article 2 does, particularly §§2-326 and 2-327; these sections solve the Benedict v. Ratner problem by validating the consignor's interest only in situations where the consignee's other creditors will not be mislead by the retailer's possession of the consigned goods. If a *security interest* is intended then Article 9 *must* be complied with (perfection by filing, etc.).[1]

PROBLEM 4

The Perfect Party Hats Company consigned a shipment of party hats to Nellie's Novelty Store, reserving title to the hats in itself. Nellie agreed to pay for the hats whether or not the novelty store could sell them. The state had a *sign law* that perfected a true consignor's

1. There are significant practical differences if Article 2 as opposed to Article 9 applies. The statutes of frauds are not the same (compare §2-201 with §9-203), and the priorities over later creditors are different. A *true consignor* not complying with §2-326 loses to all later creditors (even general creditors; this is because of the broad §1-201(12) definition of *creditor*), while a *security consignor* who fails to perfect as required by Article 9 only loses to the parties listed in §9-301.

interest if a sign was posted at the consignee's store stating that the consignor owned the goods in question. This was duly done, but Perfect Party Hats did not file an Article 9 financing statement. Nellie's Novelty Store went bankrupt and, under §544 of the Bankruptcy Code, the trustee claimed the status of a lien creditor without notice of the consignor's interest. Who is entitled to the goods? Read §§1-201(37), 2-326, 9-102, and 9-301(1)(b).

Consignment cases under both Article 2 and Article 9 are collected in 40 A.L.R.3d 1978 (1978); see also Winship, The "True" Consignment Under the UCC and Related Peccadilloes, 29 S.W.L.J. 825 (1975-1976).

In re Fabers, Inc.

12 U.C.C. Rep. Serv. 126 (D. Conn. 1972)

Seidman, Ref. Bankr. The bankrupt is a retail carpet and rug merchant. On May 31, 1971, the petitioner, Mehdi Dilmaghani & Company, Inc. (dealer), shipped oriental rugs to the bankrupt on consignment. Subsequent deliveries of rugs on a similar basis were made on May 5, 1971, October 4, 1971, October 5, 1971, October 7, 1971, December 6, 1971, and December 23, 1971. All of the rugs so shipped had an identifying label attached. On each label was printed "MD. & CO., INC., Reg. No. R.N. 22956, 100% wool pile, No. ______, Quality ______, Size ______, Sq. Feet ______, Made in Iran." The consignment agreement provided that title to the rugs remained in the dealer until fully paid for; that the consignee had the right to sell the rugs in the ordinary course of business and only at a price in excess of the invoice price; that the proceeds of any sale were the property of the dealer and held in trust for the dealer; that the proceeds of any sale were to be remitted to the dealer immediately with a report of the sale; that all rugs were held at the risk of the consignee.

No effort was made to comply with the provisions of the Uniform Commercial Code relating to security interests. The dealer does not assert a security interest in the rugs, claiming only that the rugs are and always were the property of the dealer under a "true consignment" and, therefore, not subject to the provisions of the Code relating to security interests. . . .

The dealer's claim is that the consignment was not intended for security and is, therefore, not subject to the requirements of Article 9. The logic of this argument escapes the court. If the dealer did not want the agreement to provide it with security for either the payment of the rugs or their return, what other purpose could there have been? The agreement describes the rugs as belonging to the dealer, but the risk of loss or damage is on the consignee. This is inconsistent with the liability of a bailee. The proceeds of the sales were to be the property of the dealer but the consignee is described as holding the proceeds in trust. A trustee has *title* to the trust estate. The agreement impliedly permitted the consignee to mingle the proceeds with his own funds before remitting. At any rate, there was no requirement of a separate account. This is inconsistent with a true trust. . . .

The principal claim of the dealer is that the transaction was a true consignment, that at all times the consignee was acting as the agent of the dealer and, therefore, the transaction came under the exception allowed in §2-326. [The court quoted §2-326.]

The instant transaction is a "sale or return" as described in §2-326(1) since the goods were delivered for resale. Ordinarily, goods held on "sale or return" are subject to the claims of creditors of the buyer, §2-326(2). To protect itself from the claims of creditors, the dealer could have complied with the filing provisions of Article 9, §2-326(3)(c), but it admittedly did not. The only other exceptions are compliance with an applicable Connecticut law providing for a consignor's interest by a sign (there apparently is no such law) or establishing that the consignee-bankrupt was generally known by his creditors to be substantially engaged in selling the goods of others.

In support of the latter theory, evidence was submitted that the dealer never dealt in oriental rugs prior to May 1971 and that an advertisement in the local newspapers on October 12, 1971, included a picture of Mr. Mehdi Dilmaghani together with the narrative: "By Special Arrangement, we proudly introduce: A distinctive collection of Mehdi Dilmaghani . . . renown importer of genuine handmade Oriental, India, and Petit-Point Rugs. . . ." This hardly complies with the requirement that the bankrupt "is generally known *by his creditors* to be substantially engaged in selling the goods of others." (Emphasis added.) There was no evidence of any notification to any of the bankrupt's creditors to that effect. In fact, it is found that the contrary was true. The bankrupt was not substantially engaged in selling the goods of others.

The dealer argues that the oriental rugs were not the kind of goods in which the bankrupt dealt. They may not have been of the same quality or price range as the other rugs and carpets sold by the bankrupt, but they were all of the same kind of goods — to wit: floor coverings. The trade name of the bankrupt was "Faber's World of Carpets." Other than the reference to the collection by Dilmaghani in the newspaper advertisement there was nothing to suggest any possible connection with the dealer. In fact, this advertisement is no different from that of a department store advertising a full line of "Frigidaire" appliances, or a collection of Pierre Cardin's new spring line. This is a far cry from the situation in In re Griffin 1 UCC Rep. Serv. 492 where the bankrupt had a sign in his window advertising used furniture and the court found that under the particular circumstances, this was notice that goods of others were being sold. In the instant case, there was no such notice.

There was evidence that the members of the Oriental Rug Dealers Association usually sold their rugs on consignment. This was well known to the members of the association. There was no evidence that this was the universal invariable practice in the trade, or that the creditors of the bankrupt who apparently did not deal in oriental rugs knew anything about the custom of the members of the Oriental Rug Association. As between the parties, the transaction was a consignment agreement. As to the creditors, it was a sale or return and bound by the provisions of Section 2-326. Since the petitioner does not come under the exceptions in this section, it was required to comply with the filing provisions of Article 9 to preserve its secured position. Admittedly, this was not done.

It is found that the agreement was intended for security and subject to the requirements of §2-326. There was no perfection of the security interest and the agreement did not come under the exceptions set forth in §2-326(3). Accordingly, it is held that the goods are subject to the claims of creditors, §2-326(2). The reclamation petition is denied, and it is so ordered.

In re Webb

13 U.C.C. Rep. Serv. 394 (S.D. Tex. 1973)

Patton, Jr., Ref. Bankr. The court here considers several separate applications, but since all turn on the primary question of the status of personal property in possession of the bankrupt at the time of bankruptcy they will all be considered together. The applications consist of two by the trustee to sell the bankrupt's inventory free and clear of liens, the objections of Corpus Christi Bank & Trust (hereinafter "Bank") and of the Small Business Administration (hereinafter "SBA") to the sale and their applications to abandon, and applications of Jerry L. Pinkard, dba Rector-Pinkard Company (hereinafter "Pinkard") and Devon Corporation, dba The Pathfinder Company (hereinafter "Pathfinder") to abandon or reclaim a portion of the property.

The primary problems arise from transactions between Pathfinder and Pinkard and the bankrupt whereby those two companies consigned goods to the bankrupt under written agreements. These instruments are in evidence as Trustee's Exhibits 1 and 2. In accordance with those agreements the consignors delivered goods to the bankrupt for sale by him but retained title to the property. Subsequent thereto the bankrupt, on May 5, 1972, executed a security agreement with the Bank covering, among other things, "all inventory now owned, to be purchased with a portion of the loan proceeds, and thereafter acquired." Government Exhibit 2. This security interest was perfected by properly filing a financing statement using the same language to describe the security interest in inventory. Government Exhibit 3. The SBA succeeded to the rights of the Bank and the interests of both will sometimes hereafter be designated by referring only to SBA.

A voluntary petition in bankruptcy was filed on October 10, 1972 and the trustee was duly appointed and qualified.

The heart of the problem is the determination of the rights of Pathfinder, Pinkard, SBA and the trustee to the property consigned by Pathfinder and Pinkard to the bankrupt and in the possession of the bankrupt at the time of bankruptcy.

The rights of all parties must be determined by the application of the Texas Business and Commerce Code (hereinafter UCC). At the outset there is posed the question of which sections of the UCC control and more particularly the application of Chapter 2 dealing with sales and Chapter 9 dealing with secured transactions.

Section 2-326 UCC provides that if delivered goods may be returned to the seller even though they conform to the contract the transaction may be designated a "sale or return" and that such goods may be subject to the claims of the buyer's creditors while in the buyer's possession. It further provides, that when goods are delivered to a person for sale and such person maintains a place of business at which he deals in goods of the kind involved, under a name other than the person making delivery, then, with respect to claims of creditors, the goods are deemed to be on sale or return even if title is reserved by the consignment agreement. However, the goods are not subject to the claims of creditors if the consignor does one of three things. He may comply with the applicable sign law, or establish that the consignee is "generally known by his creditors to be substantially engaged in the selling of the goods of others," or he may comply with the provisions of Chapter 9 regarding secured transactions.

Section 1-201(37) UCC provides that "security interest" means an interest in personal property which secures payment of an obligation and further provides that unless a "consignment is intended as security, reservation of title thereunder is not a 'security interest' but a consignment is in any event subject to the provisions on consignment sales," (i.e. §2-326).

Section 9-102(2) UCC provides that Chapter 9 dealing with secured transactions applies to a consignment intended as security.

Section 9-113 UCC provides, in effect, that if the debtor is in lawful possession of the goods a security interest arising under Chapter 2 is governed by Chapter 9. See Columbia International Corp. v. Kempler, 175 N.W.2d 465, 7 UCC Rep. Serv. 650 (Wisconsin Sup. Ct. 1970).

The trustee has raised the question of whether the transactions between Pathfinder and Pinkard and the bankrupt were intended as security or whether they were "true consignments." The contention is made that if they were true consignments the transaction is governed by §2-326, but if they were transactions intended as security they are governed by the provisions of Chapter 9. But, as will be demonstrated, the end result in this case is the same.

First, let us assume that the agreements between Pathfinder and Pinkard and the bankrupt were true consignments, i.e. not intended as security. In such a case goods delivered by Pathfinder and Pinkard are subject to the claims of the bankrupt's creditors if the consignors did not comply with §2-326. The merits of this issue will be later discussed.

On the other hand, if the transactions were ones intended as security Pathfinder and Pinkard did not perfect their security interest as required by Chapter 9, security interests subsequently attaching and perfected are superior to the rights of Pathfinder and Pinkard.

We will next examine the application of §2-326 to the transactions with Pathfinder and Pinkard.

There can be no question but what the goods of Pathfinder and Pinkard were delivered to the bankrupt primarily for sale. Though there was evidence that the bankrupt was engaged in other types of activities as well as selling goods of the type here involved, the court is compelled to find as a fact that the bankrupt maintained a place of business at which he dealt in goods of the kind involved, and under a name other than Pathfinder and Pinkard. It follows that the goods so delivered were for "sale or return" even though title was reserved in the consignors. Therefore, under §2-326 the goods so delivered were subject to the claims of creditors unless Pathfinder and Pinkard did one or more of the following:

(1) complied with an applicable sign law providing for a consignor's interest or the like to be evidenced by a sign, or

(2) established that the bankrupt was generally known by his creditors to be substantially engaged in selling the goods of others, or

(3) complied with the filing provisions of Chapter 9.

There is no showing that any sign law as contemplated in (1) above exists in Texas and it is undisputed that Pathfinder and Pinkard did not comply with the Code requirements to protect a security interest as provided by Chapter 9. This leaves as the only question whether the consignors established that the bankrupt was "generally known by his creditors to be substantially engaged in selling the goods of others."

According to the American College Dictionary the word "generally" means with or respect to the larger part, or for the most part; usually, commonly, or ordinary. "Substantial" is defined as meaning of ample or considerable amount, quantity or size. It therefore is Pathfinder's and Pinkard's burden to show that most of the bankrupt's creditors knew that a considerable amount of the bankrupt's business was selling the goods of others. The bankrupt scheduled 76 unsecured creditors and 8 secured creditors. By the bankrupt's testimony perhaps as many as 15 of his creditors either knew or might have known that he was handling consigned goods. Though the amount owed to those 15 creditors may have constituted more than half of the total indebtedness, §2-326 clearly does not speak to the amount of indebtedness but to "creditors." The bankrupt further testified that he was primarily known as a sandblaster and painter and that he did not know what percentage of his gross was accounted for by the sale of consigned goods from Pathfinder because it varied from 30% to 50% or as low as 10% and that the sale of Pinkard goods was a very small portion of the business.

Section 2-326(3)(b) places the burden on the consignor to establish the exception and the court finds that under the evidence neither Pathfinder nor Pinkard has established that the bankrupt was generally known by his creditors to be substantially engaged in selling the goods of others.

Having thus determined that under §2-326 the consigned goods were subject to the claims of creditors we turn to the alternative contention that if the agreements were intended solely as security then only Chapter 9 applies. However, even if the consignments were intended as security agreements they were not perfected under Chapter 9 and subsequent security interests will prevail. Under §9-312 an unperfected security interest is subordinate to a perfected security interest. Section 9-202 provides that the title to collateral is immaterial.

This now leads us to the question of what rights the SBA acquired in the consigned goods. The trustee takes the position that the financing agreement between the bankrupt and the Bank, which was later assigned to the SBA, does not reach the goods delivered by Pathfinder and Pinkard. The court agrees that it does not, although not for exactly the same reasons expressed by the trustee. The security agreement between the Bank and the bankrupt is ambiguous on its face. It grants to the Bank a security interest in "all inventory now owned, to be purchased with a portion of the loan proceeds, and thereafter acquired." A logical interpretation would be that such grant is the same as if it stated "all inventory now owned, all inventory to be purchased with a portion of the loan proceeds, and all inventory thereafter acquired." Inventory by definition means goods "held by a person who holds them for sale or lease." Section 9-109(4) UCC.

Had the agreement simply referred to "inventory" it probably would have covered all goods delivered by Pathfinder and Pinkard to the bankrupt, regardless of title. But by limiting the grant to "inventory now owned" it appears clearly that the parties did not intend to grant a security interest in non-owned inventory — i.e. goods held for sale but not owned by the debtor as of the time of the agreement. That this was the intent is shown further by the list of personal property attached to the agreement which did not include the goods on consignment.

The second phrase "to be purchased with a portion of the loan proceeds" clearly does not apply to the consigned goods and need not be considered here. The third phrase "all inventory . . . thereafter acquired" must be analyzed. "Acquired" is a word susceptible of more than one meaning. According to the American College Dictionary it means: "1. to come into possession of; get as one's own; to acquire property, a title, etc." According to Black's Law Dictionary, Third Edition, it means: "In the law of contracts and of descents. To become the owner of property; to make property one's own."

It therefore appears that the reference to "inventory thereafter acquired" could have been intended to cover inventory which the bankrupt thereafter acquired and which he owned or had title or it possibly could refer to inventory which merely came into his possession. The problem thus is trying to determine the true intent of the parties to the agreement.

It being the court's conclusion that the contract is ambiguous as to the property intended to be the subject of the agreement, parol evidence is admissible to determine the true intent of the parties. . . .

The SBA and the Bank admitted that at the time the loan was made the Bank had knowledge of the agreement between the bankrupt and Pathfinder and that the bankrupt had advised that he had a distributorship agreement with Pinkard. The bankrupt testified, without any objection from any party, that he did not intend to grant to the Bank (or the SBA) a security interest in the consigned goods. Neither the Bank nor the SBA offered any evidence of a different intent. Accordingly, the court finds that the security agreement between the Bank and the bankrupt does not give to the Bank nor the SBA any security interest in the goods consigned to the bankrupt by Pathfinder or Pinkard, but that it does have a valid security interest in the remainder of the inventory.

However, this does not dispose of the question of the rights of the trustee to this property. It having already been determined that Pathfinder and Pinkard did not comply with the requirements of §2-326 UCC it follows that the goods are subject to the claims of the bankrupt's creditors while in his possession. Under §70c [now §544(a)] of the Bankruptcy Act the trustee has the rights and powers of the so-called "perfect lien creditor" and it therefore follows that as such he has a valid security interest in the consigned goods. If the consignment agreement was intended as a security agreement and §2-326 is not applicable then the trustee will still prevail. Section 9-301 UCC provides that an unperfected security interest is subordinate to a person who becomes a lien creditor without knowledge of the security interest and before it is perfected. A lien creditor is specifically defined in that section to include a trustee in bankruptcy from the date of the filing of the petition and it is further provided as follows: "Unless all the creditors represented had knowledge of the security interest such a representative of creditors [trustee] is a lien creditor without knowledge even though he personally has knowledge of the security interest." It being undisputed that not all of the creditors had knowledge of any possible security interest of Pathfinder and Pinkard it follows that the claim of the trustee is superior to that of Pathfinder and Pinkard.

To summarize, the court finds that the SBA has a perfected security interest in all of the inventory of the bankrupt except those goods that were consigned to the bankrupt by Pathfinder and Pinkard, and that the trustee has a superior right to that of Pathfinder and Pinkard to the proceeds of the sale of the consigned goods. Accordingly, the applications of Pathfinder and Pinkard to reclaim or to abandon will be denied, the application of the SBA to abandon is granted as to all inventory except the goods consigned to the bankrupt by Pathfinder and Pinkard, and the application of the trustee to sell the inventory free and clear of liens is granted, but only as to the goods consigned to the bankrupt by Pathfinder and Pinkard.

In closing the court cannot help but comment that the result as far as Pathfinder and Pinkard is concerned is indeed harsh. However, it seems that the Uniform Commercial Code requires the holding here made and that Pathfinder and Pinkard must suffer the consequences of having failed to protect their position by compliance with the provisions of the Code.

The trustee will prepare orders in conformity with this memorandum and submit the same to opposing counsel within ten days for approval as to form.

Those states that have adopted the 1972 version of the Code have a special section (§9-114) dealing with the priorities between an existing creditor with a perfected security interest in the debtor's inventory (which includes *after-acquired inventory,* that is inventory added to that existing at the time of the original loan) and a later consignor. To prevail over the prior interest, even the true consignor must give the existing creditor the notice provided for by §9-114, a provision we will explore later in the book.

For a while, one major test for telling a true consignment from a security consignment was to ask if the arrangement was desired by the consignor primarily to fix the retail price (a *true consignment*) or merely to reserve a security interest in the consignor (*security consignment*). This test was first suggested by Professor Hawkland in Consignments Under The UCC: Sales or Security?, U.C.C. Coordinator 395 (1963), and was picked up by the Wisconsin Supreme Court in Colombia International Corp. v. Kempler, 46 Wis. 2d 550, 175 N.W.2d 465, 7 U.C.C. Rep. Serv. 650 (1970). The test has been criticized because it fails to take account of federal decisions like Simpson v. Union Oil Co., 377 U.S. 13 (1964), and United States v. General Elec. Co., 358 F. Supp. 731 (S.D.N.Y. 1973), which hold that a price-fixing consignment violates the anti-trust law; see Duesenberg, Consignments Under the UCC: Comment on Emerging Principles, 26 Bus. Law. 565 (1970). Undaunted, Wisconsin still adheres to the test: Clark Oil & Ref. Co. v. Liddicoat, 65 Wis. 2d 612, 223 N.W.2d 530, 15 U.C.C. Rep. Serv. 1145 (1974) (also holding that where the consignee had the right and duty to establish the price at which the consigned goods would be sold a security consignment and not a true one resulted).

C. LEASES

A problem similar to the applicability of Article 9 to consignments occurs when the parties masquerade a secured sale as a lease.

PROBLEM 5

B.I.G. Machines, Inc. leased a duplicating machine to Connie's Print Shop ("Printing While You Wait"). The lease was for five years and the rental payments over this period exactly equaled the current market price of the machine. The lease contract further provided that at the end of the five years Connie's Print Shop might purchase the machine outright by paying B.I.G. Machines $5.00. B.I.G. Machines did not file an Article 9 financing statement. Thereafter Connie's Print Shop borrowed money from the Octopus National Bank and signed a security agreement with the bank granting it an interest in all of the print shop's "equipment." Octopus National duly perfected its security interest by filing a financing statement in the appropriate place. When Connie's Print Shop failed to repay the loan, Octopus National seized all the shop's equipment including the duplicating machine. In the lawsuit Octopus Nat. Bank v. B.I.G. Mach., Inc., who gets the machine? Read §§1-201(37) and 9-102. Would it make a difference if the lease gave Connie's Print Shop a right to terminate at any time in the five years and return the machine to the lessor without further obligation? See In re Royer's Bakers, Inc., 56 Berks Co. L.J. 48, 4 Installment Credit Guide (CCH) ¶99,274, 1 U.C.C. Rep. Serv. 342 (Bankr. E.D. Pa. 1963) (saying this clause didn't help create a true lease), and Coogan, Leases of Equipment and Some Other Unconventional Security Devices: An Analysis of UCC Section 1-201(37) and Article 9, 1973 Duke L.J. 909, 916-924 (saying it should have).

Parties may wish to cast a transaction as a lease rather than a sale for many reasons. Prior to the adoption of §168(f)(8) of the Internal Revenue Code of 1954, as added by the Economic Recovery Tax Act of 1981, which eliminated the distinction between disguised sales and *true leases,* rental payments on a *true lease* could be deducted from gross income, but in a *sale* the "lessee" could only take depreciation on the object purchased. Tax lawyers developed much experience wrestling with the distinctions between a true lease and a disguised sale, witness:

> At the time of this writing, the use of many millions (and probably billions) of dollars' worth of equipment is being obtained through a medium of tax-oriented leases where the ability of the lessor to take accelerated depreciation and obtain the Investment Tax Credit are so crucial that the lease will not be entered into without a ruling by the Commissioner on this point, or at the very least, an unqualified opinion by tax counsel, who necessarily must err only on the side of caution. Tax counsel and administrators have developed a lore of their own for distinguishing a true lease from a disguised sale. One point of interest is their emphasis upon the necessity for the lessor's retention of a residual of significant and measurable value. Although this element is seldom stressed as such in chattel security literature, it is suggested that if UCC draftsmen ever deem it feasible to devise something better than

> either old USCA section 1(2) or abandoned section 7-403, study should be directed toward the possibility of devising a formula based on the value of the residual to be returned at the end of the lease term. A rule of thumb in tax rulings and in super-cautious opinions of lessors' tax counsel if (1) that the lease must come to an end at a time when at least two years or twenty percent of the useful life of the leased item remains, and (2) that this residual must be valued at not less than fifteen percent of the purchase price. The lessor's tax counsel is likely to insist that there be no options, or only an option to purchase at the market value as determined when the option is exercised. This position is based on the premise that risk of an increase or decrease in value of the residual is an incident of the lessor's ownership and that he should, therefore, bear this risk.

Coogan, id. at 966-967. For other IRS tests see Rev. Rul. 55-540, 1955-2 Cum. Bull. 39, and Rev. Proc. 75-21, 26 C.F.R. 601.201 (1975). The same issue comes up when books must be maintained:

> From an accounting point of view, the true lease has had the advantage to the lessee of providing him with "off balance sheet financing." That is to say, the lease obligates him to pay rent and not to buy goods. Accordingly, the leased property is not shown as an asset on the lessee's balance sheet, and, consistently, the obligation to pay rent is not listed as a liability. This treatment tends to improve the balance sheet ratios commonly used in determining the lessee's financial strength. Additionally, the obligations of a lessee under a true lease usually are not subject to restrictions on the amount of money he may borrow contained in existing loan agreements, corporate charters and so forth.

Hawkland, The Proposed Amendments to Article 9 of the UCC — Part 5: Consignments and Equipment Leases, 77 Com. L.J. 108, 113 (1972). The tax/accounting tests tend to focus on the "intention" of the parties and two other factors: (1) the "equity" the lessee builds in the leased property, and (2) the value of the property surrendered to the lessor at the end of the term.

All the UCC commentators agree that pre-Code decisions on the subject (particularly those under the old Uniform Conditional Sales Act) are highly relevant to deciding the same question under Article 9. The student/lawyer researching the issue is well advised to consult the state's prior lease/sale cases. In addition there is a growing body of Article 9 cases on this much litigated subject. One of the earliest established these measuring factors:

1. The facts in each case control to show intention of the parties to create a security interest.
2. Reservation of title in a lease or option to purchase appurtenant to or included in the lease does not in and of itself make the lease a security agreement.
3. Lease agreement which permits the lessee to become the owner at the end of the term of the lease for a nominal or for no additional consideration is deemed intended as a security agreement as a matter of law.
4. The percentage that option purchase price bears to the list price, especially if it is less than 25%, is to be considered as showing the intent of the parties to make a lease as security.
5. Where the terms of the lease and option to purchase are such that the only sensible course for the lessee at the end of the lease term is to exercise the option and become the owner of the goods, the lease was intended to create a security interest.
6. The character of a transaction as a true lease is indicated by:
   (a) Provision specifying purchase option price which is approximately the market value at the time of the exercise of the option.
   (b) Rental charges indicating an intention to compensate lessor for loss of value over the term of the lease due to aging, wear and obsolescence.
   (c) Rentals which are not excessive and option purchase price which is not too low.
   (d) Facts showing that the lessee is acquiring no equity in leased article during the term of lease.

In re Alpha Creamery Co., 4 U.C.C. Rep. Serv. 794, 797-798 (Bankr. W.D. Mich. 1967).

In re Gehrke Enterprises, Inc.

1 B.R. 647, 28 U.C.C. Rep. Serv. 794 (W.D. Wis. 1979)

MARTIN, Bankr. J. This adversary proceeding seeking reclamation on six Freightliner semi-tractors was tried to the court on November 20, 1979. The essential facts were proved as follows:

The defendant, debtor, Gehrke Enterprises, Inc. ("Gehrke") entered into agreements (collectively referred to herein as "the Agreements") with General Leasing Services Co., Inc. which on January 26, 1979, changed its name to that of the plaintiff, United General Leasing, Inc. ("Leasing"), on the dates and according to the terms summarized as follows:

Agreement A. November 8, 1978, Vehicle Lease Agreement, 1979 Freightliner, No. CA213HP152128, 48 monthly payments of $1,168.25;

Agreement B. November 8, 1978, Vehicle Lease Agreement, No. 7053-1, 1979 Freightliner, No. CA213HP152126, 48 monthly payments of $1,168.25;

Agreement C. November 8, 1979, Vehicle Lease Agreement, No. 7053-2, 1979 Freightliner, No. CA213HP152127, 48 monthly payments of $1,168.25;

Agreement D. October 8, 1977, Lease of Personal Property, one Freightliner tractor, No. CA213HM140341, 48 monthly payments of $991.74;

Agreement F. October 27, 1977, Lease of Personal Property, 1978 Freightliner, No. CA213HM4032, 48 monthly payments of $991.74; and

Agreement G. October 28, 1977, Lease of Personal Property, 1978 Freightliner tractor, No. CA213HM140343, 48 monthly payments of $991.74.

Each of the Agreements, in addition to other printed terms on the form, contained the following typed paragraph (the "residual guaranty clause"):

> After expiration of lease, Lessor shall cause the vehicle to be sold. Should the sale price be greater than $12,500.00 the overage shall be refunded to the Lessee as a reduction of rental. Should the sale price be less than $12,500.00 the difference shall be paid within 10 days of the sale to the Lessor as additional rental.

The residual guaranty clause characterized by Leasing's employee, John J. Tomann, as the "finance lease clause" is included by Leasing to provide some flexibility for lessees in the amount of monthly rental payments under the lease. If the guaranty price is high, the monthly rental payments can be lower. On the Gehrke Agreements, the sum of $12,500.00 was used to approximate the remainder of the purchase price of the truck plus financing costs which would not be amortized by the monthly rental payments.

The subject of each Agreement was a new semi-tractor selected by Gehrke from a dealer's inventory. Those tractors of the 1978 model year had suggested factory prices of approximately $48,-729.00. Those of the 1979 model year had suggested factory prices of approximately $55,444.00. There was no evidence presented as to the actual purchase price of the vehicles. Testimony was undisputed that retail sales are usually at somewhat less than suggested factory prices, but otherwise approximate those prices.

No payments due Leasing from Gehrke on Agreements A, B and C, on June 1, 1979, or thereafter; on Agreement D on June 5, 1979, or thereafter; and on Agreements F and G due on July 1, 1979, or thereafter, have been paid.

Each of the Agreements by its terms grants plaintiff the right to possession of the subject vehicles in the event of default in performance of its terms and, specifically, in the event of failure to make monthly payments as provided by the Agreement. Each of the Agreements contains terms designating the filing of an insolvency proceeding a default under the Agreement.

On August 10, 1979, Gehrke filed a petition commencing a Chapter XI proceeding under the Bankruptcy Act. Gehrke has since that date, pursuant to §342 of the Bankruptcy Act, acted as debtor-in-possession. At the time of filing of the petition commencing this Chapter XI proceeding, Gehrke had in its possession each of the six vehicles subject to the Agreements. Subsequent to filing this chapter proceeding, Gehrke, acting as debtor-in-possession, has refused Leasing's demand for surrender of possession of the subject vehicles, has continued to use the vehicles and has taken no action to disavow the Agreements. No payments have been made to Leasing by the debtor-in-possession.

On or about September 21, 1979, proceeds from the sale of shares of common stock having a net value of $26,804.99, which had been delivered to Leasing by Robert H. Gehrke as guarantor of the Agreements, were applied to Gehrke's indebtedness to Leasing, including the application of the following: $4,673.00 on Agreement A; $4,673.00 on Agreement B; $4,673.00 on Agreement C; $3,966.96 on Agreement D; $2,975.22 on Agreement F; and $2,868.59 on Agreement G.

On September 21, 1979, Leasing commenced this adversary proceeding praying that Gehrke be ordered to surrender possession of the subject vehicles to Leasing.

To determine whether Leasing is entitled to the relief it seeks, the source of its potential remedies must be explored. If the Agreements are determined to be true leases, those remedies can be determined from the terms of the Agreements and the law of bailment for hire.[2] However, if the Agreements are in the nature

2. See Ronald M. DeKoven, Proceedings After Default by Lessee Under a True Lease of Equipment, Chapter 29B, Secured Transactions, Bender's Uniform Commercial Code Service reprinted in Equipment Leasing, 1976 (Commercial Law and Practice Court Handbook Series 154).

of security leases or conditional sales within the UCC definition of security interests, the Agreements are subject to the requirements of the UCC. . . . and the remedies are those set forth in Wis Stat §§9-501–507.

In its essence, the distinction between a true lease and a security lease is that by a true lease the lessor seeks to dispose of the use of the subject property while retaining incidents of ownership and by a security lease the lessor seeks to dispose of most or all of the incidents of ownership of the property, while retaining only sufficient interest in the property to assure payment of the contract obligation. The difficulty in making this distinction has given rise to considerable judicial and scholarly comment. Cases finding one or another term of a lease agreement or the totality of several such terms to be the accurate indication of the lessor and lessee's intention suggest a variety of tests.[3]

The search for a concise test of the distinction between a security lease and a true lease has been largely fruitless. The deceptively simple test suggested by Peter Coogan after a close analysis of UCC §1-201(37) and its statutory predecessors actually provides a thorough set of guidelines:

> [W]here the lessee has agreed to pay an amount substantially equal to the value of the goods of which he is to become the owner (or has the option to become the owner), the parties have entered into a conditional sale agreement.[4]

The leading commentator on equipment leasing has elaborated on Coogan's test,

> Coogan's test established the following three elements as the sine qua non for determining whether a lease is a finance lease: (1)

3. Among the terms found to be exclusive or primary for such tests are: A nominal purchase option, Peco, Inc. v. Hartbauer Tool & Die Co., 262 Ore 573, 200 P2d 708 (1972), In re Samoset Associates, 24 UCC Rep Serv 510 (Bkcy, J., D Me 1978), Appleway Leasing, Inc. v. Wilken, 26 UCC Rep Serv 209 (Ore Ct App, 1979); a lease term equivalent to economic life of equipment, In re Lakeshore Transit — Kenosha, Inc., 7 UCC Rep Serv 607 (Ref Bkcy, ED Wis, 1969), Atlas Industries, Inc. v. National Cash Register Co., 216 Kan 213, 531 P2d 41 (1975); and obligation to pay full purchase price, Leasing Service Corp. v. American National Bank & Trust Co., 19 UCC Rep Serv 252 (DNJ 1976), National Equipment Rental Ltd. v. Priority Electronics Corp., 435 F Supp 236 (EDNY 1977), Citizens & Southern Equipment Leasing, Inc. v. Atlanta Federal Savings & Loan Ass'n, 144 Ga App 800, 243 SE2d 243 (1978).

4. Coogan, Leases of Equipment and Some Other Unconventional Security Devices: An Analysis of UCC Section 1-201(37) and Article 9, 1 Bender's Secured Transactions Under the Uniform Commercial Code §4A.07[1].

there must be an agreement by the lessee to pay the lessor a set amount; [13] (2) such amount must be equivalent to the value of the leased goods; and (3) the lessee must become the owner or have the option to become the owner of the leased goods. If any one of these elements is lacking, the lease is not a finance lease, but a true lease. The test is of great significance as it not only determines the nature of the transaction, but it also determines the law applicable to the enforceability of the rights and remedies of the parties thereto.

[16][I]f a lease contains an option in the lessee to terminate, then there is no obligation to pay an amount substantially equal to the purchase price and thus no conditional sale under pre-Code law as well as no security interest under the UCC. [Coogan, §4A.01[5][c].[5]]

The Coogan test as amplified by DeKoven presents a fair summary of the legislative philosophy reflected in the adoption of UCC §1-201(37) and the rationale of the better reasoned opinions. Although no case controlling this court has applied the precise test suggested, its adoption appears to be appropriate for consideration of the present case.

Each of the Agreements in this case provides at the election of Leasing immediate acceleration of all indebtedness under the Agreement if lessee defaults. In addition, none of the Agreements provide any terms for a voluntary termination of the Agreement by Gehrke prior to its stated term as a means of reducing Gehrke's obligation. Therefore, Gehrke was obligated to pay the full amount of rental called for in the lease and the first element of the test is therefore met.

A calculation of the rentals due under each of the Agreements indicates that the 48 monthly payments, together with the residual guaranty rental payment of $12,500.00 upon termination, represent a sum substantially in excess of the suggested factory prices of the subject vehicles. The excess in each case approximates the cost of financing the suggested factory price for a period of 48 months. The uncontroverted testimony of John J. Tomann, an employee of the plaintiff, who supervised the subject lease Agreements supports the conclusion that Leasing did in fact calculate the rental payments to recover the full value of the leased vehicles within the terms of each Agreement, together with the finance costs and administration costs relating to the purchase of the

5. Ronald M. DeKoven, Leases of Equipment: Puritan Leasing Company v. August, a Dangerous Decision, 12 University of San Francisco Law Review, page 259 (1978).

vehicles and the administration of the Agreements. Thus, the amount Gehrke was obligated to pay Leasing under the Agreements was equivalent to the value of the leased goods and the second element of the test is met.

The final element of the test is less easily met in the present case. None of the agreements by their express terms provide for the transfer of ownership upon termination of the lease to Gehrke nor do they provide any option to Gehrke to purchase the subject vehicles for nominal or essentially nominal consideration at the termination of the lease. Gehrke has suggested that the residual guaranty clause in the lease is effectively an offer to sell and that the guaranteed amount of $12,500.00 is a nominal purchase price in the circumstances. Neither of those contentions has substantial merit. Although the residual guaranty clause requires a disposition of the vehicles by sale at the termination of the Agreements, there is nothing in the language of the clause nor anything that may be imputed to the clause which indicates that the sale need be made to Gehrke. Furthermore, although there was some conflict of testimony as to what the value of the vehicles might be at the end of 48 months, there was no credible evidence that $12,500.00 would be less than half of the retail value of the vehicles at that time and, therefore, cannot be considered nominal.

The absence of an express transfer or option does not dispose of the question. As has been noted, "Since the parties to these transactions are often clever in their attempts to disguise a finance transaction as a true lease, ownership should be liberally defined."[6] Leasing did not own the vehicles prior to the Agreements. During the term of the Agreements, Gehrke was responsible for all of the normal maintenance and insurance obligations which under other circumstances might be incidents of ownership. Although the Agreements specify that the title to and primary licenses on the vehicles will be maintained in Leasing, Leasing retained no other substantial incidents of ownership during the term of the Agreements. Upon termination of the Agreements, Leasing was obligated to dispose of the vehicle by sale pursuant to the residual guaranty clause and, therefore, did not recover use of the vehicles. Thus, upon the termination of the Agreement, Leasing was required to transfer title and thereby terminate the sole significant incident of ownership it has possessed to that point.

Sale pursuant to the residual guaranty clause would not pro-

6. DeKoven, supra, note 5 at page 262.

duce for Leasing the value of the title to the vehicles. Leasing would not receive the value of the vehicles in excess of the $12,500.00 amount set at the time the Agreement was signed as the amount necessary to pay the unpaid principal, interest and costs for the initial purchase of the vehicle. Similarly, Leasing would suffer no loss or deficiency upon the sale. Thus, "the lessor has no opportunity to obtain any meaningful residual value . . . since the lessee is entitled to the 'surplus' and is obligated for the 'deficiency.' "[7] Gehrke, therefore, would effectively bear the loss or reap the benefit which would be due to an owner. With the reservation of record title, Leasing by the Agreements, transferred all significant incidents of ownership to Gehrke at the time the Agreements were entered into and thereby, Gehrke became the owner of the vehicles for the purposes of analysis under the test we have adopted.

Because the Agreements have met all of the elements of the Coogan test for finance leases or conditional sales, the Agreements are subject to the requirements of Article 2 and Article 9 of the UCC. In determining Leasing's rights under the UCC its retention of title is immaterial. Section 9-202. There is no evidence that Leasing availed itself of the protection of §9-408 to make a protective filing under §9-401 to §9-409 to perfect its lien by filing. The certificates of title are not in evidence and, therefore, the compliance of Leasing with the provisions of the Vehicle Title and Anti-theft Law, Wis Stat §342.19 through §342.24, which relate to the perfection of security interests in vehicles cannot be determined. . . .

By virtue of §342 of the Bankruptcy Act, Gehrke, as debtor-in-possession, has all the rights and title to property of a trustee appointed under §44(a) of the Bankruptcy Act and Rule 209 of the Bankruptcy Rules. The applicable rights to property are set out in §70 of the Bankruptcy Act which provides at §70(c),

> The trustee shall have as of the date of bankruptcy the rights and powers of: (1) a creditor who obtained a judgment against the bankrupt upon the date of bankruptcy, whether or not such a creditor exists, (2) a creditor who upon the date of bankruptcy obtained an execution returned unsatisfied against the bankrupt, whether or not such a creditor exists, and (3) a creditor who upon the date of bankruptcy obtained a lien by legal or equitable pro-

7. Burke, Annual Survey — Secured Transactions, 34 Business Lawyer, 1547, 1550 (1979).

> ceedings upon all property, whether or not coming into possession or control of the court, upon which a creditor of the bankrupt upon a simple contract could have obtained such a lien, whether or not such a creditor exists . . .[8]

Thus, the debtor-in-possession has rights to all personal property in its possession, superior to all but those who have complied with the perfection requirements of the applicable statutes. Leasing has failed to prove that as of August 10, 1979, it had perfected its security interest in the vehicles. Absent that proof, Leasing is not entitled to the relief it requested in this proceeding.

Upon the foregoing which shall constitute my Findings of Fact and Conclusions of Law in this matter, it is hereby

Ordered that the complaint of the plaintiff be and hereby is dismissed.

In close cases the advising attorney may wish to tell the lessor (or the consignor in consignment problems) to play it safe and file a financing statement even if it is believed that a true lease/consignment has been created. This may create a danger, however, that the Article 9 filing is an admission (for tax/accounting purposes) that only a secured transaction is involved. To avoid this admission problem the 1972 version of Article 9 includes a new section, §9-408, which you should read.

D. *OTHER TRANSACTIONS*

PROBLEM 6

When Mercy Hospital's administrators decided to build a new addition, they hired a general contractor named Crash Construction Co. and required it to get a surety to guarantee the performance of the construction job and the payment of all the workers and material suppliers (so they would not get a mechanic's lien on the hospital). Standard Surety issued such a performance and payment bond covering Crash's obligation to Mercy Hospital. To finance the construc-

8. With some alterations this provision is now §544(a) of the Bankruptcy Reform Act. —ed.

tion, Crash borrowed money from Octopus National Bank and gave as collateral the right to collect the progress payments from Mercy Hospital as they came due. ONB duly filed an Article 9 financing statement. Halfway through the job, Crash went bankrupt and Standard Surety had to finish and pay off the employees and suppliers. At this point, by virtue of the common law right to *subrogation* (the equitable right given to sureties to step into the legal shoes of persons they have paid), Standard Surety claimed a superior right to unpaid monies retained by Mercy Hospital which were to be paid to Crash. ONB also claimed this fund, pointed to its filed security interest, and stated that Standard Surety's subrogation right was only an unfiled Article 9 security interest. Who should win? See the following case and Comment, Equitable Subrogation — Too Hardy A Plant To Be Uprooted By Article 9 of the UCC?, 1971 U. Pitt. L. Rev. 580.

United States Fidelity & Guaranty Co. v. First State Bank of Salina

494 P.2d 1149, 10 U.C.C. Rep. Serv. 682 (Kan. 1972)

FOTH, C. This case represents another round in the perennial struggle for priority between the surety on the performance bond of a defaulting building contractor and a bank which has advanced money to the contractor on the faith of an assignment of the contract proceeds. The new element here is the presence of the Uniform Commercial Code (UCC), KSA, Ch. 84. The primary question we are called upon to decide is the effect, if any, the UCC has on the priorities which would otherwise obtain — although there is some preliminary dispute as to just what those priorities should be.

The facts were stipulated below and are not in dispute.

The L.R. Foy Construction Co., Inc. ("Foy") of Hutchinson, Kansas, was awarded a contract in January, 1967, to construct a student dormitory at Chadron State College, Chadron, Nebraska. (The parties are in agreement that Kansas law should control.) Foy's role in this litigation is that of stakeholder, a role assumed in most cases of this character by the owner.

On January 25, 1967, Foy entered into a subcontract with Mid-Continent Fireproofing and Insulating Co., Inc. ("Mid-Continent") to furnish and install insulation and wall board for a contract price of $13,451.50. The contract called for periodic partial payments on approved estimates, with 10% as the retained percentage pending completion. Mid-Continent agreed to pay for all labor and materials and hold Foy harmless from any claims arising out of its failure to comply with the terms of the contract. In the event there arose any claim for which Foy or the Owner "might become liable," Foy was entitled to retain from moneys then or thereafter due Mid-Continent enough to indemnify itself. Mid-Continent was required to furnish a bond or bonds "guaranteeing performance and payment of labor and material bills."

The required bond was furnished by the appellant United States Fidelity and Guaranty Company (the "surety") on January 31, 1967. By its contract the surety bound itself to Foy on the condition that Mid-Continent faithfully perform its subcontract, which was incorporated by reference. No question is raised but that the surety's guarantee included Mid-Continent's contractual obligation to pay laborers and materialmen — i.e., that it was a "payment" bond as well as a "performance" bond.

The relevant default provision was that, if the surety should be required to remedy a default, so much as might be required to reimburse the surety for its outlays should be paid to the surety out of the balance of the subcontract price then in the hands of Foy "at the times and in the manner as said sums should have been payable to [Mid-Continent] had there been no default under the subcontract." This provision is considered by the parties as a contractual assignment of Mid-Continent's interest in its contract with Foy to secure the surety — albeit a conditional assignment. The failure of the surety to file under the UCC the bond containing this "security agreement" is appellee's most strongly urged claim to priority in this case.

In customary fashion, Mid-Continent went contract-in-hand to the appellee, The First State Bank of Salina (the "bank") to secure a line of credit to carry out its contract. There, on February 13, 1967, it executed a security agreement, assigning to the bank all its rights under its contract with Foy, to secure any and all obligations it might then or thereafter have to the bank. The bank gave Foy timely notice of the assignment, requesting that Foy make any payments under the contract payable jointly to Mid-Continent and the bank. It is stipulated that the bank's *purpose* in agreeing to extend credit (apart from its 7% interest) was to enable Mid-Continent to pay for materials and labor needed to fulfill the contract with Foy.

Mid-Continent had had prior dealings with the bank. Almost a year before, on April 13, 1966, the bank had lent money to

Mid-Continent in an unrelated transaction, and had duly filed a "financing statement" under the UCC covering Mid-Continent's "Accounts receivable for goods sold or for services rendered together with equipment used by the business." It is agreed that this financing statement was broad enough to include the "security agreement" (assignment) of February 13, 1967, covering as an "account receivable" Mid-Continent's interest in the Foy contract.

The bank relying on its security agreement backed by the filed financing statement, commenced lending money to Mid-Continent on February 28, 1967, taking a series of notes. The trial court concluded that the bank had an "attached" security interest in Mid-Continent's contract with Foy as of that date, and that conclusion is not contested. (We note here that a creditor's security interest "attaches" under UCC §9-204(1) when "value is given, and the debtor has rights in the collateral." As to the collateral, the proceeds of the contract, the debtor Mid-Continent acquired "rights" as and when it performed. This was certainly no *earlier* than February 28, 1967.)

In due course Mid-Continent defaulted; Foy terminated its contract with Mid-Continent and completed the work itself. After deducting its cost of completion from the balance of Mid-Continent's contract price Foy holds $3492.24 which would have been due Mid-Continent had it not defaulted. This is the prize for which the parties here are competing.

The surety was presented with and, on February 2, 1968, paid claims of materialmen who had furnished Mid-Continent with material for the project which, by our calculation, amounted to $7409.19, taking assignments of the materialmen's claims and remedies. The bank lent Mid-Continent money at various times from February 28 to June 23, 1967, and after deducting payments on account, claims a balance due it as of July 9, 1967 of $2647.40.

The surety sued Foy for the balance in Foy's hands, asserting its right of subrogation, and joined the bank as a potential claimant to the fund. Foy tendered the money in its hands into court; the bank in its answer asserted its assignment (security agreement) as a lien with priority over the claim of the surety. [The trial court found in favor of the bank and the surety appealed.]

Our first effort, then, is to determine the status of surety vis-à-vis bank, without regard to the UCC. Perhaps the leading authorities in this area are a series of cases decided by the United States Supreme Court involving government building projects, beginning with Prairie State Bank v. United States, 164 U.S. 227,

41 L. Ed. 412, 17 S. Ct. 142 (1896), and running through Pearlman v. Reliance Inc. Co., 371 U.S. 132, 9 L. Ed. 2d 190, 83 S. Ct. 232 (1962). This judicial saga was recounted in the latter case (in which the surety on a payment bond was claiming priority over the contractor's trustee in bankruptcy to the retained percentage in the government's hands). The Court said (371 U.S., at 137-8):

> In the *Prairie Bank* Case a surety who had been compelled to complete a government contract upon the contractor's default in performance claimed that he was entitled to be reimbursed for his expenditure out of a fund that arose from the Government's retention of 10% of the estimated value of the work done under the terms of the contract between the original contractor and the Government. That contract contained almost the same provisions for retention of the fund as the contract presently before us. The Prairie Bank, contesting the surety's claim, asserted that it had a superior equitable lien arising from moneys advanced by the bank to the contractor before the surety began to complete the work. The Court, in a well-reasoned opinion by Mr. Justice White, held that this fund materially tended to protect the surety, that its creation raised an equity in the surety's favor, that the surety, by asserting the right of subrogation, could protect itself by resort to the same securities and same remedies which had been available to the United States for its protection against the contractor. The Court then went on to quote with obvious approval this statement from a state case:
>
> "The law upon this subject seems to be, the reserved per cent to be withheld until the completion of the work to be done is as much for the indemnity of him who may be a guarantor of the performance of the contract as for him for whom it is to be performed. And there is great justness in the rule adopted. Equitably, therefore, the sureties in such cases are entitled to have the sum agreed upon held as a fund out of which they may be indemnified, and if the principal releases it without their consent it discharges them from their undertaking." 164 U.S., at 239, quoting from Finney v. Condon, 86 Ill. 78, 81 (1877).
>
> The *Prairie Bank* Case thus followed an already established doctrine that a surety who completes a contract has an "equitable right" to indemnification out of a retained fund such as the one claimed by the surety in the present case. The only difference in the two cases is that here the surety incurred his losses by paying debts for the contractor rather than by finishing the contract.

As to the distinguishing feature noted in the last sentence quoted, the Court went on to observe that in Henningsen v. U.S

Fidelity & Guaranty Co., 208 U.S. 404, 52 L. Ed. 547, 28 S. Ct. 389, the distinction between a surety who *performs* and one who *pays* was obliterated, saying (371 U.S., at 139):

> . . . This Court applied the equitable principles declared in the *Prairie Bank* Case so as to entitle the surety to the same equitable claim to the retained fund that the surety in the Prairie Bank case was held to have. Thus the same equitable rules as to subrogation and property interests in a retained fund were held to exist whether a surety completes a contract or whether, though not called upon to complete the contract, it pays the laborers and materialmen. These two cases therefore, together with other cases that have followed them, establish the surety's right to subrogation in such a fund whether its bond be for performance or payment. Unless this rule has been changed, the surety here has a right to this retained fund. . . .

Finally, the Court dispelled any questions raised by dicta contained in United States v. Munsey Trust Co., 332 U.S. 234, 91 L. Ed. 2022, 67 S. Ct. 1599, by limiting its effect to the narrow holding that the government could exercise "the well-established common-law right of debtors to offset claims of their own against their creditors," and thereby defeat a surety's equitable claim to money in the government's hands. (*Munsey Trust* had, however, extended the surety's claim to earned but unpaid progress payments as well as the retained percentages.)

The result was (371 U.S., at 141):

> We therefore hold in accord with the established legal principles stated above that the Government had a right to use the retained fund to pay laborers and materialmen; that the laborers and materialmen had a right to be paid out of the fund; that the contractor, had he completed his job and paid his laborers and materialmen, would have become entitled to the fund; and that the surety, having paid the laborers and materialmen, is entitled to the benefit of all these rights to the extent necessary to reimburse it. . . .

This holding is squarely applicable here, reading "Foy" for "the Government" and "Mid-Continent" for "the contractor." While the holding itself would appear to subrogate the surety to the rights of all three — the Government, the laborers and materialmen and the contractor — three members of the *Pearlman* court concurred specially, putting their reliance on the right of the surety to stand in the shoes of the *government,* rather than in those of the laborers and materialmen it paid under what they read the majority rationale to be. Either way, the result is the same, and it is generally held that the surety may do both, as well as acquiring the rights of its principal, the contractor.

The First Circuit has referred to this as a "unique accumulation of subrogation rights," serving to "induce a function that is neither ordinary insurance nor ordinary financing." (National Shawmut Bk. of Boston v. New Amsterdam Cas. Co., 411 F.2d 843 [1st Cir. 1969].)

The function thus "induced," that of guaranteeing completion of building contracts, is one which is vital both to government and to our economy, dictated by statute in the case of public projects and by prudence in the private sector. Rights are given to the surety, however, neither as a reward nor as an inducement, but because equity requires it. Those rights are described in the following language from *National Shawmut Bk.,* supra:

> . . . But the surety in cases like this undertakes duties which entitle it to step into three sets of shoes. When, on default of the contractor, it pays all the bills of the job to date and completes the job, it stands in the shoes of the contractor insofar as there are receivables due it; in the shoes of laborers and material men who have been paid by the surety — who may have had liens; and, not least, in the shoes of the government, for whom the job was completed. [(Ibid.)]

From our examination of the numerous authorities cited to us we are convinced that the foregoing represents the general rule, accepted overwhelmingly if not universally throughout the various jurisdictions in this country. No contrary decisions have come to our attention. Applying it here, we have the surety asserting the rights of Mid-Continent, of the materialmen, and of Foy. Mid-Continent's claim is non-existent here, because of its assignment to the bank. The materialmen had their equitable claim upon the retained amounts. *Henningsen,* supra; *Pearlman,* supra. Foy had an equitable obligation to pay for material used in the project and for which it was compensated by the owner. In addition it had a right of set off under its subcontract with Mid-Continent, allowing it to apply any money in its hands otherwise due Mid-Continent to any claims for labor or material for which it or the owner "might become liable." . . .

The net result is that, barring the UCC, the surety had an

equitable lien through its right of subrogation dating back to the time it executed the bond, January 31, 1967; the bank's security interest attached no earlier than February 28, 1967. The remaining question is whether the surety lost the priority of its lien by failing to file under the UCC.

The parties agree that the doctrine of subrogation, as such, survived the enactment of the UCC, citing §1-103 that: "Unless displaced by the particular provisions of this act, the principles of law and equity . . . shall supplement its provisions."

The bank argues, however, that *priorities* are governed by the Code, and particularly Article 9. This might well be so if the surety were relying on its contractual assignments of the rights of Mid-Continent or the materialmen. It might then be argued that it was claiming a "security interest" (defined in §1-201(37)) in a "contract right" (defined in §9-106 as amended), in which case it would be covered (§9-102) and filing would be necessary to "perfect" the lien (§9-302, as amended). But the surety here prefers to abandon whatever *contractual* rights it may have, and to bottom its claim wholly on its purely *equitable* right of subrogation.

We have long recognized the distinction between "conventional" subrogation, based on contract, and "legal" or "equitable" subrogation which arises by operation of law without regard to any contractual relationship. We once put it this way:

> . . . Subrogation is a creature of equity invented to prevent a failure of justice, and is broad enough to include an instance in which one party is required to pay what is, between them, the debt of another. It does not depend upon contract nor the absence of contract, but is founded upon principles of natural justice. (New v. Smith, 94 Kan. 6, 16, 145 Pac. 880; Olson v. Peterson, 88 Kan. 350, 128 Pac. 191; Crippen v. Chappel, 35 Kan. 495, 11 Pac 453.) . . . [(Blitz v. Metzger, 119 Kan. 760, 767 241 Pac. 259.)]

And, more directly, in United States Fidelity & Guaranty Co. v. Maryland Cas. Co., 186 Kan. 637, 643, 352 P.2d 70, we said:

> It has recently been recognized that the right to legal subrogation as distinguished from conventional subrogation arises by operation of law and does not depend upon contract, assignment or agreement. [(Fenly v. Revell, 170 Kan. 705, 709, 228 P.2d 905.)] . . .

The surety's right, then, does not depend on contract, while UCC §9-102(2) says that Article 9 applies to security interests "created by contract." It follows that a surety's claim to legal or equitable subrogation is not a "security interest" under Article 9 of the UCC, and is not affected by the surety's failure to file a financing statement.

Although this proposition is new to this court, it has been considered elsewhere with near unanimous results. One of the most recent is Canter v. Schlager, — Mass. — , 267 N.E.2d 492 (1971), which surveys the decision and effectively deals with the few mavericks among them. The controversy there was between a non-filing surety and the contractor's trustee in bankruptcy who, the court noted, had the rights of a lien creditor. In holding the UCC inapplicable the Massachusetts Supreme Judicial Court quoted with approval from Jacobs v. Northeastern Corp., 416 Pa. 417, 429, 206 A.2d 49, 55 (1965):

> . . . Of basic importance is the general rule of Section 9-102(2) that Article 9 "applies to security interests *created by contract.*" Rights of subrogation, although growing out of a contractual setting and ofttimes articulated by the contract, do not depend for their existence on a grant in the contract, but are created by law to avoid injustice. Therefore, subrogation rights are not "security interests" within the meaning of Article 9. . . . [(Emphasis supplied.)] . . .

Some courts which have reached this conclusion have been impressed, as are we, by the rejection from the Code as adopted of a proposed §9-312(7) which would have specifically subordinated the lien of a surety to that of a later lender with a perfected security interest. The Editorial Board's reasons for the deletion of this proposal from the Code were:

> The Surety Companies' representatives convincingly took the position that subsection (7) as it stands is a complete reversal of the case law not only of the Supreme Court of the United States but also of the highest courts of most of the states. . . .
>
> The typical case involved is a case in which a surety company, as a prerequisite to the execution of a performance bond, required a contractor to make an assignment of all moneys coming to the contractor from the owner. Later, the contractor goes to a bank and obtains a loan presumably or actually for the purpose of enabling him to perform his contract.
>
> Under the cited case law, the surety's rights come first as to the funds owing by the owner unless the surety has subordinated its right to the bank. Subsection (7) of the Code as written would reverse the situation and give the bank priority in all cases.

> Under existing case law, both the contractor and the bank are in a position to bargain with the surety which may or may not be willing to subordinate its claim. Under subsection (7) as written in the Code the surety company would have nothing to bargain about.
>
> It was the feeling of the Editorial Board that existing law should not be disturbed particularly as the proposed change would be likely to be a point of controversy in every legislature in which the Code is introduced. [(Uniform Laws Annotated, Uniform Commercial Code, Changes in Text and Comments, at 25-26 [1953].)]

We thus have a clear recognition of the prevailing rule on the part of the draftsmen of the Code and a considered and deliberate decision, made only after reaching a tentative conclusion to the contrary, that they should not propose a change. We think this convincingly demonstrates an intent, imputed to the legislature which adopted it, that the Code should not be applicable to or alter the long established proprieties in this area. As the First Circuit put it (National Shawmut Bk. of Boston v. New Amsterdam Cas. Co., supra, 411 F.2d at 849):

> . . . It may well be — although we express no opinion — that to subject sureties to the filing requirements of the Code would improve and rationalize the system of financing public contracts. But equitable subrogation is too hardy a plant to be uprooted by a Code which speaks around but not to the issue.

We therefore conclude that the trial court erred in finding that the bank had a first and prior right to the contract proceeds in the hands of Foy. The surety, having paid out more than that amount, is entitled to the entire fund.

PROBLEM 7

Farmer Brown borrowed money from Octopus National Bank and used it to plant his crops, giving ONB a perfected security interest in the unharvested crops. When it came time for spraying, Windspeed Crop Dusters (hereinafter WCD) said it would do the job on credit, but only if ONB would agree (which it did) that WCD should be paid first out of the crop proceeds when they were sold (this is called a *subordination agreement*). The crops were then dusted and eventually sold. Before Farmer Brown could pay anyone, ONB went bankrupt. Is the subordination agreement valid against the bank's trustee or is it merely an unperfected security interest? See §9-316. The problem was first suggested by Professor G. Gilmore in Security Interests in Personal Property ch. 37 (1965) (hereinafter cited as G. Gilmore). In the 1966 version of the Code the drafters added §1-209; does it solve the problem?

E. EXCLUSIONS FROM ARTICLE 9

Read §9-104.

1. Federal Statutes

It is no surprise that the Uniform Commercial Code, a state statute, cannot displace federal law. From the way §9-104(a) is worded, however, note that the UCC *does* apply to the extent that the federal statute does not answer the problem presented. See G. Gilmore, ch. 13; for a list of such statutes, see J. White & R. Summers, Uniform Commercial Code §22-11 (1980) (hereinafter White & Summers). With the exception of the federal tax lien statute, I.R.C. §§6321-6325, most federal statutes (the Ship Mortgage Act of 1920, the Civil Aeronautics Act's provisions on security interests in aircraft, etc.) do not cover the field and are constantly supplemented by Article 9 provisions in litigation.

In United States v. Kimbell Foods, 440 U.S. 715, 26 U.C.C. Rep. Serv. 1 (1979), the Supreme Court decided that, as a matter of *federal* law, the relative priority of private consensual liens arising in favor of the U.S. government under various lending programs is to be decided under non-discriminatory state law (i.e., the UCC), unless a federal statute clearly provides otherwise.

For the practitioner the important thing to remember is that certain matters must be researched on a federal as well as state level. Ship mortgages, aircraft titles, patents and copyrights, railroad equipment, and some interstate commercial vehicles (like trucks and buses registered with the Interstate Commerce Commission) are, in part, governed by federal statutes. Creditors (and their attorneys) who think simply an Article 9 filing will perfect their interest in, say, an airplane end up as unsecured creditors whose only cause of action may be against their state-law-minded attorneys; see Feldman v. Chase Manhattan Bank, N.A., 368 F.

Supp. 1327, 13 U.C.C. Rep. Serv. 1333 (S.D.N.Y. 1974) (assignment of airplane lease with Article 9 filing not effective against bankruptcy trustee where creditor failed to file with FAA as required by Federal Aviation Act).

Further, certain federal statutes may void some security interests. Section 125 of the Truth in Lending Act, 15 U.S.C. §1635 (1980), for instance, destroys any security interest taken in a consumer's home as part of a credit transaction if the credit seller does not notify the consumer of a three day right to rescind the contract (and supply the consumer with other truth-in-lending disclosures).

2. *Landlord's Lien and Other Statutory Liens*

Subsections (b) and (c) exclude statutory liens (like the one in Problem 2), and subsection (i) excludes the common law right of *setoff* which a bank has against its depositors' accounts from Article 9; but what about the following situation?

PROBLEM 8

When Christopher Morley opened his bookshop, the landlord wanted security for the rent. They signed a lease agreement providing that all of the inventory (the books) would be subject to a lien in the landlord's favor and could be repossessed and sold if Christopher defaulted in the rent payments. Is the landlord's lien required to be perfected under Article 9? See In re Leckie Freeburn Coal Co., 405 F.2d 1043, 6 U.C.C. Rep. Serv. 15 (6th Cir. 1968): White & Summers §22-6, at 891.

3. *Wage Assignments*

Claims to wages were once a fertile source of collateral, but special statutory regulation has all but killed off wage assignments. Thus some states absolutely prohibit the assignment of future wages (see Code of Ala., tit. 39, §201; such assignments are *void*), some permit them in limited circumstances if the employer consents (see Del. Code Ann., tit. 5 §2115; N.C. Gen. Stat. §95-31), and some states require the consent of both the employer and spouse (Ind. Code of 1971, §22-2-7). Employers always disliked having to mess with direct payments to an employee's creditors (and further disliked the idea that employees had little or no equity left in their own paychecks). The special statutes on the matter survive the enactment of Article 9; §9-104(d).

PROBLEM 9

Carl Jugular was an independent insurance agent who sold policies for many companies, though his primary sales were the life and automobile policies of the Montana Insurance Association (hereinafter MIA). In order to float a loan to buy a car, Carl gave the lending bank a security interest in "all present and future commissions earned or to be earned" from MIA. Does Article 9 cover this assignment? See Massachusetts Mutual Life Ins. Co. v. Central Penn. Natl. Bank, 372 F. Supp. 1027, 14 U.C.C. Rep. Serv. 212 (E.D. Pa. 1974).

4. *Non-financing Assignments*

The §9-104(f) exclusion of some transfers of accounts and chattel paper is meant to be an exclusion of all such assignments of a non-financing nature. See G. Gilmore §10-5; compare §9-102(1)(b).

5. *Real Estate*

Except for fixtures (§9-313), real estate security interests are not covered by Article 9, but what happens when the documents creating them are used as security?

PROBLEM 10

Local Loan Company (LLC) needed to borrow money, and Octopus National Bank agreed to loan it the requisite amount, taking into ONB's possession as collateral the real property mortgages and accompanying promissory notes given to LLC by its borrowers. Need ONB do anything in either the real property recording office or under the UCC's Article 9 to protect its interest in this collateral? Compare §§9-104(j) and 9-102(3); read the latter's Official Comment 4; see the helpful discussion in Bowman, Real Estate Interests as Security Under the UCC: The Scope of Article Nine, 12 U.C.C.L.J. 99 (1979);

see also In re Freeborn, 94 Wash. 2d 336, 617 P.2d 424, 29 U.C.C. Rep. Serv. 1625 (1980).

6. *Other Exclusions*

Official Comment 8 to §9-104 states the other excluded matters that "do not customarily serve as commercial collateral." As a result, if a consumer wants to use a savings account passbook as collateral that is possible, but common law and not Article 9 will straighten out the resulting legal rights (§9-104(k)).

CHAPTER 3

THE CREATION OF A SECURITY INTEREST

A. *CLASSIFYING THE COLLATERAL*

Article 9 divides collateral (defined in §9-105(1)(c)) into nine different categories:

Goods: (§9-105(1)(h); cf. §2-105);
Consumer Goods (read §9-109(1)); 77 A.L.R.3d 1225;
Equipment (read §9-109(2));
Farm Products (read §9-109(3)); and
Inventory (read §9-109(4)); 77 A.L.R.3d 1226;

Quasi-Tangible Property:
Instruments (read §§9-105(1)(i), 3-104, and 8-102);
Documents (read §§9-105(1)(f) and 1-201(15)); and
Chattel Paper (read §9-105(1)(b)); and

Intangible Property:
Accounts (read §9-106); and
General Intangibles (read §9-106).

Note that *equipment* is defined to have not only its usual meaning, but also as a catch-all category for any *goods* that do not fit into the other three goods categories. Similarly *general intangibles* includes all intangible collateral not falling into another category.

Classification of the collateral is important because many provisions of Article 9 make legal distinctions based on the type of collateral. For example, the technical steps required to *perfect* a security interest in a negotiable instrument (§9-304(1)), a family car (§9-302(1)(d)), or a hardware store's inventory (§§9-302 and 9-312(3)) are completely different; see §9-109, Official Comment 1.

PROBLEM 11

Fill in the blanks with the proper classifications of these items of collateral:

(a) A professional pianist's piano: ________ (see In re Symons, 5 U.C.C. Rep. Serv. 262 (Ref. Bankr. E.D. Mich. 1967)).

(b) Cattle fattened by a farmer for sale: ________ (see In re Cadwell, Martin Meat Co., 10 U.C.C. Rep. Serv. 710 (Ref. Bankr. E.D. Cal. 1970)); the farmer's tractor: ________ (see Central Nat. Bank v. Wonderland Realty Corp., 38 Mich. App. 76 195 N.W.2d 768, 10 U.C.C. Rep. Serv. 1117 (1972)); the farmer's chickens: ________ (see §9-109, Official Comment 4; United States v. Pete Brown Enterp., Inc., 328 F. Supp. 600, 9 U.C.C. Rep. Serv. 734 (N.D. Miss. 1971)); manure from the dairy herd: ________ (see Miller, Farm Collateral Under the UCC: "Those Are Some Mighty Tall Silos, Ain't They Fella?," 20 S.D.L. Rev. 514, 526 (1975)).

(c) A mobile home: ________ (see White & Summers at 924-925).

(d) A right to sue someone for breach of contract: ________ (see Friedman, Lobe & Block v. C.L.W. Corp., 512 P.2d 769, 13 U.C.C. Rep. Serv. 136 (Wash. App. 1973)); for negligence: ________ (see §9-104(k)); a security interest in a lawsuit plaintiff has already won: ________ (see §9-104(h)).

(e) Pencils and other stationery supplies used by Sears or a similar large retailer in its credit offices: ________ (see §9-109, Official Comment 3).

(f) A liquor license: ________ (see In re Branding Iron, Inc., 7 B.R. 729, 30 U.C.C. Rep. Serv. 1687 (Bankr. E.D. Pa. 1980)); a right to the return of a security deposit held by a landlord: ________ (see United States v. Samel Ref. Corp., 461 F.2d 941, 10 U.C.C. Rep. Serv. 1232 (3d Cir. 1972)); a newspaper carrier's right to payments for papers already delivered: ________.

(g) Curtains bought by a lawyer for the law office: ________ (see In re Bonnema, 4 U.C.C. Rep. Serv. 894 (N.D. Ohio 1967)). What if after purchasing the curtains the lawyer decides to use them at home? Do they become consumer goods? See the next case; compare In re McClain, 447 F.2d 241, 9 U.C.C. Rep. Serv. 545 (10th Cir. 1971); White & Summers §23-13.

In re Morton

9 U.C.C. Rep. Serv. 1147 (D. Me. 1971)

Cyr, Ref. Bankr. Upon his voluntary adjudication in bankruptcy Philip Morton was in possession of a 1968 Ford Bronco subject to the purchase money security interest now under attack by the trustee in bankruptcy. When he purchased the Bronco the bankrupt was employed as an unlicensed surveyor by Knox Mining and Surveying Company. He bought the Bronco to replace an aging Chevrolet station wagon, which had been used primarily for personal and household purposes. Several months after the purchase of the Bronco, Knox Mining & Surveying Company contracted to reimburse the bankrupt on a mileage basis for transporting surveying equipment. Thereafter, the Bronco was used primarily for that purpose, although it was used to a lesser extent for other purposes as well.

When Maine National Bank's security interest attached by virtue of the execution of a valid security agreement between Harold B. Stetson, the seller, and the bankrupt, the bankrupt was residing in Union, Maine. On October 10, 1969, the same day the security agreement was executed, the seller caused a sufficient financing statement to be filed with the Town Clerk of Union.

The court is satisfied, on the basis of the evidence presented, that the bankrupt bought this vehicle primarily for personal and household purposes, but that the actual use to which it was put was of other than a personal, family, or household nature. The Bronco was used primarily in connection with the bankrupt's employment and in furtherance of his employer's surveying business.

Conclusions of Law

The filing of the financing statement in the office of the clerk of the municipality where the debtor resided at the time the security interest attached on October 10, 1969 perfected the Bank's purchase money security interest, providing the collateral constituted consumer goods. In re O'Donnell, 7 UCC Rep. Serv. 888

(D. Me. 1970). But if the vehicle was neither used nor bought for use primarily for personal, family or household purposes, it was incumbent upon the secured party to cause an additional financing statement to be filed in the office of the Secretary of State. Since the bankrupt bought the vehicle primarily for personal purposes, it constituted consumer goods. The filing of a sufficient financing statement with the Town Clerk of Union sufficed to perfect the purchase money security interest, despite the fact that the vehicle was used thereafter primarily for other than personal, family and household purposes.

There is a measure of commercial expediency inherent in gauging compliance with Code perfection requirements by recourse to the *extrinsic circumstances prevailing at the time the security interest attaches.*[1] In re O'Donnell, 7 UCC Rep. Serv. 888 (D. Me. 1970); In re Pelletier, 5 UCC Rep. Serv. 327 (D. Me. 1968). While §9-109(1) seems to restrict the court's determination of the buyer's

1. The protection afforded by §9-401(3) precludes a filing made in the proper place from being struck down later because of a change in the collateral's *actual* use. Furthermore, although §9-401(3) makes no reference to the *intended* use of the collateral, subsections (1) & (2) of §9-109 seem to fix the moment of purchase as the relevant point for inquiry into the buyer's intention. It is difficult to conceive of a circumstance in which the purchase of the collateral will not precede the attachment of the security interest, except as to collateral which was never purchased. Often collateral which was never purchased by the debtor or any predecessor in title will be inventory or farm products, whose classifications do not depend on the application of §9-109 (1) & (2). Where it is otherwise, the shortcoming inherent in the statute lies in the use of the phraseology "*bought for use*," which seems necessarily to imply the occurrence of a purchase and the presence of a buyer-debtor, neither of which will always be found in any given secured transaction. Provided the moment of the attachment of the security interest is selected as the critical point at which collateral use is tested, there can be no period following the attachment of the security interest in which a change of collateral use could render ineffective a filing accomplished in response to circumstances which existed at the moment of attachment. It is otherwise, of course, if the time of filing is the critical point, since filing may follow by a substantial period but is seldom simultaneous with either the purchase of, or the attachment of a security interest in, the collateral. A more serious problem in terms of the notice function with Code filing is supposed to serve, is that a filing made in contemplation of a security agreement will be insulated by §9-401(3) from later attack regardless how dissimilar the debtor's circumstances were at the time of filing as compared to those which obtained when he acquired rights in the collateral, or possession of the collateral, or granted a security in erest in the collateral. "The purpose of notice filing is not to notify the world of the debtor's place of residence at the time of filing, but to inform it of the existence of a security interest in collateral which arose while the debtor resided in the place where the filing is made." In re Pelletier, 5 UCC Rep. Serv. 327, 335 (D. Me. 1968).

intended use of the collateral to the time of purchase,[2] it is not so necessarily as concerns the actual use to which the collateral is put. Therefore, serious judicial consideration should be given to applying the collateral use tests prescribed by §9-109(1) and (2) in the circumstances prevailing *when the security interest attaches*. Cf. In re Pelletier, 5 UCC Rep. Serv. 327 (D. Me. 1968). But cf. Bender's UCC Service, Willier & Hart, UCC Reporter-Digest, §9-401, A20 (Matthew Bender & Co.). In terms of facilitating commerce it would be cumbersome to require secured parties to maintain a continuing surveillance of debtors and their collateral beyond the time when the security interest attached.[3] Less awkward collateral policing requirements were thought commercially unacceptable before the advent of the Uniform Commercial Code. It seems doubtful, therefore, that the Code architects intended to inhibit commercial transactions by making filing or the occurrence of some event other than the attachment of the security

2. The wording of §9-109(1) could be more precise. The purchase of the collateral will by no means always occur when the security interest attaches. Security interests commonly attach long after the purchase of the collateral. Nor is the debtor always a "buyer," in which event the *debtor's intended use* of the collateral could be deemed irrelevant. This combination of possibilities suggests the wisdom of "redundant" filing on collateral the debtor either does not buy or buys long before or after the security agreement. The quandary reaches bar examination dimensions when the interrelationship of §§9-109(1) & (2), 9-401(1)(b) & (c) and 9-401(2) & (3) is considered. See also UCC Comment 2, following 11 MRSA §9-109.

Section 9-109(1) & (2) might read:

"Goods are

"(1) Consumer goods. 'Consumer goods,' if, at the time the security interest attaches, they are used or intended by the debtor for use primarily for personal, family or household purposes. . . ."

3. It should not be overlooked that the test prescribed by §9-109(1) is of enormous importance in many jurisdictions where not only the place of filing but *the very necessity for filing* may depend upon whether or not the collateral constitutes consumer goods.

"Presumably it can be agreed that the determination of the need for filing is not to be made at the time of filing. Section 9-109 defines the various types of collateral principally on the basis of the primary use to which they are put or for which they are bought. Upon this determination turns in part the selection of the place of filing. It seems clear enough that one cannot determine the purpose or use for which collateral was acquired before it either exists or is acquired. If we concede that such decisions as what constitutes 'goods' and what constitutes 'consumer' goods often cannot be made at the time of filing and that the very necessity for filing and the place of filing turn upon such considerations, it seems both consistent and reasonably convenient, and therefore, desirable, to require that the decision as to the debtor's residence be made in like fashion." In re Pelletier, 5 UCC Rep. Serv. 327, 335-36 (D. Me. 1968).

interest the critical time to apply the collateral use test; however curious it is that neither §9-109 itself nor the Official Comments evidence awareness of the problem.

Accordingly, it is ordered, adjudged and decreed that the purchase money security interest of Maine National Bank be and it is hereby determined perfected, and it is further.

Ordered, adjudged and decreed that the application of the trustee in bankruptcy be and it is hereby dismissed, with prejudice.

QUESTION

What will be the result where a car buyer tells the salesman he wants the car for personal family use, but is lying and really plans to resell it on his own lot? See Balon v. Cadillac Automobile Co., 303 A.2d 194, 12 U.C.C. Rep. Serv. 397 (N.H. 1973).

PROBLEM 12

Fill in the blanks with the proper collateral classifications:

(a) Milk in the hands of the farmer: ________: in the hands of the grocery store: ________, in the hands of the grocery store's customer who is buying for consumption: ________. Would your answer to the second question change if "restaurant" were used in place of "grocery store"?

(b) A certificate of deposit issued by a bank: ________(compare §3-104(2)(c), §9-104(l), and Southview Corp. v. Kleberg First Nat. Bank, 512 S.W.2d 817, 15 U.C.C. Rep. Serv. 408 (Tex. Civ. App. 1974)); a written contract in which a credit car buyer promises to pay the car dealership for the car and grants the dealership a security interest in the car: ________; an "airbill" issued by an airline as a receipt for frozen shrimp shipped by air: ________(see §1-201(6)); the receipt given to a farmer by a silo operator when the farmer stored grain there: ________.

(c) Rare coins bought by a hobbyist for addition to his collection: ________(see In re Midas Coin Co., 264 F. Supp. 193, 4 U.C.C. Rep. Serv. 220 (E.D. Mo. 1967), *aff'd,* 387 F.2d 118, 4 U.C.C. Rep. Serv. 908 (8th Cir. 1968)).

PROBLEM 13

David Merry loved speculative investments, which he financed through his lucrative art business. When the late Elvis Presley died,

Merry managed to acquire one of the singer's guitars, deciding to keep it for years as it appreciated in value (he did not himself play the guitar). If Merry uses the guitar as collateral for a loan to his art business, how is the guitar classified?

B. TECHNICAL VALIDITY OF THE FORMS

The creation of an Article 9 security interest typically involves two documents: the *security agreement* and the *financing statement.* The security agreement is the *contract* between the debtor and creditor by which the debtor grants to the creditor (the *secured party*) a security interest in the collateral; see §9-105(1)(e). The financing statement is the *notice* that is filed in the place specified in §9-401 in order to give later creditors an awareness that the collateral is encumbered. Thus the purpose of the security agreement is to create rights between the debtor and creditor, and the purpose of a financing statement is to create rights in the creditor against most of the rest of the world.

This section of the book explores the technical requirements for valid security agreements and financing statements. Read §§9-203(1) and 9-402(1) and (3).

1. The Security Agreement

Where the collateral is in the possession of the secured party, no written security agreement is required. But where the property is to leave the creditor's control §9-203 becomes relevant and creates technical problems.

Section 9-203, according to the Official Comment (which you should read), is a Statute of Frauds. If the security agreement is oral (thereby creating what the common law called an *equitable lien*), it is usually unenforceable even between the parties. (The absolute anti-equitable lien language of Comment 5 has been retracted by Grant Gilmore, its author, who has stated that he "overshot the mark" and that "§9-203 will be no more successful than any other Statute of Frauds has ever been in making hard problems go away" (G. Gilmore §11.4).)

If the collateral is not in the secured party's possession, the §9-

203 writing must (a) be signed by the debtor and (b) describe the collateral (plus the land if crops or timber are involved). The security agreement need not be in any particular form or contain any particular words (cf. §1-201(3), defining *agreement*). It needn't call itself a security agreement; see Official Comment 4 to §9-203 on the admissibility of parol evidence to establish the security nature of apparently absolute transactions.

PROBLEM 14

When Frederick Bean bought a new typewriter on credit from Centerboro Office Supply, the store made him sign a "Conditional Sale Contract" by which he agreed that title to the typewriter would remain with the store until he had fully paid for it. The contract described the typewriter but nowhere did it mention a security interest. Does the contract qualify as a security agreement under §9-203? See §§1-201(37) and 2-401(1) — the second sentence in each is relevant; Sommers v. International Bus. Mach., 640 F.2d 686, 30 U.C.C. Rep. Serv. 1757 (5th Cir. 1981).

A good security agreement will of course spell out much more than §9-203 requires. It should identify the parties, describe the collateral, contain a *grant* by the debtor to the creditor of a security interest in the collateral, and specify the contractual understandings of the parties, particularly naming what events will constitute *default* so as to permit the creditor to realize on the security interest by repossessing the collateral.

2. *The Financing Statement*

The financing statement is the document filed by the creditor (secured party) to *perfect* the creditor's rights in the collateral against later parties. It must contain (a) the signatures of the debtor, (b) the mailing addresses of both parties (so that those searching the files know where to go to get more information; cf. §9-208), and (c) a description of the collateral (and the land if timber, minerals, fixtures, or crops are involved). See the sample form in §9-402(3).

Security agreements and financing statements serve different purposes, but they have several problems in common: who is the *debtor*, what is a sufficient description of the collateral, etc. Some of these questions are answered identically for both documents and some are not. The most common specific problems are explored next.

3. *The Debtor's Identity*

The debtor must sign both the security agreement and the financing statement.[4]

PROBLEM 15

Carla Debtor misread the financing statement form the creditor gave her and failed to sign her name in the appropriate spot. However, Carla did dictate an order to her secretary to type her name onto the signature blank. Has she "signed" the financing statement? See §1-201(39), defining *signed* (and see Official Comment 39 thereto), and Benedict v. Lebowitz, 346 F.2d 120, 2 U.C.C. Rep. Serv. 747 (2d Cir. 1965); see also §9-402(8); Annot., 3 A.L.R. 4th 502 (1981). If the security agreement was signed by the debtor and is filed along with an unsigned financing statement, will that solve the problem? See §9-402(1) and Sommers v. International Bus. Mach., 640 F.2d 686, 30 U.C.C. Rep. Serv. 1757 (5th Cir. 1981).

When the financing statement is filed (typically in the Secretary of State's office) it will be indexed under the debtor's name. Since later possible creditors will search the records under that name, it is particularly important that it be correct; see 99 A.L.R.3d 478 (1980).

PROBLEM 16

Harry Grownup ran a movie theatre called the "Grownup Adult Theatre," but since he was the sole proprietor that was a trade name. He gave a security interest in the business' equipment to Sharkteeth Finance Company. The financing statement calls for a listing of the "debtor's name."

(a) Should the parties use the business name or individual name?

4. The exception is on the financing statement in the situations envisioned by §9-402(2), where only the secured party need sign.

Read §9-402(7); see Citizens Bank v. Ansley, 467 F. Supp. 51, 26 U.C.C. Rep. Serv. 223 (M.D. Ga. 1979).

(b) If Sharkteeth files under the wrong name, is its security interest saved if the filing officer at the Secretary of State's office maintains a cross-index and indexes the statement under both names? Compare In re Wishart, 10 U.C.C. Rep. Serv. 1296 (Ref. Bankr. W.D. Mich. 1972), with In re Green Mill Inn, Inc., 474 F.2d 14, 12 U.C.C. Rep. Serv. 184 (9th Cir. 1973).

(c) If the theatre were run as a partnership, would the partnership's name be used as the debtor's name? See §9-402(7). One court has formulated this general rule: "A financing statement, in order to perfect a security interest, must, in the case of an individual, or individuals, doing business under a trade name show the name of the individual legally responsible for the debt unless the trade name and the individual debtor's name are so similar that a prospective creditor, upon seeing the trade name in the records, would be alerted that there might be a prior security interest in the involved collateral." In re Fowler, 407 F. Supp. 799, 803, 19 U.C.C. Rep. Serv. 322, 328 (W.D. Okla. 1975).

In re Hatfield Construction Company

10 U.C.C. Rep. Serv. 907 (M.D. Ga. 1971)

[The debtor was the bankrupt corporation of Hatfield Construction Company, and the problem was that the financing statement gave the debtor's name as "Hatfield, Wayne L.," the corporation's president. The bankruptcy trustee claimed that the security interest was therefore unperfected since the financing statement was indexed under the wrong debtor's name. After quoting U.C.C. §1-102 about "liberal construction," Bankruptcy Judge Truett Smith continued as follows.]

The scheme of the Uniform Commercial Code for this State — and other states also — is to establish a system of notice filing. Filing requirements have been simplified. Statutory requirements are designed to develop commercial transactions, not legal literary style. There is no requirement for filing the security agreement. A simple notice must be filed indicating that the secured party may have a security interest in the collateral described. Additionally, inquiry beyond filing is contemplated. The system of notice filing does not call for verbosity. In re Excel Stores, Inc., 2 Cir., 1965, 341 F.2d 961. Notice filing eliminates persnicketiness but does not eliminate certainty. Spivack, Secured Transactions, pp. 2, 3 (1963). So the key to perfection of a security interest against a debtor's property is notice and to accomplish that the financing statement must give the name of the debtor. In re Platt, D.C. Penn., 1966, 257 F. Supp. 478. See also In re Brown, D.C. Ohio, 1950, 88 F. Supp. 297. Thus in searching an index a name is important. The law will not have accomplished anything if in eliminating refined reading there is substituted guess and surmise. The purpose of notice filing is to furnish a public record with content satisfying the need to warn a person liable to be affected that there may be an earlier security interest. In re Grandmont, D.C. Conn., 1970, 310 F. Supp. 968; John Deere Co. of Baltimore v. William C. Pahl C. Co., 59 Misc. 2d 872, 300 N.Y.S.2d 701 (1969). Bearing in mind that a system of notice filing has been adopted, the effect of Ga. Code Anno. §109A-402(5), when its application is sought, is based upon the reality of each event.

In Wilkinson County a creditor has access to the indexing and to financing statements that are filed. Thus, a creditor does not have to rely upon the filing officer, who in this State is the Clerk of the Superior Court. Any interested creditor searching the index encountering the name of a debtor can examine the financing statement which he is led to examine that is indexed.

The court is guided to its result here by Silver v. Gulf City Body & Trailer Works, 5 Cir., 1970, 432 F.2d 992, and concludes under the facts and circumstances enough information can reasonably be picked out from the public record to enable those desiring to learn of the status of the property of the bankrupt to do so. It was held in that case that the address "Box 2146, Ft. Worth, Texas" was a substantial compliance with the requirement of Alabama's Uniform Commercial Code governing the content of financing statements. That case drew support from Pennsylvania where it has been held in *Platt,* supra, that a financing statement which identified the name of the debtor as Platt Fur Co. instead of as Henry Platt required those who made a search of the record to make further investigation because subsequent creditors were alerted by name similarity. In addition, *Silver,* supra, favorably viewed In re Bennett, D.C. Mich., 1969, 6 UCC Rep. Serv. 551, which court takes a more liberal view of errors and misnomers in financing statements than some other courts are taking. Hilman, Drafting Financing Statements, 44 Ref. J. 102, 104 (1970).

The relation in name similarity is in the same degree here as in *Platt,* supra. The only difference is the facts here are exactly reversed as to what was indexed and as to what was not indexed. Mr. Hatfield was the president of the bankrupt. In re Colorado Mercantile Co., D.C. Colo., 1969, 299 F. Supp. 55. On file since early 1970 with the Clerk of the Superior Court of Wilkinson County in accordance with Ga. Code Anno. §22-803 are documents of incorporation of the bankrupt. This shows Wayne L. Hatfield with his address as the name of the bankrupt's initial registered agent, as an incorporator of the bankrupt and as a member of the initial board of directors of the bankrupt. The mailing address of Mr. Hatfield on the financing statement is that of the bankrupt and this assured proper delivery of mail. Wilkinson County is not a large body of people. Its population according to the 1970 Census in 9393. The index would not deal with great numbers of financing statements compared to an index for a large community. For the reasons given the court holds that the notice filing requirements of Georgia's Uniform Commercial Code have been complied with. See Stafford v. Admiral Credit Corp., D.C.N.C., 1968, 280 F. Supp. 818; In re Thomas, D.C. Cal., 1970, 310 F. Supp. 338; Plemens v. Diddle-Glasser, Inc., 244 Md. 556, 224 A.2d 464, 469-470 (1966). The correctness of this conclusion is seen in a commendable statement counsel for the trustee made in his oral argument. He stated the scope of a search he would make of the index in Wilkinson County would lead him to the name of Wayne L. Hatfield but he urges that every person would not make a search of such scope as he would make. This may be true but his statement is in support of the court's conclusion that a creditor desiring to come to the name of Wayne L. Hatfield may do so.

PROBLEM 17

The debtor's correct name was "Raymond F. Sargent, Inc." but the financing statement listed the debtor's name as "Raymond F. Sargent Co., Inc.," and it was so indexed. Is the financing statement effective? See §9-402(8). In re Raymond F. Sargent, Inc., 8 U.C.C. Rep. Serv. 583 (Bankr. D. Me. 1970) (a case identical to the case cited in Official Comment 9 to §9-402; see White & Summers §23-16, and Comment, The Effect of Errors and Changes In the Debtor's Name on Article Nine Security Interests, 1975 Duke L.J. 148, 153-154). See also In re Lockwood, 16 U.C.C. Rep. Serv. 195 (Bankr. D. Conn. 1974) ("Farm House Market" listed for "Farm House Country Store" held OK); In re Gibson's Discount Pharmacy of Bristol, Tenn., Inc., 15

U.C.C. Rep. Serv. 233 (Bankr. E.D. Tenn. 1974) (bankrupt corporation listed on financing statement as "Gibco Discount Drugs" held insufficient, the court saying that "liberality in overlooking minor errors in names ceases when the errors eliminate notice"). For a good discussion of the consequences of reversing the debtor's first and last names and the practical workings of a filing office, see In re Graham, 18 U.C.C. Rep. Serv. 1318 (Bankr. W.D. Mich. 1975). Of course similar errors occur in describing the collateral.

Central National Bank & Trust Co. v. Community Bank & Trust Co.

528 P.2d 710, 16 U.C.C. Rep. Serv. 244 (Okla. 1974)

WILLIAMS, C.J. This appeal presents a question of priority of liens as between two Enid banks, Community Bank & Trust Company and Central National Bank and Trust Company, hereinafter referred to as Community and Central respectively. Both banks made loans to the same debtor with the same automobile, a 1972 Ford LTD, Serial No. 2G68S176503, as security. Although Community's security agreement was taken and filed earlier, the trial court's judgment accorded priority to the Central security agreement and Community appeals. All other parties in the trial court either defaulted or filed disclaimers and only the relative rights of the two banks are involved on appeal.

The pertinent facts are not in dispute. After a series of loan transactions with the debtor Anderson, under the name of "Lee Anderson," Community made a loan to "Lee Anderson," taking a security agreement on the new automobile which it properly filed in the County Clerk's office, where it was indexed under the name of "Lee Anderson." Community did not examine the manufacturer's statement of origin, issued three days earlier to James Anderson, and took no steps to assure itself that the car title papers would be issued in the name of Lee Anderson. The same day Anderson, whose full name was James Lee Anderson, applied for and received an Oklahoma certificate of title in the name of James L. Anderson. His excise tax receipt was issued in the same name.

About six months later Central also made a loan to Anderson, as "James L. Anderson," taking and filing a security agreement covering the same automobile. Before doing so it made a telephone check with the County Clerk's office and determined correctly that no prior liens on the automobile had been filed against James L. Anderson, the name shown on the certificate of title.

In a lengthy journal entry of judgment, the trial court made findings of facts which, in addition to the matters above summarized, included the following:

> *That although no one at the trial of this case, or in the briefs, made mention of the identifying serial number* of the automobile in question, it is clear to the Court, upon careful examination of the exhibits that the proper serial number was and is 2G68S176503 . . . but the Community Bank original note and security agreement . . . as well as its filing copy . . . shows that Community Bank took security upon a car with a Serial Number 2G685176503. . . .[(Emphasis added.)]

In a corresponding conclusion of law, the trial court held that because of the mistake in the serial number, Community's ". . . alleged lien upon this car was not perfected."

We agree with Community that its lien is not to be defeated solely because of the 1-digit mistake in the serial number. Under §9-110, ". . . any description of personal property or real estate is sufficient whether or not it is specific if it reasonably identifies what is described." The Uniform Commercial Code Comment under this section includes the following:

> The test of sufficiency of a description laid down by this Section is that the description do the job assigned to it — that it make possible the identification of the thing described. Under this rule courts should refuse to follow the holdings, often found in the older chattel mortgage cases, that descriptions are insufficient unless they are of the most exact and detailed nature, the so-called "serial number" test.

The security agreements in this case were filed as financing statements under §9-402, subsection 5 of which provides that "A financing statement substantially complying with the requirements of this section is effective even though it contains minor errors which are not seriously misleading."

In this connection, see Bank of North America v. Bank of Nutley, 94 N.J. Super. 220, 227 A.2d 535, in which a 1-digit mistake in an 11-digit serial number was held to be "a minor error which is not seriously misleading" in a case applying the New York version of the Uniform Commercial Code.

The wisdom of this rule is well illustrated by the facts in this case in which it appears that neither the parties, their witnesses, nor their counsel noticed the discrepancy in the serial number until it was called to their attention by the trial judge after trial briefs had been filed and the case submitted for decision.

Although the court's holding that Community's lien was not perfected because of the error in the serial number was erroneous, it does not follow that the judgment must be reversed. The court also found in effect that Community was negligent in not examining the manufacturer's statement of origin, and in not assuring itself that the certificate of title had been, or would be, issued in the name of Lee Anderson. The court further found that Community ". . . had the means to protect itself, and did not, or by its conduct created the circumstances which enabled Mr. Anderson to perpetrate additional wrongs and later obtaining three additional loans from two other banks, on the strength and security of this same automobile." The court then held, in effect, that Community's lien, although filed first, did not constitute notice to Central because it was filed under a different name, and accorded precedence to Central's lien under the rule stated as follows in Bankers Investment Co. v. Humphrey, Okl., 369 P.2d 608:

> . . . Where one of two innocent parties must suffer through the act or negligence of a third party, the loss should fall upon the one who by his conduct created the circumstances which enabled the third party to perpetrate the wrong or cause the loss.

In a reply brief, Community argues that the quoted rule from Bankers should not be applied because (1) the facts were different in that case, in which two different people, and not merely two different names of the same person, were involved, and (2) this case should be governed entirely by the provisions of the Uniform Commercial Code and equitable principles should not be applied.

As to (1) above, we do not agree that the *pertinent* facts were different. In both cases, the prior claimant filed a lien under a name not shown on the car title papers, and without examining the certificate of title or the manufacturer's statement of origin. In both cases, the subsequent claimant properly relied upon the name shown on the certificate of title.

As to (2) above, Community argues that it was guilty of no intentional wrong, and that it did all that was required by the applicable provisions of the Uniform Commercial Code in taking and filing its security agreement. This is true, but only as to automobiles owned by *Lee* Anderson. Clearly, Community's failure to file its lien in the name shown on the certificate of title was responsible for Central's later determination, justified by the lien records of the County Clerk, that there was no prior lien on record against an automobile owned by *James* L. Anderson.

The quoted rule from Bankers, also called the doctrine of estoppel by negligence and the "two innocent persons" principle, is admittedly of equitable origin. See 28 Am. Jur. 2d Estoppel and Waiver, §62 and 27 Am. Jur. 2d Equity, §147. Under §1-103, ". . . the principles of . . . equity, including . . . estoppel . . . shall supplement . . ." the provisions of the Uniform Commercial Code unless displaced by particular provisions of that Code.

We hold that the quoted rule from Bankers was properly applied in this case.

Community also argues that since Anderson's mailing address was the same on both security agreements, Central should have known that the debtor was the same. However, since the lien records of the County Clerk are indexed alphabetically according to the debtor's name, and not according to the mailing address, Central was not charged with notice of that fact. We agree with the conclusion of the trial court that ". . . reasonable diligence, in this case, would not require Central National Bank to examine all the secured transaction index under the name of 'Anderson.' "

The judgment of the trial court is affirmed.

QUESTION

If Community Bank were your client, how would you advise it to avoid this problem in the future?

PROBLEM 18

Barbara Song borrowed $50,000 from Octopus National Bank in order to start a business called "Barb's Interiors," interior design being her specialty. ONB and Ms. Song signed a security agreement and a financing statement showing her as the debtor and giving ONB an interest in the inventory and equipment; ONB duly filed the financing statement. Subsequently Ms. Song married Fred Dancer and she changed her name to Barbara Dancer. She then incorporated the business. She borrowed another $50,000 from the Foxlike Finance

Company, which loaned her the money after searching the records under both "Dancer" and "Barb's Interiors, Inc." and finding no prior encumbrances on the business' inventory and equipment. Did ONB lose its security interest because it failed to refile when her name (or the business' nature and name) changed? See §9-402(7); 99 A.L.R.3d 1194 (1980). Does it matter whether or not the creditor learns of the change in name? Compare In re Kittyhawk Television Corp., 516 F.2d 24, 16 U.C.C. Rep. Serv. 1401 (6th Cir. 1975) (doesn't matter), with In re Kalamazoo Steel Process, Inc., 503 F.2d 1218, 15 U.C.C. Rep. Serv. 571 (6th Cir. 1974) (UCC's general requirement of "good faith," §1-203, does require refiling where creditor knows of upcoming name change at the time the original security agreement is signed).

PROBLEM 19

The Last National Bank filed a financing statement in the proper place to perfect its security interest in the inventory of the American Electronics Store. When the latter ran into financial difficulty, its assets were sold to a new electronics concern, Voice of Japan, which moved into the same retail location. Must Last National refile to keep its security interest perfected in (a) the inventory actually transferred by American Electronics to Voice of Japan or (b) the inventory therefore acquired by Voice of Japan with the proceeds of the sale from the original? See §9-402(7)'s last sentence and its Official Comment 8; In Re Matto's Inc., 8 B.R. 485, 30 U.C.C. Rep. Serv. 1750 (Bankr. E.D. Mich. 1981). What if the opposite happens and the debtor remains the same but Last National assigns its interest in the debtor's inventory to Octopus National Bank; need the records be changed? Read §9-405 and its Official Comment. If this procedure is followed is ONB's interest superior to Last National's creditors? See §9-102(1); White & Summers at 959.

4. *Description of the Collateral*

One of the great fears of those opposed to Article 9's adoption would be that it would lead to creditor overreaching in demanding too much collateral.

PROBLEM 20

Peter Poor signed a security agreement and financing statement in favor of the Total Finance Company giving the company a security interest in "All personal property debtor now owns or ever owns or even hopes to own between now and the end of the world or his death whichever occurs first." Does this perfect an interest in his guitar? In re Lockwood, 16 U.C.C. Rep. Serv. 195 (Bankr. D. Conn. 1974) ("All presently owned and hereafter acquired tangible personal property" held too broad); In re Fuqua, 461 F.2d 1186, 10 U.C.C. Rep. Serv. 936 (10th Cir. 1972) ("All personal property" too broad); In re Johnson, 13 U.C.C. Rep. Serv. 953 (Bankr. D. Neb. 1973) ("All household and consumer goods located on debtor's premises" held OK); In Re Turnage, 493 F.2d 505, 14 U.C.C. Rep. Serv. 1051 (5th Cir. 1974) ("All consumer goods" held OK); In re Woods, 9 U.C.C. Rep. Serv. 116 (D. Kan. 1971) ("Consumer Goods" not OK since §9-402 requires description by "type" or "item"); Mammoth Cave Prod. Credit Assn. v. York, 429 S.W.2d 26, 5 U.C.C. Rep. Serv. 11 (Ky. 1968) ("All farm equipment" held too vague).

Section 9-110 (read same along with its Official Comment) speaks to the faulty description problem in both the security agreement and the financing statement. The cases are annotated in 100 A.L.R.3d 10 (sufficiency of description in financing statement) and 100 A.L.R.3d 940 (security agreement) (both 1980). The test adopted by the courts is "whether the description does the job assigned to it, i.e., make possible the identification of the thing described." Marine Midland Bank–Eastern Nat. Assn. v. Conerty Pontiac-Buick, Inc., 352 N.Y.S.2d 953, 14 U.C.C. Rep. Serv. 814 (Sup. Ct. 1974). Or, since the later potential creditors will be doing the records searching, would a "reasonable man" be put on inquiry as to the identity of the collateral? Ray v. City Bank & Trust Co., 358 F. Supp. 630, 13 U.C.C. Rep. Serv. 355 (S.D. Ohio 1973). The UCC, however, adopts a system of "notice filing" so that the description in the financing statement[5] need only be sufficient to alert the searcher to the necessity for further inquiry (thus the reason for the address §9-402 demands). "The description need only inform, it need not educate." *Marine* case, supra at 960. Read §§9-208 and 9-402(8).

5. Many courts hold that the description need not be as exact in the financing statement as in the security agreement. See, e.g., In re Laminated Veneers, Inc., 471 F.2d 1124, 11 U.C.C. Rep. Serv. 911 (2d Cir. 1973). The reason is that the financing statement's function is to serve as a warning to later potential lenders that the details of the earlier transaction need exploration; the security agreement's function is to describe those very details. See White & Summers §23-2, at 910.

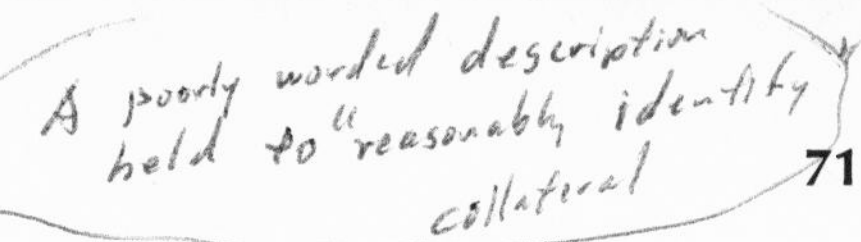

In re Sarex Corporation

509 F.2d 689, 16 U.C.C. Rep. Serv. 497 (2d Cir. 1975)

OAKES, J. As long as the language of law is ambiguous as it so often is, and so long as lawyers (or laymen) fail to take the time or omit to exercise the acuity necessary to eliminate or reduce that ambiguity, there will be law suits like this one that could have been avoided. The question on this appeal relates to the meaning of a security agreement and the sufficiency of its description of the property secured. Like the bankruptcy judge, Roy Babitt, and the district court judge, Lawrence W. Pierce, of the United States District Court for the Southern District of New York, we hold for the secured party (Selena Goudeau) and accordingly affirm the order directing the trustee of the bankrupt Sarex Corporation (Sarex) to turn over to her the proceeds received from a sale of the property secured necessary to pay the secured balance due.

Sarex, a New Jersey corporation, sold plastic cassette covers and bases and proposed to manufacture them from molds. In early 1970 it agreed to buy some 5 million covers and bases, and for manufacturing purposes two molds, a "1 × 1 cavity mold" and a "2 × 2 cavity mold," from E.G.L. Enterprises Ltd. (EGL) in Montreal. It was stipulated that until paid for the molds were not to be removed from EGL's premises. EGL proceeded to obtain a $7,500 Canadian default judgment against Sarex for failure to take delivery of and pay for the covers and bases. EGL seized and sold the molds to satisfy the judgment and subsequently bought them back. To have EGL resume production of the covers and bases, transfer title to the "2 × 2" mold and agree to transfer title to the "1 × 1" mold on payment for the final shipment of cassette covers and bases, Sarex needed $10,000.

Sarex's president, O. Louis Seda, borrowed on its behalf the necessary $10,000 from his wife, the appellee here. Evidencing the security agreement (chattel mortgage) duly executed July 15, 1970, which contained the following schedule:

> *Schedule*
>
> Describe items of collateral, the address where each item will be located and describe any prior liens, etc., and the amounts due thereon. If items are crops or goods affixed or to be affixed to real estate describe the real estate and state the name and address of the owner of record thereof.

Items

Machinery, equipment and fixtures; Molds, tools, dies, component parts including specifically the:

1 × 1 two cavity cassette cover and base mold.
2 × 2 four cavity cassette cover and base mold.
One twenty-four cavity roller mold.
One sixteen cavity hub mold.

Location, etc.

To be located either at the Debtor's plant in North Bergen, New Jersey; and in the case of the molds also at the plants of contractors who may be using said molds in the manufacture of products for the Debtor.

The appropriate financing statement was duly filed on July 23, 1970. Subsequently, the "1 × 1" mold was released from the lien and a termination statement filed as to it. Sarex filed a Chapter XI petition in August, 1970, under §322 of the Bankruptcy Act, 11 USC §722. Sarex was adjudicated a bankrupt on April 13, 1972. A lien sale of machinery, equipment, tools and molds was held on May 1, 1972, and of the $40,000 proceeds that were realized apparently only $40 was attributable to the molds itemized in the schedule.

The appellant trustee argues that only the scheduled molds were covered, relying principally upon our In re Laminated Veneers Co., 471 F2d 1124 (2d Cir. 1973). That case held security agreements to be governed by New York Uniform Commercial Code §9-110 (McKinney 1964) (the Code is hereinafter cited as UCC), which states that a description of personal property is sufficient "whether or not it is specific if it reasonably identifies what is described." There, because a truck (but not the two automobiles in question) was included in a schedule of specifically pledged items, the generic word "equipment" in an omnibus clause was held not to include the two automobiles, the court saying that "Any examining creditor would conclude that the truck as the only vehicle mentioned was the only one intended to be covered." 471 F2d at 1125.

Appellant argues that not to limit the security agreement coverage to molds (and presumably "tools, dies, component parts" which we take it refer to the molds) is to rewrite the schedule so as to make it read "All machinery, equipment and fixtures, including, but not limited to molds, tools, etc." In a sense this is how we interpret the agreement, particularly as the word "including" is often used (and construed) as a term of enlargement, not of limitation. E.g., American Surety Co. v. Marotta, 287 US 513, 517 (1933). Appellant's own construction, however, would have us give no effect whatsoever to the words "Machinery, equipment and fixtures." It would have us treat the semicolon that follows the phrase in the schedule as if it were a colon, and the molds as simply designations of the kind of machinery, equipment and fixtures.

We recognize, however, that the first phrase in the "location" section of the security agreement is ambiguous in at least one respect: the use of the words "To be located" rather than "now or hereafter located" implies that the machinery, equipment and fixtures covered were not at the date of execution of the agreement at Sarex's New Jersey plant. But the second portion of the location clause indicated that the molds might also be located at the plant of contractors (such as EGL) who might be using the molds in manufacture. If only molds were to be covered by the security agreement, as appellant would have it, this part of the "location" clause would not have included the phrase "and in the case of the molds." At least this is so in the absence of an indication that molds were to be differentiated from "tools, dies, component parts," an indication that we do not have.

Laminated Veneers does not stand for the proposition that the use of generic terms in a security agreement description will be given no effect. It does stand for the proposition that the generic term "equipment" used in reference to a lumber business does not include within it two automobiles, at least where a truck is specifically itemized in the schedule. Our case would be closer to Laminated Veneers if in question was coverage of some other mold than those specifically listed; even then, however, a "mold" is a more specific designation, more readily alerting a creditor than the broader term "equipment."

Here a reasonable draftsman could have considered, at least out of an abundance of caution, that molds (and their components) were not part of "machinery," "equipment" or "fixtures." By referring to the molds specifically we hold that he did not render meaningless the previous reference to "machinery, equipment and fixtures; . . ." The ultimate question is whether the description "reasonably identifies" what is described. UCC §9-110. The drafters of the Code told us that this requirement is "evidentiary", i.e., it depends on the proof in each case; but caution us not to require "exact and detailed" descriptions and thereby to use the so-called "serial number" test. UCC §9-110 Official Comments. See P. Coogan, W. Hogan & D. Vagts, Secured Transactions Under the Uniform Commercial Code §4.06, at 289-90 (Bender's Uniform Commercial Code Service Vol. 1, 1968). *Laminated Veneers* tells us that reliance purely on generic terminology may, however, be insufficient. This case lies in between and, for reasons stated, we hold the language in question to have reasonably specified and therefore identified the collateral in question.

Judgement affirmed.

PROBLEM 21

The financing statement's description said "Various Equipment, see attached list." No list was attached. Is the statement sufficient to perfect a security interest in the debtor's equipment? In re Stegman, 15 U.C.C. Rep. Serv. 225 (S.D. Fla. 1974) (Yes); J.K. Gill Co. v. Fireside Realty, Inc., 499 P.2d 813, 11 U.C.C. Rep. Serv. 202 (Ore. 1972) (No).

PROBLEM 22

The financing statement said the collateral was a "1969 COF 4070A." Does this perfect a security interest in a tractor having that number? See In re Richards, 455 F.2d 281, 10 U.C.C. Rep. Serv. 191 (6th Cir. 1972); compare Sherman v. Upton, Inc., 242 N.W.2d 666, 19 U.C.C. Rep. Serv. 694 (S.D. 1976) ("We have no intention of going back into the morass of nit picking from which the U.C.C. has refreshingly lead us.").

5. *Mailing Addresses*

PROBLEM 23

The financing statement contained no address for the debtor or creditor but both were well-known in the state. Is this a §9-402(8) "minor error" that is not "seriously misleading"? See White & Summers at 960-961; compare Rooney v. Mason, 394 F.2d 250, 5 U.C.C. Rep. Serv. 308 (10th Cir. 1968) (statement valid), with In re HGS Tech. Assoc., Inc., 14 U.C.C. Rep. Serv. 237 (Ref. Bankr. E.D. Tenn. 1972) (statement invalid); see also 99 A.L.R.3d 807 (1980).

The secured party's address listed only the city and state, with no street address or zip code. Is this ok? Compare In re Bengtson, 3 U.C.C. Rep. Serv. 283 (Bankr. D. Conn. 1965) (ok, since the telephone book would supply the street address), with Burlington Natl. Bank v. Strauss, 50 Wis. 2d 270, 184 N.W.2d 122, 8 U.C.C. Rep. Serv. 944 (1971) (Not ok; test is whether an address is sufficient "to enable a prudent man using reasonable care to locate the secured party"); 99 A.L.R.3d 1080 (1980).

6. *Financing Statement as Security Agreement*

If the lawyer or the creditor has been careless in filling out the forms the security agreement may be nonexistent or fatally defective (no signature of debtor, for instance). The saving factor may be the financing statement itself. Since it is a signed writing giving some evidence of the underlying agreement, can it replace or act as the security agreement? A well-known case, American Card Co. v. H.M.H. Co., has caused a lot of problems.

American Card Company v. H.M.H. Company

97 R.I. 59, 196 A.2d 150, 1 U.C.C. Rep. Serv. 447 (1963)

CONDON, C.J. The sole question for our determination is whether the Superior Court erred in holding that §9-203(b) of the Code requires in a case of this kind a written security agreement between the debtor and the secured party before a prior security interest in any collateral can attach. The claimants, Oscar A. Hillman & Sons, a co-partnership, contend that a separate agreement in writing is not necessary if the written financing statement which was filed contains the debtor's signature and a description of the collateral. In support of that position they point out that §9-402, recognizes that a security agreement and a financing statement can be one and the same document. They further argue that "under the unique circumstances that exist in this case" the minimum requirements of §9-203 are satisfied by the agreed statement of facts and by exhibits A, B, and C appended thereto.

Those circumstances may be summarized as follows. On February 21, 1962 the debtor corporation executed a promissory note in the sum of $12,373.33 payable to claimants. On March 14, 1962 the corporation as debtor and claimants as secured parties signed a financing statement form provided by the office of the

Secretary of State and filed it in that office in accordance with the provisions of the Uniform Commercial Code, §9-402.

On July 2, 1962 Melvin A. Chernick and George F. Treanor were appointed co-receivers of the debtor corporation. On October 6, 1962 claimants duly filed their proof of debt and asserted therein a security interest against certain tools and dies of the debtor which were mentioned in the financing statement as collateral. Finally, there is in addition to the agreed statement of facts testimony of claimants' agent who attempted to collect the debt. He testified that the treasurer of the debtor corporation admitted the inability of the debtor to pay the debt and agreed to the execution of the promissory note and to the designation of the tools and dies as collateral security therefor.

The claimants argue that the Code requires no " 'magic words,' no precise, formalistic language which must be put in writing in order for a security interest to be enforceable." And they further argue that "the definition of a security agreement indicates, the question of whether or not a security interest is 'created or provided for' is a question of fact which must be decided upon the basis of the words and deeds of the parties." They rely on the definition of "agreement" in §9-105(h) for support of this latter contention.

Upon consideration of those provisions of the Code, we are of the opinion that they are not decisive of the special problem posed in the instant case. The receivers contend here, as they did successfully before the Superior Court, that the controlling section of the Code is, in the circumstances, §9-203(b) and that in order to establish a security interest in any collateral the secured party must show that "the debtor has signed a security agreement which contains a description of the collateral. . . ." They concede that such a signed agreement may serve as a financing statement if it also contains the requirements thereof, but they deny that a financing statement, absent an agreement therein, can be treated as the equivalent of a security agreement.

The pertinent language of §9-402 in this regard is, "A copy of the security agreement is sufficient as a financing statement if it contains the above information and is signed by both parties." In other words, while it is possible for a financing statement and a security agreement to be one and the same document as argued by claimants, it is not possible for a financing statement which does not contain the debtor's grant of a security interest to serve as a security agreement. . . .

The financing statement which the claimants filed clearly fails to qualify also as a security agreement because nowhere in the form is there any evidence of an agreement by the debtor to grant claimants a security interest. As for the testimony of the claimants' agent upon which they also rely to prove the intention of the debtor to make such a grant, our answer is that his testimony is without probative force to supply the absence of a required security agreement in writing. Therefore the Trial Justice did not err in holding as she did that the financing statement and the evidence before her did not prove the existence of a security agreement within the contemplation of the language of the statute.

NOTES

American Card has been denounced by all the commentators (G. Gilmore in §11.4, at 347, called it "an unfortunate decision"; see White & Summers at 907 n.34; Note, 27 Okla. L. Rev. 469, 476-477 (1974)), and by more than one court (see, e.g., Kreiger v. Hartig, 527 P.2d 483, 15 U.C.C. Rep. Serv. 938 (Wash. App. 1974); In re Amex-Protein Development Corp., 504 F.2d 1056, 15 U.C.C. Rep. Serv. 286 (9th Cir. 1974)), but the vast majority of the courts have agreed that §9-203 requires "granting" language so that an ordinary financing statement does not qualify (see, e.g., Mosley v. Dallas Entertainment Co., 496 S.W.2d 237, 12 U.C.C. Rep. Serv. 735 (Tex. Civ. App. 1973), and In re Shelton, 472 F.2d 1118, 11 U.C.C. Rep. Serv. 1239 (8th Cir. 1973), and the cases cited therein). Exactly where does §9-203 state that a specific "grant" of the security interest is required?

PROBLEM 24

The security agreement stated that the tractor buyer granted a security interest to: "____________," but the seller forgot to fill in his name. He later filed a financing statement which both parties signed showing he had a secured interest in the buyer's tractor. Is the purported document with the blank a §9-203 security agreement? What about the financing statement? What about both?

If the financing statement is insufficient to create a security agreement, some courts have been willing to construct one out of other documents (such as a promissory note) whenever the course of performance shows a clear intent to produce a secured transaction; see discussions in In re Modern Engineering & Tool Co., 25 U.C.C. Rep. Serv. 580 (Bankr. D. Conn. 1978); Casco Bank & Trust Co. v. Col Cloutier, 388 A.2d 224, 26 U.C.C. Rep. Serv. 499 (Me. 1979); In re Taylor Mobile Homes, Inc., 17 U.C.C. Rep. Serv. 565 (Bankr. E.D. Mich. 1975).

In re Bollinger Corporation

614 F.2d 924, 28 U.C.C. Rep. Serv. 289 (3d Cir. 1980)

ROSSEN, J. This appeal from a district court review of an order in bankruptcy presents a question that has troubled courts since the enactment of Article Nine of the Uniform Commercial Code (UCC) governing secured transactions. Can a creditor assert a secured claim against the debtor when no formal security agreement was ever signed, but where various documents executed in connection with a loan evince an intent to create a security interest? The district court answered this question in the affirmative and permitted the creditor, Zimmerman & Jansen, to assert a secured claim against the debtor, bankrupt Bollinger Corporation, in the amount of $150,000. We affirm.

I

The facts of this case are not in dispute. Industrial Credit Corporation (ICC) made a loan to Bollinger Corporation (Bollinger) on January 13, 1972, in the amount of $150,000. As evidence of the loan, Bollinger executed a promissory note in the sum of $150,000 and signed a security agreement with ICC giving it a security interest in certain machinery and equipment. ICC in due course perfected its security interest in the collateral by filing a financing statement in accordance with Pennsylvania's enactment of Article Nine of the UCC.

Bollinger faithfully met its obligations under the note and by December 4, 1974, had repaid $85,000 of the loan, leaving $65,000 in unpaid principal. Bollinger, however, required additional capital and on December 5, 1974, entered into a loan agreement with Zimmerman & Jansen, Inc. (Z & J), by which Z & J agreed to lend Bollinger $150,000. Z & J undertook as part of this transaction to pay off the $65,000 still owed to ICC in return for an assignment by ICC to Z & J of the original note and security agreement between Bollinger and ICC. Bollinger executed a promissory note to Z & J, evidencing the agreement containing the following provision:

> Security. This promissory note is secured by security interests in a certain security agreement between Bollinger and Industrial Credit Company . . . and in a financing statement filed by [ICC] . . . , and is further secured by security interests in certain security agreement to be delivered by Bollinger to Z and J with this promissory note covering the identical machinery and equipment as identified in the ICC security agreement and with identical schedule attached in the principal amount of Eighty-Five Thousand Dollars ($85,000).

No formal security agreement was ever executed between Bollinger and Z & J. Z & J did, however, in connection with the promissory note, record a new financing statement signed by Bollinger, containing a detailed list of the machinery and equipment originally taken as collateral by ICC for its loan to Bollinger.

Bollinger filed a petition for an arrangement under Chapter XI of the Bankruptcy Act in March, 1975 and was adjudicated bankrupt one year later. In administrating the bankrupt's estate, the receiver sold some of Bollinger's equipment but agreed that Z & J would receive a $10,000 credit on its secured claim.

Z & J asserted a secured claim against the bankrupt in the amount of $150,000, arguing that although it never signed a security agreement with Bollinger, the parties had intended that a security interest in the sum of $150,000 be created to protect the loan. The trustee in bankruptcy conceded that the assignment to Z & J of ICC's original security agreement with Bollinger gave Z & J a secured claim in the amount of $65,000, the balance owed by Bollinger to ICC at the time of the assignment. The trustee, however, refused to recognize Z & J's asserted claim of an additional secured claim of $85,000 because of the absence of a security agreement between Bollinger and Z & J. The bankruptcy court agreed and entered judgment for Z & J in the amount of $55,000, representing a secured claim in the amount of $65,000 less $10,000 credit received by Z & J.

Z & J appealed to the United States District Court for the Western District of Pennsylvania, which reversed the bankruptcy court and entered judgment for Z & J in the full amount of the asserted $150,000 secured claim. The trustee in bankruptcy appeals.

II

Under Article Nine of the UCC, two documents are generally required to create a perfected security interest in a debtor's collateral. First, there must be a "security agreement" giving the creditor an interest in the collateral. Section 9-203(1)(b) contains minimal requirements for the creation of a security agreement. In order to create a security agreement, there must be: (1) a writing (2) signed by the debtor (3) containing a description of the collateral or the types of collateral. Section 9-203, Comment 1. The requirements of §9-203(1)(b) further two basic policies. First, an evidentiary function is served by requiring a signed security agreement and second, a written agreement also obviates any Statute of Frauds problems with the debtor-creditor relationship. Id. Comments 3, 5. The second document generally required is a "financing statement," which is a document signed by both parties and filed for public record. The financing statement serves the purpose of giving public notice to other creditors that a security interest is claimed in the debtor's collateral.

Despite the minimal formal requirements set forth in §9-203 for the creation of a security agreement, the commercial world has frequently neglected to comply with this simple Code provision. Soon after Article Nine's enactment, creditors who had failed to obtain formal security agreements, but who nevertheless had obtained and filed financing agreements, sought to enforce secured claims. Under §9-402, a security agreement may serve as a financing statement if it is signed by both parties. The question arises whether the converse is true: Can a signed financing statement operate as a security agreement? The earliest case to consider this question was American Card Company v. H.N.H. Co., 196 A.2d 150, 152 (RI 1963) which held that a financing statement could *not* operate as a security agreement because there was no language *granting* a security interest to a creditor. Although §9-203(1)(b) makes no mention of such a grant language requirement, the court in *American Card* thought that implicit in the definition of "security agreement" under §9-105(1)(h) was such a requirement; some grant language was necessary to "create or provide security." This view also was adopted by the Tenth Circuit in Shelton v. Erwin, 472 F.2d 1118, 1120 (8th Cir. 1973). Thus, under the holdings of these cases, the creditor's assertion of a secured claim must fall in the absence of language connoting a grant of a security interest.

The Ninth Circuit in In Re Amex-Protein Development Corporation, 504 F.2d 1056 (9th Cir. 1975), echoed criticism by commentators of the *American Card* rule. The court wrote: "There is no support in legislative history or grammatical logic for the substitution of the word grant for the phrase creates or provides for." Id. at 1059. It concluded that as long as the financing statement contains a description of the collateral signed by the debtor, the financing statement may serve as the security agreement and the formal requirements of §9-203(1)(b) are met. The tack pursued by the Ninth Circuit is supported by legal commentary on the issue. See G. Gilmore, Security Interests in Personal Property, §11.4 at 347-48 (1965).

Some courts have declined to follow the Ninth Circuit's liberal rule allowing the financing statement alone to stand as the security agreement, but have permitted the financing statement, when read in conjunction with other documents executed by the parties, to satisfy the requirements of §9-203(1)(b). The court in In re Numeric Corp., 485 F.2d 1328 (1st Cir. 1973) held that a financing statement coupled with a board of directors' resolution revealing an intent to create a security interest were sufficient to act as a security agreement. The court concluded from its reading of the Code that there appears no need to insist upon a separate document entitled "security agreement" as a prerequisite for an otherwise valid security interest.

> A writing or writings, regardless of label, which adequately describes the collateral, carries the signature of the debtor, and establishes that in fact a security interest was agreed upon, would satisfy both the formal requirements of the statute and the policies behind it. [Id. at 1331.]

The court went on to hold that "although a standard form financing statement by itself cannot be considered a security agreement, an adequate agreement can be found when a financing statement is considered together with other documents." Id. at 1332. See In re Penn Housing Corp., 367 F. Supp. 663 (WD Pa. 1973); but see Union National Bank of Pittsburgh v. Providence Washington Insurance Co., 21 UCC Rep. Serv. 1163 (WD Pa. 1977).

More recently, the Supreme Court of Maine in Casco Bank & Trust Co. v. Cloutier, 398 A.2d 1224, 1231-32 (Me. 1979) considered the question of whether composite documents were sufficient to create a security interest within the terms of the Code.

Writing for the court, Justice Wernick allowed a financing statement to be joined with a promissory note for purposes of determining whether the note contained an adequate description of the collateral to create a security agreement. The court indicated that the evidentiary and Statute of Frauds policies behind §9-203(1)(b) were satisfied by reading the note and financing statement together as the security agreement.

In the case before us, the district court went a step further and held that the promissory note executed by Bollinger in favor of Z & J, standing alone, was sufficient to act as the security agreement between the parties. In so doing, the court implicitly rejected the *American Card* rule requiring grant language before a security agreement arises under §9-203(1)(b). The parties have not referred to any Pennsylvania state cases on the question and our independent research has failed to uncover any. But although we agree that no formal grant of a security interest need exist before a security agreement arises, we do not think that the promissory note standing alone would be sufficient under Pennsylvania law to act as the security agreement. We believe, however, that the promissory note, read in conjunction with the financing statement duly filed and supported, as it is here, by correspondence during the course of the transaction between the parties, would be sufficient under Pennsylvania law to establish a valid security agreement.

III

We think Pennsylvania courts would accept the logic behind the First and Ninth Circuit rule and reject the *American Card* rule imposing the requirement of a formal grant of a security interest before a security agreement may exist. When the parties have neglected to sign a separate security agreement, it would appear that the better and more practical view is to look at the transaction as a whole in order to determine if there is a writing, or writings, signed by the debtor describing the collateral which demonstrates an intent to create a security interest in the collateral.[6] In connection with Z & J's loan of $150,000 to Bollinger, the relevant

6. We do not intend in any way to encourage the commercial community to dispense with signing security agreements as a normal part of establishing a secured transaction. Lawsuits over the existence of a security agreement may be avoided by executing a separate security agreement conforming to the minimal requirements of §9-203(1)(b). Our decision today only predicts, after our examination of the relevant case law, that Pennsylvania courts would adopt a

writings to be considered are: (1) the promissory note; (2) the financing statement; (3) a group of letters constituting the course of dealing between the parties. The district court focused solely on the promissory note finding it sufficient to constitute the security agreement. Reference, however, to the language in the note reveals that the note standing alone cannot serve as the security agreement. The note recites that along with the assigned 1972 security agreement between Bollinger and ICC, the Z & J loan is "further secured by security interests in a certain Security Agreement *to be delivered* by Bollinger to Z & J with this Promissory Note, . . ." (Emphasis added.) The bankruptcy judge correctly reasoned that "[t]he intention to create a separate security agreement negates any inference that the debtor intended that the promissory note constitute the security agreement." At best, the note is some evidence that a security agreement was contemplated by the parties, but by its own terms, plainly indicates that it is not the security agreement.

Looking beyond the promissory note, Z & J did file a financing statement signed by Bollinger containing a detailed list of all the collateral intended to secure the $150,000 loan to Bollinger. The financing statement alone meets the basic §9-203(1)(b) requirements of a writing, signed by the debtor, describing the collateral. However, the financing statement provides only an inferential basis for concluding that the parties intended a security agreement. There would be little reason to file such a detailed financing statement unless the parties intended to create a security interest.[7] The intention of the parties to create a security interest may be gleaned from the expression of future intent to create one in the promissory note and the intention of the parties as expressed in letters constituting their course of dealing.

The promissory note was executed by Bollinger in favor of Z & J in December 1974. Prior to the consummation of the loan, Z & J sent a letter to Bollinger on May 30, 1974, indicating that the loan would be made "provided" Bollinger secured the loan by a mortgage on its machinery and equipment. Bollinger sent a letter to Z & J on September 19, 1974, indicating:

---

pragmatic view of the issue raised here and recognize the intention of the parties expressed in the composite documents and not exalt form over substance.

7. Z & J would not have had to file a financing statement for the $65,000 covered by the 1972 security agreement between ICC and Bollinger, inasmuch as the assignee of a security interest is protected by the assignor's filing. Section 9-302(2).

> With your [Z & J's] stated desire to obtain security for material and funds advanced, it would appear that the use of the note would answer both our problems. Since the draft forwarded to you offers full collateralization for the funds to be advanced under it and bears normal interest during its terms, it should offer you maximum security.

Subsequent to the execution of the promissory note, Bollinger sent to Z & J a list of the equipment and machinery intended as collateral under the security agreement which was to be, but never was, delivered to Z & J. In November 1975, the parties exchanged letters clarifying whether Bollinger could substitute or replace equipment in the ordinary course of business without Z & J's consent. Such a clarification would not have been necessary had a security interest not been intended by the parties. Finally, a letter of November 18, 1975, from Bollinger to Z & J indicated that "any attempted impairment of the collateral would constitute an event of default."

From the course of dealing between Z & J and Bollinger, we conclude there is sufficient evidence that the parties intended a security agreement to be created separate from the assigned ICC agreement with Bollinger. All the evidence points towards the intended creation of such an agreement and since the financing statement contains a detailed list of the collateral, signed by Bollinger, we hold that a valid Article Nine security agreement existed under Pennsylvania law between the parties which secured Z & J in the full amount of the loan to Bollinger.

IV

The minimal formal requirements of §9-203(1)(b) were met by the financing statement and the promissory note, and the course of dealing between the parties indicated the intent to create a security interest. The judgment of the district court recognizing Z & J's secured claim in the amount of $150,000 will be affirmed.

Each side to bear their own costs.

PRACTICAL NOTE

To meet all the above objections, the wise creditor will:

(a) Make sure all the forms are correctly filled out in all particulars;

(b) Check the debtor's technical legal name now and in the immediate past, and make sure it is correctly listed on all the documents,

(c) Refile if the debtor's name changes in any way,

(d) Describe the collateral as accurately and completely as possible in all documents,

(e) Make sure that both the security agreement and the financing statement contain a *granting* clause (so if the security agreement falls through the financing statement can replace it),

(f) Make sure the mailing addresses are complete and right on the financing statement, and

(g) Inquire into the source of the debtor's title to insure that the former owner's creditors have no valid claims.

C. ATTACHMENT OF THE SECURITY INTEREST

Attachment is the process by which the security interest in favor of the creditor becomes effective against the *debtor. Perfection* is the process by which the creditor's security interest becomes effective against most of the rest of the world. The steps involved in attachment are described in §9-203; they are: (a) a security agreement, (b) the creditor must give *value* (defined in §1-201(44)) to the debtor (after all, you shouldn't get a security interest unless you've done something to deserve it), and (c) the debtor must have some rights in the collateral (one cannot give a security interest in property one does not own or have some legal interest in). Read both §§9-203 and 9-204.

PROBLEM 25

Roy Gabriel decided to go into the music business and borrowed $35,000 from Octopus National Bank in order to open his shop, named "Gabriel's Trumpets." On January 6, he signed a security agreement with the bank giving ONB an interest in all "existing and after acquired inventory in the store"; that same day he received the money. On January 6 his inventory consisted of four guitars and a pitch pipe. Gabriel did have a contract with Tinny Trumpet Manufacturing Company (hereinafter TTMC) to sell him 40 trumpets, which he paid for in advance of the delivery date (March 30). On March

15, TTMC packaged the 40 trumpets and marked them "For Shipment to Gabriel's Trumpet Store." On March 30 it shipped them to Gabriel who received them that day and displayed them in the store.

(a) On what day or days did the bank's security interest *attach* (that is, become effective) to the guitars, pitch pipe, and trumpets? Read §2-501 (why is it relevant?).

(b) Does your answer change if we add the fact that the bank filed a proper financing statement covering Gabriel's inventory on January 7? Can a financing statement be filed before the security agreement is signed? Attached? See §9-402(1). Why would a creditor wish to file a financing statement before the security interest had attached? See §9-312(5)(a).

(c) If the bank did not advance any money until March 31 (the date the bank actually saw the trumpets in the store), when did the security interest attach?

Manger v. Davis

619 P.2d 687, 30 U.C.C. Rep. Serv. 515 (Utah 1980)

MAUGHAN, J. Plaintiff, alleging her ownership of a valuable diamond ring, initiated this action to recover possession from Word Making Productions, Ltd., hereinafter "W.M.P." Plaintiff's consignee, Steven Davis, authorized Jack Anderson and Michael Allred to pledge the ring to W.M.P. The trial court ruled plaintiff's ownership was subject to the perfected security interest of W.M.P. in the ring, securing sums advanced by the pledgee. The judgment of the trial court is reversed, and the cause is remanded to the trial court for disposition in accordance with this opinion. All statutory references are to Utah Code Annotated, 1953, as amended, unless otherwise indicated.

Plaintiff is an octogenarian and widow of an academy award recipient, movie star Warner Baxter. In the 1930s he gave her a diamond ring containing an emerald cut diamond of approximately 9.72 carats with six baguettes totalling .967 of a carat. Plaintiff met Davis at a dinner party given by her niece, whose husband was a successful Hollywood producer and friend of Davis. Plaintiff was in need of funds and Davis, a recent graduate of a school of gemology, informed her he could find a buyer for the ring. She gave him possession and a writing, which stated:

Dear Mr. Davis — It would please me so much — if you would sell my emerald cut diamond ring for me — at whatever percent you consider OK. It was nice meeting you and your charming wife.

4/18/76

Sincerely
Winifred Manger

There was an explicit understanding between plaintiff and Davis that any offer to purchase was to be submitted to plaintiff for approval. Davis made a brief attempt to sell the ring in San Francisco, but the offer to purchase was unsatisfactory. Davis took the ring to Salt Lake City, where he assured plaintiff, through telephonic communication, that it was secured in a vault in a bank. From time to time he informed plaintiff of prospective sales, but the transaction always failed.

Without plaintiff's knowledge or consent Davis embarked on a peculiar course of action. He testified that he did not apprise her of his actions because she was too old to understand. Davis had met two promoters named Jack Anderson and Michael Allred, who owned stock in a local company, CD & M. The promoters explained that if they effected certain mergers of CD & M with companies in Colorado and Texas, they would be able to borrow money to purchase the ring. Davis gave possession of the ring to Anderson, who without the knowledge or authority of Davis, took the ring to Zions Bank, represented it was his property and pledged it to secure a personal loan for $10,000. The promoters gave Davis some stock certificates they represented to be worth $200,000.00. He determined the stock was worthless and returned it on October 12, 1976.

Thereafter, Allred approached James B. Medlin, president of W.M.P., which is a close corporation, to seek further loans, offering a valuable ring as security. Allred was indebted to Medlin, who knew Allred had few assets, and Medlin was suspicious about the proffered security. Allred explained that Davis was the owner of the ring and had consented to the pledge. Subsequently, Anderson, Allred, and Davis met with Medlin to arrange the loan and pledge. At this time Medlin required Davis to execute an affidavit, which provided:

Steve Davis, being first duly sworn on oath, deposes and says: As full payment for services rendered to the Estate of Winifred

> Manger, on or about August, 1975, I received the following described ring: . . .
>
> The ring has been appraised with a retail replacement value of approximately $140,000.00.
>
> I am a certified diamond appraiser and have been duly certified by the Gemalogical Institute of America. My appraised value was $165,000.00.
>
> I have entered into an agreement with Michael Allred and Jack Anderson to allow them to use my ring as collateral to raise money for their private ventures in exchange for securities which they have allowed me to use as collateral for my own private ventures.
>
> I understand that Jack Anderson and Michael Allred may be using the above-described ring as collateral to borrow money from Word Making Productions and/or James B. Medlin, and agree that said ring may be used as collateral for said loan in any manner in which Jack Anderson and Michael Allred see fit to use it.
>
> Dated this 18th day of October, 1976.
>
> *Steve Davis.*

Medlin, who is also an attorney, did not inquire what type of services were rendered by Davis, who was a young man, to receive this substantial compensation. Neither was Medlin curious about verification of the existence of such an estate, which he was informed was in Los Angeles, nor the unorthodox manner of compensation for services. He testified he relied on the statements of Allred and Anderson that the father of Davis was a prominent business man to verify the ownership of the ring. Medlin was similarly disinterested as to the motive of Davis to exchange a valuable asset with the promoters, one of whom was a debtor of Medlin and without assets, to further his own business interests. Medlin further arranged an agreement to notify the bank holding the ring as security for Anderson's loan of his subsequent security interest and appointing the bank as escrow agent to hold possession as a means of perfecting Medlin's security interest.

Plaintiff's ring was thus pledged to W.M.P. by the promoters to secure a loan of $20,000. Allred paid $5,000 of this loan to Medlin to discharge his prior indebtedness. Subsequently, Allred, alone, received an additional advance of $10,000, which was also secured by the pledge.

The promoters defaulted on all the loans and Anderson died. W.M.P. paid the bank $10,625 to discharge the prior indebtedness and took possession of the ring. The trial court ruled W.M.P. had a perfected security interest, securing payment of the following amounts: $10,625, plus interest; $20,450, plus interest; and $10,000, plus interest and court costs.

Since the other defendants do not claim any interest in the ring, only plaintiff and W.M.P. are involved in this appeal.

The trial court found the ring was delivered to Davis on a consignment to sell in April, 1976, and plaintiff did not file a financing statement or take any other action designed to perfect a security interest in the collateral. There was a finding that plaintiff had no knowledge of any of the transactions except for the delivery to Davis for purpose of sale. Davis was found not to be a merchant dealing in diamond rings or goods of that kind, and there was no valid or effective sale of the ring ever made to CD & M Co.

In its conclusions of law, the trial court ruled that W.M.P., as a lender and pledgee, was a purchaser of the ring as defined in §1-201(32). The court further ruled that pursuant to the following provisions of the Uniform Commercial Code in Title 70A: 2-104(1), 2-403(2), 1-201(19), 2-401, 2-403(1), 2-403(3), 2-403(4), 9-102, 9-105, 9-112, 9-113, 9-302, 9-501, W.M.P. had a perfected security interest in the ring by possession, which was prior to plaintiff's ownership interest. The lien of W.M.P. was obtained prior to any attempt by plaintiff to withdraw or rescind the authority of her agent, Davis. As a purchaser, W.M.P.'s lien rights applied to and secured payment of the loans. W.M.P. made the loans and took its lien in good faith without any knowledge of any claim of plaintiff. Davis was not a merchant dealing in diamond rings or goods of that kind as defined by the UCC. The trial court finally concluded that no valid or effective sale of the ring was ever made to CD & M and CD & M Company acquired no interest therein.

The essence of the dispute between the parties involves whether Davis, the consignee, had a voidable title. Respondent persuaded the trial court that Davis had such a title and a provision in §2-403(1) was controlling, namely, ". . . A person with voidable title has power to transfer a good title to a good faith purchaser for value . . ." Since "purchase" includes taking by pledge, §1-201(32), the trial court found the loan transaction, secured by a pledge of the ring to W.M.P., to be a good faith purchase for value.

In an analysis of this rather complex case, the appropriate point to begin is §9-204(1), which provides that a security interest cannot attach until the debtor has rights in the collateral. Unless Davis had rights in the ring, so he could authorize the pledge by Allred and Anderson, the security interest of W.M.P. could not attach.

The Code does not clearly establish the meaning of "rights in the collateral." Although a debtor has possession of the collateral, that fact does not give him rights. If a security transaction relates to a sale, Article 2 may determine whether the debtor has rights.[8] If there be no authority to subject property to a security interest, the creditor has no security interest therein.[9]

Concededly, under §9-305, a security interest in goods may be perfected by the secured party's taking possession of the collateral. Further, if the collateral, as herein, is held by a bailee, the secured party is deemed to have possession from the time the bailee (Zions Bank) received notification of the secured party's [W.M.P.] interest. However, Article 9 does not govern the creation of property rights, which may have arisen as a result of a sale of goods or under general principles of law which are not displaced by particular provisions of the Code §1-103.[10]

The trial court found the transaction to be a consignment to sell between plaintiff and Davis. There is a degree of confusion in the findings and conclusions of law of the trial court in regard to this relationship. On the other hand, the term "consignment" connotes an agency relationship and not a sale, and the court refers to Davis as an agent. On the other hand, the court found plaintiff had not filed a financing statement or taken any other action designed to perfect a security interest in the collateral. The court cited §2-401, which would indicate a sale, viz., plaintiff was a seller and Davis was a buyer, and upon delivery of the ring to Davis, any retention or reservation of title by plaintiff would be limited in effect to a reservation of a security interest, §2-401(1). Such a transaction has been denominated as a consignment for security.

In regard to the application of the Code concerning consignments, there are three distinct consequences depending on the nature of the transaction. First, if a transaction is deemed a consignment intended as a security, it is a secured transaction and Chapter 9 applies, §9-102(2).

However, under §1-201(37) unless a consignment is intended as security, reservation of title thereunder is not a security interest,

8. Anderson, Uniform Commercial Code (2nd ed), §9-204:7, pp 179-180.
9. Id., §9-204:8, p 180.
10. Id., §9-305:3, p 290.

but a consignment is in any event subject to the provisions on consignment sales in §2-326. A security consignment has the incidents of a sale, viz., the property is delivered to the consignee, who sells it at prices fixed by him and retains the proceeds; his only obligation is to pay the consignor when the property is sold. The consignor has agreed that if the goods are not resold, they may be returned in lieu of payment.[11] If the consignment is intended as security, it is governed by Article 9, since that article governs any transaction regardless of its form, unless otherwise excluded, intended to create a security interest in personal property or fixtures, §9-102(1).

Second, if a transaction be a true consignment, the Code may or may not control the transactions, depending on the status of the consignee as set forth in §2-326(1), (2), (3). A true consignment constitutes an agency or bailment relationship between the consignor and consignee. The consignor, as principal retains the ownership, may recall the goods, and sets the sale price. The consignee (agent) receives a commission and not the profits of the sale. Since the absolute ownership of the property is in the consignor, absent a basis to apply an estoppel (including apparent or ostensible ownership), the consignee has no interest that can be transferred to his creditors or trustee in bankruptcy. Section 2-326 has modified the consequences concerning a true consignment:

> Where goods are delivered to a person for sale and such person maintains a place of business at which he deals in goods of the kind involved, under a name other than the name of the person making delivery, then with respect to claims of creditors of the person conducting the business the goods are deemed to be on sale or return . . .[(Subsection3)]

Under Section 2-326(2) goods held on sale or return are subject to the consignee's creditors, while in his possession. A consignor must take one of the three enumerated steps in §2-326-(3)(a), (b), (c) to protect his interest against the creditors of the consignee. By means of Section 2-326, the Code sought to eliminate the danger extant under pre-Code consignment transactions that credit would be extended to a dealer on the basis of ostensible ownership of inventory, which was, in fact, protected from the claims of his creditors.

11. Columbia International Corporation v. Kempler, 46 Wis 2d 500, 175 NW2d 465, 40 ALR3d 1066 (1970); District of Columbia v. Powers Gallery, Inc., DCCA, 335 A2d 244 (1975).

Third, if a transaction be a true consignment and does not fall within the purview of §2-326, it is governed by the principles of agency, since it is not displaced by any particular provision of the act, §1-103.

The undisputed evidence in this case establishes that the transaction between plaintiff and Davis was a true consignment, establishing a principal-agent relationship. Davis was given possession with authority to sell only upon the express consent of plaintiff as to the sale price. Davis was to receive a commission and not a profit on the sale. Such a transaction does not fall within the purview of §2-401, a provision cited by the trial court, for it was not a sale with title passing to the buyer. Further, Davis did not have the status of a buyer as that term is defined in §2-103(1)(a):

> 'Buyer' means a person who buys or contracts to buy goods.

In 2 Anderson, Uniform Commercial Code (2nd ed), §2-401:10, p 11, it is explained:

> The authority of an agent to transfer title is distinct from the transfer of title which is the sale. Ordinarily the agent to sell, being clothed with no more than authority to make a transfer, does not hold title to the goods . . .

To sustain its ruling, the trial court further cited the provisions in §2-403. These provisions are of no aid to W.M.P. because Davis had no title as a consignee. The basic pre-Code concept that a possessor cannot pass title was not altered by the Code, in the absence of circumstances bringing the case within the scope of §2-403. Thus, if the possession of the seller or pledgor (Davis) is that of a bailee (consignee), the loss must fall on him whose act made the loss possible so as not to benefit the pledgee or vendee, for the latter stands in no better position than a person who innocently buys, leases, or acquires property that had been stolen. The provisions in §2-403(1) are not applicable, since there was no transaction of purchase between plaintiff and Davis, wherein he could acquire voidable title.[12] The provisions in subsection (2) and (3) are inapplicable since the trial court expressly found that Davis

12. See McDonald's Chevrolet, Inc. v. Johnson, 24 UCC Rept Serv 331 (1978), Disch v. Raven Transfer & Storage Co., 17 Wash App 73, 561 P2d 1097 (1977).

was not a merchant.[13] It should be asserted parenthetically that even though the entrustment provision of §2-403 is not applicable because the entrustee is not a merchant dealing in goods of that kind, the good faith purchaser may acquire a good title under principles of estoppel. However, it is necessary to show conduct of the true owner going beyond merely entrusting the entrustee with possession of the goods transferred by the entrustee to the good faith purchaser, for the mere delivery of possession of goods to another does not give rise to an estoppel against the true owner which prevents him from asserting title as against the possessor's good faith transferee. In the instant case, W.M.P. did not plead an estoppel as required under Rule 8(c), URCP, and such a defense was therefore waived under Rule 12(h), URCP. Furthermore, there is no evidence in the record to sustain such a defense.

W.M.P. has anticipated the problem of applying either §2-403 or §2-401 to the circumstances of this transaction; therefore, it has urged in its brief that the trial court erred in its finding that Davis was not a merchant dealing in diamond rings or goods of that kind, and thus the consignment would fall within the provisions of §2-326(3). Without detailing the record, a survey thereof clearly sustains the findings of the trial court that in his participation in this transaction, Davis was not a person who maintained a place of business at which he dealt in goods of the kind involved. It is even more apparent that this provision is inapplicable when its purpose is reviewed, viz., to prevent credit from being extended to a dealer on the basis of his ostensible ownership in inventory, which was protected from the claims of creditors. The representation of Davis in the affidavit he gave to W.M.P. indicates he was the owner of the ring, which was acquired for unknown services. There was nothing to indicate the trade or business of Davis and that he was conducting business from a definite location where he dealt in diamonds, and that the ring pledged was from this stock.

At this juncture, it is apparent that the transaction between plaintiff and Davis was a true consignment, and the law of agency

13. Anderson, Uniform Commercial Code (2nd ed), §2-403:22, p 50, states: "The entrustment provision describes the entrustee merely as a merchant 'who deals in goods of that kind.' . . . it would appear relevant in establishing the good faith of the purchaser from the entrustee that the purchaser had reason to believe that he was purchasing from a regular seller rather than a casual person who might or might not be the owner or authorized agent. There is authority that in order for UCC, §2-403 to apply, it is necessary that the merchant status of the entrustee be known to both the entruster and the purchaser."

resolves the conflicting claims between plaintiff and W.M.P. Restatement, Agency (2d), §201, provides:

> (1) Apart from statute and except as stated in Subsection (3), the interests of an undisclosed principal who entrusts an agent with a chattel other than a commercial document representing a chattel or chose in action with directions to deal with it in a particular way, as by sale, barter, pledge or mortgage is not thereby affected by a transaction of a kind different from that authorized.
>
> (2) The interests of the principal are affected by an unauthorized transaction of the same kind as that authorized if it is conducted in the usual and ordinary course of business by an agent with one who reasonably believes the agent to be the owner and who pays value.
>
> (3) If the principal delivers a chattel to a dealer in such chattels to be sold or exhibited for sale, an unauthorized sale of the chattel by such dealer in accordance with the normal business practices to one who reasonably believes the dealer to be the owner, binds the owner, although the dealer was not authorized to sell it without the consent of the owner or was not authorized to sell it to the person to whom it was sold or at the price at which it was sold.

Comment (a), following §201, refers to the Comments on §175. Comment (e), following §175, states:

> What transactions are considered to be of a kind different from those authorized is a matter of degree. For the purpose of this Section, authority to barter does not give power to the agent to pledge or to mortgage the property . . .

The authority conferred on Davis by plaintiff to sell the ring did not give him the right or power to pledge it in his own interest as an incident to his express authority. The pledge to W.M.P. was a transaction of a different kind than that authorized by the plaintiff and therefore her interest in the ring was not affected thereby.[14] Since Davis had no authority to pledge the ring, the pledgee, W.M.P., did not acquire a valid security interest therein, and plaintiff is entitled to recover unencumbered possession thereof.

Costs are awarded to plaintiff.

14. Restatement, Agency, 2d Sec 201(1); Beeson v. Hegstad, 199 Or 325, 261 P2d 381, 49 ALR2d 1266 (1953); 49 ALR2d 1271, Anno: Salesman's power to pledge employer's or principal's personal property, §2[a], pp 1272-1275.

WILKINS and STEWART, JJ., concur. HALL, J., concurs in the result.

CROCKETT, C.J. (concurring in the result). I concur in the result of allowing the plaintiff to recover her ring. Because I am somewhat unsure of some of the matters recited in the main opinion, including the effect of provisions of the Uniform Commercial Code, I desire to state as succinctly as possible the reasons which persuade me to support this court's decision.

First, I acknowledge the soundness of the proposition that, generally, where a loss must be borne by one of two innocent parties, it should fall upon the one who made the loss possible; and that this would suggest that it be borne by plaintiff, Mrs. Manger, who delivered the ring into the possession of Mr. Davis. But like all general rules, its purpose is to serve the interests of justice, rather than to defeat them; and accordingly, it is subject to exceptions in circumstances where defeating justice would be the result.

The special circumstances that persuade me to support this court's decision are these:

First, the ring in question was not any ordinary item of personal property or merchandise. It was something so extraordinary in composition and value that it is properly regarded as unique.

Second, Mr. Davis was but a consignee who had no right to sell or to pledge the ring, but only to obtain a prospective purchaser.

Third, he was not regularly engaged in that business.

Because of the foregoing, the exercise of ordinary care and prudence would require that anyone dealing with such a ring should act with commensurate caution. If the defendants had adhered to that standard, they would have discovered the facts. Accordingly, they are not in a position to assert estoppel against the plaintiff. Therefore, I agree that she should be entitled to recover possession of her ring.

CHAPTER 4

PERFECTION OF THE SECURITY INTEREST

If a security interest is *perfected* it is senior to most later creditor interests (especially the trustee in bankruptcy, should the debtor go bankrupt). Read §9-303 carefully. Note particularly that a security interest must first *attach* before perfection is possible (if you think about it, this is an obvious requirement: a security interest must be effective between the debtor and the creditor before it has legal meaning as to other parties).

The UCC's most common means of perfection is by having the secured party (the creditor) file a financing statement in the appropriate place. However, the Code does permit perfection in other ways too. Perfection of security interests in tangible collateral (goods, instruments, documents, and chattel paper) may be accomplished by the creditor taking physical possession of the collateral (a common law *pledge,* see below). Further for some types of collateral the security interest is *automatically* perfected without filing *or* possession; attachment is all that is required. The legal steps involved in perfection are considered next.

A. PERFECTION BY POSSESSION (PLEDGE)

Read §9-305, and the Official Comment to §9-305.

In re Dolly Madison Industries, Inc.

351 F. Supp. 1038, 11 U.C.C. Rep. Serv. 926 (E.D. Pa. 1972)

HANNUM, J. Presently before the court is a petition by the Trustee of Dolly Madison Industries, Inc. ("DMI") for review of an order entered by the Referee in Bankruptcy acknowledging the priority of the claim of Helen K. Groff to certain shares of Witchwood Farm Country Kitchen stock.

The Referee found as a fact that on July 17, 1968, Helen K. Groff sold to American Furniture Leasing, Inc. ("AFL," later Dolly Madison Leasing and Furniture Corp., "DML & F") all of the issued and outstanding stock of Witchwood Farm Country Kitchen, Inc., being 161 shares of Class A Common Stock and 320 shares of Class B Common stock. The sale was accomplished by means of three separate documents, a purchase agreement, a promissory note, and an escrow agreement, all executed on the same date. The purchase agreement set forth, inter alia, the terms of the sale and the warranties of the seller. The unadjusted base price of the stock was established at $26,400.00. In anticipation of entering this agreement and pursuant to its terms, Mrs. Groff caused new stock certificates to be registered in the name of AFL. In return for the stock certificates, AFL paid Mrs. Groff 29% of the total purchase price in cash and gave her a promissory note for the balance. The note was payable in three equal annual installments of $53,586.21. Payments were due on January 2 of 1969, 1970 and 1971, together with 6% simple interest on the annual unpaid balance.

At the date the purchase agreement and note were executed, the stock certificates registered in its name were transferred to AFL. Thereafter Mrs. Groff, AFL, and Hugh Moulton, Esq. entered into an escrow agreement as required by and pursuant to the purchase agreement. Accordingly, AFL endorsed the new stock certificates in blank and delivered them into the possession of Hugh Moulton, Esq. As escrow agent, he was instructed by both Mrs. Groff and AFL to hold the shares until either the balance of the note was paid, whereupon he was to deliver them to AFL, or until he was given notice by Mrs. Groff of an uncured default in the payment of annual installments, whereupon he was to deliver them to Mrs. Groff.

Paragraph 1(b)(3) of the purchase agreement contained the following provision:

> In the event that AFL shall be in default in the payment of principal or interest under its promissory note . . . and if said default shall not be cured within five days after receipt by AFL of notice thereof from seller, shall deliver the certificates to seller, *whereupon* seller's rights and obligations in and to the shares represented by the certificates . . . shall be those of a secured party holding collateral under the provisions of Article IX of the Uniform Commercial Code as in effect in the Commonwealth of Pennsylvania. [(Emphasis added)]

The same provision was incorporated by reference into the escrow agreement instructions.

After the above-mentioned agreements were entered into, the January 2, 1969 and 1970 annual installments were duly paid by AFL and received by Mrs. Groff. After the January 1970 payment only one installment remained. On June 23, 1970, DMI, including DML & F, filed a Chapter X Bankruptcy Reorganization Petition. To date, the final installment of $53,586.21 due on January 2, 1971, together with interest at 6% from January 2, 1970 to January 2, 1971, has not been paid to Mrs. Groff. Mr. Moulton continues to hold the Witchwood Stock.

On January 5, 1971, the Trustee of DMI and its subsidiaries filed with this court an application for an order directing Hugh Moulton to turn over the stock in his possession to the Trustee. The court referred the matter to the Referee in Bankruptcy for a hearing. On October 14, 1971, Hugh Moulton having filed an answer and Mrs. Groff having been granted leave to intervene, the hearing was held.

On January 14, 1972, the Referee entered an opinion and order granting the Trustee's application only upon the condition that he pay Mrs. Groff in full for the balance of the purchase price, thus granting Mrs. Groff the status of a secured creditor. The Trustee has filed the present petition to review the Referee's Order.

From the established facts, there can be no doubt that the manner in which the sale was transacted was designed to provide the seller with some form of security interest in receiving the agreed upon price and the buyer with some assurance that the stock deposited as collateral was not within the unrestricted control of the seller. The present dispute concerns the nature of the security interest intended and, more importantly, the time when it was to attach.

At the hearing below, the Referee adopted the argument advanced by Mrs. Groff that the combination of agreements entered into between the parties on July 17, 1968, coupled with AFL's transfer of the stock certificates to Hugh Moulton, constituted a security agreement in the nature of a pledge. Citing §§9-304(1) and 9-305 of the Uniform Commercial Code, the Referee concluded that, "The receipt of the stock certificates by the escrow agent, Hugh G. Moulton, was in effect receipt by the Seller and the Security interest of the Seller was perfected at that time far in advance of the bankruptcy action." Assuming the validity of the Referee's conclusion, Mrs. Groff's Security interest would have attached and been perfected as of July 17, 1968, and the Trustee, having been appointed in June of 1970, would have taken title to the stock certificates subject to it.

The Trustee, on the other hand, has advanced a more intricate analysis. In his view, the July 17, 1968 purchase agreement constitutes a written security agreement within the meaning of §9-204(1). Relying upon the last sentence of that section [in the 1972 version of Art. 9, see the second sentence of §9-203(2) — ed.] he argues that although the purchase agreement provides for the creation of a security interest, the express language of the agreement postpones the time at which the interest was to attach by making attachment contingent upon (1) default by AFL followed by (2) notice to Hugh Moulton and (3) actual receipt of the stock by Mrs. Groff: "Whereupon seller's rights and obligations in and to the shares represented by the certificates . . . shall be those of a secured party holding collateral under the provisions of Article IX of the Uniform Commercial Code." Assuming the Trustee's position to be correct, Mrs. Groff would not have had a perfected security interest at the time the Trustee was appointed and therefore would not have a claim to the stock superior to his.

In this court's opinion, the legal relationship existing between the parties is more accurately described by the Trustee. Although his reliance upon a straight reading of §9-204(1) is in itself compelling, there are additional reasons supporting the court's view. They stem, for the most part, from the fact that Mrs. Groff's position completely ignores the existence of the escrow agreement.

There can be no doubt that the escrow agreement entered into on July 17, 1968 was one in fact, not merely form. There is simply no evidence that the parties intended anything otherwise. Mrs. Groff's position to the contrary notwithstanding, the simultaneous existence of an escrow and a pledge is a legal impossibility. Qualley v. Snoqualmie Valley Bank, 136 Wash. 42, 238 P. 915 (1925).

It is fundamental to the existence of a pledge that the pledgor give up possession of his property and place it in the hands or control of the pledgee. Although possession by the pledgee may be accomplished through the use of an agent, the pledgee must have absolute domain and control over the property. Qualley v. Snoqualmie Valley Bank, supra; 72 CJS Pledges §19(b)(6) (1951); see, Uniform Commercial Code §9-305, Comment 2. Fundamental to the existence of an escrow is the transfer of the escrow instrument into the hands of a third party as depository. Prior to the happening of any of the conditions upon which the escrow agreement operates, the escrow agent is not empowered to act for either party. Although he may be an agent for one of the parties in other respects, with respect to the instrument in escrow his powers are solely limited to those stipulated in the escrow agreement. Sweifach v. Scranton Lace Co., 156 F. Supp. 384, 393 (M.D. Pa. 1957); Qualley v. Snoqualmie Valley Bank, supra.

Applying these principles to the facts in the present case, it is clear that a pledge was not created as of the date the sale was transacted. Although the parties intended to provide a security interest for Mrs. Groff, it was their further intent that such security interest would not be capable of attaching until the event of an uncured default in AFL's payments. The execution of the escrow agreement and deposit of the stock certificates with the escrow agent was intended to provide for neutral custody of the stock pending such payments or default. Because there was no uncured default until January 7, 1971, Mrs. Groff's security interest was not capable of attaching until that date. The petition for reorganization and appointment of the Trustee having occurred more than six months earlier when Mrs. Groff did not possess a perfected security interest, she does not have a claim to the stock superior to that of the Trustee. The Referee's order is reversed.

It is so ordered.

NOTE

For a case discarding all the legal technicalities and permitting an escrow arrangement to operate as a pledge as the parties obviously intended, see In re Copeland, 391 F. Supp. 134, 16 U.C.C. Rep. Serv. 273 (D. Del. 1975), *aff'd* 531 F.2d 1195, 18 U.C.C.

Rep. Serv. 833 (3d Cir. 1976) (there are good policy discussions in both opinions).

PROBLEM 26

In May, Kiddie Delight, Inc. (a manufacturer of toys) wanted to borrow money and use its inventory of toys as collateral. It called up Fred's Field Warehouse Company and Fred's came to the plant, put the inventory in a locked room, and posted a sign on the door saying "Contents of Room Under Control of Fred's Field Warehouse." Fred's then issued a negotiable warehouse receipt deliverable to the order of Kiddie Delight. Fred's hired Mort Menial, the Kiddie Delight janitor, as their local warehouse custodian (Mort was paid $1.00 a week by Fred's to mind the goods; he continued to receive his normal paycheck from Kiddie Delight). Kiddie Delight pledged the warehouse receipt (a *document*) to Mammon State Bank in return for a loan. Kiddie Delight went bankrupt shortly thereafter.

(a) Does the bank have a perfected security interest in the document? In the inventory? See §§9-205 (last sentence plus Official Comment 6) and 9-304(2).

(b) If the bank and Kiddie Delight had signed a written security agreement covering the warehouse receipt and the inventory it represented and the bank gave Kiddie Delight the money, does the bank have a perfected security interest in the warehouse receipt even *before* the bank gets possession of it? See §9-304(4).

(c) If Kiddie Delight (prior to bankruptcy) wanted to get the warehouse receipt back from the bank in order to present it to the warehouseman (Mort), get the goods, clean them, return them to the field warehouse, and get back the receipt for re-hypothecation to the bank, will the bank lose its perfection if it turns the document over to the debtor? Read §9-304(5).

(d) If the bank loses its perfection, who would you advise it to sue? See §7-204(1).

PROBLEM 27

Karate, Inc. was a self-defense training school. It pledged 36 of the promissory notes given it by its customers to Nightflyer Finance Company in return for a loan. The parties signed a security agreement, and the finance company not only took possession of the notes, but also *filed* a properly executed financing statement covering the instruments. A month later Karate, Inc.'s president, Arnold Chung, asked Nightflyer to let him have back one of the notes so that he could present it to the customer for payment (an Article 3 *presentment*). The finance company gave him the note on April 6. Chung put it in his desk at the school and forgot about it. On October 12 the karate school went bankrupt. Does the bank have a perfected security interest in any or all of the promissory notes? See §9-304 and the Official Comment thereto; McIlroy Bank v. First Nat. Bank, 480 S.W.2d 127, 10 U.C.C. Rep. Serv. 1111 (Ark. 1972). What effect does the filing have? See §9-304(1) (second sentence). Would it make a difference if the collateral qualified as *chattel paper*?

NOTE

The primary use of §§9-304(4) and (5) occurs in letter of credit transactions (UCC Article 5), wherein the issuing bank receives a bill of lading (a *document*) covering the goods and turns it over to the buyer (*debtor*) so the buyer can get the goods from the carrier, sell them, and reimburse the bank. During the 21 day period the bank's security interest in the document remains perfected even though the document is out of its possession.

B. AUTOMATIC PERFECTION

1. Purchase Money Security Interests in Consumer Goods

Read §§9-302(1)(b) through (g). The reason for having an automatic purchase money security interest in consumer goods, §9-302(1)(d), without requiring either filing or possession for perfection was partly historical (it had always been done that way) and partly practical. Consumer goods are unlikely to be used as collateral *twice*, so there are rarely any later creditors to protect. Filing costs money, and it is simply not worth it for merchants to file to perfect a security interest in every nickel and dime sale (note the exemption for motor vehicles which requires other perfection steps even if they are classified as *consumer goods*). See White & Summers §23-7.

To qualify for automatic perfection under §9-302(1)(d), the security interest in consumer goods must qualify as a *purchase money* interest, a term defined in §9-107. A purchase money security interest (PMSI) is granted to sellers or lenders whose willingness to extend credit permitted the debtor to acquire the collateral. Such creditors obviously have a superior equity in the collateral vis-à-vis other creditors and the Code therefore frequently affords them special considerations.

PROBLEM 28

Bilko Siding, Inc. put aluminum siding on Mr. and Mrs. Brown's home. They signed a contract on August 4 giving the company a security interest in all their currently owned consumer goods plus those acquired in the future. On September 25 the Browns went to First Finance Company and borrowed $80 for the stated purpose of buying a sewing machine. They signed a security agreement with the finance company granting it a security interest in the machine. First Finance did not file a financing statement. The Browns bought the machine on October 11. They filed for bankruptcy on October 12. Bilko, First Finance, and their trustee all claim the machine.

(a) Did Bilko's security interest attach to the sewing machine? See §9-204(2); see In re Johnson, 13 U.C.C. Rep. Serv. 953 (Ref. Bankr., D. Neb. 1973) (creditor's bankruptcy security interest in "all consumer goods" held totally invalid because the referee found the after-acquired property clause overbroad, unconscionable, and unfair since it had an in terrorem effect on consumers).

(b) Was the loan agreement a *purchase money security agreement* even though First Finance was a *lender* and not the seller of the machine? See §9-107.

(c) Would it have been if the Browns had used the $80 to pay a liquor bill and had used $80 from their savings account to buy the sewing machine? How can finance companies protect themselves from the debtor's misuse of the funds advanced? See §3-116(b).

(d) Assuming the $80 was used for the announced purpose, who gets the sewing machine?

Coomer v. Barclays American Financial, Inc.

8 B.R. 351, 30 U.C.C. Rep. Serv. 1961 (E.D. Pa. 1980)

[The Bankruptcy Code permits a debtor to claim an exemption in household furnishings and household goods, among other property, and in doing so the debtor may avoid any non-purchase-money security interest therein.]

KELLEY, Bankr. J. The question in this proceeding concerns the character of Merit Finance's security interest in certain household goods owned by the debtors, the Coomers. The Coomers seek to avoid Merit's security interest in the household goods. They can avoid it only if it is a nonpurchase-money security interest. 11 USC §522(f)(2)(A) (1979).

The facts are simple. The Coomers had obtained a loan from Merit but had not completely repaid it. They found some new furniture that they wanted to buy from Paul Bellamy Furniture. Mr. Coomer went to Merit to obtain a loan to buy the furniture. He was told to get a list with prices from Paul Bellamy. He got the list and took it to Merit. Merit made the loan. It issued a check to Mr. Coomer for $1,421.01, which he used to pay most of the purchase price of the furniture. The Coomers themselves had to pay $62.79.

Merit "consolidated" the loan for the furniture with the old loan. At the time the Coomers owed on it $1,172.20. Credits and refunds reduced that to $938.80 which was also "lent" to the Coomers to pay off the old loan.

Merit retained a security interest in the furniture bought from Paul Bellamy and in other household goods. Merit does not contend that its security interest in the other household goods is purchase money. The issue is whether or to what extent it has a purchase money security interest in the furniture bought from Paul Bellamy.

There is no question as to perfection of its security interest since it filed a financing statement covering all of the collateral.

The Bankruptcy Code does not define nonpurchase money or purchase money security interest. Its definition of security interest is not helpful. 11 USC §101(37) (1979).

The parties and other courts have looked to Article 9 of the Uniform Commercial Code (the UCC) for the definition of purchase money security interest. Section 9-107 of the UCC in Tennessee defines it as follows.

> A security interest is a "purchase money security interest" to the extent that it is:
>
> (a) taken or retained by the seller of the collateral to secure all or part of its price; or
>
> (b) taken by a person who by making advances . . . gives value to enable the debtor to acquire rights in . . . the collateral if such value is in fact so used.

Merit's security interest at first blush appears to satisfy subsection (b)'s criteria. But there is a problem.

Merit can have a purchase money security interest in the new furniture only to the extent it made advances to enable the Coomers to buy the furniture and the money was so used. The advance to pay off, or consolidate, the old loan was not made to enable the Coomers to buy the furniture and was not so used. New furniture also secures repayment of that part of the total loan. Merit's security interest in the new furniture cannot be purchase money to the extent it secures payment of the old loan part of the debt. See Comment 2 to §9-107.

A similar problem occurs in cases under subsection (a) of the definition. Typically the seller has sold several items at different times, combined all the debts, and retained a security interest in each item to secure payment of the total debt. The courts have held that for a security interest in one item to be purchase money, the item must secure only its price. In re Manuel, 507 F2d 990, 16 UCC Rep Serv 493 (5th Cir 1975); In re Norrell, 426 F Supp 435, 21 UCC Rep Serv 1185 (MD Ga 1977); In re Staley, 426 F Supp 437, 22 UCC Rep Serv 799 (MD Ga 1977); In re Dills, No. 3-80-00366 (Bankr Ct ED Tenn Sept. 9, 1980) (J. Bare); In re Scott, 6 BCD 407, 2 CBC2d 1012, 29 UCC Rep Serv 1038 (Bankr Ct MD Pa 1980); In re Jackson, 9 UCC Rep Serv 1152 (Bankr Ct WD Mo 1971); In re Brouse, 6 UCC Rep Serv 471 (Bankr Ct WD Mich 1969). See also In re Simpson, 4 UCC Rep Serv 243 & 250 (Bankr Ct WD Mich 1966) (2 opinions).

Those cases sometimes seem to say that if an item secures any debt other than its price, then the security interest is automatically nonpurchase money. That ignores the language of the definition which makes a security interest purchase money to the extent the collateral secures its price or purchase money. There is no requirement in the definition that the secured party intend that an item secure only its purchase money.

The real problem is proving the purchase money security interest. See In re Manuel, In re Norrell, In re Staley, and In re Brouse, above. Section 9-107(a) does not completely exclude the seller's purchase money security interest, but without a method of determining its extent, the seller must be held not to have a purchase money security interest.

Likewise, there is nothing in §9-107(b) that says a lender who makes a partly purchase money loan cannot have a partly purchase money security interest. Again the problem is proving the purchase money security interest. As to mixed loans, the problem is compounded. There must be both a method of apportioning the loan between the purchase money and nonpurchase money parts and a method of applying the payments to the parts. One court has intimated that the rule in the sellers' cases is more appropriate to cases involving purchase money lenders. In re Mid-Atlantic Flange Co., Inc., 26 UCC Rep Serv 203 (Bankr Ct ED Pa 1979). See also In re Jones, 5 BR 655, 6BCD 848 (Bankr Ct ED Pa 1980), In re Mulcahy, 3 BR 454, 1 CBC2d 887 (Bankr Ct SD Ind 1979). Despite these problems the court is reluctant to hold that Merit's security interest in the new furniture is entirely nonpurchase money.

Section 522(f) applies to a common situation. The committee reports say only that it is meant to protect the debtor's exemptions. HR Rep No. 95-595, 95th Cong, 1st Sess 362; S Rep No. 95-989, 95th Cong, 2d Sess 76. The reasons are more explicit in the Report of the Commission on Bankruptcy Laws of the United States. HR Doc No. 93-197, 93 Cong, 1st Sess, Part I (1973).

The Commission took the view that nonpurchase-money security interests in household goods generally have no value to the creditor, except as a means of coercing payment by threatening repossession. Report, Part I at 169. The Commission concluded that debtors should not be denied the benefit of their exemptions in household goods because of valueless security interests. Report, Part I at 173. That idea led to §522(f) of the Bankruptcy Code. 9 Bkr L Ed §81:1; — Cong Rec E21 (daily ed Jan. 4, 1977) (remarks of Rep. Edwards).

The main reason that the Commission and Congress prescribed this treatment was their opinion that the household goods securing nonpurchase money debts generally have no substantial market value. That conclusion is most appropriate when the debtor obtained a loan and as collateral put up used household goods. The conclusion is less appropriate for new or used goods bought by the debtor on secured credit from the seller or with the proceeds of a purchase money loan.

The court believes that the purpose of §522(f)(2)(A) generally is to avoid security interests that debtors grant in their already-owned, used household goods. Merit's security interest in the Coomers' new furniture does not fit that pattern. But under case law interpreting the UCC it would be a nonpurchase money security interest. The problem in meeting the requirements of UCC §9-107(b) is a practical one — determining the amount of its purchase money still secured by the furniture.

The court should also consider the practical effects of following or not following the UCC decisions.

If Merit's security interest in the new furniture is totally avoided, then the Coomers will keep the furniture as exempt property free of Merit's claim.

On the other hand, assume that to some extent Merit has a purchase money security interest in the new furniture. That security interest cannot be avoided under §522(f). But what would be significant is the value of the furniture. If it is worth less than the purchase money part of the debt, then the Coomers would reassume the debt or redeem the furniture only for its value. See 11 USC §§506, 524(c) & (d), 722 (1979).

In this case only the furniture bought from Paul Bellamy could be subject to a non-avoidable purchase money security interest. It was bought for less than $1,500 and now is probably worth less than what was paid for it. Merit's claim is for $2,926.06, a reduction of $1,330.94 on the consolidated debt. The point is that for the purposes of §522(f) a court might at times avoid the problem of apportioning the debt and applying payments by first comparing the value of the purchase money collateral to the amount of the debt, particularly as to later purchases. In several cases a seller's or a lender's security interest in the last item purchased survived by going unchallenged. In re Manuel, In re Norrell, In re Dills, In re Mulcahy, above. In this case, however, the court cannot reach that conclusion without confronting the problem of determining the amount of the purchase money debt.

The court has expressed its reluctance to follow the UCC rule because in this case it may not properly reflect the policy behind §522(f)(2)(A). But as a general rule it is not entirely contrary to the policy behind §522(f), which is part of the policy of the bankruptcy law to give individual debtors a "fresh start."

The court is aware that the rule presents a new problem for secured creditors when applied in this context. The perfection problem under the UCC could be solved by filing a financing statement. That is no help under §522(f). But the rule is not new. When a lender consolidates a purchase money loan with a non-purchase money loan, it effectively gives up its purchase money status unless there is some method provided for determining the extent to which each item of collateral secures its purchase money. Lenders have known that for some time.

The re-emergence of the problem under §522(f) should have been expected, at least as to recent security interests. Congress was surely aware that the UCC definition and decisions under it would be used to construe "nonpurchase-money." The court cannot say that application of the rule is an unfair surprise.

Another rule might also be inconsistent with the policy of §522(f). For example, in this case Merit retained a security interest in goods other than the new furniture to secure its purchase money. Outside of bankruptcy the security interest in the other goods would be enforceable. They would also secure the purchase money part of the debt. In attempting to apply §522(f) fairly, how should the court consider that fact? The consolidation of loans may be much more complex than in this case. The policy behind §522(f)(2)(A) may often be an uncertain guide.

Furthermore, the administration of bankruptcy cases demands a workable and clear rule. Without some guidelines, legislative or contractual, the court should not be required to distill from a mass of transactions the extent to which a security interest is purchase money.

The court concludes that the rule should be applied in this case. The new furniture secures a debt for more than its purchase money. There is no method for determining the extent to which the new furniture secures only its purchase money. Accordingly, the security interest is nonpurchase money.

This memorandum constitutes findings of fact and conclusions of law. Bankruptcy Rule 752.

2. *Certain Accounts*

Read §9-302(1)(e) and Official Comment 5. The courts have split over whether the major test is "significant part" (a percentage test) or "causal or isolated transaction" (the Official Comment test). See White & Summers §23-8. A creditor is ill-advised to rely on §9-302(1)(e) and not file; it is simply too dangerous to take the chance that a court will decide the section applies. Grant Gilmore has concluded that the exemption was meant to protect assignees who don't normally take such assignments and are therefore unlikely to file. Under his test the assignee must be "both insignificant and ignorant." G. Gilmore §19.6. One court adopted this test and permitted the assignee to establish his "insignificance and ignorance" so as to have a perfected interest without filing: E. Turgeon Constr. Co. v. Elhatton Plumbing & Heating Co., 292 A.2d 230, 10 U.C.C. Rep. Serv. 1353 (R.I. 1972).

Consolidated Film Industries v. United States

547 F.2d 533, 20 UCC Rep. Serv. 1360

DOYLE, C.J. The question in this case is whether the district court erred in granting relief to appellee enjoining the United States Internal Revenue Service from enforcing a levy. A more ultimate and specific issue is whether a financing statement is required under the pertinent Uniform Commercial Code provision, Utah Statutes, §9-302(1)(e), Utah Code (1968), which section relates to requiring the filing of a financing statement in order to perfect security interests. This in turn is dependent upon construction of the exemption provision contained in the above cited provision of the Utah Uniform Commercial Code. This issue is the crucial one. If a financing statement is required, the appellee loses and the cause must be reversed. If appellee enjoyed an exemption from filing the statement, the Internal Revenue Service's levy is not enforceable and the judgment is affirmed. Section 9-302(1)(e) provides in pertinent part as follows:

> A financing statement must be filed to perfect all security interests except the following:
>
> (e) An assignment of accounts or contract rights which does not alone or in connection with other assignments to the same assignee transfer a significant part of the outstanding accounts or contract rights of the assignor.

The government's levy was served on Inflight Motion Pictures, Inc., but appellee Consolidated Film Industries is the party in interest affected by it and so the suit is brought by it.

Due to the many participants and the several assignments the facts appear complicated, but they boil down to the described conflict as to whether a financing statement was required for perfection of the assignment and so the various formal legal motions simply provide a backdrop.

Consolidated Film Industries brought the suit for injunction against the United States to enjoin it from enforcing a levy served by the government on Inflight Motion Pictures, Inc. The trial court granted the relief and the government appeals. We reverse.

In July 1971, Interwest Film Corporation, which has its principal place of business in Utah, obtained ownership rights in a film "The Ra Expedition." In order to acquire financing to enable it to market the film, Interwest entered into a sale and lease back, with an option allowing it to repurchase the contract from Lowell Berry Foundation. Under the contract Interwest sold its property in the film to Lowell Berry for $375,000. Lowell Berry in turn granted back to Interwest exclusive marketing rights in the film until March 1, 1972. Interwest retained an option to repurchase the film for $562,500 in cash and in stock, payable in installments. The option to buy back was to be exercised by Interwest's paying Lowell Berry $93,750 in cash between February 1, 1972, and March 1, 1972. This was to be followed by the payment of installments until the full purchase price was completed. The completion date was March 1, 1973.

Interwest entered into a contract with the plaintiff-appellee, Consolidated Film Industries, for the production of several prints of the film and Interwest was obligated to pay $15,484 to Consolidated Film Industries to compensate for the making of the prints. Consolidated Film is now the successor in interest to Lowell Berry's rights.

In February 1972, Interwest exercised its option to repurchase by making the stipulated payment of $93,750 to Lowell Berry, but that was the first and last payment made on the repurchase obligation. On June 27, 1972, Interwest assigned to Lowell Berry its rights in a contract it had entered into with Inflight. This allowed Inflight to show the film aboard planes for a fee or royalty. This contract was thus security and amounts received under it were to reduce Interwest's obligation to Lowell Berry. Notice of the assignment to Lowell Berry was given to Inflight by Interwest. On July 27, 1973, Lowell Berry assigned its rights in the Interwest-Inflight contract to Consolidated Film Industries. No financing statement was filed with the Utah Secretary of State evidencing either assignment of the rights in the Interwest-Inflight contract.

In the same contract in which Interwest assigned to Lowell Berry its rights in the Interwest-Inflight contract, Interwest also assigned to Lowell Berry rights which it has in a contract with Bell & Howell and, in addition, there was a provision in which Lowell Berry agreed to allow Interwest to perform screenings of the film provided Interwest remitted daily to Lowell Berry certain percentages of the gross proceeds derived from such screenings.

On June 19, 1972, the United States, through the Internal Revenue Service, assessed against Interwest for unpaid federal employment taxes in the amount of $56,548.98. A further assessment was made against Interwest for unpaid federal employment taxes in the amount of $43,376.77 on September 25, 1972. Notice and demand for payment was made on Interwest on the dates of the respective assessments. Notice of the first federal tax lien was filed September 1, 1972. On October 31, 1972, notice of levy was served on Inflight demanding that the latter pay the United States the money which it was obligated to pay on the Inflight-Interwest contract. Inflight failed to honor this levy and failed to pay the money over to Interwest, Lowell Berry or Consolidated Film Industries.

In the suit which was filed by Consolidated Film Industries (on July 30, 1973), in the United States District Court for the Central District of California, it alleged that its rights in the fund held by Inflight were superior to the rights of the United States by virtue of Interwest's assignment of its rights in the Interwest-Inflight contract to Consolidated Film Industries, the successor in interest of Lowell Berry. It sought to enjoin the United States from enforcing its levy against Inflight and to collect money damages as well. Consolidated Film Industries moved to transfer the case to the United States District Court for the District of Utah on November 26, 1973. The cause was transferred. On December 5, 1974, and on December 6, 1974, the United States and Consolidated, respectively, moved for the summary judgment. The government's contention in the action was that Interwest's assignment of its contract rights to Lowell Berry constituted the transfer of a security interest which was subject to Article 9 of the Uniform Commercial Code, and that it had not been perfected because no financing statement had been filed. Consolidated claimed that Lowell Berry's acquisition of the Interwest-Inflight contract was a purchase transaction not protected by Article 9 and hence superior to the government's levy. Subsequently, Consolidated claimed that even if the assignment was a security interest it was subject to being perfected without filing pursuant to §9-302(1)(e), supra.

The trial court (Judge Anderson) held that the assignment was a security interest covered by Article 9, but further held that there was insufficient evidence to decide whether it came within the filing exception contained in §9-302(1)(e).

After the mentioned decision of Judge Andersson, Consolidated Film Industries filed affidavits of Lowell Berry's executive vice-president together with an affidavit of Consolidated Film Industries' counsel. These showed that Lowell Berry had reason to believe that Interwest's accounts receivable and other contract rights were substantial in relation to its Inflight contract. The affidavits were, however, conclusory. In its order the district court acknowledged that there was no evidence as to the total amount of Interwest's outstanding contract rights at the time of the assignment, and noted the weakness of the affidavits filed. The court, nonetheless, ruled that the filing exception of §9-302(1)(e) was applicable. The court reasoned that Lowell Berry had no actual or constructive notice of the substantiality of Interwest's contract rights. A further reason for the court's holding that the exception applied to relieve appellee of filing was that the assignment was an isolated or casual transaction for Lowell Berry. Based on these holdings, the United States was enjoined from enforcing its levy against Inflight and it is this order which is before us for review.

Whether a financing statement was necessary depends on the meaning to be given to the words in the exemption provision, Section 9-302(1)(e), which excepts an assignment that transfers an insignificant part of the outstanding accounts or contract rights of the assignor.

We are handicapped by not having more facts. We know that Interwest transferred its property in the film to Lowell Berry for $375,000. Interwest agreed to redeem the film from Lowell Berry for $562,500. Whether this constituted a significant part of the outstanding accounts of Interwest we do not know. The extent of our knowledge is that this was the only such account, for there is no evidence of any other.[1]

The trial court also found that the evidence was insufficient to support a finding on the issue. After the initial reaction of the trial judge, affidavits were filed, but these were also remarkably short of facts. The closest that Consolidated came to furnishing facts was its saying in the affidavit that Lowell Berry "had reason to believe" that Interwest's accounts receivable and other contract rights were substantial in relation to its Inflight contract. This statement falls short of establishing substantiality in relationship to the other rights of Interwest. It is nothing more than an opin-

1. There is some vague information that Interwest had at least one other film; however, it is inconclusive. See Affidavit of Walter M. Ross, Record on Appeal at 143.

ion. If indeed facts existed, Lowell Berry ought to have produced them.

There are no Utah cases which have construed the embattled exemption clause. So we must look elsewhere for enlightenment as to what constitutes a significant part of the outstanding accounts of the assignor and, therefore, is subject to the requirement of filing a financing statement. The trial court did not give principal effect to the wording of the statute. Instead, it used what is known as the isolated or casual transaction test taken from the comments to §9-302(1), supra. The Comment says that the purpose of the exemption is to save from invalidation "casual or isolated assignments." The Comment goes on to say:

> . . . some accounts receivable statutes were so broadly drafted that all assignments, whatever their character or purpose, fell within their filing provisions. Under such statutes many assignments which no one would think of filing might have been subject to invalidation. The paragraph (1)(e) exemption goes to that type of assignment. Any person who regularly takes assignments of any debtor's accounts should file.

We are unable to accept and use this Comment since it has never been adopted in Utah. We are unwilling to follow the Comment in preference to the words of the statute and particularly so in view of the fact that Utah has not chosen to adopt it.

The cases from other jurisdictions tend to hold that the party claiming the exemption has the burden of producing proof that brings his case within the scope of the exemption.

For example, in Miller v. Wells Fargo Bank International Corp., 406 F Supp 452, 477 (SDNY 1975), the court held that a party claiming an exemption had failed to meet its burden of proof inasmuch as the assignment was substantial. It was for over one million dollars, which was approximately 20 percent of the assignor's accounts. Cf. Standard Lumber Company v. Chambers Frames Inc., 317 F Supp 837 (ED Ark 1970) (16 percent of the accounts receivable was not a significant part).

The Wyoming Supreme Court in Craig v. Gudim, 488 P2d 316 (1971), held that the person wishing to reply on the exception under this provision has the burden of showing that the assignment did not transfer a significant part of the outstanding contract rights of the assignor. In that case, as in ours, the assignee showed only the amount of the assignment to it so the exemption was not applicable.

A similar result was reached in Citizens National Bank of Okmulgee v. Chick Norton Buick Co., 8 UCC Rep 1389 (Okla Ct App 1971). Here again it was said that the assignee must bear the burden of proving that the assignment did not constitute a significant part of the outstanding accounts or contract rights of the assignor. Since the assignee failed to show what part of the total accounts the assignment to it constituted, the court said that the exception could not be relied on. If the amount of the assignment in relationship to the total contract rights at the time was relatively small as in the case of In re Consolidated Steel Corp., 11 UCC Rep 408 (MD Fla 1972), the issue as to whether the assignment was a significant part of the outstanding accounts can be determined. We are aware of only one decision which has held that the burden of proof is on the adverse party rather than the assignee to prove transfer of a significant part of the outstanding accounts or rights of the assignor. See In re Boughner, 8 UCC Rep 144 (WD Mich 1970).

The appellee relies on Professor Gilmore's statement that the exemption provision is intended to protect from invalidation casual or isolated assignments which no one would think of filing. See Gilmore, Security Interests in Personal Property, §19.6 (1965). He states further that the provision is drafted so that no assignee, engaged in the regular course of financing will ever be tempted to rely on it in order to avoid a filing which ought to be made. See also Homer Kripke and Karl Felsenfeld, A Practical Approach to Article 9 of the UCC, 17 Rutgers L Rev 168, 190 (1962).

The problem with these learned commentaries is that they are out of harmony with the plain wording of the statute. The statutory requirement is specific that the assignment be an insignificant part of the outstanding accounts or rights of the assignor. The trial judge also assumed that this could not be a practical commercial transaction. Our reaction is that the size of the transaction considered in and of itself does not suggest that this is a casual transaction or one which would ordinarily be exempt from filing. As to whether the assignment constitutes all of the outstanding accounts or rights of the assignor, we have to conclude that from all appearances this constituted most if not all of the accounts or rights of the assignor. If that is true, and there is no evidence from appellee to the contrary, it would make no difference that it may be an isolated transaction.

Accordingly, we must hold that the ruling of the district court, based as it is on a test which in the context of this case is lacking applicability, the judgment must be reversed. It is ordered that the cause be reversed and remanded with directions to vacate the judgment and enter judgment for defendant-appellant.

C. PERFECTION BY FILING

The basic supposition of §9-302 is that except for the transactions listed therein *filing* of a "financing statement" is the exclusive method of perfection of the creditor's security interest.

1. The Mechanics of Filing

Section 9-401 specifies the *place(s)* of filing in subsection (1), a matter of such complexity that the Code drafters proposed three different alternatives for possible adoption by the states. The first alternative provides for one central state-wide filing for all collateral except fixtures (which are filed in the county real estate office); the second alternative (by far the most popular with the states) has a central filing for everything except fixtures, consumer goods, and farm-related collateral, which have local county filings (plus a *dual* filing for crops); and the third alternative is like the second only it has a further provision for *dual* filings in many circumstances. In several states none of the above was adopted — the states simply went non-uniform and creatively devised their own solutions.

You should therefore spend a few minutes looking at your own state's §9-401(1) language and seeing if you can decode its meaning. This endeavor is sure to be more interesting for you if you are aware that practicing attorneys in your jurisdiction have to know and understand the local version of §9-401(1) well — filing in an obviously wrong place sounds a great deal like malpractice.

In re Kalinoski

13 U.C.C. Rep. Serv. 387 (W.D. Wis. 1973)

BESSMAN, Ref. Bankr. Petitions for reclamation were filed in this matter by Kasten Manufacturing Corporation, Sperry Rand

Corporation, John Miller Supply Company, Inc., and Avco Distributing Corporation, all secured creditors of the bankrupt. The trustee contends that the security interests were not perfected and that he is therefore entitled to retain the property in question as an asset of the estate.

The facts are undisputed. The bankrupt, who had been engaged in the farm implement business, had his place of business in Cuba City, Wisconsin. The greater part of Cuba City is located in Grant County with a small area in adjacent LaFayette County. The bankrupt's place of business was in that small area, about one thousand feet from the county line dividing LaFayette and Grant Counties. All of the petitioners filed financing statements in the office of the Wisconsin Secretary of State and in the office of the register of deeds for Grant County.

Section 409.401(1)(c), Wisconsin Statutes, the Wisconsin version of §9-401 of the Uniform Commercial Code, requires that the financing statement be filed both in the Secretary of State's office and in the register of deeds' office where the debtor's principal place of business is located. The question is whether the petitioners perfected their security interests in view of the fact that they filed their financing statements in Grant County rather than in LaFayette County, where the bankrupt had his place of business.

The testimony established that the petitioners generally refer to postal directories to determine the county in which a business is located. The postal directory, as well as the State of Wisconsin Blue Book reports that Cuba City is located in Grant County. It does not indicate that part of the city is in LaFayette County. Similarly, the official Wisconsin highway map places Cuba City entirely in Grant County.

Under the circumstances, it is not at all surprising that the petitioners made an erroneous filing. Nevertheless, a few of the bankrupt's secured creditors somehow discovered that the debtor's place of business was in LaFayette County and properly perfected their security interests by filing financing statements with its register of deeds.

However understandable the plight of the petitioners, the statute leaves no opportunity for discretion. Its requirements are plain, as the Supreme Court of Wisconsin observed In re Federal Wholesale Meats & Frozen Foods, 43 Wis. 2d 21, 24 (1969) §9-401(1)(c), and they must be satisfied with exactitude. The good faith of the petitioners in their attempt to comply with the statutory requirements cannot excuse their error, as pointed out in the cases cited in the trustee's brief.

Under §70a of the Bankruptcy Act, the trustee has the status of a judgment creditor with an execution returned unsatisfied, and he is vested with all the property upon which a creditor of the bankrupt could have obtained a lien on the date of bankruptcy, regardless whether such a creditor exists. 4A Collier on Bankruptcy §70.04 p. 59. An unperfected security interest is subordinate to a trustee in bankruptcy under §9-301(3) Wisconsin Statutes, as well as under the Bankruptcy Act.

The controlling facts in P. S. Products Corp. v. Equilease Corp., 435 F.2d 781 (2nd Cir. 1970), are virtually identical with those in the present case. Like Cuba City, the town of Farmingdale, New York, is situated in two counties, the larger part of Nassau County and a small part in Suffolk County. The bankrupt had his place of business in Suffolk County, but the secured creditor, in addition to filing with the New York Secretary of State, filed its financing statement in Nassau County. Notwithstanding, the bankrupt was listed in the Nassau County telephone directory and had leased a post office box in that county.

The New York statute, adopted without variation from the Uniform Commercial Code, requires filing "in the department of state and in addition, if the debtor has a place of business in this state and in only one county of this state, also in the office of the filing officer of such county." More liberal than the Wisconsin version, the New York creditor need file only with the secretary of state if the debtor has a place of business in more than one county. The court held that the circumstances could not justify the improper filing since the bankrupt's sole place of business was in Suffolk County and filing in that county was essential to perfection of a security interest. Accordingly, the court affirmed the judgment of the district court dismissing the creditor's petition for reclamation.

For the reasons given, the petitions for reclamation are dismissed.

PROBLEM 29

Under the local version of §9-401 filing was required "in the county where the principal place of business of the corporation is located." The corporate charter of the Peripatetic Corporation showed its original place of business was Lincoln County, but the company soon moved to a retail store outlet in Franklin County where it dealt with the public. Further the corporation was really a husband and wife type business, and they did all the corporate paperwork at their home in Madison County (where they also kept the corporate records). Their corporate stationery used their home address. When the corporation borrows money against its accounts receivable, where should the financing statement be filed? See §9-401(6); White & Summers at §23-14; in this situation what is the "chief executive office"? The courts have developed a number of tests for the principal place of business: In re Mimshell Fabrics, Ltd., 491 F.2d 21, 14 U.C.C. Rep. Serv. 227 (2d Cir. 1974) (principal place is "frequent and notorious" to "probable potential creditors"); In re Carmichael Enterprises, Inc., 334 F. Supp. 94, 9 U.C.C. Rep. Serv. 895 (5th Cir. 1972) (not necessarily same as address on corporate charter; the proper place to file is the corporation's "factual" principal place of business). See also this oft-quoted passage from In re McQuaide, 5 U.C.C. Rep. Serv. 802, 806-807 (Ref. Bankr., D. Vt. 1968):

> "Place of business" is defined in 48 CJ 1213 §3 as an agency, an office; a place actually occupied, either continually or at regular periods, by a person or his clerks, or those in his employment; a place devoted by the proprietor to the carrying on of some form of trade or commerce; a place where people generally congregate for the purpose of carrying on some sort of traffic, or where people are invited or expected to come to engage in some sort of mercantile transaction; a place where a calling for the purpose of gain or profit is conducted; a place where business is carried on by persons under their control and on their own account; some particular locality, appropriated exclusively to a local business, such as a farm, store, shop, or dwelling place; that specific place within a city or town at which a person transacts business. *An occasional use or occupation of a place for business purposes is not sufficient to constitute it as a place of business.* [Emphasis in original.]

PRACTICAL NOTE

For perfectly obvious reasons, when in doubt file everywhere.

PROBLEM 30

S. Johnson ran a coffee shop called "The Mug"; he was the sole proprietor. He borrowed $20,000 from Octopus National Bank and gave the bank a perfected security in his family automobile (a Rolls Royce) and yacht he was planning on buying in two days (a 30-footer) ("The Mug" had been doing rather well). The local §9-401 required that financing statements covering consumer goods be filed in the county of the debtor's residence, which in this case was Jefferson County. ONB duly filed there. Before he bought the yacht, however, Johnson moved to Roosevelt County (which had a large lake). Issue: since the security interest in the yacht could not *attach* until the debtor had "rights in the collateral" (bought it), hasn't the bank filed in the wrong county? Section 9-401(3) (note that there are two alternatives) may appear, at first glance, to help, but does it? What is a "proper place"? See International Harvester Credit Corp. v. Vos, 290 N.W.2d 401, 28 U.C.C. Rep. Serv. 1187 (Mich. App. 1980); In re Roy, 21 U.C.C. Rep. Serv. 325 (Ref. Bankr., N.D. Ala. 1977); White & Summers §23-14.

In re Le Mieux

362 F. Supp. 1040, 13 UCC Rep. Serv. 559 (D. Minn. 1973)

NEVILLE, D.J. Petitioner Security National Bank of Faribault, Minnesota seeks review of an order of the Referee in Bankruptcy holding that a truck with tank used by the bankrupt in his milk-hauling business was "inventory" and that if not the bankrupt was an "organization" within the meaning of the Minnesota Uniform Commercial Code, Minn. Stat. §9-401 so as to require the filing by the bank of its financing statement securing its loan with the Secretary of State of Minnesota rather than, as it did, with the Register of Deeds of the County of the bankrupt's residence.

The facts as stipulated by the parties indicate that the bankrupt was an independent contractor engaged in the contract hauling of raw milk for farmers in four or five counties in Minnesota; that the personal property here in question was used by him in his business; that at all times relevant in this proceeding the bankrupt was a resident of Faribault, Rice County, Minnesota; that a financing statement pledging the personal property here in question to secure a loan duly executed by Security National Bank and the bankrupt was filed with the Register of Deeds in Rice County, Minnesota; and that no financing statement was filed with the Secretary of State of the State of Minnesota. The Minnesota Uniform Commercial Code, Minn. Stat. §9-401 reads in relevant part:

(1) The proper place to file in order to perfect a security interest is as follows:

(a) When the collateral is . . . consumer goods, or motor vehicles *which are not inventory*, then in the office of the register of deeds in the county of the debtor's residence if the debtor is an individual who is a resident of this state but if the debtor . . . is a corporation, partnership or *other organization* then in the office of the secretary of state . . . [emphasis added]

(c) In all other cases, in the office of the secretary of state.

On the foregoing facts the Referee in Bankruptcy found that the tank truck was "inventory," but that if not, then the bankrupt was an "organization," and that for either or both of these reasons the financing statement should have been filed with the Secretary of State and not with the Register of Deeds in Rice County. As a consequence of the improper filing, the Referee held the alleged lien invalid and that the Trustee in Bankruptcy was entitled to the escrowed proceeds of the sale of the tank truck in the amount of $19,500 free and clear of any lien on the part of Security National Bank. . . .

In support of his finding that the truck was inventory, the Referee cited no cases and noted that counsel had been unable to find any controlling authority, but relied on the definition of inventory in Minn. Stat. §9-109 that "goods are 'inventory' if they are held by a person who holds them for sale or lease or to be furnished under contracts of service or if he has so furnished them. . . ." It is conceded that the tank truck was not held "for sale or lease," but the Referee found that it had been "furnished under contracts of service." It is the opinion of this court that the meaning of "furnished under contracts of service" cannot be so broadly construed as to include the tank truck in question here. To be sure, the truck was utilized by the bankrupt under a contract of service; but it cannot be said that the truck was *furnished,* which term implies some transfer from the debtor to his customer of rights to possession and/or use. Comment 3 to §9-109 of the 1962 Official Text of the Uniform Commercial Code makes clear that a transaction having at least some of the characteristics of a sale is contemplated by the word "furnished." No such sale-like transaction is involved here. The truck is more in the nature of equipment and was used merely to haul milk belonging to the bankrupt's customers for his own profit, and always remained in the exclusive control of the bankrupt; no right of control over the truck ever passed to the customers. Comment 3 cited above provides further support for this result in its statement that the definition of "inventory" (in situations where the goods are not equipment nor held for sale) includes "one class of goods which is not held for disposition to a purchaser or user . . .," i.e., "materials used or consumed in business . . . used up or consumed in a short period of time in the production of some end product." The implication of the statement is that all other classes of goods in order to be inventory must be "held for disposition to a purchaser or user," although such disposition need not have all the formal trappings of a sale. Thus, it seems clear that the bankrupt's truck, since it was not to be incorporated into some end product was not "held for disposition to a purchaser or user," was not inventory, and the finding of the Referee is accordingly in error and reversed.

The above however, does not dispose of the case. The classification of the tank truck is immaterial if the debtor is, to quote Minn. Stat. §9-401(1)(a), "a corporation, partnership or other organization." Financing statements regarding such debtors must in any event be filed with the Secretary of State in order to become perfected as a lien. The Referee found that the bankrupt, an independent contractor in the business of hauling milk, was "an individual in business operating a legal or commercial entity" and thus within the definition of "organization." "Organization" is defined in Minn. Stat. §1-201(28) as a "corporation, government or governmental subdivision or agency, business trust, estate, trust, partnership or association, two or more persons having a joint or common interest, or any other legal or commercial entity." Petitioner argues strenuously against the proposition that the bankrupt, on becoming an individual contract milk hauler, with no employees automatically changed status from an "individual" to an "organization." This court finds that the result reached by the Referee is not supported by the language of the Code. It seems clear by Minn. Stat. §1-201(28) that by "organization" the drafters of the Code contemplated an entity or interest that comprised a group or had some existence apart from or independent of, the individuals involved. That an individual was not meant to be an organization, within the meaning of the Code, is made clear by Official Comment 28 to Minn. Stat. §1-201 which states that the definition of "organization" is "the definition of every type of entity or association, *excluding an individual,* acting as such." [Emphasis added] That the draftsmen of the Code intended to distinguish between individuals and organizations is also shown by the use of the disjunctive in the Code's definition of "person" in Minn. Stat. §1-201(30) as "an individual *or* an organization." [Emphasis added]

While research discloses no reported cases dealing squarely with this issue, the court's attention has been directed to In re Eichler, 9 UCC Rep. Serv. 1400 (E.D. Wash. 1971). In *Eichler,* the financing statement had been filed against a trade name under which the debtors husband and wife, had been doing business. The secured party, faced with a line of decisions holding that filing under a trade name was inadequate and that filing must be done under the name of the individual debtor (In re Thomas, 310 F. Supp. 338 (N.D. Cal. 1970); In re Osborn, 6 UCC Rep. Serv. 227 (W.D. Mich. 1969); In re Levins, 7 UCC Rep. Serv. 1076 (E.D.N.Y. 1970); In re Brawn, 7 UCC Rep. Serv. 565 (D. Me. 1970)), argued that use of the trade name created an entity separate from the individual debtors, which entity qualified as an "organization," and hence, the financing statement was properly filed in the name of the organization. The facts in *Eichler* certainly weighed more heavily than those in this case in favor of finding an "organization": the business was not conducted under the names of the individual debtors but rather under a trade name, and further the business consisted of two individuals, husband and wife, not just one. Nevertheless, the court declined to find an "organization," saying at 1405:

> The court is of the opinion that "Carriage Card and Record Shop" is not an organization within the meaning of the statute cited, but a trade name used by the bankrupts. The use of the assumed name created no separate entity apart from the individual debtors.

This court does not believe it can find an "organization" on the much weaker set of facts presented here than in *Eichler.*

Further evidence against the Referee's position can be found in a close analysis of Minn. Stat. §9-401(1), which, as pointed out above, has no counterpart in the 1962 official UCC Text. That section enumerates both "consumer goods" and "motor vehicles which are not inventory" as classes of financing statements which must be locally filed in the county of the debtor's residence. Since the definition of consumer goods in §9-109 covers any motor vehicle used for personal or family uses, the Code must contemplate local filing for some commercially used motor vehicles if the additional reference to "motor vehicles which are not inventory" is anything more than mere surplusage. However, if one were to accept the Referee's definition of "organization" as used subsequently in §9-401(1), any owner of a motor vehicle who used it for commerial purposes would automatically become an "organization" and thus required to file with the Secretary of State. Such a result is not warranted by the language of the Code, which, it would appear, contemplates local filing for motor vehicles used by individuals even though engaged in business, as was the case here.

This court holds that the Referee in Bankruptcy was in error both with respect to his finding that the truck was "inventory" and with respect to his alternate finding that the bankrupt was an "organization." The collateral here involved was an individually owned motor vehicle not inventory, and thus the financing statement was properly filed with the local Register of Deeds. Accordingly, the lien of Security National Bank is valid, and the proceeds from the sale of the truck, amounting to $19,500.00 now in the hands of the Trustee, are subject thereto. A separate order reversing the order of the Referee in Bankruptcy dated July 12, 1973 has been entered.

PROBLEM 31

Hamlet Corporation borrowed $100,000 from the Elsinore Finance Company and gave it a security interest in its equipment. The parties properly filled out a financing statement; Hamlet Corporation's name was signed by its president, W. Shakespeare. Elsinore gave the financing statement and the filing fee to a clerk at the Secretary of State's office (the only place the local §9-401 required a filing). The clerk, Ophelia Nunnery, had just announced her engagement to her fellow office workers and was not paying attention to her job as she indexed the financing statement under "Shakespeare" instead of "Hamlet." One year later another finance company loaned Hamlet Corporation more money taking a security interest in the same equipment (the second finance company had checked the records and discovered nothing under "Hamlet Corp."). Since priority of creditors in this situation depends on order of filing (§9-312(5)(a)), did Elsinore "file" first, or did it bear the risk of clerical error? See §9-403(1); Official Comment 1 to §9-407; In re May Lee Indus., Inc., 380 F. Supp. 1, 15 U.C.C. Rep. Serv. 528 (S.D.N.Y.), *aff'd*, 501 F.2d 1407,

15 U.C.C. Rep. Serv. 532 (2d Cir. 1974) (lost financing statement); In re Royal Electrotype Corp., 485 F.2d 394, 13 U.C.C. Rep. Serv. 183 (3d Cir. 1973) (indexed under creditor's name instead of debtor); In re Butler's Tire & Battery Co., 17 U.C.C. Rep. Serv. 1363 (Bankr. D. Ore. 1975), *aff'd on opinion below,* 18 U.C.C. Rep. Serv. 1302 (D. Ore. 1976) (creditor not protected where creditor's error caused filing official's mistake). Whichever creditor loses should sue the state for negligence. Some states have set aside a fund from the filing fees with which to pay judgments against the filing officer; see, e.g., Ind. Code §26-1-9-401(6) (fund to pay "all valid judgments recovered or to be recovered against county or state filing officers or their employees for failure to properly file or furnish correct information").

PRACTICAL NOTE

When filing financing statements always pay whatever extra amount is necessary to have duplicate copies of the financing statement made, stamped, and returned to you. See §9-407(1). That way you can prove what was filed, where it was filed, and when it was filed.

2. *Other filings*

A financing statement is effective for five years and then it lapses unless a continuation statement is filed (more on this later). Read §9-403. Upon paying off the secured obligation, the debtor will want the files cleared and is entitled to a termination statement; read §9-404. If the secured party assigns the security interest to another creditor the two creditors may (it is not compulsory) file an assignment statement; read §§9-405, 9-302(2); see White & Summers §23-16, at 959-960. If the debtor and secured party want to free some of the collateral from coverage under a filed financing statement, see the procedure provided for in §9-406. Finally, read §9-407, which speaks to the rights of later potential creditors who want information from the files.

3. *Misfiling*

PROBLEM 32

Local §9-401 required a dual filing for farm products collateral: in the county where the debtor resides and in the Secretary of State's office. When attorney Sam Ambulance filed Octopus National Bank's financing statement showing a security interest in Farmer Brown's livestock, he misread the statute and filed only in the Secretary of State's office. Two years later the Antitrust National Bank wanted to lend Farmer Brown money using the same collateral, and its attorney searched both the county and state records; in the latter he came across the earlier financing statement, but found none in the county records. May the second attorney assume that ONB's security interest is unperfected and ANB will win if it is the first to file in both places? Read §9-401(2) carefully.

PROBLEM 33

What does "knowledge of the contents of such financing statement" mean in §9-401(2)? Does it mean, as in the last Problem, that the eyes of the later file searcher must have actually seen the misfiled statement, or is it enough that the *security agreement* is described to the later party before that party files? Compare White & Summers §23-15 (who, despite some disagreement between the authors, conclude that knowledge that there is a security agreement and a misfiled financing statement is not the same as knowing the "contents" of the financing statement), with the case law which goes both ways; see discussion in Security Nat. Bank & Trust Co. v. Dentsply Professional Plan, 617 P.2d 1340, 29 U.C.C. Rep. Serv. 1686 (Okla. 1980).

CHAPTER 5

MULTI-STATE TRANSACTIONS

A. *CHOICE OF LAW*

Section 1-105 is the Code's general choice of law provision. It permits *party autonomy*, so that those involved in the transaction may agree to be bound by the law of any state or nation bearing a "reasonable relation" to the transaction. Read §1-105. Article 9 has its own overriding conflicts provision §9-103, and when Article 9 dominates the problem this section is controlling. See Weintraub, Choice of Law In Secured Transactions: The Impact of Article 9 of the Uniform Commercial Code, 68 Mich. L. Rev. 684, 691-697 (1970). Whenever the collateral takes tangible form and is not the type of goods typically used in more than one location, the Code applies a "situs" theory and usually chooses the law of the jurisdiction in which the collateral is *physically located* at the time of the happening of the last event on which the claim for perfection is based; see §9-103(1)(b). When, however, the collateral is intangible or is the kind of goods commonly moved from place to place (i.e., homeless, for instance packing crates), then the Code adopts a *domicile* approach and looks to the law of the debtor's state; see §9-103(3).

B. *INTANGIBLE PROPERTY*

Obviously accounts and general intangibles have no physical location. Section 9-103(3) is meant to deal with that difficulty.

PROBLEM 34

The Hanging Gardens Construction Company had its chief place of business (and its business records) in Fargo, North Dakota. It agreed to build a municipal parking garage for the City of Nebuchadnezzar, Nevada, and it financed the construction by a loan from the Second Wonder National Bank (a Nevada Bank), giving SWNB a security interest in the money the City agreed to pay it. SWNB comes to you and asks you where it should file its financing statement. Assume North Dakota has adopted the second alternative to §9-401 and Nevada the third. See United States v. Ed Lusk Constr. Co., 504 F.2d 328, 15 U.C.C. Rep. Serv. 952 (10th Cir. 1974).

C. *MOVEABLE GOODS*

Section 9-103(3) also establishes a situs for the type of goods that frequently move from place to place. Warning: if the debtor holds a certificate of public convenience and necessity under the Interstate Commerce Act, 49 U.S.C. §313 (1974) (covering certain trucks, tractors, trailers, and buses), federal law controls (as it does in connection with ships, airplanes, and airplane accessories). See G. Gilmore ch. 13. Also if the goods are covered by a certificate of title on which liens are required to be noted as a condition of perfection, §9-103(3) will not apply; §9-103(2), covered infra, will.

PROBLEM 35

Road Hog, Inc. was in the business of building roads and clearing land for road construction. It had its chief place of business in Delaware. Its principal asset was a giant 30-story high crane, nicknamed "Big Mama," which was used to scoop up and clear enormous hunks of earth at once. It was so large it could only move 4 m.p.h. at its fastest. It was assembled in West Virginia and for the past 5 years (its whole life), Big Mama has been building a super-highway in West Virginia. Now Road Hog wants to borrow money and use Big Mama as collateral. A pledge being out of the question, where should the secured creditor file? See Official Comment 5(b) to §9-103.

PROBLEM 36

Van Fingers was a famous pianist who toured the country nine months of the year always taking along a favorite piano, Truetone. One year at tax time he needed to borrow money and he applied for a loan from a Chicago bank, using Truetone as collateral. The bank phones you for advice. Should it file the financing statement in Illinois, where Van Fingers and Truetone are playing a two week engagement — see §9-103(1)(b) — or in St. Louis, Missouri, where they are scheduled to go next — read §9-103(1)(c) — or in Newark, New Jersey, where Van Fingers has a home?

D. "LAST EVENT" TEST

The general catch-all choice-of-law rule is found in §9-103(1)(b) which chooses the law of the jurisdiction where the collateral is when the last event occurs to perfect the security interest; White & Summers §23-18, at 966-976.

PROBLEM 37

Christian Ruade decided to open a sporting goods store in Bismark, North Dakota, and went to the Snowplow State Bank for financing. There he signed a security agreement and a financing statement giving the bank a purchase money security interest in his future inventory. The bank loaned him $10,000 and promptly filed the financing statement in the places commanded by North Dakota's §9-401. Ruade then ordered the inventory from Vorlage Sporting Equipment in upstate New York, paying cash. The New York seller set aside the goods for Ruade and agreed to ship them to North Dakota in 45 days (after they were first painted with Ruade's new trademark). Forty-five days later the goods were shipped to North Dakota. Does the bank have a perfected security interest in the goods under §9-103(1)? See §2-501; see discussion of this and related "last event" problems in 1 C.

Coogan, W. Hogan, & D. Vagts, Secured Transactions Under the UCC 12-19 (Supp. 1976).

PROBLEM 38

For two years Octopus National Bank had had a perfected floating lien over the inventory of Middleman, Inc., a national food wholesaler, which had its offices in Des Moines, Iowa; the financing statement for this transaction was therefore filed in Iowa. The bank's lien was a purchase money security interest since the loans made by the bank were used to buy Middleman's inventory. On March 3, Middleman contracted to buy a carload of cereal then located in a boxcar in Battle Creek, Michigan, the cereal to be shipped to Des Moines, arriving on March 10. On March 8, Middleman ordered the carrier to reroute the shipment to Columbus, Ohio, and deliver it there to Ohio Feeds, Inc., a creditor of Middleman's who had agreed to accept the cereal as settlement of an outstanding debt. The shipment was delivered to Ohio Feeds on March 9; ONB filed a financing statement in Ohio on April 1, the date on which it located the cereal. Prior to that date Ohio Feeds had no notice of ONB's interest in the shipment. In the lawsuit Octopus Nat. Bank v. Ohio Feeds, Inc., who prevails? Read §§9-301(1)(c) and 9-103(1) carefully.

PROBLEM 39

Gerald Czech decided to go into business for himself as a breeder of turkeys. He was living in New York, but he heard that the best turkeys could be purchased in Vermont from Gobbler Farms. He bought 40 turkeys from Gobbler, with the seller understanding that Czech meant to raise the birds in New York. Gobbler took a purchase money security interest in the turkeys.

(a) How is the collateral classified: inventory, farm products, or equipment?

(b) Where should Gobbler file: New York or Vermont?

(c) What should Gobbler do if it discovers that Czech received possession of the turkeys on May 1, started for New York the next day but never left the state because of an auto accident, and is currently laid up in a Vermont hospital? It is now May 29; Gobbler had filed in New York on May 1. See Official Comment 2 to §9-103.

(d) What if the turkeys never got to New York because Czech changed his mind and took them to a place he bought in Pennsylvania? See In re Dennis Mitchell Indus., Inc., 419 F.2d 349, 6 U.C.C.

Rep. Serv. 573, 7 U.C.C. Rep. Serv. 112 (3d Cir. 1969). Would your answer to the last question change if the turkeys passed through New York on their way to Pennsylvania? See Official Comment 3 to §9-103.

PROBLEM 40

Nightflyer Finance Company agreed to lend Nancy Tumbleweeds enough money to buy a washer and dryer and took a purchase money security interest in same. When she switches states need Nightflyer file within four months there? Nightflyer did not file in the original state because of §9-302(1)(d). See §9-103(1)(d). What if she refuses to sign a new financing statement? See §9-402(2).

PROBLEM 41

When Evelyn opened her ceramics store in San Francisco she gave the Redwoods State Bank (hereinafter RSB) a security interest in the inventory. RSB filed a financing statement in the proper place under California law. Evelyn's business declined and she decided to move to Seattle, Washington, inventory and all, which she did on April 1, 1986. On April 30, 1986, she borrowed more money from a Washington bank (Apple National Bank) (hereinafter ANB), and gave it a security interest in the inventory, which ANB perfected by a proper filing under Washington's §9-401.

(a) As of May 1, 1986, which of the banks has priority over the other?

(b) Would your answer change if RSB knew at the time it loaned her money that she was planning to move the inventory to Washington within three weeks? Six months? What if she says she is going to move at the end of six months, but actually moves the inventory to Washington two weeks after RSB advances her the money?

(c) Assume RSB did not know she was leaving or that she had gone. Which creditor has priority as of October 1, 1986?

(d) If RSB never perfected in Washington, and on December 25, 1986, Evelyn moved the inventory *back* to California and ANB immediately refiled in California in the same place where RSB originally filed, which bank has priority (remember RSB's original statement is still on file in California)? See In re Miller, 14 U.C.C. Rep. Serv. 1042 (Ref. Bankr. D. Ore. 1974) ("Were the view argued by [bank in RSB's position] adopted, a prospective leader could not be assured of priority over security interests earlier perfected in other states to which the property might later be removed without a search of the filing records of all such states."); see also Henson §9-5, at 329-330.

E. *CERTIFICATES OF TITLE*

Two paragraphs from G. Gilmore §20.1, at 550-551:

> The automobile, in addition to its potentialities as an instrument of destruction and an agent of social change, has been one of the great sources of law in the twentieth century. As the most expensive chattel ever to come into general use, it generated novel methods of secured financing. Its unique mobility, combined with the high resale value of used cars, made theft both easy and profitable.
>
> From a legal point of view there is nothing interesting in the situation where A, a thief, steals B's car and sells it to C: A, if apprehended, will go to jail and C, if found, can be forced to return the car to B. However, the fact that most automobile purchases are financed under some kind of security device has led to a refined version of automobile theft which is legally much more interesting than the crude business of smash and grab. Under the refined version, A buys a car, making the smallest possible down payment and executing a chattel mortgage, a conditional sale contract or an Article 9 security agreement for the balance in favor of B. A, representing the car to be free from liens, now sells it to C, who buys it, we may assume, in good faith and without actual knowledge of B's interest. C is typically a used car dealer, so that a further complication is introduced when C resells to D, who also buys in good faith and without notice. A's behavior is criminal and legally uninteresting; if caught, he will and should go to jail. The sales to C and D, however, begin to be worth thinking about since A, who is a criminal, albeit a refined one, is also in some sense an owner of the car, with some kind of title to it, and our legal system has always sharply distinguished between the lot of the good faith purchaser from a thief without title (who gets nothing) and that of the good faith purchaser from a person with a defective title (who may get perfect title, despite the intervening fraud or crime).

Complexities concerning vehicles covered by certificates of title have caused the choice of law issues to assume nightmarish proportions. The problem is that many states require security interests in motor vehicles (and sometimes mobile homes, airplanes, and/or boats) to be noted on the certificate of title as a condition of perfection, other states require certificates of title for such vehicles but do not note lien interests thereon, and still other states do not even issue certificates of title and require only the usual steps for perfection (typically filing). Read Official Comment 4 to §9-103; see Meyers, Multi-State Motor Vehicle Transactions Under the UCC: An Update, 30 Okla. L. Rev. 834 (1977).

In re Hartberg

25 U.C.C. Rep. Serv. 1429 (E.D. Wis. 1979)

HILGENDORF, Bankr. J. The parties have submitted this case to the court for decision upon a written stipulation of facts. The sole issue is whether the defendant, Barnett Bank, has a perfected lien against the automobile of the bankrupt which is valid against the trustee in bankruptcy.

The bankrupts purchased a 1975 Oldsmobile in Florida and executed a security agreement with the Barnett Bank of Winter Park, Florida on November 9, 1976. A Florida certificate of title to the vehicle was issued on December 10, 1976 containing a notice of lien in favor of the Barnett Bank. This certificate of title was retained by the Barnett Bank and is still held by the bank. The bankrupts moved from Florida to Wisconsin in September, 1977 and established residency in Wisconsin bringing the automobile with them without securing permission from the bank to move the vehicle to Wisconsin. They continued to make monthly payments to the Barnett Bank until April 1978 after which time they defaulted. On December 3, 1977 they registered the automobile with the Motor Vehicle Department of Wisconsin and obtained Wisconsin license plates for the vehicle. Since they did not have possession of the title, the Motor Vehicle Department did not issue a Wisconsin title but issued only a certificate of registration and Wisconsin license plates. On July 3, 1978 the bankrupts filed a voluntary petition in bankruptcy in the Eastern District of Wisconsin while in possession of the vehicle. The trustee in bankruptcy contends that the lien of the Barnett Bank is not valid against the trustee because the automobile was permanently removed from Florida and remained in Wisconsin more than four months and was registered in Wisconsin. The trustee contends that the lien was never perfected in Wisconsin and is therefore invalid as to the trustee.

The applicable statutes are:

342.19 Perfection of Security Interests

(6) If a vehicle is subject to a security interest when brought into this state, §409.103(1), (2) and (3) state the rules which apply to determine the validity and perfection of the security interest in this state.

[The court quoted §9-103(2).]

341.08 Application for Registration

(3) The division may accept an application and complete registration of a vehicle when the evidence of ownership is held by a nonresident lienholder or for other reason is not immediately available and the division is satisfied as to ownership of the vehicle. The title fee shall be collected at the time of registration and retained even though certificate of title is not issued.

The defendant, Barnett Bank, contends that the automobile was removed to Wisconsin from the State of Florida without the consent of the bank and that because of the default in payments required under the security agreement, the bank was entitled to take immediate possession of the collateral. Assuming that this argument is factually correct, the simple answer to the bank's argument is that the bank may have had a right to take possession of the automobile prior to bankruptcy but failed to do so. The right to take possession of the vehicle did not deprive the bankrupts of ownership. After the petition in bankruptcy was filed the right to repossess the vehicle expired because the trustee in bankruptcy succeeded to ownership of the automobile by operation of law. Sec. 70 of the Bankruptcy Act [now §544(a) — ed.]. A trustee in bankruptcy is not required to obtain a certificate of title in order to have ownership of a vehicle. The court therefore holds that the trustee in bankruptcy acquired legal title and ownership of the 1975 Oldsmobile on July 3, 1978.

The only remaining question is whether the lien of the bank is valid against the trustee. This question requires examination of the laws of the State of Wisconsin which has adopted the Uniform Code pertaining to motor vehicles. (§9-103(2) quoted above.)

The original 1962 version of the Uniform Commercial Code relating to motor vehicles was substantially different from the 1972 official text which was adopted in Wisconsin in 1973. The 1962 Code was interpreted by most courts to grant priority to a lien holder whose lien was perfected by indication on the certificate of title regardless of where the automobile may have been taken and regardless of the period of time it remained in another jurisdiction. In other words, the 4 month rule did apply to motor vehicles removed to another state from a state which issued a certificate of title containing notice of a lien. This interpretation of the code was based upon §9-103(4) which provided:

> (4) Notwithstanding subsections (2) and (3), if personal property is covered by a certificate of title issued under a statute of this state or any other jurisdiction which requires indication on a certificate of title of any security interest in the property as a condition of perfection, then the perfection is governed by the law of the jurisdiction which issued the certificate.

The courts interpreted §9-103(4) to supersede the 4 month rule in §9-103(3) as to motor vehicles. This interpretation resulted in several decisions against a trustee in bankruptcy. See Ford Motor Credit Co. v. Ossen, 18 UCC Rep. 504 and cases cited therein; In re Friedman, 4 UCC Rep 890. In the Friedman case Bankruptcy Judge Trevethan referred to §9-103(4) of the 1962 Uniform Code as "an example of blunderous draftsmanship." Nevertheless he felt compelled to hold that the lien of the secured creditor was valid against the trustee in bankruptcy notwithstanding that the automobile had been removed to Connecticut and had remained there for more than four months without perfection of the lien in Connecticut. This interpretation of §9-103(4) of the Code also resulted in decisions by other courts holding that the lien of a secured creditor prevailed over a bona fide purchaser who relied upon a "clean" certificate of title issued by another state. See GMAC v. Whisnant, 4 UCC Rep 1016, 387 F.2d 774; In re White, 4 UCC Rep 421. Further comments on §9-103(4) may be found in the case of In re Canter, 8 UCC Rep 252, 254 where the court said:

> The lack of clarity in §9-103(4) of the Uniform Commercial Code has been the subject of comment and criticism both by courts and text writers. Professor Gilmore's observation is pertinent.
>
> "Subsection (4) was a last minute addition to Article 9; it appears to have been imperfectly thought through and is clearly defective in its drafting." Gilmore, Security Interests in Personal Property, Vol. 1, Sec. 10.10.

To correct these inequities §9-103 was amended in 1972 and the official Uniform Commercial Code text was adopted in Wisconsin in 1973 as §409.103(2) of the Wis Stats. This amendment deleted entirely subsection (4) quoted above which the courts interpreted as superseding the four month rule. In addition to deleting subsection (4), the 1962 Code was amended to include a provision relating to the "registration" of a motor vehicle in another jurisdiction. The code as amended now provides that the perfection of a lien on a motor vehicle is governed by the law of the jurisdiction issuing the certificate of title "until four months after the goods are removed from that jurisdiction and thereafter until the goods are *registered* in another jurisdiction, but in any event not beyond surrender of the certificate. After the expiration of that period, the goods are not covered by the certificate of title within the meaning of this section." (Emphasis ours.)

The purpose for this amendment is discussed in the Draftsmen's Comment to 1972 Official Text where it is stated at §9-103 p. 38:

> (c) . . . If the vehicle is registered in another jurisdiction while the secured party still holds the certificate, a danger of deception to third parties arises. The section provides that the certificate ceases to control after 4 months following removal if registration has occurred, but during the 4 months the secured party has the same protection for cases of interstate removal as is set forth in paragraph (1)(d) of the section."

The Drafters further stated at p 41:

> 7. . . . The four-month period is long enough for a secured party to discover in most cases that the collateral has been removed and refile in this state; thereafter, if he has not done so, his interest, although originally perfected in the jurisdiction from which the collateral was removed, is subject to defeat here by purchasers of the collateral. . . . It should be noted that a "purchaser" includes a secured party. Section 1-201(32) and (33). The rights of a purchaser with a security interest against an unperfected security interest are governed by Section 9-312.

A trustee in bankruptcy is not only a secured party — he is "the ideal creditor, irreproachable and without notice, armed cap-a-pie with every right and power which is conferred by the law of the state upon its most favored creditor who has acquired a lien by legal or equitable proceedings." Collier, §70.49.

In the case at bar there is no proof that the bankrupts practiced any fraud or deception. They moved their residence to Wisconsin, and as required by Wisconsin law, they registered the automobile with the Motor Vehicle Department of Wisconsin in accordance with Chapter 341 of the Wisconsin Statutes. Since they did not have possession of the Florida certificate of title, the Wisconsin Motor Vehicle Department issued only a certificate of registration and not a certificate of title. This certificate of registration enabled them to purchase Wisconsin license plates which they were required to do by law after becoming residents of Wisconsin. The stipulation of facts also establishes that the automobile remained in Wisconsin for more than four months after removal from Florida. Thus under the provisions of §9-103(2)(b) of the Wis Stats the perfection of the lien on the automobile was no longer covered by the Florida law but by the laws of Wisconsin. The Barnett Bank had four months to perfect its lien in Wisconsin by filing appropriate notice with the Wisconsin Motor Vehicle Department but failed to do so. Therefore the lien of the bank was not perfected under Wisconsin law.

Although the record does not establish whether the bank had actual knowledge that the automobile was permanently moved to Wisconsin, it does not appear that knowledge of removal is necessary. The stipulation recites that the bankrupts made monthly payments from October, 1977 through April, 1978 from Wisconsin. When such payments were received from Wisconsin for a number of months, the bank was alerted to the fact that the owners probably moved to Wisconsin. Knowledge could therefore be imputed to the bank, but as stated above, the court finds that knowledge of the removal is not required.

For the reasons stated the court holds that the automobile in question was removed from Florida to Wisconsin and remained in Wisconsin for more than four months, and in addition the vehicle was registered in the State of Wisconsin. Under the provisions of §9-103(2) of the Wis Stats for 1977 the lien of the Barnett Bank is invalid as to the trustee in bankruptcy.

It is so ordered, adjudged and decreed.

PROBLEM 42

Kansas law requires a security interest in a motor vehicle to be noted on the Kansas certificate of title to be perfected; Oklahoma's law says perfection occurs by filing only (*not* by notation on the Oklahoma certificate). A Kansas bank loaned the Burly Moving Company money with which it bought a new moving van, the Kansas bank taking a purchase money security interest therein which was duly noted on the Kansas certificate of title. The moving van traveled throughout the USA, but normally returned to Topeka, Kansas, the chief place of business of the Burly Moving Company. After one year, Burly decided to domicile this one van in Oklahoma City, Oklahoma (but it kept the other four vans it owned in Topeka). When the van was moved to Oklahoma on February 6, Burly obtained a clean certificate of title from that state, and it reflected no lien interests in favor of anyone. Burly borrowed more money from an Oklahoma bank on February 28, giving that bank a security interest, which the bank promptly filed in Oklahoma. The Kansas bank never filed in Oklahoma. Burly went bankrupt on September 1. All parties to the priority dispute (the two banks and the bankruptcy trustee) agree the van is the type of equipment described in §9-103(3). They disagree as to how §9-103 is to be applied in this situation. Decide the issue. See White & Summers §23-19; the cases are in disagreement: Associates Discount Corp. v. Reeves, 13 U.C.C. Rep. Serv. 709 (Okla. App. 1973) (first creditor should file in Oklahoma within four months of van's entry into state); In re Dobbins, 371 F. Supp. 141, 14 U.C.C. Rep. Serv. 796 (D. Kan. 1973) (first creditor protected if he *files* in Kansas). What is the best *policy* decision to protect the interests of the creditors involved? See Rohner, Autos, Title Certificates, and UCC §9-103: The Draftsmen Try Again, 27 Bus. Law. 1177 (1972).

PROBLEM 43

On May 10, Holly Tourist, a resident of Cleveland, Ohio, bought a new car on credit while on vacation in Norman, Oklahoma, from Norman Car Sales, Inc. (hereinafter NCS). Oklahoma issues certificates of title but does not note lien interests thereon, and instead requires a filing of a financing statement in the Oklahoma Secretary of State's office, which NCS did on May 12. On the day of sale NCS knew that Holly lived in Cleveland and planned to return there immediately. On May 14, Holly drove the car to Cleveland, and that same day reregistered the car there, turning in the Oklahoma certificate and receiving an Ohio one. Ohio requires lien interests to be noted on the certificate of title as a condition of perfection. The Ohio certificate of title stated on it that "This Certificate of Title May Be Subject to Liens Not Shown Hereon." On May 26, Holly sold the car to her neighbor, William Innocent, who paid full value therefore without knowledge of NCS's interest. On May 28 learning of the sale to William, NCS arranged for the car to be repossessed from in front of his house. Assuming that her resale of the car was a "default," so as to entitle NCS to repossess, decide which of them is entitled to the car. See §§9-103(1), 9-103(2), and 9-301(1)(c), and read §9-307(2) and its Official Comment 3. Note that §9-103(2)(d) favors non-business buyers; a used car lot buying an out-of-state vehicle is not entitled to the protection of this subsection.

In re Brown

5 U.C.C. Rep. Serv. 401 (W.D. Mich. 1968)

NIMS, JR., Ref. Bankr. This matter is before the court on the petition of Edward M. Yampolsky, the duly appointed and qualified trustee in bankruptcy, for an order determining the security interest of Truck Trailer Acceptance Corporation of Sunbury, Pennsylvania, in the bankrupt's 1966 Norwin semi-trailer to be invalid as against the trustee and for an order directing the bankrupt to turn over this trailer.

Except for the application for Certificate of Title and a Certificate of Residence, the only evidence adduced at the hearing on the above mentioned petition was the testimony of the bankrupt himself. According to this testimony, the bankrupt has lived at [Route] #1, Union, Michigan for ten years. He is an independent truck operator hauling steel in a territory covering the States of Illinois, Indiana and that part of Michigan south of Highway U.S. 10. On April 29, 1966, bankrupt purchased the trailer in question from Trailco Mfg. and Sales Co. of Michigan City, Indiana. He executed a security agreement which was assigned to respondent, Truck Trailer Acceptance Corporation. On the same date, he signed a so called certificate addressed to respondent in which he represented his legal residence to be:

Street	Rt #1
City	Union
County	Cass County
State	Michigan
County Seat	Cassopolis

Under a heading "Equipment Domicile if other than legal residence" he entered

Street	Route #1
City	Bristol
County	Elkhart
State	Indiana
County Seat	Goshen

The next day, April 30, 1966, he signed an application for an Indiana title showing the lien interest of respondent and giving his address as "RR 1, Bristol, Ind." On June 28, 1966, a Certificate of Title was issued by the State of Indiana in bankrupt's name giving his address as "RR 1, Bristol, Ind."

As of the day of purchase, the bankrupt operated out of Chicago, usually hauling for the Chicago, Michigan Express Company of Chicago. The Indiana address given to the dealer and entered on the title is the address of the bankrupt's sister who lives about one mile from the bankrupt. The bankrupt testified that he parked his trailer a number of places including his sister's place. The only other piece of equipment he had, a tractor, was licensed in Michigan. If he gave no temporary telephone number, orders would be telephoned to his residence — never to his sister's home. He often used his residential telephone for business calls. Many of his telephone calls were made on the road. He admitted that the address given to the Indiana authorities was false but stated that he wanted to register in Indiana to save $600.00 on license and sales tax charges which he would have to pay in Michigan. The only purpose in giving the Indiana domicile was to obtain an Indiana title and he only parked the trailer at his sister's enough to get the Indiana title. He had no place of business which he rented in Indiana or Illinois. His situation was no different at the time he applied for his tractor license in Michigan. When not on the road, the tractor was kept at bankrupt's house. The address given to Chicago, Michigan Express Company was his residence in Michigan.

On May 10, 1966, bankrupt filed his petition for adjudication as a voluntary bankrupt. On May 16, 1966, respondent filed its financing statement in the office of the Register of Deeds for Cass County Michigan. . . .

[The court quoted the 1962 UCC Code section that was the equivalent to the current §9-103(3).]

It is the claim of respondent that the chief place of business of this debtor was Indiana. I cannot agree. His place of business was at his residence in Michigan. No other place has any characteristics of a place of business other than those of other places except that bankrupt gave his sister's address to the dealer as the domicile of his trailer and the State of Indiana as his address. But, he admits this was done solely to qualify for the savings to be realized by not obtaining a Michigan license. It is not necessary to review the facts stated above. A mere reiteration should be sufficient to support a finding of fact that the chief place of business was bankrupt's residence.

Respondent claims that the trustee is estopped from claiming the chief place of business is other than in Indiana. If the trustee were relying on Section 70a of the Bankruptcy Act, 11 USC §110a, this might be true. But, the trustee claims as the hypothetical creditor with judgment and lien under §70c of the Bankruptcy Act, 11 USC §110c and the bankrupt cannot bind him by his acts. Anyway, the bankrupt never represented that his chief place of business was in Indiana — only that the domicile of the truck would be Indiana. There is a real distinction. [The court quoted Official Comment 3 to §9-103.]

I thus find as a matter of fact and law that the bankrupt's chief place of business was Michigan. . . .

[The court quoted the 1962 Code's equivalent to §9-103(1).]

Respondent states that there is no evidence that the trailer was in fact brought into Michigan within 30 days after the purchase. But, neither is there any evidence that the trailer was to be kept in Indiana. It was because of the problems involving "automotive equipment, rolling stock," etc., that the drafters of the UCC provided for the "chief place of business" test. Subparagraph (3) expressly excludes personal property "governed by subsections (1) and (2)." Thus I find that subparagraph (3) does not apply. . . .

[The court quoted the 1962 equivalent to §9-103(2).]

Our first question here is whether Indiana is a jurisdiction which requires indication on a certificate of title of any security interest in the property as a condition of perfection. The Uniform Commercial Code of Indiana, Burns Ind. Statutes, Sec. 9-302(3) provides:

> The filing provisions of this Article (Chapter) do not apply to a security interest in property subject to a statute . . . (b) of this State which provides for central filing of security interests in such property, or in a motor vehicle which is not inventory held for sale for which a certificate of title is required under the statutes of this State if a notation of such a security interest can be indicated by a public official on a certificate or a duplicate thereof.

According to the annotator, there has been some question on whether a security interest can be indicated by a public official on the certificate. The conclusion of the annotator after a long discussion is that the perfection of a security interest is controlled by the certificate title law and not by the UCC. But, for the purpose of this opinion, I assume that Indiana is a State which qualifies under subparagraph (4).

Problems w 9-103(4)

Reading subparagraph (4) literally, the security interest of respondent would have been properly perfected. But, are we to read this literally? I cannot believe that this was the intent of the drafters or the legislature of either Indiana or Michigan. Trouble with subparagraph (4) has been anticipated. Judge Brennan in In Re White, 266 F. Supp. 863 (D.C.N.D.N.Y. 1967) at p. 865 refers to subsection (4) and states:

> That the above language lacks the clarity desirable in the statute may well be admitted. The criticism thereof, expressed in Benders Uniform Commercial Code Service in the volume entitled Reporter-Digest Case Annotations at page 2-828 may, at least in part, be justified.

Referee Bobier in Battle v. General Motors Acceptance Corporation, No. 65-8436 (E.D. Mich. 1967) [4 UCC Rep. Serv. 1180] stated, in considering the same subsection:

> It is unfortunate indeed that the framers of the UCC could labor so long and produce a statute lacking clarity in the degree that they did in the statute under consideration in this case. Especially is it regretful that in the comments of the committee there was an absence of clarifying language.

In In the Matter of George M. Caraway, No. 28858 (D.C.W.D. Mich. S.D. — 1968) I also indicated, "I would anticipate that section 9-103(4) will cause many problems in the future. . . ."

One writer, and I don't recall who it was or where I read his comments, passed over the situation with which we are here faced by saying it was presumed that no State would issue a Certificate of Title unless it was the proper State of registration. But, here the bankrupt deliberately misled the State authorities by entering a false address so as to profit by the lower taxes and fees in Indiana. The application form of Indiana is somewhat vague as it calls only for the "address." The bankrupt claims that his sister's place could be his address. Perhaps he is right. Webster's Seventh New Collegiate Dictionary defines address as "a place where a person or organization may be communicated with." This is about as helpful as respondent's use of the word "domicile" in connection with a motor vehicle (at least under the above authority, Webster's Collegiate Dictionary, only man can have a domicile). If we read the statute literally, a trucker could pick any state in which to obtain his title and one searching the records would only be safe if he checked each of fifty states.

As I stated In the Matter of Paul Lavern Vaughan, No. 28465 (D.C.W.D. Mich. 1967),

> The entire key to Article 9 is *Notice*. As stated in the Comments of National Conference of Commissioners and American Law Institute in reference to §9-402 (see annotation following MSA Sec. 9.9402);
>
> "Purposes:
>
> "2. This section adopts the system of 'notice filing' which has proved successful under the Uniform Trust Receipts Act. What is required to be filed is not, as under chattel mortgage and conditional sales acts, the security agreement itself, but only a simple notice which may be filed before the security interest attaches or thereafter. The notice itself indicates merely that the secured party who has filed may have a security interest in the collateral described. Further inquiry from the parties concerned will be necessary to disclose the complete state of affairs. Section 9-208 provides a statutory procedure under which the secured party, at the debtor's request, may be required to make disclosure. Notice filing has proved to be of great use in financing transactions involving inventory, accounts and chattel paper, since it obviates the necessity of refiling on each of a series of transactions in a continuing arrangement where the collateral changes from day to day. Where other types of collateral are involved, the alternative procedure of filing a signed copy of the security agreement may prove to be the simplest solution."

It was on this broad concept that I found security interests perfected in In the Matter of Paul Lavern Vaughan, supra, and again in In the Matter of William James Kulesza, No. 28415 (D.C.W.D. Mich. 1967). But if notice is a governing factor of the UCC, notice must be given where it can be reasonably found and not hidden from the world because of misrepresentations of the debtor or carelessness by State employees and secured parties.

It was because of this purpose of notice that §9-103(2) was

inserted in the code for as was stated above, the "Chief Place of Business" is the place "where the person dealing with the debtor *would normally look* for credit information . . ." (emphasis added).

The only conclusion that seems to me to be reasonable is that it was the intent of the drafters of the UCC that §9-103 be read as a whole. Section 9-103(4) would only apply if the security interest had been properly perfected by indicating it on the title in an appropriate State *if* the State issuing the certificate of title is the proper State under 9-103(2) or 9-103(3). Thus, *if* Indiana had been the "Chief Place of Business" of the bankrupt and *if* Indiana is a State requiring indication on a certificate of title of any security interest in the property as a condition of perfection, then the indicating of the security interest on the title would perfect that interest whether the debtor remained in Indiana (§9-103(2)) or moved his Chief Place of Business to Michigan (§9-103(4)). Since the bankrupt has never changed his chief place of business, Michigan laws would govern. . . .

Thus, I must hold that the security interest of respondent was not perfected as of the date of bankruptcy in the proper State, Michigan, and therefore the interest is subordinate to the interest of the trustee. The bankrupt has no right to the possession of the trailer. An order may be entered requiring the bankrupt to turn over the trailer to the trustee forthwith and holding that the trustee holds said trailer free and clear of any security interest in respondent.

NOTE:

In re Brown raises what has come to be known as Professor Gilmore's "Lichtenstein certificate" problem:

> [I]f the . . . principality of Lichtenstein issues a certificate of title covering a truck owned by a debtor whose chief place of business is in Massachusetts (a Code state) and if the truck has never been operated in . . . Lichtenstein, then the purported "certificate of title" is merely waste paper and nothing in [the UCC] gives it any "jural significance." The certificate of title must then be "validly" issued, but nothing in the Code casts any light on "validly."

G. Gilmore §10.10, at 327. He concludes that "obviously the issuing state must have, on some theory, sufficient contact with or control over the property or its owner to make the issuance a reasonable exercise of state power." G. Gilmore §22.7, at 621. The problem has not been resolved by the 1972 amendments; see the article by Professor Rohner cited in Problem 42, supra, at 1190-1191. Other courts and commentators have not been troubled by the apparent difficulties presented by a Lichtenstein certificate; see Henson §9-8, at 343-344; In re Dawson, 21 U.C.C. Rep. Serv. 293 (Bankr. E.D. Mo. 1976) ("any lender . . . will most assuredly ask his prospective debtor for his registration and title papers to such vehicle, and begin his credit investigation, in respect of liens, in the certificating state"). As a practical matter how should the trailer dealership protect itself in the future? After losing this one to the bankruptcy trustee, the dealership will turn to its lawyer to make sure it doesn't happen again. What would you advise?

PROBLEM 44

Joseph Weakleg bought a car in a state that did not use certificates of title and required filing for perfection, which step the financing bank (Octopus National) duly took. Weakleg then moved to a state that required all security interests to be noted on certificates of title issued by that state, but he never took the trouble to get such a certificate. Does ONB's perfection in the second state last indefinitely or only four months? What if the opposite situation occurs: Weakleg starts in a title state and ONB's interest is noted on that state's certificate. Weakleg moves to a state that has no certificates of title at all and ONB never files there, and Weakleg never re-registers the car.

CHAPTER 6

PRIORITY PROBLEMS

A. *SIMPLE DISPUTES*

When the debtor's financial situation collapses, the creditors all jump on the debtor's assets. The legal issue of *priority* decides which creditor gets what. A basic priority provision is §9-301. Read it and these problems:

PROBLEM 45

Epstein's Bookstore borrowed $10,000 from Octopus National Bank, signing a security agreement giving the bank a floating lien over the store's inventory. ONB, due to negligence, never got around to filing the financing statement. Martin's Travel Service was an unpaid creditor of the bookstore, and it sued on the debt and recovered a judgment against the store. It then had the sheriff levy on the inventory. ONB learned of this and calls you, ONB's attorney. Does ONB or Martin's Travel Service get paid first when the inventory is sold? See §9-301(1)(b). If, instead of a judgment creditor seizing on the goods, Epstein's Bookstore had filed a bankruptcy petition while ONB was still unperfected, what result? See §9-301(3).

PROBLEM 46

When David More, a professional magician, needed money he asked his next door neighbor, Alfred Less, for a loan. Less agreed, but only if More granted him an interest in More's right to receive payments for future performances at private parties. More and Less signed such an agreement but it was never filed (Less was a dentist and had never heard of the UCC). Later More needed more money and used the same future payments as collateral for a loan from Finance City Trust Company, which did get a security agreement and a financing statement (the latter it filed in the proper §9-401 spot). More couldn't pay his debts and disappeared, but his prior performances had created collateral of the type envisioned by both security agreements. Who gets paid first when More's accounts are collected? See Official Comment 2 to §9-301.

The major Article 9 priority section is §9-312, which you should read after you finish this paragraph. It is not as bad as it looks, fortunately, since the primary part is subsection (5). Subsection (5) should be used to resolve the problems that follow.

PROBLEM 47

Jay Eastriver ran a clothing store and needed money. He went to two banks, the First National Bank and the Second State Bank, and asked each to loan him money using his inventory as collateral. They each made him sign a security agreement and a financing statement. First National Bank filed first, on September 25, but did not loan Eastriver any money until November 10. On October 2, Second State both loaned Eastriver the money and filed the financing statement. Eastriver paid neither bank. Answer these questions:

(a) Did both banks have a perfected security interest assuming they filed in the proper place?

(b) Remembering that attachment is a prerequisite to perfection, §9-303, and that attachment cannot occur until the creditor gives value, decide which bank has the superior right to the inventory.

In re Smith

326 F. Supp. 1311, 9 U.C.C. Rep. Serv. 549 (D. Minn. 1971)

LARSON, J. On or about April 14, 1969, one Bruce A. Smith purchased a 1968 Plymouth automobile from Southtown Chrysler in Minneapolis, Minnesota. At that time he executed a conditional sales contract which was assigned by the seller to the First National Bank of Minneapolis. Neither the seller nor assignee filed a financing statement evidencing the security interest.

In July of 1969 Community Credit Co. lent Mr. Smith money. Mr. Smith at that time executed a chattel mortgage on the Plymouth automobile in favor of the lender. The lender filed a financing statement evidencing the chattel mortgage on July 14, 1969, with the Hennepin County Register of Deeds. At the time of this transaction Community Credit Co. had actual knowledge of the unperfected security interest of the First National Bank of Minneapolis in the automobile.

Bruce A. Smith was duly adjudicated a bankrupt on May 7, 1970, after the filing of a voluntary petition in bankruptcy. The trustee in bankruptcy is given the power of a perfect lien creditor by Section 70(c) of the Bankruptcy Act [now §544(a) — ed.]. He therefore takes a priority over and is entitled to avoid the unperfected security interest of the First National Bank of Minneapolis.

Pursuant to the order of the Referee in Bankruptcy the automobile was sold to Community Credit. The sale proceeds are held by the trustee subject to the claim of security interest by Community Credit.

The trustee, however, chose to exercise the option made available to him by Section 70(e)(2) of the Bankruptcy Act [now §551 — ed.]. That provision permitted him to preserve the Bank's interest for the benefit of the estate and to assert it against the subsequent lien taken by Community Credit.

There is no dispute that the bank's security interest is not good against the trustee in bankruptcy. Since it was not perfected either by possession or filing, it remains subject to the rights of the trustee as a perfected lien creditor. The trustee by preserving the Bank's interest and asserting it for the benefit of the estate steps into the shoes of the Bank. His rights are determined by what position the Bank would have been in had there been no bankruptcy proceedings.

The situation presented is one involving conflicting security interests in the same collateral. Community Credit holds a security perfected by filing. The Bank's interest is prior in time but is unperfected either by filing or possession. It is conceded by all parties that Community Credit as holder of the perfected security interest would prevail if it had not had actual knowledge of the

Bank's prior unperfected interest. Hence the issue raised before the Referee in Bankruptcy and which now faces this court is whether actual knowledge on the part of Community Credit of the Bank's prior interest prevents it from achieving priority which would have otherwise been obtained by being the first to file. The Referee answered this question in the affirmative and gave priority to the Bank's lien.

The portion of the Minnesota Uniform Commercial Code which governs this situation is MSA §9-312(5).

[The court quoted §9-312(5).]

This provision nowhere makes lack of knowledge (good faith) a requirement for obtaining priority. The statute on its face provides for a race to the filing office with actual knowledge of a prior unperfected security interest apparently being irrelevant if one perfects first by filing. Such an approach by the Uniform Commercial Code would clearly be a change in the pre-existing law. Under precode commercial law, actual notice of an earlier unperfected interest in the property would prevent the second interest from obtaining priority. This was true even if the second interest was perfected first by filing.

The change would be one effected by omission rather than an affirmative statement of change. It is the absence of any reference to knowledge or good faith which raises the presumption that it is not relevant. There is no positive statement in §9-312(5) that knowledge of the earlier interest has no bearing on priority. Under these circumstances, a conclusion that knowledge is not a factor in establishing priorities under §9-312(5) is predicated on the underlying assumption that the omission of any reference to knowledge was a deliberate one. The Referee in Bankruptcy refused to make that assumption. He came, in fact, to the opposite conclusion, namely, that the absence of any reference to knowledge was unintentional on the part of the code draftsmen. Hence, the instant controversy is casus omissus and must be interpreted in light of the common law. As was previously noted, the common law made good faith a critical factor in achieving priority.

The Referee, in reaching his decision that the omission was unintentional, relied heavily on Professor Grant Gilmore's interpretation of the drafting history of §9-312(5) of the UCC. II Gilmore, Security Interests in Personal Property §34.2 (pp. 898-902) 1965. Professor Gilmore acknowledges that Article 9 appears to have discarded good faith as a factor in determining priorities under §9-312 of the UCC. However, he makes an argument that the result is not clearly an intentional and deliberate one on the part of the draftsmen. Professor Gilmore's analysis fairly questions whether or not the elimination of the good faith provision was a calculated one on the part of the draftsmen of the UCC. However, this court feels that the Referee in Bankruptcy's reliance on that analysis to imply a good cause [sic] provision in §9-312(5) is misplaced.

It is true that Professor Gilmore suggested implying a good cause [sic] provision as one way of approaching §9-312(5). To the contrary he also pointed out that there were some good reasons for disregarding knowledge and creating a race to file situation. One is the protection of the integrity of the filing system. Gilmore, pp. 901-902. It is desirable that perfection of interests take place promptly. It is appropriate then to provide that a secured party who fails to file runs the risk of subordination to a later but more diligent party. In this regard it should be pointed out that filing is of particular importance with respect to notice to other parties. It is agreed that where the later party has actual notice there is no need to rely upon a filing to notify him of a prior interest. The problem, however, cannot be analyzed in this narrow context. Some parties may rely on the record in extending credit and obtaining a security agreement in collateral. Although they will prevail over the unperfected prior interest in time if a dispute arises, it is entirely possible that they wanted to avoid the dispute altogether. In other words, they may not have relied on the complete absence of a prior interest perfected or otherwise out of which a dispute could arise. The only way this kind of record expectation can be protected is by prompt perfection of all security interests.

Professor Gilmore also recognizes the fact that a good faith requirement creates evidentiary problems.

> [T]he presence or absence of "knowledge" is a subjective question of fact, difficult to prove. Unless there is an overwhelming policy argument in favor of using such a criterion, it is always wise to discard it and to make decision turn on some easily determinable objective event — as, for example, the date of filing. [Gilmore, p. 502.]

The only way to effectively produce the above result is to make "knowledge" irrelevant and rely solely on perfection to establish priority.

Finally, Professor Gilmore admits that Example 2 in the Official Comment to §9-312(5) seems to indicate that the apparent result was intended. It reads as follows insofar as relevant:

> *Example 2.* A and B make non-purchase money advances against the same collateral. The collateral is in the debtor's possession and neither interest is perfected when the second advance is made. Whichever secured party first perfects his interest (by taking possession of the collateral or by filing) takes priority and it makes no difference whether or not he knows of the other interest at the time he perfects his own.
>
> Subsections (5)(a) and (5)(b) both lead to this result. It may be regarded as an adoption, in this type of situation, of the idea, deeply rooted at common law, of a race of diligence among creditors. . . .

The comment is not directly in point because it deals with knowledge at time of perfection and not at the time of attachment. Subsections (5)(a) and (5)(b), however, give priority whether perfection is before or after attachment. Thus, if attachment came after perfection, knowledge at time of perfection would also mean knowledge at time of attachment. Presumably Example 2 would control in that situation also (although it is not certain since under Example 2's facts, attachment was clearly prior to perfection.) This conclusion is supported by Example 1.

> *Example 1.* A files against X (debtor) on February 1. B files against X on March 1. B makes a non-purchase money advance against certain collateral on April 1. A makes an advance against the same collateral on May 1. A has priority even though B's advance was made earlier and was perfected when made. *It makes no difference whether or not A knew of B's interest when he made his advance.* . . . [(Emphasis added.)]

This example makes clear that once priority has been achieved by being the first to file, that priority will not be destroyed as to an advance made with the knowledge that a second party has made a prior advance secured by a perfected security interest in the same collateral. This is the case, apparently, even if it is the first advance made under the prior perfected agreement. Similar treatment should be accorded any interest which attached after filing.

It can be seen from the foregoing that Professor Gilmore's

position is not an unequivocal one. Furthermore, Professor Gilmore himself admits that the Code Comment to §9-312(5) tends to indicate that the drafters of the code were aware of and intended that knowledge be irrelevant in determining priorities under that section. Under these circumstances this court feels that the conclusion of the Referee in Bankruptcy that good faith should be read into Minn. Stat. Ann. §9-312(5) is unwarranted.

There are some other practical reasons why this court feels constrained to reverse the Referee in Bankruptcy. First of all, there are other commentators who have argued that the elimination of the good faith provision was intentional. See Felsenfeld, Knowledge as a Factor in Determining Priorities Under the Uniform Commercial Code, 42 N.Y.U.L. Rev. 246, 248-50 (1967).

Secondly, the assumption of most of the commentators has been that §9-312(5) operated without regard to knowledge of the perfecting party of a prior unperfected security interest. See Coogan, Hogan, Vagts, Secured Transactions Under the UCC 177. The Minnesota Code Comment referring to §9-312(5) says:

> Notice of a prior security interest does not invalidate a subsequent interest which is otherwise entitled to priority under this subsection. . . . This changes prior Minnesota law as to security interests in the nature of chattel mortgages and conditional sales, since subsequent mortgagees under prior law had the burden of proving "good faith" (i.e., lack of notice) as against prior mortgagees or conditional vendors whose mortgages or conditional sales contracts are unfiled. . . .

It is clear that the assumption of the Minnesota legislature when they adopted the code was that it changed prior law.

Finally, all the cases which have dealt with the problem indicate by holding or dicta that knowledge is irrelevant to the operation of §9-312(5). Bloom v. Hilty, 427 Pa. 463, 234 A.2d 860 (1967); First National Bank and Trust Company of Vinita, Okla. v. Atlas Credit Corp., 417 F.2d 1081, at 1082, fn. 1, 1083 (10th Cir. 1969); In re Gunderson, 4 UCC Rep. Serv. 358, 359 (D.C. Ill. 1967).

The attitude of the commentators and the weight of recorded decisions clearly indicated that knowledge could be disregarded in the operation of §9-312(5). The instant situation is evidence that there has been reliance on the apparent meaning of the statute as it has been interpreted by commentators and the courts.

To permit the decision of the Referee in Bankruptcy to stand would be to disrupt substantially expectations under §9-312(5).

Furthermore, it would create a split in authority and destroy the uniformity the code seeks to achieve. This is not to say that if the current interpretations were clearly contrary to the intent of the drafters that a split in authority would not be appropriate. That, however, is clearly not the situation presented. The only individual who seriously asserts that the elimination of a good faith requirement was unintentional is Professor Gilmore and his position is not an unequivocal one.

Under the circumstances this court cannot permit to stand a decision which goes against the weight of authority and reasonable expectations under the statute. The decision of the Referee in Bankruptcy must therefore be reversed.

Next comes the *Coin-O-Matic* problem. The following case is another example of a Rhode Island court having to deal with a new UCC Article 9 problem and creating a precedent many courts disagree with (and, it should be noted, all the commentators disagree; White & Summers at 1038-1040). Is the court right or wrong in your opinion? Right: Texas Kenworth Co. v. First Natl. Bank, 564 P.2d 222, 21 U.C.C. Rep. Serv. 1512 (Okla. 1977); In re Hagler, 10 U.C.C. Rep. Serv. 1285 (Bankr., E.D. Tenn. 1972); Wrong: In re Rivet, 299 F. Supp. 374, 6 U.C.C. Rep. Serv. 460 (E.D. Mich. 1969) (splendid opinion); James Talcott, Inc. v. Franklin Natl. Bank 194 N.W.2d 775, 10 U.C.C. Rep. Serv. 11 (Minn. 1972) (the "first to file rule" is "basic and essential to the certainty that Article 9 seeks to achieve"); In re Gruder, 392 N.Y.S.2d 203, 21 U.C.C. Rep. Serv. 287 (Sur. Ct. 1977); see also In re Nason, 31 U.C.C. Rep. Serv. 1739 (Bankr. D. R.I. 1981).

Coin-O-Matic Service Co. v. Rhode Island Hospital Trust Co.

3 U.C.C. Rep. Serv. 1112 (R.I. Superior Ct. 1966)

LICHT, J. This matter is before the court on an agreed statement of facts. The following is a summary of the facts which will help place the case in proper perspective.

On July 11, 1963, Munroe Doroff purchased a motor vehicle from Warwick Motors, Inc. on a time payment basis (Exhibit "A"). The security agreement representing the purchase was assigned to the Rhode Island Hospital Trust Company. The security agreement did not have any provision for after-acquired property or future advances. It described the collateral as one Chevrolet Station Wagon Greenbrier 1963. The financing statement filed July 16, 1963 contained a reference to the same Chevrolet Greenbrier Station Wagon (Exhibit "B").

On October 2, 1964 Doroff became indebted to Coin-O-Matic Service Company in the sum of $5600.00 represented by a promissory note and secured by a security agreement (Exhibits "C" and "D"). A financing agreement was filed October 23, 1964 (Exhibit "E"). On November 13, 1964, Doroff owed the Hospital Trust Company $302.77 on the security agreement of July 11, 1963 and on that date Rhode Island Hospital Trust Company loaned Doroff the sum of $1,000.00 from which sum he paid to Rhode Island Hospital Trust Company $302.77 in full satisfaction of his July 11, 1963 obligation. Rhode Island Hospital Trust Company thereupon cancelled the old agreement. Doroff executed a new promissory note secured by a security agreement (Exhibit "F"). A new financing statement was filed on November 17, 1964 (Exhibit "G"). On December 7, 1964 Doroff went into bankruptcy. It was stipulated that the value of the motor vehicle at the time it came into Rhode Island Hospital Trust Company's possession was $1200.00. It was further stipulated that the automobile was used in Doroff's business and there is no question that the automobile was part of the collateral given to Coin-O-Matic Service Company, the plaintiff. . . .

The defendant contends that its original financing statement was sufficient not only to protect the original conditional sales agreement but the subsequent agreement despite the fact that there intervened a security agreement between Doroff and Coin-O-Matic and a filed financing statement in connection therewith.

The issues raised require a consideration of the Uniform Commercial Code. There is no dispute that the word "equipment" used in the security agreement between Doroff and Coin-O-Matic was within Section 9-109(2).

[The court quoted §9-312(5)(a).]

The defendant relies wholly upon what it considers the compelling literal meaning of the language of the section. That is to say, that having entered into a security transaction which covered the 1963 Chevrolet Greenbrier Station Wagon and having filed a financing statement it comes ahead of the plaintiff who had a security interest in the same collateral but whose filing of a financing statement was subsequent in time to the original filing and ahead of defendant's second filing. Obviously with respect to the original transaction there is no dispute that the prior filing of the financial statement would govern. But the defendant carries its argument a step further and contends that the original financing statement is an umbrella which gives the defendant a priority with respect to its second security transaction notwithstanding that the plaintiff's security interest was established in point of time prior to defendant's second security transaction.

The defendant contends that as long as there is a financing statement on file the whole world is given notice that the debtor is obligated; that there is a security interest in the particular collateral and that the debtor may at any time after the original transaction become further indebted and enter into an additional security agreement with respect to the collateral. In support of this position the defendant cites a colloquy betweeen Peter Coogan, a member of the Permanent Editorial Board of the Uniform Commercial Code, and a member of the bar at a panel discussion conducted under the auspices of the American Bar Association in August of 1963. The following in colloquy which is one of such interest that the court in order to place the matter in its proper perspective sets it forth as follows:

> *Mr. Kripke:* Before you go on, let us take a hard case. Let us suppose you had this original mortgage for a dollar and then you have another intervening contractual chattel mortgage, and Sydney has no future advance clause but takes a third mortgage instrument for the half million dollars on the same property and there has already been an intervening filing with respect to it. Now where does Sydney rank?
>
> *Mr. Coogan:* Let's see if I follow you —
>
> *Mr. Kripke:* You have an original chattel mortgage for a dollar, perfected by a notice which says "industrial equipment." You have an intervening chattel mortgage for another lender on the same equipment for a hundred thousand dollars, let us say. Then Sydney takes a third piece of paper, a chattel mortgage on the same piece of equipment — one never in the original contemplation of the parties. Where do their parties rank?
>
> *Mr. Coogan:* Sydney comes ahead of everybody. This is an illustration of the first-to-file rule. Where two security interests have both been perfected through filing, and no specific priority rule applies the priorities date from the time of the filing.
>
> *Mr. Kripke:* You mean the original notice determines priorities as of its date even for a transaction that was not contemplated at the time?
>
> *Mr. Coogan:* That is correct.

Mr. Kripke: It would cover an advance which was not even covered by a future advance clause?
Mr. Coogan: That is correct. [19 Bus. Law 20, 52 (1963)].

It will be observed as already noted that the original conditional sales agreement between Doroff and Warwick Motors, Inc. which was assigned to the defendant has no provision for future advances.

Section 9-204, subsection (5) provides:

> Obligations covered by a security agreement may include future advances or other value whether or not the advances or value are given pursuant to commitment.

Defendant contends that this provision merely permits a lender to include a provision for future advances in the original security agreement and that when this is so provided it obviates the necessity of executing subsequent security agreements with respect to the collateral in question but that it does not in any way affect the priority with respect to future advances as long as the financing statement covering the collateral in question is prior in time and additional security agreements are obtained with each new loan. This is, according to the defendant, the thrust of Mr. Coogan's remarks to which reference has already been made. If this is so, it places a lender in an unusually strong position, vis-à-vis, the debtor and any subsequent lenders. In fact, it gives the lender a throttle hold on the debtor. For example, a debtor borrows $25,000.00 from a lender to be paid over a three-year period without any right of anticipation. The security is the equipment of the debtor. No provision is made for future advances. The financing statement is filed. The debtor reduces the obligation to $12,500.00 and now seeks to borrow an additional $5,000.00. The original lender is not interested in making a second loan. The debtor is in no position to pay off the loan without borrowing from another lender. The original lender does not desire to liquidate the obligation except in strict accordance with the agreement. Under the theory advanced by the defendant the original debtor cannot borrow from the second lender because no second lender can safely advance the money as long as there is a possibility that a future advance by the original lender would have priority in the collateral over the second lender. The interpretation contended for by the defendant does not appear to this court to be necessary for the protection of lenders nor does it seem necessary for facilitating commercial transactions. Defendant's counsel does not deny that this is so but contends that it makes no difference because Section 9-312(5)(a) gives the original lender such protection. Counsel for the defendant concedes a difference in a case in which the lender is paid off, the balance on the original transaction is reduced to zero and in which the financing statement is not terminated by a termination agreement as provided in §9-404 but it distinguishes the instant case from such a situation. The termination statement section provides in part as follows:

> Termination Statement. — (1) Whenever there is no outstanding secured obligations and no commitment to make advances, incur obligations or otherwise give value, the secured party must on written demand by the debtor send the debtor a statement that he no longer claims a security interest under the financing statement, which shall be identified by file number. . . .

It seems, however, that the defendant, notwithstanding his recognition of a difference in the illustration put forth should nevertheless take the position that as long as the financing statement is not terminated the lender is protected even when the original balance is liquidated, provided that additional funds are loaned and a new security agreement is entered into between the original lender and debtor. In such a case the original lender would come ahead of an intervening security transaction in which a financing statement had been filed for the same collateral. But why should the law be so interpreted to produce such a result? In all of these cases a lender can protect himself against the situation involved herein by providing in the original security agreement for future advances. In other words, the conclusion urged upon this court by the defendant is not required in the interest of facilitating commercial transactions particularly in the light of the fact that the Code provides for future advances in §9-204(5).

[The court quoted Official Comment 8 to §9-204 and example 4 to §9-312, Official Comment 5.] It will be observed that under this example the advance is made pursuant to the original security agreement, meaning thereby that the original security agreement contains a future advance provision. . . .

This is a case of first impression. No case has been cited to this court but counsel informed the court that there is no decided case involving the precise issue presented herein.

But Hart and Willier, Forms and Procedures under UCC, has the following interesting comment:

> *91A.08 Description of the Collateral*
> Secured transactions between the same secured party and debtor probably will follow one of several general procedures:
>
> (1) A single transaction; subsequent transactions are not originally contemplated and, if entered into, each would be separate and distinct.
> (2) A continuing series of transactions, each by a separate security agreement with its own collateral.
> (3) A secured transaction under one blanket security agreement covering a broad category of present and after-acquired collateral which may or may not contemplate future advances by the secured party or acts of the debtor identifying, segregating, substituting or transferring the collateral from time to time.
>
> In the first situation, a new filing will be required for each transaction. . . .

The provisions of the Code with respect to notice is, in the judgment of this court, helpful in the matter of interpreting §9-312(5).

Section 9-402 provides for the financing statement and the filing.

Section 9-208 provides that a debtor may request information from the lender as to the amount due on the obligation and the collateral covered by the security agreement. If the secured party, without reasonable excuse, fails to comply with the request he is liable for any loss caused to the debtor thereby and if the debtor has properly included in his request a good faith statement of the obligation or a list of the collateral or both, the secured party may claim a security interest only as shown in the statement against persons misled by his failure to comply.

If the Code gives the lender an interest in the collateral for future advances even though no provision is made for such future advances, then the information secured by the debtor and given to a subsequent lender is of little value because the second creditor surely could not rely upon the information. If the defendant's interpretation of the Code is correct, there seems to be hardly any substantive reason why the original lender should be bound to comply with the borrower's request for information concerning a correct statement of the outstanding balance and the collateral covered under the security agreement.

It should be observed that the defendant and the original debtor believed that the original conditional sales transaction was a single transaction and did not provide for future advances by virtue of the original financing statement. This is clear from an examination of the agreed financing statement and the exhibits attached thereto. When, on November 15th, Doroff's balance with the Hospital Trust was $302.77 on the security agreement of July 11, 1963, and when, on that date, the defendant loaned Doroff $1,000.00 which paid off the original balance and the old agreement was cancelled, Doroff executed a new promissory note secured by new security agreement and a new financing statement was filed with the Secretary of State on November 17, 1964.

It would seem to this court that without a consideration of the meaning of §9-312(5) this case might properly be decided on what the parties themselves did and what the parties themselves intended. Insofar as Doroff and the Rhode Island Hospital Trust Company were concerned these parties intended an entirely new transaction when the additional loan was made and they considered the original transaction as terminated. They did not intend to affect an intervening creditor. Certainly Doroff, although he subsequently went into bankruptcy, might well have not agreed to a new transaction if such new transaction was to have the effect of cutting out the intervening creditor. What these parties intended was a completely separate transaction and the claim now that the defendant is entitled to the protection of the original financing statement comes, in the judgment of this court, as an after-thought.

It is the considered judgment of the court after a careful consideration of the agreed statement of facts and the applicable provisions of the Commercial Code that particularly in this case the defendant is not entitled to rely upon the original financing statement in order to bring its subsequent loan ahead of that of the intervening creditor. This is said not because of the application of the principles of estoppel or waiver but because the parties surely are not prohibited under the Code from treating their transactions as separate and unrelated transactions. See §§1-102(2) and 1-201(3).

Section 9-312(5) deals with priority between conflicting security interests in the same collateral and gives a priority in the order of the filing but that obviously does not relate to separate and distinct security transactions. Moreover, a careful examination of §9-312 and the other applicable provisions of the Code lead to the conclusion that the reasonable interpretation of §9-312 is that a security agreement which does not provide for future advances is a single transaction and in the case of subsequent security agreement there is required a new financing statement. That is to say, a single financing statement in connection with a security agreement when no provision is made for future advances is not an umbrella for future advances based upon new security agreements, notwithstanding the fact that involved is the same collateral.

For the foregoing reasons decision is entered for the plaintiff in the sum of $1,000.00 plus interest and costs and the Clerk is directed to enter judgment forthwith and to give notice thereof to the parties pursuant to the Rules of Civil Procedure and Rules of Practice of the Superior Court.

QUESTION

What practical step does this case suggest for attorneys drafting a security agreement? Read §9-204(3). The Article Nine Review Committee, which disapproved of *Coin-O-Matic;* see E-39 of the "General Comment on the Approach of the Review Committee for Article 9." Does 1972's §9-312(7) solve this problem? See Allis-Chambers Credit Corp. v. Cheney Inv., Inc., 227 Kan. 4, 605 P.2d 525, 28 U.C.C. Rep. Serv. 574 (1980), and Coogan, The New Article 9, 86 Harv. L. Rev. 477, 509-511 (1973) (a valuable reference work for exploring the major changes made by the 1972 revision).

PROBLEM 48

Woody Timbers was the sole proprietor of a lumber business named "Timbers' Timbers." He was also a desperate man because the business was going under. On October 4, he granted Octopus National Bank a security interest in his lumber in return for a loan. He signed a financing statement, but ONB's loan officer lost it before it could be placed on file. On November 12, Woody signed an identical security agreement and financing statement with Nightflyer Finance Company, which loaned him more money. On November 13 (a Friday) the institutions learned of each other's claim to the inventory. Since Woody had missed payments on both debts, ONB immediately sent 12 burly men to Timbers' Timbers to take possession of the lumber. They arrived at 10:30 A.M. with a truck and, shooing off potential customers and Woody's protests, placed a guard on the lumber until their truck arrived at 11:00 A.M., when they began loading. They finished at 11:30 A.M. Nightflyer filed its financing statement in the proper place at 10:45 A.M. on the same day. Which creditor is entitled to the goods? See Transport Equip. Co. v. Guaranty St. Bank, 518 F.2d 377, 17 U.C.C. Rep. Serv. 1 (10th Cir. 1975) (the court defined "possession as meaning 'physical control' " and stated that it required "as open and notorious a change of possession as the nature of the property permitted in order to give plain and public notice to other creditors or purchasers of the secured party's claim against the property.").

PROBLEM 49

Phillip Philately pledged his valuable stamp collection to the Collectors National Bank (hereinafter CNB) in return for a loan (he gave CNB an oral security interest in the collateral; no financing statement was signed). The bank put the stamp collection in their vault. Philately later borrowed money from his father, Filbert Philately, and gave him a signed security agreement in the same stamp collection. The father filed a financing statement in the proper place. Answer these questions:

(a) Who has priority between CNB and the father?

(b) If Phillip goes to the bank and takes the collection home so that he can add new stamps, but does then return it, does the answer change? At common law the pledgee could return the collateral to the pledgor for a "temporary and limited purpose" without losing its perfection. See G. Gilmore §14.5. Has this doctrine survived the enactment of the Code? See §9-305; is §9-304(5) relevant?

(c) If CNB makes Phillip sign a security agreement and then turns the collection over to him but never files a financing statement, who wins? See §9-303(2). What should CNB have done?

(d) If, while retaining a possession, CNB makes *another* advance to Phillip after the transaction between the father and son, does the interest created by the second advance also prevail over the father (that is, does it *relate back* to the time of the original perfection)? See §9-312(7); see also (5) of the "Reasons For 1972 Change" for a discussion of this issue.

Section 9-204(3) broadly authorizes future advance clauses in the security agreement. Does it also give the drafters' imprimatur to the so-called dragnet clause, a clause purporting to expand the security interest to cover unrelated obligations owed by the debtor to the creditor? Professor Gilmore thinks not, and in §35.6 of his treatise proposes that the courts develop a test based upon the intention of the parties, and a requirement that the later obligation be "related," "similar," or "of the same class" as the original transaction.

PROBLEM 50

Howard "Red" Poll decided to go into the cattle business and borrowed $15,000 from the Brangus National Bank to finance part of the purchase of the initial herd. Poll signed a security agreement using the cattle as collateral for this "and all other obligations now or hereafter owed to the bank." A financing statement covering this transaction was filed in the appropriate place. Two years later Poll received a charge card from the same bank and used it to finance a trip to Australia to look over cattle ranching there. When he failed to pay the credit card bill the bank repossessed the cattle (even though his payments on the cattle purchase loan were current). Did the bank's security interest in the cattle encompass the credit card obligation? See John Miller Supply Co. v. Western St. Bank, 55 Wis. 2d 385, 199 N.W.2d 161, 10 U.C.C. Rep. Serv. 1329 (1972) (adopts the Gilmore tests); Kimbell Foods, Inc. v. Republic Nat. Bank, 401 F. Supp. 316, 18 U.C.C. Rep. Serv. 507 (N.D. Tex. 1975) ("The true intention of the parties is really the sole and controlling factor in determining whether future advances were covered by the original agreement . . . [or] would have to be reperfected."); In re Johnson, 31 U.C.C. Rep. Serv. 291 (Ref. Bky., M.D. Tenn. 1981) (consumer goods held not to secure future advances of a business nature in spite of dragnet clause); Note, Future Advances Financing Under the UCC: Curbing the Abuses of the Dragnet Clause, 34 U. Pitt. L. Rev. 691 (1973).

B. PURCHASE MONEY SECURITY INTERESTS

The seller who extends credit to the buyer or the lender who advances the money to enable the buyer to purchase the collateral has a special equity in it in the eyes of the law. If the parties sign a security agreement the seller/lender gets a "purchase money security interest." Read §9-107. Even though the goods become subject to an existing security interest when they come into the buyer's possession, the purchase money security interest is given priority. This is true in spite of the fact that the purchase money security interest is later in time. Where the collateral is consumer goods no further steps are required for a purchase money security interest therein to prevail over prior or later interests; see §9-302(1)(d). All other purchase money security interests are automatically perfected only during a 10-day "grace period" following the buyer's possession of the goods. They must be reperfected during the 10-day period or their perfection lapses and their priority is lost. Read §9-301(2) and 9-312(4) carefully. Section 9-312(3) has a special rule for purchase money security interests taken in goods that are to become part of the buyer's inventory; we'll defer consideration of it for a few pages.

PROBLEM 51

When Paramount Homes finished building "Utopia, Ltd.," its newest fancy apartment complex, it had to furnish the club house, and so it sent its construction manager, Bill Gilbert to Sophy's Interiors, a furniture store, where he made $2000 worth of credit purchases and signed a security agreement on behalf of Paramount Homes in favor of the seller. The agreement was signed on June 8; the goods were delivered that same day. Bill failed to mention that all his employer's assets (equipment and inventory) were designated as collateral on an existing security agreement and filed financing statement in favor of Sullivan National Bank. This agreement contained an "after-acquired property" clause stating that later similar collateral coming into the buyer's estate would automatically fall under the bank's security interest (see §9-204(1)). It was Sophy's Interiors' policy not to file financing statements for its credit furniture sales.

(a) Why might it have such a policy? Is it wise here?

(b) On June 10, which creditor will have priority in the furniture? On June 19?

(c) Would it make a difference if Bill had told Sophy's Interiors' salesman that he was buying the goods for his own home? See In re Morton, supra at p. 55; Balon v. Cadillac Auto. Co., 303 A.2d 194, 12 U.C.C. Rep. Serv. 397 (N.H. 1973).

Galleon Industries, Inc. v. Lewyn Machinery Co.

50 Ala. App. 334, 279 So. 2d 137, 12 U.C.C. Rep. Serv. 1224 (Ala. 1973)

Wright, P.J. Galleon Industries, Incorporated, and Central Bank and Trust Company, Incorporated, were defendants below in an action in detinue. From a verdict and judgment in favor of plaintiff for the property sued for, after denial of motion for new trial, defendants each have appealed. . . .

The facts giving rise to plaintiff's suit are generally as follows: A representative of Lewyn Machinery Company, with offices in Atlanta, Georgia, came to the place of business of Galleon Industries in Pell City, Alabama, and discussed the sale by Lewyn and purchase by Galleon of certain items of equipment. A decision was made as to the items to be purchased subject to arrangement of financing. Upon investigation of Galleon's credit standing, Lewyn notified Galleon that no credit could be extended and that the items could be purchased for cash at Lewyn's office in Atlanta and delivered to Galleon there. Galleon subsequently went to Lewyn's office in Atlanta, paid cash, and accepted delivery of all items except one. This one item was a machine which Lewyn did not have on hand, but which was to be obtained by them from the manufacturer, J. M. Lancaster, located in North Carolina. Galleon was informed that when the machine was received by Lewyn he could return to Atlanta, pay cash, and accept delivery. The price was to be $2800.00 Through mistake or misunderstanding, the machine was subsequently shipped by the manufacturer, Lancaster, directly to Galleon in Pell City. Lancaster notified Lewyn of the shipment. Lewyn then sent to Galleon an invoice on the machine stating thereon the terms of "net 30 days." Shipment by Lancaster to Galleon was shown to be June 22, 1970. Lewyn's invoice was dated the same day. Actual receipt of the machine by Galleon was apparently about July 5, 1970.

On November 21, 1969, a security agreement had been entered into by Galleon with Central Bank and Trust Company. This agreement included as collateral all equipment and inventory owned or to be thereafter acquired by Galleon. A financing statement was filed thereon on December 1, 1969. On July 13, 1970, the loan of Central being in default, Central foreclosed its security agreement and took possession of Galleon's property, including the machine which is the subject of this suit.

Appellee's testimony was that after notice of shipment by Lancaster to Galleon, Galleon was contacted by phone at least twice and a check for the machine was requested. Such check was promised but did not arrive. After several days the owner of Lewyn Machinery Company came to Pell City and learned of the taking of possession by Central. He retained counsel and brought suit in detinue against Galleon and Central. . . .

Plaintiff, Lewyn, presented his case on the theory that title to the machine did not pass to Galleon until it had been paid for and since Galleon never paid, the title, and thus the right to possession, remained in Lewyn. We consider that the vesting of rights, as required under §9-204 of the Uniform Commercial Code, and not the passing of title (§2-401) is the question to be determined on this appeal. The provisions of §2-401 are explicitly subject to the provisions of Article 9 — therefore, the question being the effect of Central's after-acquired property clause, we will limit our discussion to whether or not sufficient rights did in fact vest in the buyer Galleon, for Central's perfected security interest to attach.

It is without dispute in the evidence that the machine was shipped by the manufacturer to the buyer, Galleon. Lewyn stated that such shipment was by mistake, and that it was orally agreed between Galleon and Lewyn that delivery was not to be made except upon payment. However, after receiving notice of the shipment, Lewyn sent to Galleon an invoice requiring payment "net in 30 days." Thus any prior agreement as to delivery and payment was modified or waived by Lewyn and Galleon became a credit buyer. We do not decide here the application of §2-201, the Statute of Frauds, to the sales agreement. The effect of delivery, together with the invoice, was to limit any retention of rights or title to an explicit security agreement subject to the provisions of Article 9 of the Uniform Commercial Code as to perfection and priority. Harvey v. Spellman, 113 Ill. App. 2d 463, 251 N.E.2d 265; §2-401, Title 7A, Code 1940, recompiled.

Section 9-202 states "Each provision of this Article with regards to rights, obligations or remedies applies whether title to collateral is in the secured party or in the debtor." It is stated in Anderson, Uniform Commercial Code, 2d Edition, Volume 2, page 26: "If it is the desire of the parties to effect a reservation of title until the purchase price be paid, a secured transaction should be entered into and a proper filing made if required to protect the creditor's interest as against third persons."

Section 9-204 provides for a security agreement covering after-acquired property such as that held by Central. This section also provides the manner in which such security interest shall attach. In the case of the security interest of Central, it attached when the debtor, Galleon, acquired "rights" in the collateral covered by the security agreement. As we have previously stated, the delivery of the machine and the forwarding of the invoice stating "net 30 days" made Galleon a credit buyer. A credit buyer acquires "rights" in the property when possession is received from the seller. In re Ten Brock, 4 UCC Rep. Serv. 712.

Lewyn, if retaining title until payment, by delivery to a credit buyer reserved only a purchase money security interest, such security interest was never perfected by filing as required by §9-302. Lewyn could have perfected its purchase money security interest and received priority over the perfected security interest of Central by filing a financing statement at the time of delivery, or within 10 days thereafter. Section 9-312(4). According to the evidence, Lewyn learned of the foreclosure and taking of possession by Central eight days after delivery to Galleon. There still remained two days for perfection of its security interest by filing a financing statement. Such filing would have given it priority over the perfected security interest of Central. Section 9-312(4).

Since sufficient "rights" had passed to Galleon by delivery and the sending of the invoice, the requirements of §9-204 were satisfied and the security interest of Central attached to the machine. The failure of Lewyn to perfect its security interest by filing within 10 days after delivery gave Central priority. Thus at the time of the filing of the suit in detinue, Central had a superior right to possession. . . .

Reversed and remanded.

PROBLEM 52

Albert Bullet was a circus performer whose act consisted of being shot from a cannon. The circus, which owned all of his equipment, had used all of its equipment (now or after-acquired) as collateral for a loan from the Florida Circus Bank, which had a perfected security interest in same. Bullet, as the circus' agent, went to the Big Bang Ordinance Store to buy a new cannon. He told them he wanted to have a trial use period before the circus became obligated to buy and BBOS and Bullet (as agent) signed an agreement giving him temporary possession but reserving title in the store. The circus was given an option to buy, but until it did so paid only a nominal rental of $30 a day. The cannon was delivered to the circus on April 1; the circus decided to buy on April 30, and signed a security agreement and a financing statement in favor of BBOS on that date. The store filed the same day. If the circus folds, which creditor gets the cannon? Read §2-326(2). Compare the case below, In re Ultra Precision Indus., Inc., 503 F.2d 414, 15 U.C.C. Rep. Serv. 281 (9th Cir. 1974), and Fan-Gil Corp. v. American Hosp. Supply Corp., 49 Mich. App. 106, 211 N.W.2d 561, 13 U.C.C. Rep. Serv. 733 (1973), with James Talcott, Inc. v. Associates Capital Co., 491 F.2d 879, 14 U.C.C. Rep. Serv. 202 (6th Cir. 1974).

Brodie Hotel Supply, Inc. v. United States

431 F.2d 1316, 8 U.C.C. Rep. Serv. 113 (9th Cir. 1970)

HAMLEY, C.J. Brodie Hotel Supply, Inc. (Brodie), brought this action against the United States to determine which of the parties had priority, under their respective chattel mortgages, to the proceeds of the sale of certain restaurant equipment. The facts were stipulated and the property was sold and proceeds impounded by agreement. The district court granted summary judgment for Brodie and the United States appeals.

In 1959, Brodie sold the restaurant equipment to Standard Management Company, Inc., for use in a restaurant at Anchorage, Alaska. Standard Management went bankrupt. Brodie repossessed the equipment but left it in the restaurant. With the consent of Brodie, James Lyon took possession of the restaurant and began operating it on June 1, 1964. Throughout the summer of 1964, Brodie and Lyon negotiated over the price and terms under which Lyon was to purchase the equipment.

On November 2, 1964, Lyon borrowed seventeen thousand dollars from the National Bank of Alaska and, as security for the loan, which was evidenced by a promissory note, executed a chattel mortgage covering the restaurant equipment. This equipment consisted of 159 separate types of items, including a refrigerator, a dishwasher, an ice cream cabinet, spoons, forks, cups, ladles, pots, pans, and assorted glassware and chinaware. The bank assigned its mortgage to the Small Business Administration (SBA), represented in this action by the United States. On November 4, 1964, the bank filed a financing statement, showing the SBA as assignee.

On November 12, Brodie delivered to Lyon a bill of sale covering the equipment. On the same day Lyon executed a chattel mortgage on the equipment, naming Brodie as mortgagee. This mortgage was given to secure the unpaid purchase price of the equipment. Brodie filed a financing statement on November 23, 1964.

Alaska had adopted the Uniform Commercial Code (Code). Under §9-312(5)(a) of the Code the general rule of priority, if both interests are perfected by filing, is that the secured party who first files a financing statement (in this case SBA as assignee of the bank) prevails, regardless of when his security interest attached. However, there is a special exception for purchase-money security interests in collateral other than inventory. Brodie had such an interest. Under this exception, the purchase-money security interest prevails over conflicting interests in non-inventory collateral if "the purchase money security interest is perfected [i.e., here it was perfected by filing a financing statement] at the time the debtor receives possession of the collateral or within 10 days after the debtor receives possession." (Code, §9-312(4)).

On the basis of these stipulated facts, Brodie moved for summary judgment. Brodie contended that although Lyon received possession of the restaurant equipment on June 1, 1964, over five months before Brodie's financing statement was filed, Lyon did not become a "debtor," and the equipment did not become "collateral" until November 12, 1964, when Lyon received the bill of sale and executed Brodie's chattel mortgage. Accordingly, Brodie contended, it was not until November 12, that "the debtor [Lyon] receive[d] possession of the collateral" within the meaning of the statute referred to above. As already indicated, Brodie's financing statement was filed within ten days of that date. The district court agreed with this analysis in granting summary judgment for Brodie.

If, in §9-312(4), the term "debtor" is given the meaning ascribed to it in §9-105(1)(d), Brodie was entitled to priority. It was not until November 12, 1964, that Lyon purchased the equipment and became obligated to pay the purchase price. Until that obligation came into being, Lyon was not Brodie's debtor with power to mortgage the restaurant equipment as collateral for the unpaid purchase price.

But the United States argues that in the context of this case the priority statute, §9-312(4), is ambiguous as to whether "debtor" is used in the sense defined in §9-105(1)(d), or whether it is used merely to identify an individual in possession, who ultimately becomes indebted to the purchase-money mortgagee. In contending that this "ambiguity" should be resolved in favor of the latter construction, the United States refers to the history and underlying purposes and policies of the Code, the assertedly different language of the prior Uniform Conditional Sales Act, and the fact that, under §9-402(1) a financing statement may be filed before a security agreement is made or a security interest otherwise attaches, notwithstanding the fact that this section refers to "debtor," "secured party," and "security interest."

We are not persuaded that either recourse to the history or consideration of the underlying purposes of the Code supports Government's position. In our view, the term "debtor" as it is used in this particular priority statute, §9-312(4), means "the person who owes payment or other performance of the obligation secured." Code §9-105(1)(d). Although Lyon might have been liable for the reasonable rental of the equipment or for its return to Brodie, he did not owe performance of an "obligation secured" by the collateral in question until November 12, 1964, and therefore was not a "debtor" for purposes of §9-312(4). Brodie's filing was therefore within the ten-day period and Brodie has priority over the conflicting security interest held by SBA.

The Government has urged us to look at the policy and the purposes of the Code to resolve what it considers to be the ambiguous meaning of "debtor." The Code has granted a specially favored position to the holder of a purchase-money security interest in non-inventory collateral. The holder of such an interest need not follow the notice procedures which are prescribed for the holders of purchase-money interests in inventory. Code, §9-312(3). Such a holder is also given a special priority position. His interest, perfected second, but within the ten-day grace period, will prevail over any previously perfected security interest. This priority exists even though the framers of the Code knew that the holder of the conflicting security interest would be relying on the possession of the collateral and upon the absence of a prior filing. Similarly, the holder of a purchase-money security interest in non-inventory collateral will have priority over a previously perfected security interest which includes the collateral by virtue of an after-acquired property clause. Code, §9-312(4), Official Comment 3. Such a holder therefore is not required to search the files to determine the existence of such a conflicting interest in order to be sure of his priority.

The protection which the Code confers upon a purchase-money

interest in non-inventory collateral is not unduly extended by a decision giving priority to Brodie's interest. Although it is true that Brodie could have filed a financing statement as soon as Lyon went into possession and thus protected itself, it is also true that the bank, SBA's assignor, could have protected itself by inquiring into Lyon's interest in the equipment before accepting his chattel mortgage. Due to the favored status given by the Code to the holder of a purchase-money interest in non-inventory collateral, we are not convinced that the trial court erred in refusing to impose this burden on Brodie.

Affirmed.

C. *INVENTORY*

The inventory financier will have a perfected interest in existing and after-acquired inventory, in effect a floating lien over the mass of changing goods available for sale by the debtor to others. If the debtor buys new inventory and gives the seller a purchase money security interest therein, the original financier is seriously hurt if (a) it does not know of the purchase money interest but instead thinks *all* the inventory is collateral in which it has priority, and (b) the purchase money interest is held to prevail over the already perfected interest in after-acquired inventory. To protect the first creditor §9-312(3) provides a notification procedure that the purchase money secured creditor must follow in order to take the normal priority. See White & Summers §25-5; G. Gilmore §29.3; Henson §5-4.

PROBLEM 53

The Merchants Credit Assn. held a perfected security interest in Harold's Clothing Store's inventory. Harold went to a fashion showing in New York and contracted to buy $4000 worth of new clothes for resale; the seller was to be Madam Belinda's Fashions, Inc., which took a purchase money security interest in the clothes on December 10, the date of sale. Madam Belinda herself wrote the Merchant's Credit Assn. on December 11, and informed the credit manager of the sale. He protested, but did nothing. Madam Belinda filed on December 11; the goods were delivered to the store on December 12.

(a) Who has priority?

(b) Would your answer change if Madam Belinda's notice wasn't received until December 13th?

(c) If the notice was received on the 11th, as above, is it sufficient to permit Madam Belinda to keep selling goods to Harold for an indefinite period thereafter or only for this one transaction? See §9-312(3)(c).

PROBLEM 54

Hans Racing Equipment bought much of its inventory from Standard Auto Wholesales, Inc., which always took a purchase money security interest in the goods sold to Hans and which filed a financing statement on the same day. Hans also borrowed money from the Matching Dishes National Bank to finance the purchase of inventory from wholesalers, part of which was used to pay off Standard Auto; MDNB filed a financing statement claiming a security interest in Hans' inventory. On March 28, Hans contracted to buy $3000 in goods from Standard, making a down payment of $1500 and giving Standard a purchase money security interest in the goods for the rest. On that same day he borrowed the $1500 down payment from MDNB and also gave the bank a purchase money security interest in the same goods. Both creditors knew of the other, so they both sent written notice to each other. The goods were delivered to Hans on April 2. Which creditor has priority?[1]

Similar problems arise of course with consignments. Even true consigners hoping to prevail over perfected interests in the inventory of the consignee must follow a notification procedure of this type. Read §9-114.

PROBLEM 55

Barbara Shipek was pleased and flattered when Tim Isle, owner of Isle's Fine Art Works, asked her if he could exhibit and sell some of

1. G. Gilmore §29-3, at 790 has this answer: "Section 9-312(3) sensibly makes no attempt to answer these wild-eyed hypotheticals. In such a situation, A and B, once they have become aware of each other's presence, will be well advised to sit down together and come to an agreement: the notification mechanism will not solve their problems for them. If, in defiance of common sense, they engage in a battle of notifications, they should both be hung. It is not worth anyone's time to try to figure out the priorities between them."

Henson §5-4 solves the problem by reference to §9-312(5), though he can see an analogy to the result found in §9-315(2) (the "commingling" section).

her pottery. She gave him five of her favorite pieces. The next day she took a party of friends down to the store to see the display, and was astounded to learn that Octopus National Bank, which had a perfected floating lien on the store's inventory, had foreclosed and seized everything in the store, including Barb's pottery. Can ONB do this to her? See §9-114.

D. BUYERS

Section 9-201 states what White & Summers call Article 9's "Golden Rule" (White & Summers at 1064):

> Except as otherwise provided by this Act a security agreement is effective according to its terms between the parties, against purchasers of the collateral and against creditors. . . .

Section 9-307 is one of the sections that fits in the "except" language of §9-201; so is §9-301(1) which lists other parties who win out over the *unperfected* secured party in some circumstances (particularly see §§9-301(1)(c) and (d) which delineate the purchasers of collateral who prevail over unperfected interests). A corollary to §9-201's "Golden Rule" is §9-306(2):

> (2) Except where this Article otherwise provides, a security interest continues in collateral notwithstanding sale, exchange or other disposition thereof by the debtor unless his action was authorized by the secured party in the security agreement or otherwise, and also continues in any identifiable proceeds including collections received by the debtor.

PROBLEM 56

Betty Consumer bought a television set from Distortion TV, Inc., a retail store. A month later Distortion went bankrupt and a minor functionary from the Octopus National Bank showed up on her stoop and asked her to turn over the set. He explained that ONB held a perfected security interest in all of Distortion's inventory and since Distortion had not paid off its debts to ONB, the bank was repossessing.

(a) What should Ms. Consumer tell the bank's flunky? See §9-307.

(b) Would it matter if she had known that ONB had a perfected security interest in Distortion's inventory? See White & Summers §25-13; Official Comment 2 to §9-307.

(c) What if Ms. Consumer had put the TV on "lay-away" and she had paid 50% of the price but permitted Distortion to keep the TV (she signed a contract obligating herself to pay the balance)? Read §2-502; see International Harvester Credit Corp. v. Associates Financial Serv. Co., 133 Ga. App. 488, 211 S.E.2d 430, 16 U.C.C. Rep. Serv. 396 (1974); Chrysler Credit Corp. v. Sharp, 56 Misc. 2d 261, 288 N.Y.S.2d 525; 5 U.C.C. Rep. Serv. 226 (1968). The Bankruptcy Reform Act gives such consumers some relief in §507(a)(5) which gives layaway buyers a fifth priority payment up to the amount of $900 per individual.

International Harvester Co. v. Glendenning

505 S.W.2d. 320, 14 U.C.C. Rep. Serv. 837 (Tex. 1974)

WILLIAMS, Ch. J. This appeal is from a take nothing judgment in a suit to recover damages for wrongful conversion of three tractors.

International Harvester Company and International Harvester Credit Corporation (both hereinafter referred to as International) brought this action against Don Glendenning in which it was alleged that International was the holder of a duly perfected security interest in three new International Harvester tractors; that such security agreements had been executed in favor of International by Jack L. Barnes, doing business as Barnes Equipment Company, an International Harvester dealer; that Barnes and Glendenning had entered into a fraudulent conspiracy wherein Glendenning had wrongfully purchased the three tractors from Barnes; that Glendenning was not a buyer in the ordinary course of business; that he did not act in a commercially reasonable manner and did not act honestly, therefore taking the tractors subject to International's security interest. It was further alleged that Barnes and Glendenning had wrongfully conspired to convert the ownership of the tractors and to deprive International, by fraud and deceit, of its ownership of the tractors by virtue of their security interest therein in that (1) Glendenning acquiesced in falsifying a retail order form so that it was made to indicate receipt of $16,000 in cash and the trade-in of two used tractors allegedly worth a total of $8,700, while in fact both Glendenning and Barnes knew that Glendenning had only paid the sum of $16,000 in cash, a sum far below the market value of the tractors; (2) that Glendenning in the furtherance of the conspiracy and unlawful conversion, represented to a representative of International that he, Glendenning had, in fact, traded certain used tractors to Barnes, which was untrue; and (3) Glendenning removed the new tractors in which International had a security interest to the State of Louisiana where he sold the same and converted the proceeds to his own use and benefit. International sought damages in the sum of $24,049.99 which was alleged to be the reasonable value of the tractors on the date of conversion.

Glendenning answered by a general denial and with the special defense to the effect that he purchased the tractors in the ordinary course of business and that such purchase was made in good faith and without any knowledge of any security interest held by International. . . .

> Do you find from a preponderance of the evidence that on the time and occasion in question, the defendant, Don Glendenning, was a buyer in the ordinary course of business?

In connection with this issue the court instructed the jury that the term "buyer in ordinary course of business" means "a person who in good faith and without knowledge that the sale to him is in violation of the ownership rights or security interest of the third party in the goods buys in the ordinary course from a person in the business of selling goods of that kind."

The court instructed the jury that the term "good faith" means "honesty in fact in the conduct or transaction concerned."

The jury answered the special issue "Yes." . . .

[The court quoted §§9-307(1), 1-209(9), and 1-201(19), and noted that "whether a sale is in the ordinary course of business is a mixed question of law and fact."]

The material testimony presented to the court and jury may be summarized, as follows:

At the time of the trial of this case appellee Glendenning was a farmer in Collin County. He described himself as being not only a farmer but a trader. He said that he frequently traded tractors and other farm equipment as well as anything else from which he could make a profit. He has had almost twenty years' experience in the business of buying and selling farm tractors. In the early 1950s he owned an International Harvester dealership in Frisco, Collin County, Texas. From 1956 to 1960 he was a salesman for International Harvester. After leaving International he began trading farm equipment of his own, using some of the implements on his own farm and holding others strictly for resale. For many years he had been familiar with International Harvester's custom of "floor-planning" tractors and other farm equipment. By this plan International would supply tractors and other equipment to the dealers who, in turn, would give International a note and security agreement to protect International in its investment. When a dealer sold a piece of equipment from the floor he would pay International the amount due. He also testified that he knew that when used tractors were taken as trade-ins by International Harvester dealers such used tractors were also mortgaged or covered by the security agreement to International. He admitted that International Harvester always kept close tabs to see what was wrong with the used tractors and that International always wanted to know what its dealers traded for in connection with new equipment sales. Glendenning acknowledged that any false information contained on a retail order form would provide incorrect information concerning the transactions to International Harvester, or any other lender.

Glendenning said that he had known Jack L. Barnes, an International Harvester dealer, for two or three years and during that time he had bought several tractors from him. In the early part of July 1971 Barnes, and Joe Willard, another friend, came to his home in Collin County and talked to him about buying some tractors. He said that Barnes had eight tractors to sell but that he was only interested in buying three of the machines. Barnes described the tractors and told Glendenning that he wanted $18,500 for the three. Glendenning declined that offer but told Barnes that he would give $16,000 cash for the three. Barnes accepted the offer.

At the time of this transaction Glendenning knew that the three tractors were reasonably worth $22,500. Willard went to Vernon, Texas, and got the tractors and delivered them to Mr. Glendenning's home. Glendenning asked Willard to bring him a bill of sale when he returned with the tractors. Willard received from Barnes an instrument entitled "Retail Order Form" dated July 5, 1971, which recited that Glendenning had purchased from Barnes three tractors for the total price of $24,700 with a cash payment of $16,000 leaving a balance of $8,700. The instrument recited that Glendenning had traded in four tractors with values totaling $8,700 so that the total consideration of $24,700 was shown to have been paid.

Glendenning said that the next day Barnes came to his home to get payment for the tractors. At that time Glendenning requested a "bill of sale" and he watched Barnes fill in another retail order form similar to the one that he had obtained from Willard the day before. This order form stated that Glendenning had traded in four tractors worth $8,700 in addition to payment of $16,000 in cash making a total purchase of $24,700. After Barnes had completed filling out this form and signed the same Glendenning said that he put his signature on the instrument also. He then gave Barnes $16,000.

Concerning the contents of the retail order form Glendenning said that at the time Barnes filled in the blanks indicating that Glendenning was trading in four tractors he knew that he was not trading anything and that he did not question Barnes about the trade-in information contained in the form. He admitted that he did not ask Barnes whether the tractors which he purchased were free and clear nor did he call International to determine whether or not such company had a mortgage on the tractors. Glendenning admitted that he knew that the information contained in the printed form concerning trade-ins and total consideration for the sale of the three new tractors was false; that he knew of this falsification when he signed the order form; and that he also knew that such falsification would mislead any creditors relying on the document such as a dealer, a manufacturer or a bank lending money with the equipment as collateral. He admitted that at the time of the transaction in question Barnes was probably "trying to come out even" or that he did it to make his books balance. Glendenning admitted that he was suspicious of the manner in which Barnes prepared the order form and confessed that his actions amounted to dishonesty. He said that to his knowledge he had never before signed an order form with false trade-ins. He admitted that such action was "unusual."

A few days after the transaction a Mr. McKinney, collection manager for International Harvester Company, and a representative of International Harvester Credit Corporation, telephoned Glendenning concerning the transaction in question. In that conversation Glendenning told McKinney that he had traded four tractors to Barnes in addition to paying $16,000 cash for the three new International tractors. Glendenning testified that he knew that he had lied to Mr. McKinney concerning the trade-ins and that such oral misrepresentation or lie was dishonest.

After receiving the tractors Glendenning removed them to a barn near Alexandria, Louisiana, although it was his usual practice to place equipment on his own premises or at another dealer's place of business. He subsequently sold the three tractors in Louisiana.

As a part of his direct examination Glendenning testified that he considered the deal to be a purchase of three tractors for $16,000; that he had no side agreement with Barnes; that he thought he was making a good deal; and that he was acting in good faith.

At the very beginning of this trial appellee Glendenning confessed the validity of appellant's cause of action against him based upon fraud, conspiracy and conversion, but sought to evade legal liability by assuming, pursuant to Tex. R. Civ. P. 266, the burden of going forward and establishing his sole defense that he was a buyer in ordinary course of business within the meaning of §9.307(a) (1968). This assumption carried with it the additional burden of establishing by competent evidence that Glendenning acted in good faith and without knowledge that the sale to him was in violation of the ownership rights or security interest of a third party. Good faith, as the court correctly charged the jury, means honesty in fact in the conduct or transaction concerned. In an effort to establish this affirmative defense and thereby evade liability, appellee Glendenning testified on direct examination with the broad conclusory statement that he had acted in good faith. However, this subjective and conclusory statement was immediately annihilated by factual evidence falling from the lips of Glendenning himself.

Appellee Glendenning's own testimony immediately removes him from the category of an innocent Collin County farmer who seeks to purchase one or more tractors in the ordinary course of business. By his own testimony he has had many years of experience as a tractor dealer, a salesman and one of the most active traders of farm equipment in Collin County. Based upon this experience he is knowledgeable in the very nature of business done by International by "floor-planning" its equipment. With all of this knowledge and information in his possession he purchased the equipment for considerably less than its value, made no investigation of International's security interest, acquiesced in the falsification of the retail order form showing nonexistent trade-ins, and misrepresented the particulars of the transaction to International's representative by stating that there were, in fact, trade-ins. He confesses that his actions were dishonest.

Thus it is evident to us that Glendenning's own testimony, which is the only material testimony offered, is entirely devoid of honesty in fact and completely negates his contention that he was a buyer in the ordinary course of business within the meaning of the Texas Business & Commerce Code.

While we have been unable to find any Texas authorities decided under this specific provision of the Business & Commerce Code a recent Uniform Commercial Code release notes that the good faith requirement was added "to make it clear that one who buys dishonestly is not within the definition. The 'without knowledge' addition spells out one important type of dishonesty." UCC Release No. 27-1973, 6 Bender's Uniform Commercial Code Service §1-201 at 1-29 (1965).

The complete picture revealed by all of the material testimony in this case reveals a definite pattern of lies, deceit, dishonesty and bad faith. We find no competent evidence in this record to support the jury's answer to the special issue submitted and therefore the same should have been set aside and disregarded by the trial court. . . .

PROBLEM 57

Deering Milliken was a textile manufacturer. It routinely sold textiles on credit to Mill Fabrics, a firm which finished the textiles into dyed and patterned fabrics. It was Mill Fabrics' practice to resell the fabrics to Tanbro Fabrics, a wholesaler. While the textiles were still in Deering's warehouse, Mill Fabrics contracted to buy them from Deering, signing a security agreement to that effect. In turn Mill Fabrics sold the textiles to Tanbro, which paid Mill Fabrics for them, but delayed taking delivery for a few weeks. Deals of this kind were common in the textile industry, and all parties knew of the others' interests. Unfortunately Mill Fabrics became insolvent and never paid Deering for the textiles, and Deering therefore refused to deliver them to Tanbro. The latter sued. Who should prevail? See Tanbro Fabrics Corp. v. Deering Milliken, Inc., 39 N.Y.2d 632, 385 N.Y.S.2d 260, 350 N.E.2d 590, 19 U.C.C. Rep. Serv. 385 (1976).

White & Summers list six conditions (culled from §9-307 and §1-201's definition of "buyer in the ordinary course of business" that a §9-307 buyer must meet to purchase free of the prior security interest:

(1) He must be a buyer in the ordinary course

(2) who does not buy in bulk and does not take his interest as security for or in total or partial satisfaction of a pre-existing debt (that is, he must give some form of "new" value)

(3) who buys from one in the business of selling goods of that kind (that is, cars from a car dealer, i.e. inventory);

(4) who buys in good faith and without knowledge that his purchase is in violation of others' ownership rights or security interests, and

(5) does not buy farm products from a person engaged in farming operations, and

(6) the competing security interest must be one "created by his seller."

White & Summers §25-13, at 1067.

PROBLEM 58

Octopus National Bank had a perfected security interest in all cars on Smiles Motors' lot. Smiles owed $5000 in past due insurance premiums to its insurance agent, Howard Teeth, who showed up one morning to buy a new car from Smiles. The president of Smiles first gave Howard a check for $5000, but Howard indorsed it back over to Smiles when he saw a new car he wanted to buy. Is Howard a §1-201(9) "buyer in the ordinary course of business" so as to take free of ONB's security interest? See Chrysler Credit Corp. v. Malone, 502 S.W.2d 910, 13 U.C.C. Rep. Serv. 964 (Tex. Civ. App. 1973).

PROBLEM 59

Wonder Spa, Inc. pledged 50 of its promissory notes to the Conservative State Bank and Trust Company (hereinafter CSB) in return for a loan. The bank took possession of the notes. (Possession, you will recall, is the *only* way to perfect a security interest in an instrument; §9-304(1).) The spa asked to have 10 of the notes back for presentment to the makers for payment, and the bank duly turned over the notes, which Wonder Spa sold (*discounted*) to Octopus National Bank, a bona fide purchaser without knowledge of CSB's interest. This resale was in direct violation of the spa's agreement with CSB. Which bank is entitled to the instruments? Read §§9-

304(5)(b) and 9-309. Is ONB one of the parties protected by §9-309? See §§3-302 and 3-305. Would the result change if the instruments were technically non-negotiable or were attached to retail sales contracts containing security agreements so that they become chattel paper under §9-105(1)(b)? Read §9-308; see North Central Kansas Prod. Credit Assn. v. Boese, 19 U.C.C. Rep. Serv. 179 (D. Kan. 1976).

Subsection (2) to §9-307 appears at first glance to apply to more situations than it really fits. It is meant to cover only a rare transaction: a sale by a consumer to a consumer. White & Summers §25-14; Balon v. Cadillac Auto. Co., 303 A.2d 194, 12 U.C.C. Rep. Serv. 397 (N.H. 1973); Everett Natl. Bank v. Deschuiteneer, 109 N.H. 112, 244 A.2d 196, 5 U.C.C. Rep. Serv. 561 (1968). In such a sale the buyer takes free of the seller's creditor's security interest only if the buyer is ignorant of it and if there is no financing statement on file.

PROBLEM 60

Andy Audio bought a stereo receiver on credit from Voice of Japan, Inc., an electronics store, giving it a purchase money security interest in the receiver. Voice of Japan did not file a financing statement. Six months later when Andy still owed Voice of Japan $300, he held a garage sale and sold the receiver to Nancy Neighbor for $200 cash. If Andy stops making payments to Voice of Japan, can it repossess the receiver from Nancy? See §9-307(2), and its Official Comment 3.

PROBLEM 61

The Repossession Finance Company had a perfected (filed) security interest in White Truck Ice Cream, Inc.'s (hereafter WTIC) equipment (the company sold ice cream to children from trucks that traveled through the city's neighborhoods). Though technically a corporation, WTIC was in actuality a family business, and Bill White-Truck himself was frequently the driver of one of the trucks. One day while making his rounds, Bill met Frank Family, a consumer who asked about buying an ice cream making machine for his family. Bill promptly sold him one of the machines the company owned, for which Frank paid cash. When WTIC failed to make its payments, the finance company lived up to its name and repossessed all equipment. When

Frank refused to turn over the ice cream machine, Repossession sued him for conversion (a tort that does not require "scienter" or guilty knowledge for its commission). Does he lose? Compare §§9-201, 9-311, 9-306(2), and Production Credit Assn. v. Nowatzski, 90 Wis. 2d 344, 280 N.W.2d 118, 26 U.C.C. Rep. Serv. 1338 (1979).

PROBLEM 62

Burroughs Bank had a perfected security interest in John Clayton's car. When the vehicle was totaled in an accident, the Porter Insurance Company sent John a check for the value of the car. Is Porter Insurance (in effect a buyer of the car) guilty of conversion? See Judah AMC & Jeep, Inc. v. Old Rep. Ins. Co., 293 N.W.2d 212, 29 U.C.C. Rep. Serv. 687 (Iowa 1980) (no), and Terra W. Corp. v. Berry & Co., 207 Neb. 28, 295 N.W.2d 693, 29 U.C.C. Rep. Serv. 1046 (1980) (no).

PROBLEM 63

Paul Pop was a rock singer to whom Octopus National Bank loaned $8000 so he could buy stereo equipment. On April 2, Paul purchased the equipment, and on April 10, ONB filed its financing statement in the proper place. However in the interim, on April 8, Paul sold the equipment to Used Stereo Heaven, which bought with no knowledge of the bank's purchase money security interest. Does ONB or Used Stereo Heaven have the superior claim to the equipment? Compare §§2-403, 9-201, 9-301, and 9-312(4).

PROBLEM 64

Farmer Carl sold eggs and vegetables from a roadside stand. All his farm products were covered by a perfected (filed) security interest in favor of the Farmers Friend Financing Company (hereinafter FFFC). Betty Consumer bought a large number of eggs from the stand one Monday morning (she was gathering ingredients for an orgy of baking — it was state fair time). That afternoon Carl filed for bankruptcy and FFFC sent a truck around to Betty's house demanding the eggs back. Legally must she turn them over? See United States v. Pete Brown Enterp., Inc., 328 F. Supp. 600, 9 U.C.C. Rep. Serv. 734 (N.D. Miss. 1971). FFFC's position is stronger if it can point to a provision in the security agreement whereby Farmer Carl agreed not to sell the farm products without the consent of FFFC. But what if they knew he was violating this provision? Can a security interest be *waived*?

Clovis National Bank v. Thomas

77 N.M. 554, 425 P.2d 726, 4 U.C.C. Rep. Serv. 137 (N.M. 1967)

OMAN, J. This is a suit by plaintiff-appellant for alleged conversion of cattle by defendant-appellee. The parties operate their respective businesses in Clovis, Curry County, New Mexico, and will be referred to as plaintiff and defendant.

In its capacity as a bank, plaintiff, on March 27, 1963, loaned the sum of $8,800 to a Mr. W. D. Bunch. To evidence and secure the indebtedness he gave plaintiff a promissory note and a security agreement by which he granted a security interest in about 46 head of cattle belonging to him and branded "W D Bar." On April 11, 1963 a further security agreement, granting a security interest in 102 head of cattle, was given by him to plaintiff as additional security for the loan of March 27, and as security for additional loans to be made to him by plaintiff from time to time.

On July 29, 1963, he deposited $3,507 with plaintiff. This money represented proceeds from the sale by him of 35 head of cattle covered by the security agreements. $3,300 of this amount was applied by plaintiff on the indebtedness then owing by him.

On October 29, 1963, he deposited with plaintiff the sum of $5,613.17, the total amount of which was applied to his indebtedness, and which amount represented proceeds from the sale by him of 56 head of cattle covered by the security agreements. This deposit consisted of two checks given by defendant, who is a licensed commission house and market agency and as such handled the sale of the cattle for him.

Plaintiff admitted to being aware that Mr. Bunch was making sales of cattle covered by the security agreements.

In about September 1963, he made application to plaintiff for an additional loan with which to purchase additional cattle and with which to carry his cattle through the winter. An investigation was made by plaintiff during September, to determine the feasibility of granting this additional loan. Plaintiff approved the loan, and cattle were acquired by him and paid for by drafts drawn on plaintiff. By November 12, 1963, the additional cattle had been acquired.

On November 12, a new note in the principal amount of $21,500 and a new security agreement covering 283 head of cattle branded W D Bar were given by him to plaintiff to evidence and secure his then indebtedness. This indebtedness in the amount of $21,500 represented $2,007.67 still owing on the original note of March 27, $2,743.10 credited to his checking account on November 12, and amounts loaned or advanced to him during the intervening period. The security agreement was duly recorded in both Curry and Quay counties and in part provided:

> DEBTOR FURTHER REPRESENTS, WARRANTS, AND AGREES THAT: . . .
>
> Without the prior written consent of Secured Party, Debtor will not sell, . . . or otherwise dispose of the collateral. . . .

Thereafter, cattle covered by the November 12 security agreement were consigned to defendant by Mr. Bunch for sale on his behalf at public auction. The plaintiff had no actual knowledge of these sales and had not given any express consent to Mr. Bunch to make the sales. He remitted no part of the proceeds from these sales to the plaintiff for application on his indebtedness. The sales were of 45 head of cattle on February 20, 1964, 95 head on May 14, 1964, and one head on May 21, 1964. The total value of these cattle was $16,450.34, and plaintiff sought recovery from defendant of this amount under the first cause of action of its complaint.

Mr. Bunch has a son by the name of William D. Bunch, Jr., also known as Bill Bunch, Jr., who will be referred to either by name or as the son. The son was the owner of a brand referred to as "Swastika K." Some time prior to July 15, 1964, at least 90 head of cattle were acquired by either Mr. Bunch or his son and were branded Swastika K. There was some evidence tending to show that these cattle, at least to some extent, were actually property of the father. No security agreement was ever given by either the father or the son by which a security interest in cattle branded Swastika K was granted to the plaintiff, unless in some way it can be held that they were covered by the security agreement of November 12.

On July 15, 1964, plaintiff requested that Mr. Bunch sell the remainder of his cattle, including the Swastika K cattle. On the following day, 90 head of Swastika K cattle were trucked to defendant's place of business for sale and were carried on the defendant's records as belonging to Bill Bunch, Jr. Plaintiff knew the cattle were at defendant's place of business to be sold and told defendant that plaintiff claimed some interest in the cattle. Defendant was not told the nature or extent of the claimed interest of plaintiff in these cattle.

The cattle were sold on July 16. Plaintiff was aware of the sale and advised defendant that it would be "nice" if the check in payment for these cattle could be made payable to one or both of the Bunches and to the plaintiff. At no time did the plaintiff demand payment or request that defendant not make payment to Bill Bunch, Jr.

Bill Bunch, Jr., consulted the local brand inspector and solicited his aid in securing payment from the defendant. The brand inspector advised defendant that the Swastika K brand was recorded in the name of Bill Bunch, Jr., and that insofar as the Cattle Sanitary Board was concerned, payment could be made to him.

An attorney also called defendant on behalf of Bill Bunch, Jr., concerning payment for the cattle, and demand was made by Bill Bunch, Jr., upon defendant to pay him the proceeds from the sale of the cattle. This the defendant did on July 22. This payment was in the amount of $7,777.84, which is the amount of plaintiff's claim against defendant under the second cause of action.

On this same date, plaintiff filed suit against W. D. Bunch and William D. Bunch, Jr., wherein plaintiff sought to recover from the father on the note of November 12, and sought to recover from the son the said sum of $7,777.84. In this proceeding plaintiff filed an affidavit in support of an application for a writ of garnishment, wherein it was asserted that the defendant was indebted to William D. Bunch, Jr. No claim was made that the proceeds from the sale belonged to plaintiff, but rather plaintiff asserted that the proceeds belonged to William D. Bunch, Jr., and, as already stated, tried to reach these proceeds by garnishment, which came too late. The present suit was then filed against defendant on August 31, 1964.

The plaintiff asserts thirteen separate points relied upon for reversal. However, the ultimate conclusions upon which the judgment for defendant rests are (1) the plaintiff consented to the sales of W D Bar cattle covered by the security agreement of November 12, and thus waived any possessory rights it may have had in these cattle, and (2) the plaintiff had no perfected security interest in the Swastika K cattle, and failed to prove an unperfected security interest in these cattle of which defendant had knowledge.

Insofar as the sales of the W D Bar cattle are concerned, the trial court found plaintiff, as a matter of common practice, usage and procedure, permitted Mr. Bunch to sell cattle covered by the security agreements of March 27 and April 11, and consented to receipt of the sale proceeds by Mr. Bunch. It also found that plaintiff, by common practice, custom, usage and procedure, permitted and consented to the sales of W D Bar cattle covered by the security agreement of November 12, and permitted and consented to the receipt by Mr. Bunch of the proceeds from these sales.

The trial court concluded that plaintiff had permitted, acquiesced in, and consented to these sales; that by its conduct, plaintiff had waived any possessory rights it may have had in and to these cattle; that defendant did not wrongfully convert cattle in which plaintiff had an enforceable security interest; and that defendant was not responsible for the debtor's failure to remit the proceeds of the sales to plaintiff.

We agree with the findings and conclusions of trial court. Insofar as consent and waiver on behalf of plaintiff are concerned, in addition to the facts recited above, the plaintiff's officers testified that it was the custom and practice of plaintiff to permit a debtor, who has given cattle as collateral, to retain possession and to sell the collateral without ever obtaining prior written consent of plaintiff, and that at no time in its dealings with Mr. Bunch between the time of the making of the note on November 12, 1963, and the sale of cattle on May 21, 1964, did plaintiff demand of him that he obtain prior written consent before making a sale.

It is true there was some testimony that the collateral was not released from the lien until the debtor actually delivered the proceeds of the sale to plaintiff, but, as testified to by one of the plaintiff's officers, the debtor never contacts the plaintiff and secures permission to make a sale, but the sale is made and plaintiff relies upon the debtor to bring the proceeds to plaintiff to be applied on the indebtedness. This practice is followed because 99% of the people with whom plaintiff deals are honest and take care of their obligations.

The general rule of liability of an auctioneer, who sells, in behalf of his principal, property subject to a mortgage lien, is stated as follows in the annotation at 96 ALR2d 208, 212 (1964):

> According to the overwhelming weight of authority, an auctioneer who sells property on behalf of a principal who has not title thereto, or who holds the property subject to a mortgage or other lien, or who for other reasons has no right to sell such property, is personally liable to the true owner or mortgagee for conversion regardless of whether he had knowledge, actual or constructive of the principal's lack of title or want of authority to sell, in the absence

> of facts creating an estoppel or showing acquiescence or consent on the part of the true owner or mortgagee. . . .

The trial court, in addition to holding plaintiff had consented to and acquiesced in the sales and had waived his possessory rights in the cattle, concluded plaintiff was estopped from recovery by reason of its conduct. The plaintiff and the amicus curiae have both made strong attacks on this conclusion. We are inclined to agree that the essential elements of an estoppel are lacking. We do not, however, predicate our decision upon estoppel, but rather upon consent and waiver.

The plaintiff, if not expressly consenting to the questioned sales, certainly impliedly acquiesced in and consented thereto. It not only permitted Mr. Bunch, but permitted all its other debtors who granted security interests in cattle, to retain possession of the cattle and to sell the same from time to time as the debtor chose, and it relied upon the honesty of each debtor to bring in the proceeds from his sales to be applied on his indebtedness.

Plaintiff was fully aware of its right to require its written authority to sell or otherwise dispose of the collateral, but it elected to waive this right. Waiver is the intentional abandonment or relinquishment of a known right. Smith v. New York Life Ins. Co., 26 N.M. 408, 193 Pac. 67; Miller v. Phoenix Assur. Co. Ltd., 52 N.M. 68, 191 P.2d 993.

In Farmers' Nat. Bank v. Missouri Livestock Comm. Co., 53 F.2d 991 (8th Cir. 1931), suit was brought by the holder of chattel mortgages for alleged conversion of cattle by a livestock commission house. Although the facts are dissimilar from those of the present case, that case does stand for the principle that consent may be established by implication arising from a course of conduct as well as by express words, and that consent to a sale operates as a waiver of the lien or security interest. See also Moffet Bros. & Andrews Comm. Co. v. Kent, 5 S.W.2d 395 (Mo. 1928).

In First Nat. Bank & Trust Co. v. Stock Yards Loan Co., 65 F.2d 226 (8th Cir. 1933), the effect of a course of conduct on the part of a mortgagee, such as was followed by the mortgagee in that case and such as was followed by plaintiff in the present case, was stated to be:

> . . . When a mortgagee under a chattel mortgage allows the mortgagor to retain possession of the property and to sell the same at will, the mortgagee waives his lien, and this is true whether the purchaser knew of the existence of the chattel mortgage or not.

The fact that plaintiff may have intended that the proceeds from the sales of cattle covered by the security agreements should be remitted to plaintiff by Mr. Bunch for application on his indebtedness did not change the waiver. When plaintiff consented to the sales and the collection of the proceeds of the sales by him, it lost its security interest in the collateral and was then looking to him personally for payment.

The collateral here in question — livestock, falls within the classification of "farm products," and these products are expressly excluded from the classifications of "equipment" and "inventory." Section 9-109(3), NMSA 1953. By excluding "farm products" from the classifications of "equipment" and "inventory," and by expressly providing in §9-307(1), NMSA 1953, that a buyer in the ordinary course of business of farm products from a person engaged in farming operations does not take free of a security interest created by the seller, the draftsmen of the code apparently intended "to freeze the agricultural mortgagee into the special status he has achieved under the pre-code case law." 2 Gilmore, Security Interests in Personal Property 714 (1965).

It would only seem logical and consistent that if the buyer from one engaged in farming operations takes subject to the security interest, then the selling agent is subject to the rights of the secured party in the collateral. This is consistent with the foregoing cited authorities. See also United States v. Union Livestock Sales Co., 298 F.2d 755 (4th Cir. 1962); United States v. Matthews, 244 F.2d 626 (9th Cir. 1957).

Section 9-306(2), NMSA 1953 provides:

> Except where this article otherwise provides, a security interest continues in collateral notwithstanding sale, exchange or other disposition thereof by the debtor unless his action was authorized by the secured party in the security agreement or otherwise, and also continues in any identifiable proceeds including collections received by the debtor.

No section of the code provides otherwise as to farm products. Thus, the holder of the security interest in farm products has the same protection under the code which he had under the pre-code law, and the cattle broker is still liable to the secured party for conversion of the collateral. United States v. Sommerville, 211 F. Supp. 843 (W.D. Pa. 1962), *aff'd on other grounds,* 324 F.2d 712 (3rd Cir. 1963), *cert. denied* 376 U.S. 909 (1964). See also 2 Gilmore, Security Interests in Personal Property 715 (1965).

Also, under the code the secured party may consent to the sale of the collateral, and thereby waive his rights in the same. See Official Comment No. 3, §9-306, and Official Comment No. 2, §9-307. There being no particular provision of the Code which displaces the law of waiver, and particularly waiver by implied acquiescence or consent, the code provisions are supplemented thereby. Section 1-103, NMSA 1953. The defendant cannot be held liable for a conversion of the W D Bar cattle, because plaintiff consented to and acquiesced on the sales thereof, and thereby waived its rights in this collateral. . . .

It follows from what has been stated that the judgment should be affirmed. It is so ordered.

CHAVEZ, C.J., NOBLE COMPTON, J.J. concur. CARMODY, J. (dissenting). [Omitted.]

NOTE

The New Mexico legislature responded by amending the UCC to provide that course of dealing or trade usage could not have the effect of waiving a security interest in farm products. The court did not consider the effect of §1-205(4); had it, would the result have changed? Compare Official Comment 2 to §1-205 with §2-208(3). Later courts have generally (though not always) followed *Clovis*. See the case law summary in Hedrick Sav. Bank v. Myers, 229 N.W.2d 252, 16 U.C.C. Rep. Serv. 1412 (Iowa 1975). Some courts have developed a "conditional consent" test whereby the waiver is ineffective unless the condition under which it was made (typically payment of the proceeds to the secured party) is complied with; see, e.g., Farmers St. Bank v. Edison Non-Stock Coop., 190 Neb. 789, 212 N.E.2d 625, 13 U.C.C. Rep. Serv. 728 (1973); Baker Prod. Credit Assn. v. Long Creek Meat Co., 97 Ore. 1372, 513 P.2d 1129, 13 U.C.C. Rep. Serv. 531 (1973). Other courts, noting that the bank's "waiver" is really nothing more than the acceptance of a fait accompli ("I sold the collateral even though I said I wouldn't; here's the money"), have not permitted such a "course of dealing" to override the express selling prohibition of the security agreement; see §1-205(4); Wabasso St. Bank v. Caldwell Packing Co., 251 N.W.2d 321, 19 U.C.C. Rep. Serv. 315 (Minn. 1976). At the time of many of these decisions the revised version of Article 9 was not in effect. How does the new language of §9-402(7)'s last sentence affect the waiver argument? See In re Matto's, Inc., 8 B.R. 485, 30 U.C.C. Rep. Serv. 1750 (Ref. Bankr., E.D. Mich. 1981). One other note: fair or not, it is the rule that no agent of the United States government has actual or apparent authority to waive the government's security interests. United

States v. Hughes, 340 F. Supp. 539, 10 U.C.C. Rep. Serv. 697 (N.D. Miss. 1972).

For an informative discussion of the meaning of "conversion" in Article 9, see Mammoth Cave Prod. Credit Assn. v. Oldham, 569 S.W.2d 833, 25 U.C.C. Rep. Serv. 603 (Tenn. App. 1977).

PROBLEM 65

Mr. and Mrs. Halyard purchased a large sailboat with money borrowed from the Boilerplate National Bank (hereinafter BNB), which took a security interest therein and promptly filed a financing statement in the proper place. The Halyards sold the boat to Oil Slick Boat Sales, Inc., a used boat concern, telling Oil Slick of the bank's interest and of the necessity of making monthly payments to the bank. Oil Slick turned around and resold the boat to Mr. and Mrs. Blink, innocent people who paid full value for the boat believing Oil Slick had clear title. When BNB did not receive its usual monthly payment it investigated, found the boat, and repossessed it. Has the Blinks' property been converted or don't they fit into §9-307? What does "created by his seller" mean in §9-307(1)? See White & Summers at 1070-1071. Does Article 2's "entrusting" rule, §9-403, help the Blinks? What is §2-403 relationship with Article 9? See White & Summers §25-15; National Shawmut Bank v. Jones, 108 N.H. 386, 236 A.2d 484, 4 U.C.C. Rep. Serv. 1021 (1967). The actual case on which this problem is based is Security Pac. Nat. Bank v. Goodman, 100 Cal. Rptr. 763, 10 U.C.C. Rep. Serv. 529 (Cal. App. 1972). The "created by his seller" language will often cause trouble for buyers buying goods from a used merchandise dealer. Where no Article 9 security agreement is involved, §2-403 always controls problems involving purchases in the ordinary course of business. Apeco Corp. v. Bishop Mobile Homes, Inc., 506 S.W.2d 711, 14 U.C.C Rep. Ser. 680 (Tex. Civ. App. 1974); Simpson v. Moon, 137 Ga. App. 82, 222 S.E.2d 873, 18 U.C.C. Rep. Serv. 1191 (1975). If the Blinks lose this lawsuit, they should sue Oil Slick for breach of the warranty of title found in §2-312.

E. *ARTICLE 2 CLAIMANTS*

PROBLEM 66

Jack Gladhand was a traveling salesman. He needed new luggage and bought a set from Alligator Fashions, which reserved a security interest therein and had him sign a financing statement. The store, however, did not file the financing statement since it assumed the luggage was meant to be consumer goods. Jack had said nothing to create this impression; in fact he planned to use the luggage to carry his samples in. A month later, in the middle of a hot sales deal, Jack sold all of his samples *and* the luggage to Mark Impulse, a compulsive buyer. Jack told Mark (who paid cash for the goods) that the luggage was genuine alligator (a lie — he knew it was lizard). When Mark discovered the truth he revoked his acceptance of the goods pursuant to §2-608 and claimed a security interest in the goods. Read §2-711(3). On learning of Jack's resale to Mark and of the latter's revocation of acceptance, Alligator Fashions quickly filed its financing statement in the appropriate place. Who is entitled to the luggage? See §§9-113 and 9-312(5). If Alligator Fashions had filed before Mark revoked acceptance, who would prevail?

The rights of an unpaid seller are governed by both Article 2 and Article 9. If the seller gets a security agreement, a purchase money security interest (§9-107) arises and Article 9 handles the priority in §§9-312(3) and (4). If the seller extends credit to the buyer but fails to reserve a security interest, §2-702 applies. Finally if the buyer gets the goods and pays with a check that is then dishonored ("N.S.F." — "not sufficient funds"), the seller's rights are governed by §§2-403, 2-507, and 2-511 (which you should now read), and not §2-702. Section 2-702 applies only to credit sales, and where the seller took a check only a cash transaction was intended. At common law the *cash sale* doctrine permitted the seller to recover the goods when the check bounced. The continued vitality of this doctrine under the UCC is a much debated issue. Read the Official Comments to §2-403 and In re Samuels & Co., Inc., below, the leading (and controversial) case.

In re Samuels & Co., Inc.

510 F.2d 139, 16 U.C.C. Rep. Serv. 577 (5th Cir. 1975)

INGRAHAM, J. . . . Samuels & Co., Inc., is a Texas meatpacking firm that purchases, processes and packages meat and sells the meat within and without the State of Texas. Since 1963 Samuels' operations, including its cattle purchases, have been financed on a weekly basis by C.I.T. Corporation. To secure its financing,

C.I.T. has properly perfected a lien on Samuels' assets, inventory and all after-acquired property, including livestock that is from time to time purchased for slaughter and processing.

From May 12 through May 23, 1969, the appellants, fifteen cattle farmers, delivered their cattle to Samuels. Although the sellers did not receive payment for the sale simultaneously with delivery of the cattle, checks were subsequently issued to the sellers. On May 23, 1969, before these checks had been paid, C.I.T., believing itself to be insecure, refused to advance any more funds to Samuels for the operation of the packing plant. On that same day Samuels filed a petition in bankruptcy. Since C.I.T. refused to advance more funds, although apparently aware that there were unpaid checks outstanding, the appellants' checks issued in payment for cattle were dishonored by the drawee bank.

Because of the fungible nature of the cattle, the beef has long since been butchered and processed and sold through the normal course of business. The proceeds from the cattle sales have been deposited with the trustee in bankruptcy pending the outcome of this litigation. The issues in this case concern the priority of interest in these proceeds between a creditor of the debtor, which holds a perfected security interest in the debtor's after-acquired property, and a seller of goods to the debtor. Since the sellers have not been paid, they claim a superior right to the deposited proceeds and argue that they are now entitled to payment out of these proceeds. The finance corporation, on the other hand, contends that the sellers are merely unsecured creditors of the bankrupt and are not entitled to a prior claim to the funds, and alternately that the finance corporation qualified as a good faith purchaser of the cattle and is therefore immune to the sellers' claims of non-payment. For the reasons that follow, we conclude that the sellers should prevail.

I

In order to determine which provisions of the Texas Business & Commerce Code govern the relationships among the parties, the first question that must be resolved is whether this commercial venture was a cash or credit transaction. The significance of classifying a sale as a cash or credit transaction relates back to the common law and the historical passing of title concept. Under the common law, a sale for cash, as opposed to a sale on credit, meant that the seller of goods implicitly reserved the incidents of ownership or title to the goods until payment was made in full. If the buyer failed to make payment, the seller could regain possession of the goods by instituting an action in replevin. Additionally, since the buyer of goods for cash did not obtain title to the goods until the seller was paid, the defaulting buyer was incapable of passing title to a third party. Based on the cash sale doctrine, an unpaid seller could even reclaim goods sold by an intermediary to one who otherwise qualified as a bona fide purchaser.

When the owner of goods sold them on credit, however, all the incidents of ownership, including title, passed to the buyer. If the buyer subsequently failed to make payment, the seller's rights were only those of a creditor for the purchase price, and he had no right against the merchandise. Since in a sale on credit the buyer obtained all the incidents of ownership in the goods, including title, he was able to convey his interest in the goods, absolute ownership, to a third party without recourse on behalf of the seller. Corman, Cash Sales, Worthless Checks and the Bona Fide Purchaser, 10 Vanderbilt Law Review 55 (1956); Gilmore, The Commercial Doctrine of Good Faith Purchaser, 63 Yale L.J. 1057, 1060 & n.10 (1954).

Underlying the different characteristics and consequences of cash and credit sales are the expectations and intentions of the three parties concerned. When goods are sold for cash, the seller is assuming virtually no risk of loss because he believes that he has full payment for the goods in his hands. When the sale is for credit, however, the seller assumes a far more substantial risk and voluntarily relinquishes the incidents of ownership to the buyer. The buyer, possessed of these incidents of ownership, is capable of conveying title to a bona fide purchaser, completely terminating the rights of the seller in the goods. The credit seller recognizes that he will receive full payment for his merchandise only if the business of the buyer progresses normally and sales are made to third parties in the normal course of business. Note, The Owner's Intent and the Negotiability of Chattels: A Critique of Section 2-403 of the Uniform Commercial Code, 72 Yale L.J. 1205, 1220 (1963). Although commercial transactions and the law governing such relationships has developed significantly since the conception of these doctrines, this reasoning with respect to the different risks assumed by the different sellers underlie and differentiate the two concepts and is as valid a distinction today as it was when the doctrines were originally conceived.

The Uniform Commercial Code as adopted by the State of

Texas has to some extent modified the common law doctrines of cash and credit sales. It is clear that the historical concept of passing title to goods is not emphasized in the Code, and the location of title generally is not regarded as being determinative of the rights of adverse parties. Helstad, Deemphasis of Title Under the Uniform Commercial Code, 1964 Wisconsin L.R. 362. Instead of implementing the fictional concept of title, the countervailing interests of the parties are sometimes defined in terms of various rights, privileges, powers and immunities.

But even though the title concept is so reduced in significance, the Code recognizes and adopts the fundamental distinctions of the common law between cash and credit sales, at least with respect to the rights of the unpaid seller against the defaulting buyer. The Code deals with a sale on credit in provisions separate from those dealing with cash sales. Section 2-702 specifically sets forth the credit seller's remedy and provides that when "the seller discovers that the buyer has received goods on credit while insolvent, he may reclaim the goods upon demand made within ten days after receipt . . ." Texas Business and Commerce Code, §2-702(2), VTCA (1968). This provision goes on to define the seller's priority rights against other specific parties, providing that "[t]he seller's right to reclaim under Subsection (b) is subject to the rights of a buyer in the ordinary course or other good faith purchaser or lien creditor under this chapter (Section 2-403)." Id. §2-702(3). Although this section authorizes a limited right against the goods, it generally recognizes that when the sale is on a credit basis, all the incidents of ownership pass to the buyer who may then convey this interest to certain third parties. The seller stands merely as a general creditor for the purchase price.

With respect to cash sales, however, §2-507 of the Code explicitly recognizes that "unless otherwise agreed," "[w]here payment is due and demanded on the delivery to the buyer of goods . . . , [the buyer's] right as against the seller to retain or dispose of them is conditional upon his making payment due." Texas Business and Commerce Code, §2-507(2) (1968). Like the cash sale doctrine at common law, §2-507 provides that when the buyer is to pay cash for the goods, the validity of the transaction is dependent upon his making payment, and when the buyer fails to pay, he does not even have the right to possess the goods. Absolute ownership does not pass to the buyer until payment is complete.

The limited interest conveyed to the buyer prior to payment under §2-507(2) is reemphasized in §2-511(3), which deals specifically with the situation where payment for goods is made by check that is later dishonored. Section 2-511(3) provides that payment by check "is conditional and is defeated as between the parties by dishonor of the check on due presentment." Texas Business and Commerce Code, §2-511(3) (1968). Underlying this provision is the principle that, in order to encourage and facilitate commercial sales and economic growth generally, the recipient of a check in payment for goods "is not to be penalized in any way" for accepting this commercially acceptable mode of payment. Id. Comment 4.

Even though the Code deemphasizes the title concept of the common law, these two provisions strongly suggest that the underlying philosophy of the common law cash sale doctrine has been embodied here. Like the traditional cash sale doctrine, the existence of a valid contractual relationship between the buyer and seller is dependent upon the buyer's completing his part of the bargain and paying for the merchandise. When the buyer fails to pay, he no longer has even the right to possess the goods.

Mindful of these principles we turn to the facts of the instant case to determine whether the sale of the cattle to the packing house was on a cash or credit basis. This sale of goods must be regarded as a cash transaction rather than a credit transaction because of the established course of dealing between the buyer and sellers. A course of dealing, as defined by the Texas Commercial Code, is a "sequence of previous conduct between the parties to a particular transaction which is fairly to be regarded as establishing a common basis of understanding for interpreting their expressions and other conduct." Texas Business and Commercial Code, §1-205(1) (1968).

According to the [Packers and Stockyards] Act and regulations, when a cattle grower sells his livestock on what is termed a "grade and yield" basis, the contract price to be paid is left open because it has yet to be determined. Before the purchase price can be determined, the cattle must be slaughtered and the carcasses chilled for twenty-four hours. After the meat is chilled, the Department of Agriculture grades it and determines the yield, and at that time the contract price can be set. When the price is set, a point sometime after delivery, a check is issued to the seller, 9 CFR §§201.43(b)-99.

While a lapse of time occurring between delivery of the cattle and payment, even if only a day, might be considered an extension of credit, the course of dealing between the parties establishes that this was a sale for cash. The delay between delivery and payment was not credit, but rather was a result of a procedure mandated by the Act and regulations that governed the relationship between the buyer and seller when cattle are sold on a grade and yield basis. This procedure apparently had been followed since the inception of the regulations requiring such conduct. Moreover, not only do the Act and regulations prescribe such a course of conduct, all the cattle sellers regarded this commercial venture as a cash transaction, and there is nothing in the record to suggest that the buyer regarded the delay in issuing the check as credit. The course of conduct prescribed by the Act and regulations, coupled with the undisputed intent of the cattle sellers, compels the conclusion that this was a cash and not a credit affair. Engstrom v. Wiley, 191 F.2d 634 (9th Cir. 1951); In re Helms Veneer Corp., 287 F. Supp. 840 (WD Va, 1968).

Having so concluded, we turn to §§2-507 and 2-511 in order to define the cash seller's rights and remedies. Although §2-702, dealing solely with credit sales, specifically outlines the seller's right to reclaim the property and sets forth priorities as to certain third parties, neither §§2-507 or 2-511 explicitly define the cash seller's rights or priorities. The only indication of the seller's rights is in the comment following §2-507, which implicitly authorizes the seller's right to reclaim and simultaneously imposes a ten day limit on that right when the buyer is insolvent. In re Mort, 208 F. Supp. 309 (E.D. Pa., 1962); Greater Louisville Auto Auction v. Ogle Buick, Inc., 387 S.W.2d 17 (Ky. Ct. App. 1965); J. White & R. Summers, The Uniform Commercial Code, 98 (1972); Kinyon, Outline of Buyer-Seller Rights and Remedies in Default and Breach Situations Under the UCC, 53 Minn. L.R. 729, 731 (1969).

While armed with a right to reclaim the cattle, the sellers failed to comply with the ten day limitation on that right. The record shows that the sellers did not file a petition for reclamation for almost a year. The Code does not arbitrarily impose this limitation on the seller's rights, but does so in order to conform with the fundamental policies of the Code and the Bankruptcy Act. By imposing this limitation, a creditor is required to promptly disclose and identify his claim to property in the bankrupt's estate so that other creditors will not prejudice themselves. Otherwise, a creditor might extend credit to the bankrupt subsequent to its filing a petition on the basis of a misapprehension that the bankrupt possesses unencumbered assets. Additionally, when all the claims are promptly disclosed, the objective of the Bankruptcy Act, equitable distribution of the bankrupt's assets among its creditors, is more fully assured. See J. White and R. Summers, The Uniform Commercial Code 872 (1972).

Although the sellers did not reclaim the property until sometime after the filing of Samuels' petition for bankruptcy, the purposes for imposing the limitation had been fulfilled. C.I.T. in its own behalf filed a reclamation petition on or before July 23, 1969, only about two weeks after the petition in bankruptcy was filed. A hearing was held, and on August 13, 1969, the referee in bankruptcy entered an order generally outlining C.I.T.'s claims to the assets and inventory of the bankrupt. In demonstrating its claim to Samuels' assets, there apparently was extensive disclosure of Samuels' financial affairs, all of which, as noted later, C.I.T. was intimately aware. At the end of the order, the referee noted that "the asserted lien rights other than the debtor, C.I.T. Corporation and the receiver, are in no way prejudiced hereby and the court reserves for further consideration any question pertaining to conflicting claims of liens or lien priorities."

While all the claims were not particularized in the referee's order, the hearing and order disclosed many claims against the estate and demonstrated to the parties involved the great likelihood of other claims being asserted against the assets. The record does not disclose that any creditors prejudiced themselves by extending credit on what they believed to be unencumbered assets. Indeed, because C.I.T. had such an in depth knowledge of Samuels' financial affairs, it was well aware of the claims of the cattle sellers that were unpaid as a result of its refusal to advance more money. Recognizing the many conflicting claims against the estate, the referee wisely preserved the current state of affairs and specifically refrained from adjudicating any additional disputes until a later date.

Nor does the seller's ultimate reclamation of the cattle, or rather proceeds from sale of the cattle, prejudice the rights of any creditors. When a sale is made on credit, the purchased merchandise belongs to the estate of the bankrupt and all the seller has is a security interest in the property. If the seller failed to perfect his interest, he stands as a general creditor with the rest of the unsecured creditors and is entitled only to his proportionate share of the bankrupt's estate. To allow him to recover his loss in full from the estate would prejudice the rights of the other creditors. In re Colacci's of America, Inc., Bar Control of Colorado v. Gifford, 13 UCC Rep. 1023 (10th Cir., 1973); Engstrom v. Wiley, supra, 191 F.2d at 689; Engelkes v. Farmers Co-op Co., 194 F. Supp. 319 (N.D. Iowa, 1961).

But when the sale is for cash, the merchandise belongs to the bankrupt's estate only if the buyer pays for the goods. If payment is not made, the seller is not a mere creditor and therefore is not compelled to share proportionately with the general creditors of the estate. The general creditors are not entitled to any portion of these assets because the goods do not belong to the bankrupt estate. The seller's reclamation of the goods does not remove any assets of the bankrupt in which general creditors would share and thus does not prejudice the rights of the seller on credit. Since the seller for cash is not a creditor and is not required to share with the general creditors in the estate as a creditor, he is entitled to his merchandise.

Also, C.I.T.'s initiation of the reclamation proceeding assisted in identifying the various creditors and thereby insured a more equitable distribution of the bankrupt's estate. When the various creditors and their claims are revealed at an early state, all the parties involved are able to assess the current financial status of the bankrupt and the probability of obtaining some return on the credit extended to the bankrupt. Early identification of the claims, plus the referee's preserving all creditors' rights until a later time, insured an equitable distribution of the estate.

Besides the underlying purpose of the ten day rule being satisfied, the facts show that the sellers made a faithful attempt to comply with the provisions of the Code. As pointed out by appellees, due to the sellers' misapprehension of the events culminating in Samuels' bankruptcy, the sellers' reclamation petition was not filed until almost a year after the filing of Samuels' bankruptcy petition. The sellers apparently believed that after Samuels filed the petition in bankruptcy on May 23, 1969, the packing house conducted normal operations. Only shortly after Samuels was adjudicated bankrupt on May 6, 1970, did the sellers file their petition for reclamation. Apparently the sellers thought that there was no need for them to assert their rights under the Code until after the adjudication of straight bankruptcy.

To add to the confusion, it is not clear from the Code that the sellers had any remedy to seek at all. While the Code sets forth the sellers' right to reclaim, under the peculiar facts of this case assertion of that right would seem futile. As pointed out earlier, the Packers and Stockyards Act and regulations issued thereunder require that when livestock is sold on a grade and yield basis, it must be slaughtered almost immediately and the carcasses chilled so that the purchase price can be determined. Through the normal processing thereafter the carcasses are butchered and packaged and the identity of the cattle is lost. Since each owner's property could not be identified, it would seem to have been futile to assert the right to reclaim. A conclusion requiring such an exercise in futility certainly would not conform with reason. Additionally, the sellers never even had the opportunity to protect their property by reclamation because the identity of most of the cattle was destroyed when the petition in bankruptcy was filed.

Under these circumstances, strict application of a ten day limitation on the right to reclaim is unwarranted. The fundamental purposes of imposing the ten day limitation on the sellers' rights have been fulfilled and the sellers made an attempt to comply with the Code's terms. Reason and logic mandate that we not require a futile gesture on behalf of the sellers to reclaim their cattle when it had already lost its identity. The right to reclaim under §2-507, we think, has been properly preserved.

II

Having concluded that as between the seller and buyer, the seller is entitled to prevail, we turn to the sellers' rights as against the finance corporation. Relying basically on Article 9 provisions that outline priorities between perfected and unperfected security interests, C.I.T. first argues that any attempt by the sellers to retain title to the goods merely reserves an unperfected security interest and that this unperfected interest is subordinate to its perfected security interest covering Samuels' after-acquired property. Texas Business and Commerce Code, §9-301(1)(a) (1968); See Hogan, Unperfected Security Interests and the Floating Lien, 44 Tex. L.R. 713, 714 (1966).

It is true that §2-401(1) of the Code modifies an attempt to retain title to the retention of an unperfected security interest in the goods. And, indeed, if this interest was the only interest of the sellers, the application of Article 9 provisions would seem to cut off the sellers' rights. But closer examination of the Code provisions and the Code's underlying philosophy leads to the conclusion that these provisions do not contemplate a situation in which the sale is for cash and thus do not control the outcome of the litigation at hand.

Section 2-401(1) deals with the situation in which the seller of goods attempts to retain title to the goods, but the sale is nevertheless a credit transaction, not cash. A common example of this type of transaction is when goods are sold to a buyer, and the buyer is obligated to make periodic payments for the goods. Title to the goods, however, is not supposed to pass to the buyer until the last payment is made at the end of the term. See The Sherer-Gillett Co. v. Long, 318 Ill. 432, 149 N.E. 225 (1925).

But this simply is not the case when a sale is made for cash. In a cash sale the seller believes, and not unreasonably, that he has his payment in hand. The only phase of the transaction left uncompleted is the seller's cashing the check. All he has to do is put the check in the mail and wait for it to be cleared at the bank, or take the check directly to the bank and cash it. Because the limited time sequence, extending from the receipt of the check to its being cashed, is so short, it would be unreasonable to require the cash seller to follow the litany of the Code and take measures to perfect an alleged security interest. See Corman, Cash Sales, Worthless Checks and the Bona Fide Purchaser, 10 Vanderbilt L.R. 55, 65 (1965).

Presumably, any shifting of the loss from the purchaser to the seller that might be contemplated by the Code is based on the Code's provisions that authorize the seller to follow the prescribed steps and protect himself against loss. But because of the limited time sequence involved, the seller does not have the opportunity to protect himself. It would take more time and effort to protect his interest under the Code than to simply collect on the check. The reasons for limiting a sellers interest to an unperfected security interest simply do not exist in the cash sale transaction.[2]

2. In the event that a conflict among secured interest holders arises, the Code clearly provides that generally the unperfected interest will always be subordinate to the perfected interest. The only exception to this rule is the purchase money security interest. When the transaction involves inventory, the Code gives this particular interest priority over the perfected lien if, and only if, the holder perfects its interest when the buyer takes possession of the goods and the seller gives notice to the financer. Texas Business and Commerce Code, §§9-312(3)(a)-(b) (1968); Hogan, Unperfected Security Interests and the Floating Lien, 44 Tex. L.R. 713, 720 (1966).

But these requirements just further demonstrate the impracticality of requiring a cash seller to take steps to perfect and protect his interest in the goods sold. Plainly the cash seller need only cash his check and his interests are totally and undeniably protected, rather than follow the often confusing and more

Supporting the conclusion that the seller's rights are not cut off under Article 9 are the explicit provisions of the Code. Section 9-102 and the accompanying comments broadly define the scope of Article 9, but carefully limit its application to commercial transactions in which the parties intend to create security interests. As found by the referee, and it has not been contested in this court, each of the cattle sellers involved in this litigation regarded the sale to Samuels as a cash transaction, and there is nothing in the record to suggest that any of the parties involved thought it was anything but a cash sale. Selling goods on a credit basis involved the assumption of a far greater risk on the part of the seller than when the goods are sold for cash. To summarily label these sellers as holders of unperfected security interests would change entirely the nature of the transaction as it was intended by the parties, and alter the cash seller's status to one who thinks he has full payment for his goods to one in which he stands as a mere unsecured creditor. The Code was designed to supplement the agreement between the parties in commercial transactions where the parties failed to provide, not completely change the character of an existing relationship. See Bunn, Freedom of Contract Under the Uniform Commercial Code, 2 BC Ind. & Com. L.R. 59 (1960); J. White and R. Summers, The Uniform Commercial Code 6 (1972).

Even assuming the validity of C.I.T.'s argument that the sellers have only an unperfected security interest that is subordinate to their perfected interest, the finance corporation is still not entitled to prevail over the sellers. In order for C.I.T. to have a valid security interest in the cattle, three fundamental requirements must be met. First, the debtor and creditor must enter into an agreement and that agreement must be reduced to writing. The record is clear that C.I.T. had been financing Samuels' operations at least since 1963 and had a security interest in Samuels' assets and inventory. Second, the creditor must give value. The Code makes clear that an antecedent debt will constitute value. Third, the debtor must acquire rights in the collateral to which the lien

demanding provisions of the Code. Moreover, because at least some of the sellers delivered their cattle immediately prior to Samuels filing a petition for bankruptcy, it was practically impossible for them to comply with the requirements of the Code before Samuels closed its doors and C.I.T. asserted its claims to the cattle. Because of the impracticality demonstrated by an analysis of these provisions in light of the limited element, we do not think that the Code intended to limit the cash seller's rights only to an unperfected security interest and subject the seller to the consequences of holding such an undesirable interest.

can attach. It is with respect to the third element making up an enforceable security interest that gives rise to the difficulty in the case at hand.

Less than absolute ownership of goods has been deemed by the courts to be sufficient rights in property to which a lien on after-acquired property can attach. Although the location of title to the goods generally does not determine the rights of the parties, the Code provides that the title to goods follows their possession. Consequently if the presence of title made any difference, which it does not, title would seem to be in the debtor Samuels. In addition to possession of the cattle, Samuels had other rights incident to mere possession such as the right to begin slaughtering the cattle and processing and packaging the meat.

But even assuming that the debtor had sufficient rights in the collateral to which C.I.T.'s lien attached, C.I.T.'s rights in the collateral, like the rights of the debtor, were only conditional. Since the Code provides that the rights of the creditor stem from the debtor's obtaining rights in the collateral, it seems that the creditor's rights are derived from, and are no greater than, the rights of the debtor. J. White and R. Summers, The Uniform Commercial Code 795 (1968). When the debtor's rights in the collateral are only conditional, the rights of the creditor are also so limited. The only source of rights upon which Samuels could rely to claim any rights in the goods, including mere possession, was the contract of purchase between itself and the sellers. When Samuels failed to fulfill its part of the bargain by not paying, this contractual relationship came to an end, and thus Samuels had absolutely no right to retain or dispose of the merchandise. Since under Texas law the debtor had only a defeasible interest in the property that was terminated when it failed to pay, the lienholder's right, derived solely from the rights of the debtor, also terminated.

This is not to say that a security interest cannot continue to exist with respect to collateral in the event that the debtor sells, exchanges or otherwise disposes of the goods. Texas Business and Commerce Code, §9-306(2) (1968). This extension of a secured party's rights in goods contemplates a sale or disposition to a fourth party. It does not anticipate a termination of the right of a debtor in goods with respect to the source from which the debtor procured the goods. . . .

III

The third question is whether C.I.T. qualifies as a good faith purchaser. Under §2-403 of the Code, the buyer of goods from a seller is vested with a limited interest that it can convey to a good faith purchaser and thus create in the purchaser a greater right to the goods than the buyer itself had. This is possible even when the buyer obtains the goods as a result of giving a check that is later dishonored or when the purchase was made for cash. But in order to attain this status, the proponent must be a purchaser that gives value and acts in good faith. While C.I.T. gave value for the goods within the meaning of the Code, it failed to meet the test of a purchaser or one acting in good faith.

With regard to C.I.T.'s status as a purchaser, the Code broadly defines this term as one who takes "by sale, discount, negotiation, mortgage, pledge, lien, issue or reissue, gift or any other voluntary transaction creating an interest in property." Texas Business and Commerce Code, §1-201(32) (1968); see id. §1-201(33). As noted earlier, C.I.T. does not have an interest in the cattle because its rights in the collateral are derivative of its debtor's rights in it. When Samuels failed to pay for the cattle, its rights in the cattle terminated and thus so did C.I.T.'s. C.I.T.'s status as a good faith purchaser is also defeated with regard to its acting in good faith. The Code defines good faith as "honesty in fact in the conduct or transaction concerned." Texas Business and Commerce Code, §1-201(19) (1968). Implicit in the term "good faith" is the requirement that C.I.T. take its interest in the cattle without notice of the outstanding claims of others. . . .

It is true that the evidence does not reveal any breach of an express obligation on C.I.T.'s behalf to continue financing the packing house after Samuels filed a petition in bankruptcy. Nor does the good faith element require the creditor to continue to finance the operation of a business when it is apparent that the business is unprofitable and is going bankrupt. But because of the integral relationship between C.I.T. and Samuels, we do not see how C.I.T. could have kept from knowing of the outstanding claims of others. C.I.T. maintained close scrutiny over the financial affairs of Samuels' operations. C.I.T. had been financing Samuels' packing house operations for at least six years, and the financing involved the flow of millions of dollars. The amount of cash advances made to Samuels was not predetermined or determined arbitrarily, but was calculated only after C.I.T. examined weekly the outstanding accounts and the current inventory of the business. From such a continuous and prolonged study of the business to determine the amount of each weekly advance, C.I.T. must have been intricately aware of the operations and financial status of the business.

Since C.I.T. was so intimately involved in Samuels' financial affairs it must have known that when it refused to advance additional funds, unpaid checks issued to cattle sellers by Samuels' would be dishonored. Samuels' operations were totally dependent on the financing of C.I.T. and both parties knew it. From its enduring involvement in the weekly financing, C.I.T. apparently knew that Samuels was purchasing and processing cattle up until the very time of filing the petition. Knowing that cattle had been purchased and processed immediately preceding its refusal to advance more money, C.I.T. must have known as a result of this refusal that some cattle sellers who had recently delivered their cattle to Samuels would not be paid. Because C.I.T. and Samuels were so intertwined in the management of the financial affairs of the business, we do not think that C.I.T. can plausibly claim, in complete honesty, that it was unaware of the claims of the unpaid cattle sellers. Since C.I.T. was aware of these outstanding claims, it does not qualify as a good faith purchaser.

IV

We now turn to the unpaid cattle sellers' rights as against the trustee in bankruptcy. It is true that under §70c of the Bankruptcy Act[3] the trustee, as a hypothetical lien creditor, will cut off the rights of the sellers as holders of unperfected security interests. But as pointed out earlier, the sellers' rights are not limited merely to the retention of an unperfected security interest, for they also have the right to reclaim the cattle. Thus the question becomes whether the trustee's lien gives him a priority of interest in the proceeds of sale of the cattle as against the sellers' rights to reclaim.

Turning again to §2-507 of the Code in order to define the sellers' rights, we see that the section and accompanying comments implicitly give the sellers the right to reclaim, but it expressly subordinates that right only to a good faith purchaser. There is no mention of a subordination of the reclamation rights to the trustee in bankruptcy, nor is there any suggestion in this provision, the following comments, or otherwise that the drafters of the Code intended that the sellers' right to reclaim be so subordinated. Indeed, in view of the historical developments leading to the drafting and subsequent amendment of §2-702, an analogous provision which deals solely with credit sales and not cash, irresistible logic

3. [Now §544(a) — ed.]

compels the conclusion that the Code draftsmen intended for the sellers' reclamation rights to prevail over the trustee's lien.

When §2-702 was originally written, it spelled out that a seller's right to reclaim was subordinate to "a buyer in ordinary course or other good faith purchaser or lien creditor . . ." Texas Business and Commerce Code, §2-702(3) (1968). Construing this provision, the Third Circuit in In re Kravitz, 278 F.2d 820 (1960), held that a trustee in bankruptcy fell within the definition of lien creditor. Since the Code did not set out the priorities of a lien creditor as against the seller's right to reclaim, the court turned to Pennsylvania law and concluded that under the law of that state, the lien creditor should prevail. Consequently the sellers' attempts to reclaim their property were unsuccessful.

Kravitz and its implications have been widely discussed. Peters, Remedies for Breach of Contracts Relating to the Sale of Goods under the Uniform Commercial Code: A Road Map for Article 2, 73 Yale L.J. 199, 219, n.64 (1963). Although the permanent editorial board in 1962 rejected a proposed amendment to §2-702 based on the Kravitz decision that would have deleted the words "lien creditor," the board in 1966 adopted the amendment and deleted this party as one to which reclamation rights would be subordinated. J. White and R. Summers, The Uniform Commercial Code, 243 (1972). This amendment, obviously thoroughly considered, amply demonstrates that the provisions of the Code were not intended to subordinate the sellers' reclamation rights to those of the trustee in bankruptcy.

But even assuming the continuing vitality of Kravitz, that decision does not control the outcome of this litigation. The litigants in Kravitz dealt on the basis of a credit transaction and thus §2-702, dealing solely with credit transactions, defined the rights of the sellers as against the trustee in bankruptcy. Under the facts of the instant case, however, we are concerned with a cash sale, and thus the sellers' rights are defined by §2-507. Nowhere in that provision, the accompanying comments, or the law of Texas, is the sellers' rights to reclaim subordinated to a lien creditor or a trustee in bankruptcy. The sellers' right to reclaim having been properly preserved, the cattle farmers are entitled to exercise it now.

V

We believe it inequitable to deny the claims of the stock farmers who produced and delivered the cattle, in favor of the mortgagee who refused to advance the money before bankruptcy. We adhere to the teachings of Bank of Marin v. England, 385 U.S. 99, 103, 87 S. Ct. 274, 277, 17 L. Ed. 2d 197 (1966): ". . . There is an overriding consideration that equitable principles govern the exercise of bankruptcy jurisdiction . . ."

It is our firm belief that the approach to the Code outlined above is eminently reasonable and conforms with the Code's express provisions and underlying policies. We do not believe that the drafters of the Code intended for the unpaid sellers to walk away from this transaction with nothing, neither their goods nor the purchase price, while the mortgagee enjoys a preferred lien on that for which it refused to advance payment. Based on our understanding of the Code, such a result is insupportable.

We again reverse the judgment of the district court.

GODBOLD, J. (dissenting). I dissent.

This case raises one primary question: under the Uniform Commercial Code as adopted in Texas, is the interest of an unpaid cash seller in goods already delivered to a buyer superior or subordinate to the interest of a holder of a perfected security interest in those same goods? In my opinion, under Article Nine, the perfected security interest is unquestionably superior to the interest of the seller. Moreover, the perfected lender is protected from the seller's claims by two independent and theoretically distinct Article Two provisions. My result is not the product of revealed truth, but rather of a meticulous and dispassionate reading of Articles Two and Nine and an understanding that the Code is an integrated statute whose Articles and Sections overlap and flow into one another in an effort to encourage specific types of commercial behavior. The Code's overall plan, which typically favors good faith purchasers, and which encourages notice filing of nonpossessory security interests in personalty through the imposition of stringent penalties for nonfiling, compels a finding that the perfected secured party here should prevail.

My brothers have not concealed that their orientation in the case before us is to somehow reach a result in favor of the sellers of cattle, assumed by them to be "little fellows," and against a large corporate lender, because it seems the "fair" thing to do. We do not sit as federal chancellors confecting ways to escape the state law of commercial transactions when that law produces a result not to our tastes. Doing what seems fair is heady stuff. But the next seller may be a tremendous corporate conglomerate engaged in the cattle feeding business, and the next lender a small town Texas bank. Today's heady draught may give the majority a euphoric feeling, but it can produce tomorrow's hangover.

I. Rights Under §2-403

My analysis begins with an examination of the relative rights of seller and secured party under §2-403(1).

Section 2-403 gives certain transferors power to pass greater title than they themselves claim. Section 2-403(1) gives good faith purchasers of even fraudulent buyers-transferors greater rights than the defrauded seller can assert. This harsh rule is designed to promote the greatest range of freedom possible to commercial vendors and purchasers.

The provision anticipates a situation where (1) a cash seller has delivered goods to a buyer who has paid by a check which is subsequently dishonored, §2-403(1)(b), (c), and where (2) the defaulting buyer transfers title to a Code-defined "good faith purchaser." The interest of the good faith purchaser is protected pro tanto against the claims of the aggrieved seller. §§2-403(1); 2-403, Comment 1. The Code expressly recognizes the power of the defaulting buyer to transfer good title to such a purchaser even though the transfer is wrongful as against the seller. The buyer is granted the power to transfer good title despite the fact that under §2-507 he lacks the right to do so.

The Code definition of "purchaser" is broad, and includes not only one taking by sale but also covers persons taking by gift or by voluntary mortgage, pledge or lien. §1-201(32), (33). It is therefore broad enough to include an Article Nine secured party. §§1-201(37); 9-101, Comment; 9-102(1), (2). Thus if C.I.T. holds a valid Article Nine security interest, it is by virtue of that status also a purchaser under §2-403(1). . . .

Attachment of an Article Nine interest takes place when (1) there is agreement that the interest attach to the collateral; (2) the secured party has given value; and (3) the debtor has rights in the collateral sufficient to permit attachment. §9-204(1).

(1) The agreement: In 1963, Samuels initially authorized C.I.T.'s lien in its after-acquired inventory. The agreement between these parties remained in effect throughout the period of delivery of Stowers' cattle to Samuels.

(2) Value: At the time of Stowers' delivery, Samuels' indebtedness to C.I.T. exceeded $1.8 million. This pre-existing indebtedness to the lender constituted "value" under the Code. §1-201(44).

(3) Rights in the collateral: Finally, upon delivery, Samuels acquired rights in the cattle sufficient to allow attachment of C.I.T.'s lien. The fact that the holder of a voluntary lien — including an Article Nine interest — is a "purchaser" under the Code is of great significance to a proper understanding and resolution of this case under Article Two and Article Nine. The Code establishes that purchasers can take from a defaulting cash buyer, §2-403(1). Lien creditors are included in the definition of purchasers, §1-201(32), (33). A lien is an Article Nine interest, §§9-101, Comment; 9-102(2); 9-102 Comment. The existence of an Article Nine interest presupposes the debtor's having rights in the collateral sufficient to permit attachment, §9-204(1). Therefore, since a defaulting cash buyer has the power to transfer a security interest to a lien creditor, including an Article Nine secured party, the buyer's rights in the property, however marginal, must be sufficient to allow attachment of a lien. And this is true even if, arguendo, I were to agree that the cash seller is granted reclamation rights under Article Two. See First National Bank of Elkhart Cty. v. Smoker, 11 UCC Rept. Serv. 10, 19 (Ind. Ct. App., 1972); Evans Products Co. v. Jorgensen, 245 Or. 362, 421 P.2d 978 (1966).

If the Article Nine secured party acted in good faith, it is prior under §2-403(1) to an aggrieved seller. Under the facts before us, I think that C.I.T. acted in good faith. The Code's good faith provision requires "honesty in fact," §1-201(19), which, for Article Two purposes, is "expressly defined as . . . reasonable commercial standards of fair dealing." §§1-201, Comment 19; 2-103(1)(b). There is no evidence that C.I.T. acted in bad faith in its dealings with Samuels, or that Stowers' loss resulted from any breach of obligation by C.I.T. There is no claim that the 1963 security agreement was the product of bad faith. The lender's interest had been perfected and was of record for six years when Stower's delivery to Samuels occurred. There is no suggestion that the $1.8 million debt owing from Samuels to C.I.T. was the result of bad faith or of a desire to defeat Stowers' $50,000 claim. There is no claim that C.I.T. exercised or was able to exercise control over Samuels' business operations. There is no evidence that C.I.T. authorized or ordered or suggested that Samuels dishonor Stowers' check. There is no contention that C.I.T.'s refusal to extend credit on May 23, the date Samuels filed a voluntary petition on bankruptcy at a time when it owed C.I.T. more than $1.8 million, was violative of an obligatory future advance clause.

The Code's good faith provision requires "honesty in fact," §1-201(19); it hardly requires a secured party to continue financing a doomed business enterprise.

The majority deny that C.I.T. acted in good faith because, they claim, the lender had "intimate" knowledge of Samuels' business operations. The majority's source of information on the scope of C.I.T.'s knowledge is a little puzzling. The Referee in Bankruptcy found only that "C.I.T. knew or should have known of the manner by which the bankrupt bought livestock . . . on a grade and yield basis." In the Matter of Samuels & Co., Inc., No BK 3-1314 (N.D. Tex. order of Jan. 19, 1972). This factual finding was affirmed by the District Court which reversed the Referee and upheld C.I.T.'s priority over Stowers. Id., orders of Nov. 24, 1972, and Jan. 16, 1973. Neither the Referee nor the District Court found, nor have the parties alleged, that C.I.T.'s knowledge of Samuels' business extended to knowledge of the debtor's obligations to third party creditors.

However, even if evidence had established that C.I.T. knew of Samuels' nonpayment and of Stowers' claim, C.I.T.'s status as an Article Two good faith purchaser would be unaffected. Lack of knowledge of outstanding claims is necessary to the common law BFP, and is similarly expressly required in many Code BFP and priority provisions. See e.g., §§3-302; 6-110; 8-301, 8-302; 9-301(1)(b). But the Code's definition of an Article Two good faith purchaser does not expressly or impliedly include lack of knowledge of third-party claims as an element. The detailed definition of the Article's counterpart of the common law BFP requires only honesty in fact, reasonable commercial behavior, fair dealing. And this describes precisely C.I.T.'s dealings with Samuels: during the period May 13-22 — the time when the bulk of Stowers' cattle were delivered and the time of the issuance of the NSF checks — C.I.T.'s advances to Samuels totalled $1 million. The advances were curtailed on May 23 because of Samuels' taking voluntary bankruptcy at a time when its indebtedness to C.I.T. was enormous. The decision to terminate further funding was clearly reasonable. It was also fair, and honest, and, as the majority have failed to grasp, was not the cause of Stowers' suffering. As I note infra in my analysis of rights under Article Nine, the sellers' loss was avoidable through perfection of their security interests in the cattle. If they had perfected, they would not only have been prior to C.I.T. as an Article Nine lender, §9-312, but also protected against C.I.T. as an Article Two purchaser, §9-201. As it happens, Stowers did not perfect. I believe the sellers cannot now be permitted to force an innocent, if prosperous, secured creditor to shoulder their loss for them.

II. Rights Under §2-507

The majority opinion devotes much of its concentration and energy to an analysis of the sellers' "reclamation right" under §2-507 and §2-702. Relying on an expansive reading of these Sections, the opinion concludes that a cash seller whose right to payment is frustrated through a check ultimately dishonored can "reclaim" proceeds of goods delivered to the buyer despite an interim third-party interest, and despite a year-long delay in seeking reclamation. I am unable to accept this reading of Code policy and requirements.

Although the Code expressly grants a credit seller the right and power to reclaim goods from a breaching buyer, the right is triggered only by specific and limited circumstances; it can be asserted only if an exacting procedure is followed; and the right can never be asserted to defeat the interests of certain third parties who have dealt with the defaulting buyer. §2-702(2), (3). There is no Code Section expressly granting a similar reclamation right to a cash seller.

The seller's remedies upon breach are enumerated in §2-703. These provisions do not include or suggest a right or power in a cash seller to recover goods already delivered to a breaching buyer. Nevertheless the courts have read a reclamation right into the Code. It is this judicially-confected right to reclaim goods in which the majority's reclamation analysis is grounded. However, the majority take the reclamation right beyond anything intimated by the Code or heretofore permitted by courts recognizing a cash seller's reclamation right.

The cash seller's right to reclaim has been drawn from the language of §2-507(2) and §2-507, Comment 3. I note, first, that the remedy granted by §2-507(2) is one of seller against buyer, see In re Helms Veneer Corp., 287 F. Supp. 840 (W.D. Va., 1968). It does not concern rights of seller against third parties. Section 2-507, Comment 3 explains that the seller's rights under §2-507 must "conform with the policy set forth in the bona fide purchase section of this Article," i.e., with §2-403. As I have noted above, under this provision the rights of an aggrieved cash seller are subordinated to those of the buyer's good-faith purchasers, including Article Nine lenders such as C.I.T. Thus, the Code provisions supporting a cash seller's reclamation right expressly preclude recovery by Stowers as against C.I.T. See §§2-507(2); 2-507, Comment 3; 2-702(2), (3). See also Stumbo v. Paul B. Hult Lumber Co., 251 Or. 20, 444 P.2d 564 (1968); In re Hayward Woolen Co., 3 UCC Rep. 1107 (D. Mass., 1967); Evans Products Co v. Jorgensen, 245 Or. 362, 421 P.2d 978 (1966).

Moreover, those courts which have permitted reclamation under §2-507 have invariably adhered to §2-507, Comment 3's express requirement that demand for return be made within ten days after receipt by the buyer or else be lost. See In re Colacci's of America, Inc., 490 F.2d 1118 (CA 10, 1974); In re Helms Veneer Corp., supra, Stumbo v. Paul B. Hult Lumber Co., supra; In re Mort, 208 F. Supp 309 (ED Pa., 1962).

In the instant case, demand was not made within ten days or ten weeks; it came a full year after delivery to Samuels. The majority excuse this gross noncompliance by finding that the sellers' failure was the product of innocent error, and, in any event, was not required since the "purpose" of the demand rule — protection of purchasers of the delivered goods — was served through C.I.T.'s alleged intimate knowledge of Samuels' business operations.

The Code's ten-day provision is an absolute requirement. There is no exception in the Code Sections or Comments, express or implied, to the statutory period. I would be hesitant to read any extension into a statute of limitations clear and unambiguous on its face, and particularly unwilling to allow an extension some 36 times greater than the statutory maximum. My reluctance is all the greater where the right at issue is not granted by the Code but is rather the product of judicial interpretation of a Comment which, whatever grant of power it may suggest, expressly limits that right to a ten-day life.

The spirit in which the rule was broken seems to me irrelevant. Even conceding that Stowers' noncompliance occurred in absolute good faith, it was nonetheless noncompliance. Mistake of law does not constitute excuse of mistake.

C.I.T.'s apocryphal intimate knowledge of Samuels' business operations is, I believe, also irrelevant to a determination of the validity of Stower's claim. The majority find the purpose of the ten-day rule to be one of notice to third parties that a claim exists. I have somewhat greater difficulty than my brothers in pinpointing the purpose of the ten-day rule. But I am convinced that the goal is not one of protection or notice to third-party purchasers, for their rights are secure under the Code as against the aggrieved seller even if demand is timely made. §§2-507, Comment 3; 2-702(3). The Code does not condition the purchasers' rights on a lack of knowledge of the seller's interest. With or without knowledge, the purchaser rests secure. I am therefore forced to conclude that the ten-day rule serves some function other than notifying third-party takers, and, consequently, that even if C.I.T. knew of Stowers' claim, the sellers' obligation under the ten-day rule would not have been excused. And even if knowledge by the purchaser suspended the sellers' duty to make a timely demand, the record in this case is devoid of any hint that C.I.T. knew of Samuels' breach and Stowers' reclamation right.

Moreover, §2-507 and §2-702 speak of a right to reclaim goods. Neither provision grants a right to go after proceeds of those goods. Where a right or interest in proceeds is recognized by the Code it is recognized expressly. See e.g., §9-306. The right granted by §2-507 is narrowly defined. I am unwilling to imply an extension to such a short-lived and precisely drawn remedy.

Finally, even if there were a right to reclaim proceeds, even if the right had been timely exercised, and even if it could have been exercised despite the transfer of interest to C.I.T., Stowers would have taken subject to C.I.T.'s perfected Article Nine interest. See §§9-201, 9-301, 9-306, 9-312. See also my discussion of C.I.T.'s rights and interest under Article Nine, infra.

III. Rights Under §2-511

The majority opinion states that C.I.T.'s interest cannot be found superior to Stowers' because such a finding would violate §2-511's prohibition on penalizing a seller for accepting as payment a check which is ultimately dishonored. I believe the majority have misconstrued the scope and significance of §2-511.

Like §2-507, §2-511 concerns claims of the seller as against the buyer. See §2-511(3), §2-511, Comment 4. On its face it does not affect the rights of third parties taking from the defaulting buyer. Moreover, and more important, the seller is not here "penalized" for taking an N.S.F. check. Such loss as Stowers suffered is the direct result of his failure to comply with Code provisions which, once followed — and regardless of Stowers' acceptance of Samuels' check — would have made his interest invulnerable to claims by C.I.T. See, e.g., §§9-107; 9-201; 9-301; 9-312(3).

IV. Rights Under Article Nine

I am also unable to agree with the majority's conclusion that, under the Code, Stowers' interest is different from and greater than a security interest. Similarly, I disagree with the theory that by virtue of Stowers' power under Article Two, C.I.T.'s security interest is subject to defeat since it (1) could not attach because the debtor's rights in the collateral were too slight to permit attachment and (2) was subject to defeat even if it attached because a security interest collapses if the debtor's right to the property is extinguished. The majority's result is achieved only by ignoring or circumventing the plain meaning of Article Nine and Article Two.

Prior to the enactment of the Uniform Commercial Code, seller and buyer could agree that, despite buyer's possession, title to goods sold was to remain in the seller until he was paid. Such a reservation of title under the "cash sale" doctrine would defeat not only a claim to the goods by the defaulting buyer, but also the claims of lien creditors of the buyer, for the buyer's naked possession could give rise to no interest to which a lien could attach.

However, the UCC specifically limits the seller's ability to reserve title once he has voluntarily surrendered possession to the buyer: "Any retention or reservation by the seller of the title (property) in goods shipped or delivered to the buyer is limited in effect to a reservation of a security interest." §2-401(1). See also §1-201(37). The drafters noted the theory behind this provision: "Article [Two] deals with the issues between seller and buyer in terms of step by step performance or non-performance under the contract for sale and not in terms of whether or not 'title' to the goods has passed." §2-401, Comment 1.

The majority opinion interprets §2-401(1) as applying only to "credit" sales, and of no effect where the parties have contracted a "cash" sale. However, the Code provision speaks of "any reservation of title." It does not on its face apply solely to credit sales. There is no authority under the Code for the majority's restrictive interpretation. Numerous courts have, in fact, applied §2-401 to cash sales. See e.g., Guy Martin Buick, Inc. v. Colo. Springs Nat'l

Bank, 32 Colo. App. 235, 511 P.2d 912 (1973); First Nat'l Bank of Elkhart City v. Smoker, 11 UCC Rep. 10 (Ind. App., 1972); English v. Ford, 17 Cal. App. 3d 1038, 95 Cal. Rptr. 501 (1971); Evans Products v. Jorgensen, 245 Or. 362, 421 P.2d 978 (1966). I have been unable to find even one case suggesting that §2-401 applies only to credit sales.

If the majority were correct, the section would be merely definitional, for a credit sale is but a sales transaction in which the seller reserves a security interest. However, §2-401 is not definitional. It is operational and concerns the effect of transfer of possession under a sales contract upon any reservation of title. Neither law nor logic leads me to believe that §2-401 is correctly interpreted to exclude cash sales.

The majority also suggest that Stowers' interest cannot be characterized as a security interest subject to Article Nine requirements and priorities since, the majority conclude, such interests must be "consensual." While it is true that many interests governed by Article Nine are consensual, §§9-102; 9-102, Comment, the Code clearly subjects Article Two security interests arising not by consent but by operation of law to Article Nine. See §§2-401(1); 9-113; 9-113, Comment 2. See also §§2-326; 9-114; 9-102, Comment 1.

Since Stowers' interest upon delivery of the cattle to Samuels was limited to a security interest subject to Article Nine, §§2-401(1); 9-113, the validity of C.I.T.'s Article Nine interest becomes crucial. If C.I.T. is the holder of a perfected Article Nine interest in the collateral claimed by Stowers through its unperfected §2-401 interest, C.I.T.'s interest will prevail over Stowers, §9-312(5).

The majority assert that C.I.T. cannot claim an interest in the cattle because Samuels' interest was too slight to permit attachment. See §9-204(1). As I noted in my discussion of rights under §2-403, this argument ignores the significance of §2-403(1) and §1-201(32), (33). The Code anticipates a situation where the interest of an unpaid cash seller who has delivered goods to a breaching buyer is subordinated to the interest of "purchasers" of the buyer. Lien creditors are included in the definition of "purchasers"; in order that there be lien creditors, the buyer's interest must be great enough to allow attachment. Therefore, however Samuels' interest upon delivery of the cattle is defined, and however slight or tenuous or marginal it was, it was necessarily great enough to permit attachment of a lien, including C.I.T.'s Article Nine interest.

The majority find that even if attachment occurred, C.I.T.'s interest would be defeated by Stowers' reclamation. The theory behind this argument is that the rights of the Article Nine secured party are at best coextensive with the rights of the debtor; if the debtor loses his rights, the security interest too is lost.

Upon nonpayment Samuels lost the right to retain or dispose of the property, but the Code recognizes that the breaching buyer had the power to encumber, despite nonpayment, so long as he retained possession. §§2-403(1); 1-201(32), (33). In the instant case, this power arose as a result of Stowers' delivery, and it did not terminate while the goods remained in Samuels' hands. The whole point of Article Nine is the continuity of perfected security interests once they have properly attached, despite subsequent loss of control or possession of the collateral by the debtor. §9-201. Article Nine does not except an unpaid cash seller from this overall plan. In fact it specifically provides a means for him to perfect and become prior to previous perfected security interests. §9-312(3), (4).

To hold that a reclaiming seller is given the power to sweep away a security interest which was able to attach only as a direct and Code-approved result of his voluntary act of delivery to the buyer would require ignoring the meaning and interplay of Article Two and Article Nine. Article Two recognizes the continuous vitality and priority of an Article Nine interest over the rights of an aggrieved seller. See §§2-403(1); 2-507, Comment 3; 2-702(3). It would be error to believe that a proper analysis of Article Nine could require the extinction of an identical Article Nine interest in the very circumstances specified by Article Two as triggering the priority of lienor over seller. See §§2-403(1); 2-507(2); 2-507, Comment 3; 2-702(2), (3); 9-102; 9-107(1); 9-312(3), (4).

Any seeming unfairness to Stowers resulting from the Code's operation is illusory, for the sellers could have protected their interests, even as against C.I.T.'s prior perfected interest, if they had merely complied with the UCC's purchase-money provisions. §§9-107, 9-312(3), (4). The Code favors purchase-money financing, and encourages it by granting to a seller of goods the power to defeat prior liens. The seller at most need only (1) file a financing statement and (2) notify the prior secured party of its interest before delivery of the new inventory. The procedure is not unduly complex or cumbersome. But whether cumbersome or not, a lender who chooses to ignore its provisions takes a calculated risk that a loss will result.

In the instant case Stowers did not utilize §9-312's purchase-money provision. The sellers never perfected. Thus, in a competition with a perfected secured party they are subordinated, and, in this case, lose the whole of their interests. See §§9-201, 9-301, 9-312(5).

V. Rights Under the Bankruptcy Act

C.I.T.'s perfected security interest is not subject to defeat by the Trustee in Bankruptcy Mahon. If, however, C.I.T. were to have abandoned its claim against Samuels, Stowers would nonetheless have lost in a priority contest with the Trustee.

Bankruptcy Act §70c confers the status of a hypothetical lien creditor upon the Trustee. Mahon could assert those §70 rights against Stowers, an unperfected security party, and would prevail under UCC §9-301(1)(b).

Bank of Marin v. England, 385 US 99, 87 S. Ct. 274, 17 L. Ed 2d 197 (1966), does not strengthen Stowers' claim. In that case the drawer of a check took bankruptcy after the check had been issued but before presentment. The drawee paid on the instrument without notice or knowledge of the bankruptcy. Such payment was in compliance with UCC §§4-303, 4-401 and 4-402. The Supreme Court found that an application of Bankruptcy Act §70d under these circumstances would work a hardship on the payee. *Bank of Marin* has been critically attacked by scholars, see e.g., 4A Collier on Bankruptcy, §70-68 at 755 (14th Ed. 1971). In any event, the "inequity" in *Bank of Marin* occurred when a loss resulted from the effect of a federal statute upon good faith compliance with state statute. The federal statute's operation and effect were wholly beyond the control of the innocent drawee. In the instant case Stowers' loss resulted from his own failure to comply with state law which would have enabled him to perfect his purchase money security interest. The loss could have been avoided through his own efforts. This is not the kind of loss equity protects against.

IMPORTANT NOTE

The Fifth Circuit granted an en banc rehearing on this case and then reversed the original panel and adopted Judge Godbold's dissenting opinion as the position of the Fifth Circuit. Five of the fourteen judges dissented from the Godbold result. The proceedings on the rehearing en banc are reported at 526 F.2d 1238, 18 U.C.C. Rep. Serv. 545 (1976).

Is the prevailing rule wise as a matter of policy? Isn't the court discouraging the acceptance of checks? See McDonnell, The Floating Lienor as Good Faith Purchaser, 50 S. Cal. L. Rev. 429 (1977). Shortly after this decision Congress amended the Packers and Stockyard Act to protect unpaid ranchers who protest non-payment within a short period after delivery. See 7 U.S.C. §§196, 228b, and 228c (1976). The Bankruptcy Reform Act of 1978 also codifies a federal rule similar to U.C.C. §2-702, in §546(c):

> (c) The rights and powers of the trustee under sections 544(a), 545, 547, and 549 of this title are subject to any statutory right or common law right of a seller, in the ordinary course of such seller's business, of goods to the debtor to reclaim such goods if the debtor has received such goods while insolvent, but —
>
> (1) such a seller may not reclaim any such goods unless such seller demands in writing reclamation of such goods before ten days after receipt of such goods by the debtor; and
>
> (2) the court may deny reclamation to a seller with such a right of reclamation that has made such a demand only if court —
>
> (A) grants the claim of such a seller priority as an administrative expense; or
>
> (B) secures such claim by a lien.

F. *STATUTORY LIEN HOLDERS*

Just as the buyer in the ordinary course of business is a favorite of the law, the repairman in the ordinary course of business is frequently given priority over previously perfected consensual security interests. Read §9-310 and the Official Comments thereto.

PROBLEM 67

The Repossession Finance Company (hereinafter RFC) had a perfected security interest in Hattie Mobile's car (RFC's lien was noted on the certificate of title as required by state law). The car broke down on the interstate one day and Hattie had it towed to Mike's Greasepit Garage, where it was repaired. State law gave a possessory artisan's lien to repairmen. The garage told Hattie it was claiming such a lien, but when she pleaded with the manager he let her drive the car to work after she assured him that she would return the car to the garage for storage every night (fortunately she lived across the street). Repossession found out about this practice and, deeming itself insecure (§1-208), accelerated the amount due and repossessed the car from the parking lot in front of Hattie's place of business.

(a) Which creditor has the superior interest in the car under §9-310? Forrest Cate Ford v. Fryar, 62 Tenn. App. 572, 465 S.W.2d 822, 8 U.C.C. Rep. Serv. 239 (Tenn. App. 1970).

(b) If the car had been in Mike's possession when the conflict arose, would it matter under §9-310 that the finance company never gave its consent to the repairs? See General Motor Acceptance Corp. v. Colwell Diesal Serv. & Garage, Inc., 302 A.2d 595, 12 U.C.C. Rep. Serv. 226 (Me. 1973); Nickell v. Lambrecht, 29 Mich. App. 191, 185 N.W.2d 155, 8 U.C.C. Rep. Serv. 1381 (1970); Annot., 69 A.L.R.3d 1162 (1976).

If the garage's charges are unconscionably high does the lien still prevail? See §1-203; G. Gilmore §33.5, at 888: "To be entitled to priority under §9-310 the lienor must have furnished services or materials 'in the ordinary course of his business.' This limitation should be read as tantamount to a requirement of good faith. . . .Section 9-310 is designed to protect the honest lienor and not the crook."

Balzer Machinery Co. v. Klineline Sand & Gravel Co.

533 P.2d 321, 16 U.C.C Rep. Serv. 1160 (Ore. 1975)

DENECKE, J. Does the holder of a nonpossessory artisan's lien have the priority over the holder of a prior perfected security interest? That is the principal issue.

Plaintiff, Balzer Machinery Co., brought this suit to foreclose its nonpossessory lien. The lien arose out of repairs made to certain rock crushing equipment which was being operated by defendant Klineline Sand & Gravel Co. under a lease-purchase agreement. The defendant Clark Leasing Corp. was the assignee of the lessor-vendor's interest. Clark subsequently repossessed the rock crusher and sold it to the defendant Spencer. Klineline is not involved in the appeal.

The lease-purchase agreement was entered into on April 29, 1970. It was stipulated that the lessor-vendor had a security interest in the equipment. Also, on April 29, 1970, a duly executed financing statement was filed with the appropriate government authorities. Balzer Machinery Co. performed repair work on the equipment at the request of Klineline in February 1972. Balzer then claimed a nonpossessory lien on the equipment and filed appropriate notice pursuant to ORS 87.090. On June 1, 1972, Klineline was in default on its lease-purchase agreement. Clark repossessed the equipment and sold it to Spencer.

The trial court foreclosed Balzer's lien and held it was prior to Clark's interest. Clark appeals.

[The court quoted §9-310.]

ORS 87.085 provides for a nonpossessory lien for labor or materials expended upon equipment. This is termed an artisan's lien. ORS 87.090 provides for the filing of notice of such lien.

In 1972 when these transactions occurred ORS 87.100 provided:

> . . . The lien of every person as provided in ORS 87.085 shall be superior to the rights of the person holding the title to the chattel or any lien thereon antedating the time of the expenditure provided in ORS 87.085 by such lien claimant. However, the lien filed under the provisions of ORS 87.090 shall only have such priority over a chattel mortgage duly recorded prior to the date of the expenditure claimed under the lien during the period the lien claimant retains possession of the chattel; . . .

ORS §9-102(2) provides, in part: "ORS §§9-101 to 9-507 [the Secured Transactions chapter of the Uniform Commercial Code] do not apply to statutory liens except as provided in ORS 9-310."

Clark makes several alternative arguments suggesting how these statutes should be interpreted in order to grant Clark's security interest priority over Balzer's nonpossessory lien.

Clark argues that because ORS §9-310 expressly grants an artisan's possessory lien priority over a perfected security interest, the statute impliedly denies priority to a nonpossessory lien. Clark further argues that ORS §9-130 was enacted subsequent to ORS 87.100 and by implication repealed any provisions of ORS 87.100 inconsistent with ORS §9-310.

The only decision we have been referred to precisely deciding this issue holds: "We conclude the plain import of TCA §9-310 is the repairman must retain possession of the vehicle repaired in order to maintain the *priority* of his statutory lien, acquired under TCA §64-1901 et. seq., over that of a previously perfected security interest in the same vehicle." Forrest Cate Ford, Inc. v. Fryar, 62 Tenn. App. 572, 577, 465 S.W.2d 882 (1970).

With one exception, the few writers who have discussed this subject have been in accord with this reasoning.

> To construe Section 9-310 other than restrictively is to create a threat to security interests created and perfected under Article 9. When so construed restrictively it insures that the person who contributes to the value of goods, and retains possession until paid, is protected. [Miller, Liens Created by Operation of Law: A Look at Section 9-310 of the Uniform Commercial Code, 76 Com. L.J. 221, 231 (1971).]
>
> So long as the repairman retains possession of the set, if he has a lien by statute or common law he is entitled to priority unless the lien is statutory and the statute provides otherwise. [Henson, Secured Transactions, 74 (1973).]

Gilmore has reservations:

> . . . The hard question is whether the possessory language in §9-310 should be taken to reverse priorities (and subordinate the lien) where the lien statute (expressly or by judicial construction) gives priority to the filing lienor without possession. That may be the most obvious construction of §9-310, but the unexplained appearance of the possessory language in the 1956 draft does not lead inevitably to the conclusion that the draftsmen deliberately aimed at subordinating nonpossessory liens even when the liens, quite apart from Article 9, already enjoyed a statutory or judicial priority. In the absence of judicial construction, the question must be considered open. [2 Gilmore, Security Interests in Personal Property, 888 (1965).]

Even if we construe the language "goods in the possession of such person," as used in ORS §9-310, to impliedly deny priority to a lien upon goods not in possession, two ancillary problems remain before we can accept Clark's argument.

ORS §9-310, stating that a possessory lien has priority, provides, "unless the lien is statutory and the statute expressly provides otherwise." We agree with Clark that the most likely meaning of that language and the intent of the statute is that it refers to the possessory lien statutes; that is, a "lien upon goods in the possession of that person given by statute," and not to statutes such as ORS 87.100.

The other problem is: did the legislature, in enacting ORS §9-310 of the UCC, by implication amend the nonpossessory lien stat statute, ORS 87.100? We believe the legislature necessarily did so. ORS 69-310, as we interpret it, provides that when an artisan repairs goods subject to a prior perfected security interest, the artisan's lien takes priority over the security interest only if the artisan retains possession. ORS 87.100 is to the contrary. It provides, regardless of whether the artisan lien holder retains possession, that an artisan's lien is prior to all other lien claimants except the lien of a chattel mortgagee.

Amendment by implication is not favored but "is recognized when the matter is clear." State v. Scott, 237 Or. 390, 397, 390 P.2d 328, 331 (1964). In this instance we find it to be clear. The two statutes are inconsistent and, therefore, the latter will prevail.

We construe ORS §9-310 to be the applicable statute and hold that it provides that a perfected security interest has priority over a nonpossessory artisan's lien.

We have not been able to find a substantial reason for the distinction between possessory and nonpossessory liens.[4] The Oregon Legislature, however, has made and continues to make such a distinction in ORS 87.100. Our construction is, as Gilmore admits, the most obvious construction of the language. The result we reach by such a construction is the same as would be reached under the statute as amended subsequent to the events of this case. The legislature brought ORS 87.100 into conformance with the UCC and provided that an artisan lien holder would have priority over a prior "duly perfected security interest" only if the lien holder retained possession.

Reversed.

4. For a possible reason for the distinction see 76 Yale L.J. 1649, 1656 (1967).

G. *LAPSED PRIORITY*

PROBLEM 68

Octopus National Bank had a security interest in the equipment of the Muscles Construction Company for which it filed a financing statement in the proper place on May 1, 1980. Antitrust National Bank took a security interest in the same collateral and filed its financing statement on May 2, 1980, in the same place.

(a) How long is a financing statement effective? See §9-403(2).

(b) If ONB files a continuation statement on May 1, 1984, is its perfected position continued? See §9-403(3). Pre-Code decisions called this the problem of "premature renewal"; for a UCC decision see In re Callahan Motors, Inc., 538 F.2d 76, 19 U.C.C. Rep. Serv. 963 (3d Cir. 1976).

(c) If ONB files a *financing* statement on April 1, 1985, and it is identical to the first financing statement, is that sufficient as a continuation statement? See Eastern Indiana Prod. Credit Assn. v. Farmers St. Bank, 31 Ohio App. 2d 252, 11 U.C.C. Rep. Serv. 664 (1972).

H. *PRIORITY IN CROPS*

PROBLEM 69

The Farmers' Friend Financing Co-op loaned Fred Bandanna $5000 and in May, 1984, perfected a security interest in his 1984 peanut crop and "all future peanut crops." In June, 1986, Fred needed further financing and prior to planting, borrowed $2000 from the Rural State Bank, which took a security interest in his 1986 crop and filed a financing statement in the proper place on the day before he began planting. Both debts were defaulted and the two creditors each claim the crops. Further, Fred's farm was subject to a pre-existing morgage in favor of Octopus National Bank (a mortgage that was 10 years old), which mortgage also reached "crops," though no financing statement had been filed in the proper Article 9 spot. Who gets the crop? See §9-312(2); Coates, Financing the Farmer, 20 Prac.

Law. 45 (1972); G. Gilmore ch. 32; Miller, Farm Collateral Under the UCC: "Those Are Some Mighty Tall Silos, Ain't They Fella?," 20 S.D.L. Rev. 514, 534-535 (1975). If later creditors wish to loan the farmer money, what can they do to be assured of priority over prior perfected interests in the farmer's property? See §9-316.

I. FIXTURES

Article 9 of necessity had to make special rules for the creation and perfection of a *fixture* — the legal bugaboo that hangs in limbo somewhere between chattel mobility and realty attachment. See, e.g., §9-102 ("this Article applies . . . to any transaction . . . which is intended to create a security interest in personal property or fixtures . . ."), and §9-401(1) ("The proper place to file . . . when . . . the collateral is goods which are *or are to become* fixtures [is] the office where a mortgage on the real estate would be filed or recorded").

The Code has only the most limited definition of fixtures. Read §§9-313(1)(a) and 9-313(2) and Official Comment 2. Obviously pre-Code state law defining *fixtures* is very important. State law tests ranged from a pure *annexation* test (measured by the difficulty of removal), to an "intention of the parties" test (for which the leading case is Teaff v. Hewitt, 1 Ohio St. 511 (1853)). Moreover, some courts developed different categories of fixtures. *Trade fixtures* are items of personal property necessary to the conduct of the tenant's business but not permanently affixed to the realty. They remain the tenant's and may be removed when the tenancy ends. Generally the UCC courts treat a *trade fixture* as equipment and not a true fixture, In re Factory Homes Corp., 333 F. Supp. 126, 9 U.C.C. Rep. Serv. 1330 (W.D. Ark. 1971), though the wide-awake lawyer will advise dual filings. A similar idea is the *assembled industrial plant* doctrine which has it that all items connected with the operation of a going business are fixtures (primarily a Pennsylvania way of thinking; for a doctrine's clash with the UCC see General Elec. Credit Corp. v. Pennsylvania Bank & Trust Co., 56 Pa. D. & C.2d 472, 11 U.C.C. Rep. Serv. 858 (1972)). For general treatise discussions of the meaning of *fixture*, see R. Powell, Real Property chs. 57 and 57A (Rohan ed. 1974) (chapter 57A is entitled Fixtures and the Uniform Commercial Code); G. Thompson, Real Property §§55-70 (Grimes ed. 1964); W. Burby, Real Property §11 (3d ed. 1965); R. Brown, Personal Property ch. 16 (Raushenbush 3d ed. 1975); 5 American Law of Property §§19.1-19.4 (1952).

George v. Commercial Credit Corporation

440 F.2d 551, 8 U.C.C. Rep. Serv. 1315 (7th Cir. 1971)

Duffy, J. This is an appeal from an order of the District Court affirming the decision of a Referee in Bankruptcy and sustaining a secured creditor's interest in a mobile home.

The question before us for decision is whether appellee's real estate mortgage on his mobile home may prevail against the trustee's claimed interest.

The referee and the District Court upheld the appellee's claim finding that the mobile home had become a fixture under Wisconsin law. The trustee argues that the mobile home was not a fixture, in fact, and secondly, that the law of fixtures does not apply to security interests in mobile homes.

Dale Wallace Foskett owned five acres of land in Jefferson County, Wisconsin. On December 6, 1968, he purchased a Marshfield Mobile Home, No. 9090, from Highway Mobile Home Sales, Inc. He signed an installment contract and paid $880 on the purchase price of $8,800. Added was a sales tax and interest covering a ten-year period.

Sometime in December 1968, Foskett executed a real estate mortgage to Highway Mobile Home Sales, Inc. The mortgage recites the sum of $14,227.70 and described the real estate in metes and bounds. The mortgage was assigned to Commercial Credit Corporation, the respondent-appellee herein.

The mobile home here in question could not move under its own power. It was delivered to Foskett's real property by Mobile Sales. This mobile home was never again operated on or over the highways as a motor vehicle.

The mobile home here in question was 68 feet in length, 14 feet in width and 12 feet in height. It contained six rooms and weighed 15,000 pounds.

The bankrupt owned no other home and he and his wife occupied the mobile home continuously from December 6, 1968 until forced to vacate same by order of the Trustee in Bankruptcy.

The home was set on cinder blocks three courses high. It was connected with a well. It was hooked up to a septic tank. It also was connected with electric power lines.

The bankrupt never applied for a certificate of title from the Wisconsin Motor Vehicle Department. However, he did apply for a home owner's insurance policy and he asked the seller to remove the wheels from his home. He also applied for a building permit and was told he had to construct a permanent foundation for the home. The permit was granted upon condition that the foundation be constructed within one year. However, within that period, the petition for bankruptcy was filed.

The issue before us can be thus stated: Commercial Credit Corporation argues that the mobile home was a fixture under applicable law and is not personalty. The trustee insists that the mobile home was and still is a "motor vehicle" and is personalty.

The mobile homes industry has grown rapidly in the last few years. There has been a great demand for relatively inexpensive housing by middle income families. In Wisconsin, a distinction is now recognized between mobile homes (those used as homes) and motor homes (those often used as vehicles).

In the recent case of Beaulieu v. Minnehoma Insurance Co., 44 Wis. 2d 437, 171 N.W.2d 348 (1969), the Wisconsin Supreme Court pointed out the unique character of mobile homes: "As indicated by the plaintiff, a mobile home has a dual nature. It is designed as a house; yet, unlike a house, it is also capable of being easily transported. In the instant case, it was employed solely as an economical means of housing. It was never moved, nor was moving contemplated at the time the insurance coverage was procured." (44 Wis. 2d at 439).

We look to state law to determine the applicable standards for determining when personalty becomes affixed to real property.

The Wisconsin law on the question is found in Auto Acceptance and Loan Corp. v. Kelm, 18 Wis. 2d 178, 118 N.W. 2d 175 (1962) where the Wisconsin Supreme Court reaffirmed its decision in Standard Oil Co. v. LaCrosse Super Auto Service, Inc., 217 Wis. 237, 258 N.W. 791 (1935). That case held that the three tests for determining whether facilities remain personalty or are to be considered part of the realty are (1) actual physical annexation to the realty; (2) application or adaption to the use or purpose to which the realty is devoted, and (3) intention of the person making annexation to make a permanent accession to the freehold.

In the Standard Oil Company case, supra, the court pointed out that "physical annexation" is relatively unimportant and "intention" of the parties is the principal consideration.

In Premonstratensian Fathers v. Badger Mutual Insurance Co., 46 Wis. 2d 362, 175 N.W.2d 237 (1970), the court reaffirmed its adherence to the three-fold test saying, (46 Wis. 2d at p. 367) "It is the application of these tests to the facts of a particular case which will lead to a determination of whether or not an article, otherwise considered personal property, constitutes a common-law fixture, and hence takes on the nature of real property."

Viewed in light of these Wisconsin tests, the finding of the referee and the District Court that this mobile home had become a fixture must clearly stand. The bankrupt's actual intention pointed definitely toward affixing the mobile home to the land as a permanent residence, as seen in his application for a building permit (which, by law, required him to erect a concrete slab as a permanent foundation within one year), his purchase of a home-owner's insurance policy, and his requests made to the seller to have the wheels of the home removed. Moreover, the home was clearly adapted to use as the permanent residence of the bankrupt and was never moved off of his five-acre plot.

The fact that it may have been physically possible for this mobile home to have been more securely attached to the ground should not alter our position. Physical attachment did occur by means of cinder blocks and a "C" clamp, while connections for electricity, sewage and natural gas were provided as well. Finally, we note that the very size and difficulty in transporting this mobile home further highlight the fact that this was a vehicle which was intended primarily to be placed in one position for a long period of time and to be used as an intended permanent home. . . .

Our reading of the Wisconsin Statutes is thus consistent with other statutory and common law provisions dealing with the fixture situation, such as §9-313 of the Uniform Commercial Code which takes care to state that the Code does *not* prevent creation of encumbrances upon fixtures or real estate pursuant to the law applicable to real estate. (See also 4A Collier on Bankruptcy, ¶70.20 pp. 283-295).

In view of our holding that this particular mobile home had become a fixture under Wisconsin law and that the law of fixtures may, by law, be applied to mobile homes in that state, the judgment of the District must be and is

Affirmed.

NOTE

See White & Summers §25-8 and Henson §8-4. Then there is this oft-quoted passage from Strain v. Green, 25 Wash. 2d 692, 695, 172 P.2d 216, 218 (1946):

> [W]e will not undertake to write a Treatise on the law of fixtures. Every lawyer knows that cases can be found in this field that will support any position that the facts of his particular case require him to take. . . . [T]here is a wilderness of authority. . . . Fixture cases are so conflicting that it would be profitless . . . to review . . . them.

In theory your basic Property course taught you to tell fixtures from non-fixtures. Our main concern is resolution of priority disputes between those having a security interest in the fixture and those who have or acquire an interest in the realty to which the collateral is affixed. Read §9-313 carefully then consider these problems:

PROBLEM 70

The Righton Railway went to Octopus National Bank and asked to borrow money, using as part of the collateral its extensive network of railroad track (rails and ties), which winds through 12 western states. Octopus National consults you. The track is installed in a total of 117 counties. Must it file a financing statement in each one? See §§9-401(5) and 9-105(n). If so, may *copies* be filed or must each financing statement be an original that is manually signed by both parties? See §9-402(1), last sentence. See R. Kratovil, Modern Mortgage Law and Practice §283 (1972).

PROBLEM 71

Simon Mustache decided to erect an apartment building on a vacant lot he owned, so he borrowed $4,000,000 from Construction State Bank (hereafter CSB), to which he mortgaged the real estate "and all appurtenances or things affixed thereto, now present or after-acquired." Simon and CSB signed the mortgage, which contained a legal description of the realty, and the mortgage was filed in the real property recorder's office. The mortgage contained the debtor's mailing address, but did not give CSB's address. Is the filed mortgage effective as a "financing statement" so as to create a perfected security interest in goods which later become fixtures? See §§9-402(6), 9-402(1), 9-402(5), 9-402(8).

The original version of §9-401 (where to file) stated that fixture filings were to be in the county where a real estate mortgage would be filed, but did *not* say that it should be filed in the mortgage records. Some county clerks kept separate fixture files, some placed the filings in the real estate records, some placed them in with the other Article 9 non-fixture financing statement records, and, according to Professor Gilmore, some "filed" them in desk drawers and "old shoe boxes." G. Gilmore §30.5, at 818. This non-uniformity drove title examiners to drink. Many states amended §9-401 to require filing in the real estate records or in separate fixture files, depending on the nature of the state's recording system (Torrens, etc.); see Kripke, Fixtures Under the Uniform Commercial Code, 64 Colum. L. Rev. 44, 53 (1964). The 1972 version of §9-401(1) requires filing in the real property records; see Official Comment 1 to §9-313.

PROBLEM 72

Assume CSB (last Problem) did have a perfected security interest by virtue of its recorded mortgage covering after-acquired fixtures. During construction of the apartment building, Simon Mustache bought a furnace on credit from Blast Home Supplies, giving Blast a security interest in the furnace, and signing a financing statement which described the real estate. Where should Blast file? See §§9-313(1)(b) and 9-401. Is there a technical sentence that needs to be in the financing statement? See §9-402(5); why would the drafters have added such a requirement? Even if Blast files a proper financing statement in the right place before the furnace is installed, will Blast prevail over CSB? See §§9-313(4)(a), 9-313(6) and 9-313(1)(c), and Official Comment 4(e). If CSB's interest is not perfected, will Blast prevail? See §9-313(4)(b). What can Blast do to ensure itself of priority? See §9-313(5)(a).

PROBLEM 73

Would your answer to the last Problem's priority disputes change if the object in question were a refrigerator? What if it were a typewriter that Simon purchased for use in his office (which is located in the apartment building)? (Note: Some states would consider the typewriter a *fixture* under the *industrial plant* doctrine; see discussion above.) See §§9-313(4)(b), 9-313(6).

PROBLEM 74

Simon Mustache (last Problem) failed to pay his attorney, Susan Mean, so she sued him, recovered judgment, and levied on the apartment building and its contents. Will Simon's creditors holding security interests in the fixtures prevail if they have perfected by fixture filings? See §9-313(4)(d). What if those creditors filed financing statements in all the correct places *except* the real estate records? See Official Comment 4(c) to §9-313.

PROBLEM 75

After the building was complete, Tuesday Tenant moved in; not liking the refrigerator Simon had installed, she had him remove it and she bought another refrigerator on time from Easy Credit Department Store, which reserved a security interest therein but never filed a financing statement. Assume state real property laws permits CSB's after-acquired property mortgage to reach fixtures installed by lessees (if it does not, Easy Credit will always prevail; see §9-313(5)(b)). Will Easy Credit be entitled to priority if it is forced to repossess? See §9-313(4)(c) and Official Comment 4(d).

PROBLEM 76

Assume Tuesday (last Problem) bought a trash compactor on credit from Easy Credit Department Store and had her kitchen area remodeled to accommodate it. It was installed on May 5. Easy Credit comes to you on May 7, bringing with it a financing statement signed by Tuesday. Should the statement contain Simon Mustache's name too? Why? See §§9-402(5), 9-403(7). Will Easy Credit prevail over CSB if it files on May 10? See §§9-313(4)(a) and 9-302(1)(d). Will it prevail over Simon's landlord's lien?

PROBLEM 77

Assume that Blast Home Supplies held a perfected security interest in Simon's furnace, and that this interest was entitled to priority over CSB, the real estate mortgagee. If Simon defaults on his payments, what liability does Blast have to CSB if removal (repossession) of the furnace will do $1000 damage to the building's structure and if to replace it Simon (or CSB) will have to spend $8000? See §9-313(8) and Official Comment 9. What are CSB's rights? See the last sentence to §9-313(8). Is Blast liable to Simon for the damage to the building caused by the furnace's removal?

J. ACCESSIONS AND COMMINGLING

When goods are affixed to other goods (as opposed to realty) an *accession* occurs and the rights of the creditors are regulated by §9-314. A similar problem arises when goods are so combined with other goods (eggs in a cake mix, for example) that they cannot be recovered; see §9-315 on *commingling.* Article 9's contribution to the solution of these problems can only be completely understood in light of centuries of property law development; a lawyer embroiled in litigation should review the basic common law rules. See R. Brown, Personal Property ch. VI (Assessions and Confusion) (3d ed. Raushenbush 1975). Strangely enough, there has been little accession litigation and, at the time of this writing, only one minor appellate commingling case (and it was a criminal proceeding), Sowards v. State, 137 Ga. App. 423, 224 S.E.2d 85, 19 U.C.C. Rep. Serv. 292 (1976). Professor Gilmore has a good discussion of the meaning of the Code provisions in G. Gilmore ch. 31.

PROBLEM 78

Victor Valises was a traveling salesman. He owned a 1982 Ford in which the Salesmen's Credit Union held a perfected security interest (which was filed, as required by local law, in the office of the Secretary of State). When the tires were worn out he bought new ones from the Yeti Tire Company, which claimed a security interest in the tires, though the financing statement was not filed in the secretary of state's office until *after* the tires were installed on the Ford. If Victor goes bankrupt, which of the creditors is entitled to the tires? See §9-314; In re Williams, 12 U.C.C. Rep. Serv. 990 (Bankr., E.D. Wis. 1973) (defines *accession* to exclude easily removable items like tires); compare Ford Motor Credit Co. v. Howell Bros. Truck & Auto Repairs, Inc., 325 So. 2d 562, 18 U.C.C. Rep. Serv. 798 (Ala. App. 1975). If the tire company had filed a financing statement prior to the installation of the tires and that statement covered the *product* into which the goods were incorporated, could Yeti elect to claim a superior interest in the whole Ford (up to the value of the tires)? See §9-315; G. Gilmore §31.5, at 854.

K. FEDERAL PRIORITIES FOR DEBTS AND TAXES

1. The Federal Priority Statute

Most of the federal statutes concerning secured transactions are registration acts only and say little or nothing about priorities in the collateral. There are two major exceptions: the general federal priority statute, 31 U.S.C. §191 (fondly known as "R.S. 3466"), and the Federal Tax Lien Act, which is part of the Internal Revenue Code §§6321 to 6323.

The federal priority statute is a broadly worded grant of pre-bankruptcy priority for *all* federal claims (no matter how arising: tax matters, contract debts, federal insurance loans, guaranties, etc.), so that these claims are paid first when a debtor becomes insolvent. R.S. 3466, in language unchanged since Congress adopted it in 1797, provides:

> Whenever any person indebted to the United States is insolvent, or whenever the estate of any deceased debtor, in the hands of the executors or administrators, is insufficient to pay all the debts due from the deceased, the debts due to the United States shall be first satisfied; and the priority established shall extend as well to cases in which a debtor, not having sufficient property to pay all his debts, makes a voluntary assignment thereof, or in which the estate and effects of an absconding, concealed, or absent debtor are attached by process of law, as to cases in which an act of bankruptcy is committed.

The statute makes no exceptions to absolute federal priority but the courts have subordinated the federal claim to an earlier lien (judicial, statutory, and consensual) if the lien is *choate*. The United States Supreme Court, in a maddening series of cases, has refused to clarify the meaning of *choate,* so that it is difficult to predict when an earlier perfected lien will be sufficiently *choate* to prevail over the federal R.S. 3466 debt. In Illinois ex rel. Gordon v. Campbell, 329 U.S. 362 (1946), the Court held that a lien is "choate" (and therefore superior to the federal interest) if the lien is "definite . . . in at least three respects: . . . (1) the identity of the lienor; . . . (2) the amount of the lien . . . and (3) the property to which it attaches." In the *Campbell* case the Court held that a state statutory lien for unemployment contributions that purported to cover "all the personal property . . . used . . . in business" was not "choate" since the collateral's description was too vague under test number (3) above. In a later case, United States v. Gilbert Associates, Inc., 345 U.S. 361 (1953), the Court added that a lien was "inchoate" (and thereby lost to an R.S. 3466 claim) where the lien claimant had neither title nor possession. Since the 1946 *Campbell* decision, the Court has never found a lien sufficiently *choate* to survive a R.S. 3466 challenge, though lower federal courts have held that most security interests perfected under Article 9 are sufficiently choate to come ahead of the United States' claim; Pine Builders, Inc. v. United States, 413 F. Supp. 77, 19 U.C.C. Rep. Serv. 306 (E.D. Va. 1976). There is general agreement, however, that a security arrangement claiming a floating lien on after-acquired property or claiming a priority for future advances is *inchoate* and inferior to the federal claim. G. Gilmore §40.5.

2. *Tax Liens — Basic Priority*

A federal tax lien arises on *assessment* and covers all of the taxpayer's property, real or personal, presently owned or after acquired. This is a secret lien since it may be that no one knows of the assessment except the IRS, but the tax lien nevertheless binds the property and the government wins out over all parties claiming an interest in the property except those listed in §6323(a): "any purchaser, holder of a security interest, mechanic's lienor, or judgment creditor." To prevail over such persons, the federal tax lien must be *filed* in the place designated under state law (see IRC §6323(f)).

Aetna Insurance Co. v. Texas Thermal Industries

591 F.2d 1035, 26 U.C.C. Rep. Serv. 179 (5th Cir. 1979)

Per Curiam. This interpleader action requires resolution of three competing claims to the insurance proceeds due Texas

Thermal Industries, Inc. (TTI) after its insured inventory was destroyed in a fire. The principal claimants are (1) the Small Business Administration (SBA), which bases its claim to the proceeds upon a UCC security interest in the inventory, accounts receivable, machinery and equipment of TTI, (2) the Internal Revenue Service, which is asserting various federal tax liens against all property interests belonging to TTI, and (3) Eileen Markman, to whom TTI assigned its right to receive a portion of the insurance fund.

The case was submitted to the District Court upon an agreed statement of facts. The District Court entered findings of fact and conclusions of law, reported at 436 F. Supp. 371, and held that the SBA was entitled to the entire fund. We affirm.

The SBA interest stems from two loans made by the Citizens Bank of Kilgore, Texas, in participation with the SBA, to TTI. The loans, in the amounts of $200,000 and $150,000, were disbursed on January 5, 1973, and June 15, 1973, respectively. Collateral for these loans consisted of a security interest in and to all inventory, accounts receivable, machinery, and equipment of TTI. Financing statements were filed with the County Clerk of Gregg County, Texas, on January 15, 1973, and June 21, 1973.

The loan authorization issued by the SBA on both loans required that TTI obtain hazard insurance on the mortgaged collateral with loss-payee endorsements in favor of Citizens Bank and the SBA. On October 2, 1973, Aetna Insurance Company issued a hazards insurance policy to TTI, with loss-payee endorsements in favor of Citizens Bank and the SBA. Under the second loan authorization, TTI was also required to maintain 500 units of finished goods inventory under a bonded warehouse arrangement. A large portion of this inventory was destroyed in a warehouse fire on December 18, 1973.

On April 25, 1974, Citizens Bank assigned both the $200,000 note and the $150,000 note, as well as its interest in the secured collateral, to the SBA. As of June 24, 1974, the $150,000 note had a balance of $109,885.16 plus accrued interest from that date. As of September 24, 1974, the $200,000 note had a balance of $190,437.85 plus accrued interest.

The federal tax liens asserted by the IRS stem from a number of tax liabilities incurred by TTI and assessed between September 3, 1973 and August 5, 1974. The first filing of notice of any of these federal tax liens did not occur until December 17, 1973 — well after the Citizens Bank/SBA security interests had been perfected. According to the agreed statement of facts, there remains an outstanding assessed balance of $42,744.48 plus interest.

Eileen Markman's claim to the insurance proceeds stems from a loan of $16,000 she made to TTI shortly after the fire to help pay immediate expenses and maintain the business as an operating concern. As an inducement for the loans and as security for its repayment, on December 27, 1973, TTI executed an assignment of $11,000 of its right to receive proceeds under the Aetna policy to Eileen Markman.

A controversy subsequently arose between the insurance company and TTI over the extent of the loss occasioned by the warehouse fire in December, 1973. By stipulation of all interested parties it was finally agreed after extensive negotiations that the amount of loss was $175,000, and that Aetna would deposit this sum into the Registry of the Court in an interpleader action. The District Court concluded that the SBA lien had priority as to all others, and since its claim exceeded the amount in the insurance fund, the entire $175,000 was awarded to the SBA.

The appellants (TTI and Eileen Markman) argue the following points: (1) that the federal tax lien had priority over the SBA lien because the latter was not "choate"; (2) that Texas Business & Commercial Code §9-306(1), as it existed at the time of the fire loss, excluded the fire insurance funds from the definition of "proceeds"; and (3) that Eileen Markman is entitled to a portion of the fire insurance fund. We will address each of these issues in order.

(1) The first issue to be decided is the relative priority as between the federal tax liens and the contractual SBA liens asserted under Texas law. The principal statutory provisions governing federal tax liens are Sections 6321-6323 of the Internal Revenue Code, 26 USC §§6321-6323. Section 6321 provides that a lien shall arise in favor of the United States upon all property and property rights of any taxpayer to the extent of any tax liability which that taxpayer neglects or refuses to pay after demand. By virtue of §6322, this lien arises automatically on the date of assessment. Section 6323, as overhauled by the Federal Tax Lien Act of 1966, speaks to priority conflicts and subordinates the federal tax liens created under §§6321 and 6322 to certain competing private or nonfederal liens. Of particular importance to this case are subsections (a) and (h)(1). The former provides that a federal tax lien imposed by §6321 is not valid as against the

holder of a security interest until proper notice of the federal lien has been filed. 26 USC §6323(a). "Security interest" is defined by §6323(h)(1) in the following terms:

> The term "security interest" means any interest in property acquired by contract for the purpose of securing payment or performance of an obligation or indemnifying against loss or liability. A securing interest exists at any time (A) if, at such time, the property is in existence and the interest has become protected under local law against a subsequent judgment lien arising out of an unsecured obligation, and (B) to the extent that, at such time, the holder has parted with money or money's worth.

Notice of any of the federal tax liens in this case was not filed until December 17, 1978, while the SBA security interests were perfected with the filing of the financing statements on January 5, and June 15, 1973. Thus, by the explicit terms of §6323(a) and (h)(1), the federal tax liens in this case are not valid as against the SBA liens, provided the SBA's secured interest in proceeds encompasses insurance proceeds.

The appellants however contend that despite the provisions of §6323, the SBA liens are not prime because they are not "choate." They base their argument on the long-established principle of federal common law governing priority conflicts between nonfederal or private liens or obligations and federal claims for the collection of debts owing the United States that only "choate" nonfederal liens prime competing federal claims.[5] In a series of cases between 1950 and 1963, the Supreme Court applied this choateness doctrine to questions of priority involving federal tax liens and evolved the following test: in order for a nonfederal lien to prevail over a later filed federal tax lien, the "identity of the lienor, the property subject to the lien, and the amount of the lien" must be established as of the date of filing of notice of the tax lien.[6] Appellants argue that the SBA liens do not satisfy that choateness test.

5. See generally Kennedy, The Relative Priority of the Federal Government: The Pernicious Career of the Inchoate and General Lien, 63 Yale LJ 905 (1954).

6. See, e.g., United States v. Pioneer American Ins. Co., 1963, 374 US 84, 83 S. Ct. 1651, 10 L. Ed 2d 770; United States v. New Britain, 1953, 347 US 81, 84, 74 S. Ct. 367, 98 L. Ed 520; see generally Coogan, The Effect of the Federal Tax Lien Act of 1966 Upon Security Interests Created Under the Uniform Commercial Code, 81 Harv. L. Rev. 1369, 1375-80.

That may or may not be the case, but Congress has spared us the necessity of engaging in the metaphysical analysis necessary to answer the question. As the Treasury increased its reliance upon the tax lien as a method for collecting outstanding taxes, and as the financing world increasingly relied upon security interests in inventory and accounts receivable, the harshness of the choateness rule and the vagaries of its application in the tax lien context caused increasing confusion and generated increasing criticism. The Federal Tax Lien Act of 1966, as codified at 26 USC §6323, represented a response to the problem. The purpose of the Act was, at least in large part, to "conform the lien provisions of the internal revenue laws to the concepts developed in [the] Uniform Commercial Code."[7] We therefore conclude, and hold, that whatever role the "choateness" rule of federal common law may play in other contexts, it has been supplanted by the provisions of §6323 with respect to tax lien priority questions as to which that statute provides an unambiguous federal law answer. Cf. Slodov v. United States, 1978, 436 US 238, 256-58, 98 S. Ct. 1778 56 L. Ed. 2d 251. Since §6323 specifically subordinates federal tax liens to security interests — such as those asserted by the SBA — that are perfected under the UCC provisions of state law prior to the filing of the tax lien, the SBA liens have priority, regardless whether they are "choate" or not under formerly applicable common law principles.

(2) [The court then concluded that the SBA's interest extended to the insurance proceeds.]

(3) Simple arithmetic disposes of the third issue. Since the SBA lien had priority over all other liens, and since the $175,000 fund is completely consumed by the SBA claim (which exceeds $300,000), there is simply nothing left for Eileen Markman to claim, regardless of whether her lien is equitable or not.

The judgment of the District Court is affirmed.

3. *Tax Liens and After-Acquired Property*

Problem 79

Octopus National Bank had a perfected security interest in the inventory, accounts receivable, instruments, and chattel paper of an

7. HR Rep. No. 1884, 89th Cong, 2d Sess 1 (1966).

automobile dealership named Smiles Motors, to which the bank made periodic loans. Smiles Motors failed to pay its federal taxes and the IRS filed a tax lien in the proper place on October 1, 1982. On the first days of November and December new shipments of cars arrived at Smiles' lot, and all during the rest of the year Smiles continued to sell cars on credit, generating chattel paper and accounts receivable. Does the filing of the tax lien cut off ONB's floating lien in whole or in part? Is this issue in any way affected by the bank's knowledge of the tax lien filing?

The answer to Problem 79 is that §6323(c) of the Internal Revenue Code expressly permits *commercial financing security* (defined at the end of the section) to fall under an existing perfected security arrangement and take priority over a filed federal tax lien if the new collateral is acquired by the taxpayer-debtor in the 45 days following the tax lien filing. While §6323(c)(2)(A) requires that the loan has to be made without knowledge of the tax lien filing, the lender's later discovery of the tax lien filing in no way affects the priority of its floating lien during the 45-day period; see Treas. Reg. §301.6323(c)-1(d) (1976). Section 6323(c):

> (c) Protection for certain commercial transactions financing agreements, etc. —
>
> (1) In general. — To the extent provided in this subsection, even though notice of a lien imposed by section 6321 has been filed, such lien shall not be valid with respect to a security interest which came into existence after tax lien filing but which —
>
> (A) is in qualified property covered by the terms of a written agreement entered into before tax lien filing and constituting —
>
> (i) a commercial transactions financing agreement,
>
> (ii) a real property construction or improvement financing agreement, or
>
> (iii) an obligatory disbursement agreement, and
>
> (B) is protected under local law against a judgment lien arising, as of the time of tax lien filing, out of an unsecured obligation.
>
> (2) Commercial transactions financing agreement. — For purposes of this subsection —
>
> (A) Definition. — The term "commercial transactions financing agreement" means an agreement (entered into by a person in the course of his trade or business) —
>
> (i) to make loans to the taxpayer to be secured by

commercial financing security acquired by the taxpayer in the ordinary course of his trade or business, or

(ii) to purchase commercial financing security (other than inventory) acquired by the taxpayer in the ordinary course of his trade or business;

but such an agreement shall be treated as coming within the term only to the extent that such loan or purchase is made before the 46th day of tax lien filing or (if earlier) before the lender or purchaser had actual notice or knowledge of such tax lien filing.

(B) Limitation on qualified property. — The term "qualified property," when used with respect to a commercial transactions financing agreement, includes only commercial financing security acquired by the taxpayer before the 46th day after the date of tax lien filing.

(C) Commercial financing security defined. — The term "commercial financing security" means (i) paper of a kind ordinarily arising in commercial transactions, (ii) accounts receivable, (iii) mortgages on real property, and (iv) inventory.

See Texas Oil & Gas Corp. v. United States, 466 F.2d 1040, 11 U.C.C. Rep. Serv. 575 (5th Cir. 1972), a splendid opinion that begins: "We enter with some trepidation the tortured meanderings of federal tax lien law, intersected now by the somewhat smoother byway of the Uniform Commercial Code," and concludes that the 45-day rule only applies as to property *actually acquired* by the debtor in the 45-day period:

> Of course we realize that this disposition does not afford the protection that commercial lenders who deal with after-acquired property might prefer. As the law appears to stand, the commercial lender must check the applicable records every 45 days or else seriously jeopardize his security under the varying degrees of rigor promulgated by the choateness doctrine.

466 F.2d at 1053, 11 UCC Rep. Serv. at 593.

To take advantage of this 45-day period, the drafters of the 1972 version of the Code amended §9-301(4) to conform the state law battle of secured party vs. lien creditor to the same 45-day rule. See Henson §§5-14 to 5-17.[8]

8. A similar amendment to §9-307 is new subsection (3), which protects non-ordinary course buyers from future advances made with knowledge of the purchase or more than 45 days after the purchase. See Henson §5-18.

PROBLEM 80

Six months after the IRS filed a tax lien against her, Charlene McGee bought a fire extinguisher system for her horse stables. She purchased the system on credit from King Protection Enterprises, which reserved a purchase money security interest in itself. Is the IRS's lien superior to King's purchase money security interest? See Rev. Rul. 68-57, 26 C.F.R. 301.6321-1 (1968).

4. *Tax Liens and Future Advances*

After the filing of the tax lien, the taxpayer's financing creditor may make a new loan expecting it to be secured by an existing perfected interest in the collateral listed in the security agreement. If the secured party is aware of the filed tax lien it almost certainly will refuse to make the advance, but if the lien is undiscovered and the advance given, which has priority — the IRS or the lender?

I.R.C. §6323(d) gives protection to future advances made without knowledge of the tax lien in the 45 days after its filing if the advance is collateralized by a perfected security interest in existing property of the taxpayer, such as equipment. It provides:

> (d) 45-day period for making disbursements. — Even though notice of a lien imposed by section 6321 has been filed, such lien shall not be valid with respect to a security interest which came into existence after tax lien filing by reason of disbursements made before the 46th day after the date of tax lien filing, or (if earlier) before the person making such disbursements had actual notice or knowledge of tax lien filing, but only if such security interest—
>
> (1) is in property (A) subject, at the time of tax lien filing, to the lien imposed by section 6321, and (B) covered by the terms of a written agreement entered into before tax lien filing, and
>
> (2) is protected under local law against a judgment lien arising, as of the time of tax lien filing, out of an unsecured obligation.

PROBLEM 81

Muscles Construction Company owned construction equipment worth $90,000 and used it as collateral for a $50,000 loan from Octopus National Bank. ONB, due to malpractice by its attorney, filed the financing statement in only *one* of the two places mandated by the state's version of §9-401. Muscles thereafter borrowed $20,000 from Boilerplate State Bank, using the equipment again as collateral. When searching the files prior to filing BSB's financing statement, BSB's attorney happened across the ONB partial filing. Since the collateral was worth more than both debts the attorney didn't worry about the prior transaction, and BSB's financing statement was then correctly filed in both places mandated by §9-401. Three days after the BSB filing, the IRS filed its tax lien. Muscles owed the federal government $30,000 in back taxes. The day *after* the tax lien filing, of which BSB knew nothing, BSB advanced the $20,000 to Muscles. The IRS seized the equipment and sold it for $90,000 a month later. How is the $90,000 divvied up between the three claimants? Note §9-401(2). For an exhaustive discussion of circular priority problems and the headaches they cause see G. Gilmore ch. 39.

PROBLEM 82

Marie Medici owned a hat factory. She financed her business through a series of loans from the Richelieu State Bank pursuant to an agreement by which she gave the bank a security interest in all of the factory's equipment and the bank agreed to loan her money from time to time "as it thinks prudent." A financing statement covering the equipment was filed in the proper place. On August 1, 1977, she owed the bank $1500 (having paid back most of the prior loans); the equipment consisted of two machines: the Habsburg Hat Blocker (worth $7,000) and the Huguenot Felt Press (worth $5,000). On that date the United States filed a federal tax lien against all of Medici's property. On August 31, the bank loaned her another $10,000. Answer these questions:

(a) Assuming the bank did not know of the tax lien on August 31, does the bank or the United States have priority in the equipment, and to what amount? See I.R.C. §6323(d). What if the bank did know?

(b) Assume there is no tax lien but on August 15, Louis Dupes paid Medici $5,000 cash for the Huguenot Felt Press, and on August 31, the bank loaned her the $10,000. Does the purchase cut off the bank's security interest? Does it matter whether or not the bank knew of the sale prior to the August 31 loan? See §§9-307(3), 9-105(1)(k).

(c) Instead of buying the machine as in the last paragraph, assume that Dupes is another creditor of Medici's and on August 15, he levied execution on the felt press pursuant to a judgment. If he did this with full knowledge of the bank's security interest, and with notice of his levy the bank still loans Medici the $10,000 on August 31, does Dupes or the Richelieu State Bank have the superior interest in the felt press? See §9-301 and its Official Comment 7.

CHAPTER 7

BANKRUPTCY AND ARTICLE 9

A. *THE TRUSTEE'S STATUS*

Under §544(b) of the Bankruptcy Code the trustee is imbued with the rights and position of any unsecured creditor who has a claim against the estate. In the cryptic and often criticized opinion of Moore v. Bay, 284 U.S. 4 (1931), the Supreme Court per Oliver Wendell Holmes held, however, that the trustee gets better rights than the creditor represented since the trustee's claim is not limited to the amount of the actual creditor's claim but rather is the size of the entire estate.

§544. *Trustee As Lien Creditor and As Successor To Certain Creditors and Purchasers*

(a) The trustee shall have, as of the commencement of the case, and without regard to any knowledge of the trustee or of any creditor, the rights and powers of, or may avoid any transfer of property of the debtor or any obligation incurred by the debtor that is voidable by —

(1) a creditor that extends credit to the debtor at the time of the commencement of the case, and that obtains, at such time and with respect to such credit, a judicial lien on all property on which a creditor on a simple contract could have obtained a judicial lien, whether or not such a creditor exists;

(2) a creditor that extends credit, to the debtor at the time of the commencement of the case, and obtains, at such time and with respect to such credit, an execution against the debtor that is returned unsatisfied at such time, whether or not such a creditor exists; and

(3) a bona fide purchaser of real property from the debtor, against whom applicable law permits such transfer to be perfected, that obtains the status of a bona fide purchaser at the time of the commencement of the case, whether or not such a purchaser exists.

(6) The trustee may avoid any transfer of an interest of the debtor in property or any obligation incurred by the debtor that is voidable under applicable law by a creditor holding an unsecured claim that is allowable under section 502 of this title or that is not allowable only under section 502(e) of this title.

PROBLEM 83

Vince Vagrant was the owner of the Aristides Stables, where he bred, trained, and raced horses. For a $1000 loan, he gave the Baden Baden Bank a security interest in the horses on October 27, 1982, and the bank filed a financing statement in the county recorder's office (it should have been filed in the office of the secretary of state). The Day Star Financing Company (hereinafter DSFC) loaned Vagrant $20,000 on December 4, 1982, taking a security interest in the same collateral, and filing a financing statement in the proper office. Day Star had actual knowledge of the terms of the first security agreement and had seen the improperly filed financing statement. The stables and Vagrant went under and a bankruptcy petition was filed on January 8, 1983. The trustee, Lord Murphy, an expatriated English peer now working as a lawyer in the United States, represented unsecured debts of $54,000. Under §544(a)(1) of the Bankruptcy Code, Lord Murphy has the status of a lien creditor who perfects his lien on the date of the filing of the bankruptcy petition, and can avoid any prior security interest that is not valid against such a lien creditor. What are Lord Murphy's rights against the Baden Baden Bank? See §§9-301(1)(b) and 9-301(3). Even though the trustee can use §544(a)(1) of the Bankruptcy Code to *avoid* the bank's secured position as against the bank, the trustee may nonetheless *preserve* such a position vis-à-vis other creditors and squeeze himself into it. This means that if the Baden Baden Bank wins out over the Day Star Financing Company, Lord Murphy can use §544(a)(1) to avoid BBB's security interest and then assume BBB's superior position against DSFC. Does BBB have priority over DSFC? Section 9-401(2). If Lord Murphy gets in ahead of DSFC and the horses sell for exactly $20,000, is the latter's interest cut down by $1000 and still perfected as to $19,000? See the Moore v. Bay discussion above and White & Summers §24-7.

PROBLEM 84

Lew Sun, a Korean, moved to Chicago and opened a Korean restaurant called "Seoul Food." He had many unsecured creditors (food sellers, linen services, employees, etc.), and on April 17, 1982 he applied to the International State Bank for a loan of $10,000, signing a security interest and a financing statement in favor of the bank, secured by an interest in Sun's equipment. On April 18, 1982 one hour before the bank filed the financing statement, Sun filed a bankruptcy petition in the federal court.

(a) If no new general creditors came into existence between the loan on April 17 and the petition filing on April 18, can the trustee avoid the bank's security interest under §544(a) of the Code?

(b) What result if the bank had filed its financing statement two seconds before the bankruptcy petition was filed?

(c) If the bank's interest had been a *purchase money security interest* would the filing of the bankruptcy petition have cut off the usual 10-day grace period? See §546(b) of the Code which follows.

§546. *Limitations on Avoiding Powers*

(a) An action or proceeding under section 544, 545, 547, 548, or 553 of this title may not be commenced after the earlier of —

(1) two years after the appointment of a trustee under section 702, 1104, 1163, or 1302 of this title; and

(2) the time the case is closed or dismissed.

(b) The rights and powers of the trustee under section 544, 545, or 549 of this title are subject to any generally applicable law that permits perfection of an interest in property to be effective against an entity that acquires rights in such property before the date of such perfection. If such law requires seizure of such property or commencement of an action to accomplish such perfection, and such property has not been seized or such action has not been commenced before the date of the filing of the petition, such interest in such property shall be perfected by notice within the time fixed by such law for such seizure or commencement.

B. PREFERENCES

A preference is a "transfer" (defined in the Bankruptcy Code to include the creation of a security interest in the debtor's property) made or suffered by the bankrupt to pay or secure a pre-existing debt within the 90-day period preceding the filing of the bankruptcy petition which has the effect of giving the transferee (the creditor) a greater payment than the creditor would get under the usual bankruptcy distribution. The trustee can avoid such preferential transfers under §547 of the Bankruptcy Code, reprinted in the next paragraph, if the debtor was insolvent at the time of transfer, which is presumed in the 90-day period. An Article 9 creditor who delays perfection until the 90 days before bankruptcy is frequently met with a trustee who is wielding §547 as a weapon.

If the creation of a security interest is deemed preferential, the trustee can cancel it, thus turning the preferred creditor into an unsecured (read *unpaid*) one. Other transfers of the debtor's property (for instance, a cash payment) are returned to the bankrupt's estate at the trustee's insistence.

§547. *Preferences*

(a) In this section —

(1) "inventory" means personal property leased or furnished, held for sale or lease, or to be furnished under a contract for service, raw materials, work in process, or materials used or consumed in a business, including farm products such as crops or livestock, held for sale or lease;

(2) "new value" means money or money's worth in goods, services, or new credit, or release by a transferee of property previously transferred to such transferee in a transaction that is neither void nor voidable by the debtor or the trustee under any applicable law, but does not include an obligation substituted for an existing obligation;

(3) "receivable" means right to payment, whether or not such right has been earned by performance; and

(4) a debt for a tax is incurred on the day when such tax is last payable, including any extension, without penalty.

(b) Except as provided in subsection (c) of this section, the trustee may avoid any transfer of property of the debtor —

(1) to or for the benefit of a creditor;

(2) for or on account of an antecedent debt owed by the debtor before such transfer was made;

(3) made while the debtor was insolvent;

(4) made —

(A) on or within 90 days before the date of the filing of the petition; or

(B) between 90 days and one year before the date of the filing of the petition, if such creditor, at the time of such transfer

(i) was an insider; and

(ii) had reasonable cause to believe the debtor was insolvent at the time of such transfer; and

(5) that enables such creditor to receive more than such creditor would receive if —

(A) the case were a case under chapter 7 of this title;

(B) the transfer had not been made; and

(C) such creditor received payment of such debt to the extent provided by the provisions of this title.

(c) The trustee may not avoid under this section a transfer —

(1) to the extent that such transfer was —

(A) intended by the debtor and the creditor to or for whose benefit such transfer was made to be a contemporaneous exchange for new value given to the debtor; and

(B) in fact a substantially contemporaneous exchange;

(2) to the extent that such transfer was —

(A) in payment of a debt incurred in the ordinary course of business or financial affairs of the debtor and the transferee;

(B) made not later than 45 days after such debt was incurred;

(C) made in the ordinary course of business or financial affairs of the debtor and the transferee; and

(D) made according to ordinary business terms;

(3) of a security interest in property acquired by the debtor —

(A) to the extent such security interest secures new value that was —

(i) given at or after the signing of a security agreement that contains a description of such property as collateral;

(ii) given by or on behalf of the secured party under such agreement;

(iii) given to enable the debtor to acquire such property; and

(iv) in fact used by the debtor to acquire such property; and

(B) that is perfected before 10 days after such security interest attaches;

(4) to or for the benefit of a creditor, to the extent that, after such transfer, such creditor gave new value to or for the benefit of the debtor —

(A) not secured by an otherwise unavoidable security interest; and

(B) on account of which new value the debtor did not make an otherwise unavoidable transfer to or for the benefit of such creditor;

(5) of a perfected security interest in inventory or a receivable or the proceeds of either, except to the extent that the aggregate of all such transfers to the transferee caused a reduction, as of the date of the filing of the petition and to the prejudice of other creditors holding unsecured claims, of any amount by which the debt secured by such security interest exceeded the value of all security interest for such debt on the later of —

(A)(i) with respect to a transfer to which subsection (b)(4)(A) of this section applies, 90 days before the date of the filing of the petition; or

(ii) with respect to a transfer to which subsection (b)(4)(B) of this section applies, one year before the date of the filing of the petition; and

(B) the date on which new value was first given under the security agreement creating such security interest; or

(6) that is the fixing of a statutory lien that is not avoidable under section 545 of this title.

(d) A trustee may avoid a transfer of property of the debtor transferred to secure reimbursement of a surety that furnished a bond or other obligation to dissolve a judicial lien that would have been avoidable by the trustee under subsection (b) of this section. The liability of such surety under such bond or obligation shall be discharged to the extent of the value of such property recovered by the trustee or the amount paid to the trustee.

(e) (1) For the purposes of this section —

(A) a transfer of real property other than fixtures, but including the interest of a seller or purchaser under a contract for the sale of real property, is perfected when a bona fide purchaser of such property from the debtor against whom applicable law permits such transfer to be perfected cannot acquire an interest that is superior to the interest of the transferee; and

(B) a transfer of a fixture or property other than real property is perfected when a creditor on a simple contract cannot acquire a judicial lien that is superior to the interest of the transferee.

(2) For the purposes of this section, except as provided in paragraph (3) of this subsection, a transfer is made —

(A) at the time such transfer takes effect between the transferor and the transferee, if such transfer is perfected at, or within 10 days after, such time;

(B) at the time such transfer is perfected, if such transfer is perfected after such 10 days; or

(C) immediately before the date of the filing of the petition, if such transfer is not perfected at the later of —

(i) the commencement of the case; and

(ii) 10 days after such transfer takes effect between the transferor and the transferee.

(3) For the purposes of this section, a transfer is not made until the debtor has acquired rights in the property transferred.

(f) For the purposes of this section, the debtor is presumed to have been insolvent on and during the 90 days immediately preceding the date of the filing of the petition.

PROBLEM 85

On June 8, Business Corporation borrowed $80,000 from Octopus National Bank and gave the bank a security interest in its equipment. On July 18, ONB filed a properly executed financing statement in the proper place. The next day Business Corporation filed its bankruptcy petition. Can the trustee destroy ONB's secured position and turn it into a general creditor under the theory that the delayed perfection is a preference? If ONB *had* perfected on June 8 but the bankrupt made some payments to ONB in the 90-day period before the filing of the petition, could the trustee use §547 to make ONB pay that money back into the estate? See White & Summers §24-4 at 1004.

PROBLEM 86

Mark Garvey ran a travel agency in New York. He bought a company car which he financed by a loan from the Small Business Association. The SBA took a security interest in the car, but failed to perfect it under New York law. By February 28, Garvey had missed two payments in a row and the SBA repossessed the car the next day. See §9-302(1)(a). On April 1, Garvey filed a bankruptcy petition. Can the trustee recover the car from the SBA?

PROBLEM 87

On November 1, the Piggy National Bank loaned Kermit $1000 to buy a banjo he wanted for his nightclub act, making him sign a security agreement and a financing statement. He bought the banjo on November 15, and the bank filed the financing statement in the proper place on November 20; Kermit filed his bankruptcy petition the next day. Is the *transfer* of the security interest in his banjo a preference? See §547(c)(3). If the bank's security interest were not of the *purchase money* variety, but was simply a floating lien covering all after-acquired equipment, what result using the same dates? See §547(e)(2); White & Summers §24-5, at 1006-1007.

PROBLEM 88

In early 1981, John Carter borrowed $1000 from the Barsoom World Bank; it was a *signature loan* (i.e., no collateral). On September 25, 1981, John made a $500 payment to the bank, but on October 4 he borrowed $300 more from the bank, giving it a security interest in his sword collection. The bank never filed a financing statement, and John filed a bankruptcy petition on November 8, 1981. How much, if anything, may his bankruptcy trustee recover from the bank? See §§544(a)(2) and 547(c)(4); White & Summers §24-5, at 1007.

C. *THE FLOATING LIEN IN BANKRUPTCY*

Section 60 of the former Bankruptcy Act condemned as a preference the creation of a security interest within four months of the filing of the bankruptcy petition unless the creditor advanced new money for the collateral as it was acquired. A question of immense concern to creditors who lent against inventory or accounts receivable was whether their security interest in the collateral acquired in that four-month period would be preferential. Even though the UCC clearly permits after-acquired property to be covered automatically by the security interest, the Code is drafted so that the security interest cannot *attach* or be *perfected* until the debtor acquires an interest in the property, and, arguably, *that* occurs within the four-month period; §§9-203, 9-303. Under both the prior and current versions of the Bankruptcy Act *perfection* of the security interest is the moment of "transfer" in preference disputes, and thus the argument is that the collateral first falling under the floating lien during the preference period is recoverable by the trustee as a preferential "transfer" securing an old debt.

To meet this argument by the trustee, the UCC drafters came up with §9-108, which "explains" to the federal courts that the security interest creation is not a preference even though it attaches to some parts of the inventory or accounts within the four months preceding bankruptcy because the true transfer is "deemed" to have taken place earlier. The problem with §9-108 is that it is state law, and the decision as to what is a preference is a federal bankruptcy question. Further the Code drafters surely could have thought up a better word than "deemed," which implies that although the transfer "really" takes place now, we'll all pretend it took place earlier. Read §9-108 carefully.

Everyone crossed their fingers and waited for a federal appellate court to hear a bankruptcy challenge to an Article 9 floating lien. The Seventh Circuit spoke first. In Grain Merchants of Ind., Inc. v. Union Bank & Sav. Co., 408 F.2d 209, 6 U.C.C. Rep. Serv. 1 (7th Cir. 1969), the court upheld the floating lien's validity as to the property falling under it during the preference period, though the court noted that in the case at bar there was both inflow and outgo of collateral during the relevant time period and the creditor had thus not improved its position by getting an increased amount of collateral prior to bankruptcy. The court did not rely on §9-108 to justify its pro-creditor result, though later courts have done so.

The Bankruptcy Act's solution to this after-acquired property/preference issue is found in §547(c)(5) supra; use it to solve the following.

PROBLEM 89

The Last National Bank had a perfected security interest in the inventory of the Epstein bookstore, which owed the bank $20,000. On March 1, 1985, the inventory was worth $8,000. On May 28, 1985, when Epstein filed for bankruptcy the inventory was worth $20,000 since the store had purchased several new shipments for cash in the interim. What can the trustee do about the bank's claim? What if the bank first loaned Epstein $20,000 on May 1, 1985, when the inventory was worth $12,000?

D. *FRAUDULENT CONVEYANCES*

Under §§548 or 544(b) of the Bankruptcy Code, the trustee can avoid any "transfer" (including the creation of an Article 9 security interest) that is a *fraudulent conveyance*. The law as to what is or is not a fraudulent conveyance has been developing for centuries, but is generally summarized in the Uniform Fraudulent Conveyances Act (UFCA), which many states adopted. There an existing or later creditor (and the bankruptcy trustee per §544(b)) may avoid any transfer of the insolvent debtor's property if the transferee does not give "a fair consideration" in exchange, or if the transferee has actual intent to defraud the debtor's creditors.

PROBLEM 90

When Arnold Austin retired as an international diplomat he was famous but much in debt. He decided to make money by writing his memoirs, which were certainly bestseller material. He gave a security interest in the right to receive royalty payments from his publisher to his wife as collateral for "the many debts I owe her," and she filed a financing statement in the proper place five months before Arnold filed his bankruptcy petition. Can the trustee avoid this security interest? (At common law one of the *badges of fraud* — situations in which fraud is presumed — was a voluntary transfer made by the debtor to a family member; United States v. West, 299 F. Supp. 661 (D. Del. 1969).) See G. Gilmore §45.3.1.

E. *NON-CONSENSUAL LIENS AND THE TRUSTEE*

Section 547(b) of the Bankruptcy Act condemns as preferential all judicial liens acquired by a creditor within the 90 days preceding the bankruptcy filing if taken while the bankrupt was insolvent.

As for statutory liens (the auto repairman, etc.), they are effective under §545 against the trustee if (a) they would be good against a BFP, and (b) they do not arise only on insolvency. The reason for this last rule — statutory liens which arise only on insolvency are void against the trustee — is this: originally the Bankruptcy Act permitted the separate states to specify which general creditors would get priority payments when the bankrupt's estate was distributed. When that power was taken away from the states, the states battled back by rewriting their priority statutes as statutory lien statutes, providing, for example, that unpaid employees would have an automatic lien on the employer's assets if the employer became insolvent but not otherwise. Since Congress didn't want the states to be able to dictate priorities in a federal insolvency proceeding, §545 and its predecessor were redrafted to avoid this type of statutory lien.

CHAPTER 8

PROCEEDS

A. THE MEANING OF PROCEEDS

Proceeds is defined in §9-306(1) and there subdivided into two parts: *cash proceeds* and *non-cash proceeds*. Read §9-306(1) and (2).

PROBLEM 91

When Rosetta Stone bought a new car from Champollion Motors, Inc., she traded in her five-year-old car, made a $200 downpayment by giving the salesman her check, and signed a promissory note for the balance payable to the dealership. The Rameses National Bank had a perfected security interest in Champollion Motor's inventory.

(a) Does that security interest continue in the car once it is delivered to Ms. Stone? See §9-307(1).

(b) Under §9-306(2) the bank's security interest will continue in *proceeds*, as defined in subsection (1). What are the proceeds of the car sale?

(c) Is the attachment of the bank's security interest to the proceeds automatic or need the bank take technical steps to perfect it? Read §9-306(3) carefully.

(d) If Rameses National Bank wants to file a financing statement in the 10-day period provided by §9-306, but the debtor Champollion Motors refused to sign, what should RNB do? See §9-402(2).

While Article 9 does not usually apply to security interests taken in either insurance policies or bank accounts as collateral (the common law or other statutes regulate these transactions), insurance payments or bank account monies that qualify as *proceeds* are regulated by the Code. For example, if the collateral is a car that is destroyed in a traffic mishap and the car owner receives compensation from an insurance company, the insurance money is *proceeds* and any security interest in the car attaches to these monies. Similarly if the car owner sells the car and deposits the buyer's money in a bank account, the account now is *proceeds* and the car money can be traced into the bank account and tapped by the unpaid secured creditor. Read §§9-306(2) and 9-306(3)(b); cf. §§9-104(g) and 9-104(l).

B. *PRIORITIES IN PROCEEDS*

PROBLEM 92

The Aquarius Auto Audio Shop (hereinafter AAAS) sold and installed stereo systems in cars. Its inventory was financed by the Canis Major Bank and Trust Co., which had a perfected security interest in present and after-acquired inventory. When Aquarius sold the systems it sometimes was paid cash and sometimes extended credit without signed contracts, and sometimes made credit customers sign contracts promising payment and granting AAAS a security interest in the systems. When it needed further financing, it took a later loan from the Cassiopeia Finance Company, granting the lender a security interest in its accounts receivable and its chattel paper. Cassiopeia knew all about the prior loan and inventory security interest of the Canis Major Bank at the time it filed its financing statement in the proper place. Aquarius defaulted on both loans, and both secured parties claimed the accounts and chattel paper (only Canis Major claimed the inventory). Canis Major's theory was that the accounts and chattel paper were *proceeds* of the inventory. The chattel paper was in Cassiopeia's possession; it had not yet collected any of the accounts receivable. Who should prevail? See §§9-306, 9-308, and 9-312; White & Summers §25-4, at 1040-1041, and §25-17; Henson §6-5; Bank of Beulah v. Chase, 231 N.W.2d 738, 17 U.C.C. Rep.

Serv. 259 (N.D. 1975); Rex Fin. Corp. v. Great W. Bank & Trust, 23 Ariz. App. 286, 532 P.2d 558, 16 U.C.C. Rep. Serv. 1155 (1975). What result where the accounts receivable financer filed first?

PROBLEM 93

Shadrach Heating & Air Conditioning, Inc. borrowed $15,000 from the Meshach Merchants Financing Association (hereinafter MMFA) in order to purchase a new furnace for its own home office. When one of its important clients needed an identical furnace in a hurry, Shadrach Heating sold it its own new furnace, which it installed in the client's place of business. The $17,000 check it received in payment was put into Shadrach's checking account (balance prior to this deposit: $81.00) with the Abednego State Bank. Thereafter Shadrach made one further deposit of $5000, followed a week later by a withdrawal of $5040.

(a) Are proceeds from the furnace sale still in the bank accounts? See Universal C.I.T. Credit Corp. v. Farmers Bank, 358 F. Supp. 317, 13 U.C.C. Rep. Serv. 109 (E.D. Mo. 1973) (the general rule is that "in tracing commingled funds it is presumed that any payments made were from other than funds in which another had a legally recognized interest," called the "lowest intermediate balance" rule); §9-306(2) permits tracing of *identifiable* proceeds. See also Brown & Williamson Tobacco Corp. v. First Natl. Bank, 504 F.2d 998, 15 U.C.C. Rep. Serv. 553 (7th Cir. 1974) and C.O. Funk & Son, Inc. v. Sullivan Equip. Inc., 92 Ill. App. 3d 659, 415 N.E.2d 1309, 30 U.C.C. Rep. Serv. 1459 (1981).

(b) If Shadrach Heating defaults on its loan repayment to Meshach Merchants Financing Association and also on an unsecured promissory note currently held by the Abednego State Bank, can the bank exercise its common law right of setoff and pay itself out of the checking account, or is its setoff right junior to MMFA's security interest in the proceeds? See Universal C.I.T. Credit Corp. v. Farmers Bank, supra; Commercial Discount Corp. v. Milwaukee W. Bank, 61 Wis. 2d 671, 214 N.W.2d 33, 13 U.C.C. Rep. Serv. 1202 (1974); Citizens Natl. Bank v. Mid-States Dev. Co., 380 N.E.2d 1243, 24 U.C.C. Rep. Serv. 1321 (Ind. App. 1978); Annot., 8 A.L.R.3d 235 and 3 A.L.R.4th 998 (1981).

Read §9-306(3) carefully and work your way through the following problem.

PROBLEM 94

On August 2, when the filed financing statement in favor of the Last National Bank covered "all business machines," the debtor engaged in the transactions listed below. Decide for each transaction if the bank should take action before August 12 or if the financing statement is sufficient as filed:

(a) the debtor traded a typewriter for another typewriter;

(b) the debtor traded another typewriter for a painting;

(c) the debtor traded a duplicating machine for a used car (and state law requires lien interests in vehicles to be noted on the certificate of title as the sole means of perfection);

(d) the debtor sold a calculator to a friend for cash and that same day used the cash to buy a painting;

(e) the debtor sold an adding machine for $500 and put the cash in a bank account; on August 2 the bank exercised its right of setoff against the account. Would the priorities change if the setoff occurred on August 15?

(f) the debtor sold a coffee maker for $200 and gave the money to a Salvation Army volunteer that same day. What result if the charitable donation occurs on August 15? What result if the debtor pays the $200 to another creditor on August 2? On August 15?

When the debtor becomes insolvent, §9-306(4) replaces all common law principles of tracing and gives the secured party all identifiable cash and non-cash proceeds still on hand or in non-commingled bank accounts. As to proceeds that have been commingled in bank accounts with non-proceeds, the creditor is limited to the amount produced by application of the following formula. First compute the amount of cash proceeds received by the debtor in the last 10 days before the insolvency proceedings were begun (typically the filing of a bankruptcy petition), then subtract from that amount two things: (1) the amount of non-commingled cash proceeds still on hand, and (2) any amounts paid by the debtor to the creditor in that same 10-day period. The quantity remaining is the amount of proceeds in the commingled account to which the secured creditor has priority.

PROBLEM 95

The Syringa Meditation Center, Inc. was a school offering courses in transcendental meditation. It was financed by a loan from the

Hibiscus Savings & Loan Association, to whom the school owed $50,000, and to whom it had given a security interest in its accounts receivable (and proceeds), which interest Hibiscus had duly perfected. Syringa had a checking account with the Columbine National Bank. On June 5, the morning mail brought $4000 worth of checks by students who were making payments for the TM Course. At the first class that morning the school received $2000 in cash from students, and, to its surprise, a donkey, which was presented to the school by one Hawthorn Bitterroot, a student who was heading for parts unknown and wanted to leave some form of payment behind. The school deposited all $4000 of the checks in its account with the Columbine National Bank, along with $1000 of the cash. Prior to the deposit the account contained $6000. It kept $500 of the cash in a safe at the school and paid $500 to Hibiscus Savings & Loan in reduction of the debt. The next day it filed for bankruptcy and the trustee now claims everything. Assuming §9-306(4) is not invalid as a statutory lien arising only on insolvency (as to which see G. Gilmore §45-9 and the next case), to what is Hibiscus Savings & Loan entitled under that subsection? If the school had not paid Hibiscus anything to what would the lending institution be entitled? If the school had put only the checks worth $4000 into the account and had used the $2000 cash to pay other creditors, what portion of the $10,000 in the bank account may be reached by Hibiscus?

In re Dexter Buick-GMC Truck Company

28 U.C.C. Rep. Serv. 243 (Bankr., R.I. 1980)

Votolato, Bankr. J. Heard on the complaint of General Motors Acceptance Corporation (GMAC) to impress a trust upon funds on deposit in the Debtor's corporate checking account.

The relevant facts are undisputed. In 1962, the plaintiff, GMAC, and Elliott Buick Inc., the predecessor of the Debtor, Dexter Buick, executed a security agreement covering new and used vehicles, and the proceeds from the sale of these vehicles. (Plaintiff's Exhibit No. 1). The requisite provisions of the Uniform Commercial Code were complied with, and the security interest in the collateral was perfected. Within the ten days preceding the filing of its Chapter XI petition, the Debtor sold a number of vehicles in which GMAC had a security interest, and deposited the cash proceeds of these sales ($363,026) in its corporate checking account. These proceeds were commingled with other funds in the Debtor's account, and a number of checks were drawn against that account. On the date of the filing of the petition, the corporate checking account contained approximately $205,000.

GMAC contends that the funds in the bank account of the Debtor on the date of the filing are cash proceeds from the sale of the vehicles in which it has a perfected security interest, and claims that this security interest arises under UCC §9-306(4)(d), which provides:

> In the event of insolvency proceedings instituted by or against a debtor, a secured party with a perfected security interest in proceeds has a perfected security interest; . . . (d) in all cash and bank accounts of the debtor, if other cash proceeds have been commingled or deposited in a bank account, but the perfected security interest under this paragraph (d) is . . . (ii) limited to an amount not greater than the amount of any cash proceeds received by the debtor within ten days before the institution of the insolvency proceedings and commingled or deposited in a bank account prior to the insolvency proceedings . . .

The receiver opposes the plaintiff's arguments on several grounds, his major contention being that the plaintiff's alleged security interest in the Debtor's bank account constitutes a voidable preference under §60a of the Bankruptcy Act, 11 USC §96(a), because it did not arise, under UCC §9-306(4)(d), until the filing of the Chapter XI petition. The receiver further asserts that UCC §9-306(4)(d) creates a statutory lien or a disguised state priority which may be invalidated under the Bankruptcy Act.

The issue is whether the security interest which the plaintiff claims under UCC §9-306(4)(d) is able to withstand collision with the pertinent provisions of the Bankruptcy Act.

The receiver's first contention, that the operation of UCC §9-306(4)(d) constitutes a voidable preference, is based on §60a of the Bankruptcy Act. Section 60a(1) defines a preference as

> [1] a transfer . . . of any of the property of a debtor [2] to or for the benefit of a creditor [3] for or on account of an antecedent debt, [4] made or suffered by such debtor while insolvent and [5] within four months before the filing . . . [6] the effect of which transfer will be to enable such creditor to obtain a greater percentage of his debt than some other creditor of the same class.

Section 60a(2) determines when a transfer has been made:

> (A) transfer of property . . . shall be deemed to have been made or suffered at the time when it became so far perfected that no

subsequent lien upon such property obtainable by legal or equitable proceedings on a simple contract could become superior to the rights of the transferee.

The receiver contends that a transfer took place as of the filing of the Debtor's petition, because it is at that point in time that GMAC's security interest in the Debtor's bank account was perfected under UCC §9-306(4)(d). The receiver does not dispute that GMAC has a security interest in identified proceeds from the sale of the vehicles under the original security agreement with the Debtor, which was perfected prior to the four month statutory period for a voidable preference. Rather, he contends that GMAC is asserting a security interest in all cash deposited in the Debtor's bank account within ten days of the filing of the petition, not simply in identifiable proceeds stemming from the sale of vehicles under the original security agreement. Under §60a(2) of the Bankruptcy Act, a transfer is essentially equated with the act by which priority is obtained over later creditors. DuBay v. Williams, 417 F.2d 1277, 1287 (9th Cir., 1969). A creditor attaching the bank account of the Debtor the day prior to the filing of the petition, the receiver asserts, could have obtained a lien on the Debtor's bank account superior to GMAC's. He then argues that because GMAC's security interest did not become perfected under UCC §9-306(4)(d) until the initiation of the insolvency proceeding a transfer took place at that time, for the benefit of a creditor, in payment of an antecedent debt, and made while the Debtor was insolvent — a voidable preference under §60a of the Bankruptcy Act.

The apparent conflict between UCC §9-306(4)(d) and §60 of the Bankruptcy Act, which has been the subject of much scholarly debate,[1] generally arises when a secured creditor asserts a right to both proceeds and other cash deposited in the Debtor's bank account. While the intent of the draftsmen of the Uniform Commercial Code in promulgating §9-306(4)(d) was to limit the expense and necessity of tracing proceeds that have been commingled with other funds, the literal effect of UCC §9-306(4)(d) is to give the secured party a security interest in all cash and deposits re-

1. See 4A Collier on Bankruptcy, 70.62A[4.3] (14th ed J. Moore & L. King 1976); Henson "Proceeds" Under the Uniform Commercial Code, 65 Colum L Rev 232, 242-53 (1965); Marsh, Triumph or Tragedy?: The Bankruptcy Act Amendments of 1966, 42 Wash L Rev 681, 715-17 (1967); Comment, Toward Commercial Reasonableness: An Examination of Some of the Conflicts Between Article 9 of the Uniform Commercial Code and the Bankruptcy Act, 19 Syr L Rev 939, 954-55 (1968).

ceived by the debtor within ten days of the filing of the bankruptcy petition, even though some of those proceeds may not have resulted from the sale of secured collateral. As one court described this conflict,

> [T]he problem arises in the UCC §9-306(4)(d) situation because that subsection gives the secured creditor a perfected security interest in the entire amount deposited by the debtor within ten days before bankruptcy without limiting the interest to the amount that can be identified as the proceeds from the sale of the creditor's collateral.

In re Gibson Products of Arizona, 543 F.2d 652, 655 (9th Cir., 1976).

The cases where the problem of interpreting UCC §9-306(4)(d) in conjunction with the Bankruptcy Act has arisen have generally involved the situation where a secured creditor is able to trace only a small amount of cash proceeds from the sale of collateral in which the creditor has a perfected security interest into the Debtor's bank account, and attempts to use UCC §9-306(4)(d) to claim all of the funds deposited in the account within ten days of the commencement of the insolvency proceeding. See, In re Gibson Products, supra; Fitzpatrick v. Philco Finance Corp., 491 F.2d 1288 (7th Cir., 1974). The approach adopted by these courts has been to allow the secured party to recover funds in the debtor's bank account to the extent that the creditor can trace those proceeds from the sale of collateral in which it had a perfected security interest. In In re Gibson Products, for example, the court held that

> . . . To the extent that a creditor is able to identify his proceeds to trace their path into the commingled funds, he will be able to defeat pro tanto the trustee's assertion of a preference.
>
> By this construction of Section 60 of the Bankruptcy Act and Section 9-306(4) of the UCC, we do violence neither to statute nor to substantial justice among the parties. The creditor's security interest in the whole account under Section 9-306(4) is prima facie valid, except as to the trustee, and, as to him, the creditor's security interest is presumptively preferential. The creditor can rebut the presumption by appropriately tracing his proceeds. [Supra at 657 (emphasis added).]

The approach adopted by the *Gibson* court, which we find most persuasive, essentially adopts the pre-Code requirement of tracing cash proceeds from the sale of the collateral in which a security interest has been perfected. Where the secured creditor has initially perfected its security interest in the collateral more than four months before the filing of the petition, and where the creditor can identify the proceeds to which its security interest has attached, no collision between UCC §9-306(4)(d) and the Bankruptcy Act occurs. In re Gibson Products, supra at 655.

It is undisputed in the present case that the original security agreement between GMAC and the Debtor was perfected more than four months prior to the date of the petition. The evidence presented by GMAC clearly traces the cash proceeds from the sale of vehicles by the Debtor into the corporate checking account. This evidence, consisting of cash receipt journals, car sale invoices, and bank statements of deposits at the Newport National Bank, clearly demonstrates that the major portion of the funds in question was generated by the sale of the vehicles in which GMAC had a perfected security interest. Furthermore, unlike the secured creditors in In re Gibson Products, supra, and Fitzpatrick v. Philco Finance Corp., supra, the amount of proceeds traceable from the sale of these vehicles that was deposited in the Debtor's bank account within ten days before the filing of the Chapter XI petition clearly and substantially exceeds the cash on hand in the account at the commencement of the Chapter XI proceedings. We find, therefore, that GMAC has a valid security interest in the funds in Debtor's bank account, since they consist of cash proceeds from the sale of collateral in which it had a perfected security interest, and we conclude as a matter of law that the enforcement of said security interest under UCC §9-306(4)(d) is not a voidable preference under §60a of the Bankruptcy Act.

While the Receiver places principal reliance upon his argument that plaintiff's security interest in the commingled account constitutes a voidable preference, it is also claimed that, to the extent that the original agreement did not cover the cash and bank accounts of the debtor, UCC §9-306(4) is unenforceable because it conflicts with §67(a) and §64 of the Bankruptcy Act.

The receiver argues that UCC §9-306(4)(d) creates a statutory lien which first becomes effective upon the insolvency of the debtor and hence is expressly invalidated under §67c(1)(a) of the Bankruptcy Act which provides:

> The following liens shall be invalid against the trustee: (A) Every statutory lien which first becomes effective upon the insolvency of

> the debtor, or upon distribution or liquidation of his property, or upon execution against his property levied at the instance of one other than the lienor.

The thrust of his argument is that the claimed security interest is a lien established by statute, because the original agreement did not cover monies commingled in the debtor's general account. However, the receiver's argument ignores the definition of "statutory lien" which specifically excludes "any lien provided by or dependent upon an agreement to give security . . ." 11 USC §1(29a). The Agreement between the plaintiff and the debtor clearly establishes a security interest and not a statutory lien:

> GMAC's security interest in the vehicles shall attach to the full extent provided or permitted by law to the proceeds, in whatever form, of any retail sale or lease thereof by us until such proceeds are accounted for as aforesaid, and to the proceeds of any other dispositions of said vehicles or any part thereof. [(Plaintiff's Exhibit #1 emphasis supplied).]

Because GMAC has been able to trace proceeds from the sale of the vehicles into the Debtor's general account, we conclude that its claim to those traceable proceeds is based upon the Agreement, and does not arise under state law.

Our position is consistent with Elliot v. Bumb, 356 F.2d 749, (9th Cir. 1966), which the receiver cites for the proposition that state statutory liens not accompanied by possession of or levy upon property subject to lien before filing the petitions of bankruptcy are invalidated. The court noted in that case, however, that "the state statute undertakes to dispense with the beneficiary's need to trace" and, as such, represented a disguised priority. Id. at 754. See also, In Re Faber's Inc., 360 F. Supp. 946, 949-50 (D. Conn. 1973). In the present case, even if it could be argued that the lien on the bank accounts arises under state statute, plaintiff has met the additional burden of tracing the proceeds from the sale of the secured vehicles into the general bank account of the debtor.

Finally, the receiver argues that even if UCC §9-306(4)(d) is not a statutory lien under §67c, it nevertheless is a disguised state-created priority which conflicts with §64 of the Bankruptcy Act, because the security interest in debtor's bank account became perfected only at the onset of the insolvency proceedings, and that absent UCC §9-306(4)(d) the plaintiff would be relegated to the status of unsecured creditor.

In our view, most of the considerations which we have found controlling in rejecting §60 and §67c objections have similar validity when applied separately to the question whether the priorities established in §64 are distorted or defeated by respecting GMAC's claim to the traceable proceeds. GMAC's security interest in the funds in the Debtor's bank account did not become perfected at the onset of the insolvency proceeding, but arose by virtue of its security agreement with the Debtor. This security agreement gave GMAC a perfected security interest in proceeds from the sale of the secured vehicles, which GMAC has clearly traced to the Debtor's bank account. GMAC's right to these proceeds, therefore, results from its security agreement with Dexter, and from tracing, and cannot be attributed to a disguised state priority which attempts to give GMAC rights that it would have apart from bankruptcy. See, Matter of Federal's Inc., 553 F.2d 509, 516, 518 (6th Cir. 1977); 2 G. Gilmore, Security Interests in Personal Property, ¶45.9 at 1337-38 (1965). We therefore conclude that GMAC's title to the traceable proceeds from the sale of the secured vehicles cannot be defeated by §64 of the Bankruptcy Act, either.

For the reasons stated above, Plaintiff's complaint is granted vis-à-vis the Receiver. . . .

PROBLEM 96

Balboa Bank & Trust Company floor-planned the inventory of Erickson Motors and perfected its security interest in the inventory (and proceeds) by filing in the proper place. Erickson Motors sold a car to John Smith who paid $500 down and signed a contract obligating himself to pay $5000 more. The car dealership assigned this contract to the Cartier Finance Company which took possession of the contract and notified Smith he was to make future payments to Cartier. Smith made no payments at all, and at Cartier's direction Erickson Motors repossessed the car on September 11. On September 12, a representative of Cartier Finance Company came to the dealership and took possession of the car, claiming it was *proceeds* from the contract of purchase which Cartier still had. Balboa Bank objected and claimed a superior interest in the car, pointing to §9-306(5). If you were the judge, how would you read §9-306(5) to resolve the priorities in the repossessed car? See G. Gilmore §27.5; Henson §6-6; compare Citizens & S. Factors, Inc. v. Small Bus. Ad., 375 So. 2d 351, 27 U.C.C. Rep. Serv. 569 (Ala. 1979). Would the result change if Cartier Finance had purchased accounts receivable instead of chattel paper? See §9-306(5)(c).

For a complete review of priority problems, read Official Comments 4 through 8 of §9-312. If you can understand them all you are on top of the subject matter of this course.

CHAPTER 9

DEFAULT

A. *PRE-DEFAULT DUTIES OF THE SECURED PARTY*

PROBLEM 97

Andy Doria was the owner of 100 shares of Titanic Telephone which he pledged to the Morro Castle National Bank as collateral for a $10,000 loan. At the time of the pledge the stock was selling for $100 a share. The security agreement was oral and the bank filed no financing statement.

(a) Does the bank have a perfected security interest?

(b) If the stock began to fall in value and on November 4, when it was selling at $80 a share, Andy called the bank and told the bank to sell, is the bank responsible if it does not and the stock bottoms out at $1.50 a share? Read §9-207; see Reed v. Central Natl. Bank, 421 F.2d 113, 7 U.C.C. Rep. Serv. 113 (10th Cir. 1970); Fidelity Bank & Trust Co. v. Production Metals Corp., 366 F. Supp. 613, 14 U.C.C. Rep. Serv. 219 (E.D. Pa. 1973); Hutchinson v. Southern Cal. First Natl. Bank, 27 Cal. App. 2d 572, 103 Cal. Rptr. 816, 11 U.C.C. Rep. Serv. 274 (1972); Grace v. Sterling, Grace & Co., 30 App. Div. 2d 61, 289 N.Y.S.2d 632, 5 U.C.C. Rep. Serv. 297 (1968).

(c) Would it help the bank's position if the pledge agreement contained a clause saying that the bank was not responsible for its own negligence in dealing with the stock? Read §1-102(3); see the

Reed case cited above and Brodheim v. Chase Manhattan Bank, N.A., 347 N.Y.S.2d 394, 13 U.C.C. Rep. Serv. 139 (Sup. Ct. 1973); G. Gilmore ch. 42.

(d) Andy's dealings with the bank became more complicated and eventually the bank held, as pledgee, Andy's stocks in five different companies. One of these, Lusitania Foundry, offered a stock split option that had to be exercised by December 31, so Andy wrote the Morro Castle National Bank and, explaining that his records had become confused, asked the bank how many shares of Lusitania Foundry it held. The bank replied that it possessed 50 shares (this was a typographical error; it actually held 150). Andy tendered 50 shares of equivalent stock to the bank in exchange for a return of 50 shares of Lusitania Foundry, on which he then exercised the stock option, which proved very profitable. On January 3, Andy learned he owned 100 more shares that the bank held; it was too late to take the stock option on these shares. Does Andy have a cause of action against the bank under §9-207? Under §9-208?

PROBLEM 98

Mazie Minkus borrowed $2000 from the Mount Brown State Bank, and, as collateral, pledged to the bank her stamp collection (valued at $2000). She used the money for a South American vacation. While she was away, the bank, which was located in an unstable geological area, was destroyed in an earthquake. The stamp collection went with it. Fortunately the bank was fully insured by a policy with the Gibbons Insurance Company which inter alia paid the bank $2000 for the loss of the stamp collection. Gibbons then notified Mazie that she should pay the $2000 debt to the insurance company, which was using the doctrine of subrogation to step into the shoes of the bank. Need she pay? See §9-207(2)(b); G. Gilmore §42.7.

B. DEFAULT: THE BASIC REMEDIES

PROBLEM 99

Mark Penury contracted to pay $800 in return for a three room suite sold by Plastic Furniture Mart. He signed an agreement permitting the store to retain a security interest in the furniture. He missed the first payment and the store seized the furniture and sold it at an auction for $50. Plastic Furniture Mart itself was the buyer (and the only bidder). One week later Plastic Furniture filed suit against Mark for the amount still due. Mark's attorney argued that the relevant jurisdiction had adopted the Uniform Consumer Credit Code (hereinafter UCCC) and §5-103[1] thereof destroyed Plastic Furniture Mart's security interest. Alternately, assume that Plastic Furniture did *not* repossess, and that the UCCC was not in effect in the jurisdiction. Instead when Mark missed a payment, Plastic Furniture simply filed suit against him and took judgment when he defaulted. If in the lawsuit Plastic Furniture failed to mention its security interest in the furniture has it "elected its remedy" and waived its security interest? Is the claim to the collateral now res judicata? See In re Wilson, 390 F. Supp. 1121, 17 U.C.C. Rep. Serv. 280 (D. Kan. 1975); contra In re Hill, 26 U.C.C. Rep. Serv. 1390 (Bankr. D. Kan. 1979); White & Summers §26-4. Do either or both of these arguments succeed?

Foster v. Knutson

527 P.2d 1108, 15 U.C.C. Rep. Serv. 1127 (Wash. 1974)

UTTER, J. The Superior Court, in a nonjury trial, awarded judgment in favor of Myron and Earl Foster and Janet Conrad,

1. U.C.C.C. §5.103 provides:

"(1) This section applies to a consumer credit sale of goods or services.

"(2) If the seller repossesses or voluntarily accepts surrender of goods which were the subject of the sale and in which he has a security interest and the cash price of the goods repossessed or surrendered was $1000 or less, the buyer is not personally liable to the seller for the unpaid balance of the debt arising from the sale of the goods, and the seller is not obligated to resell the collateral.

"(3) If the seller repossesses or voluntarily accepts surrender of goods which were not the subject of the sale but in which he has a security interest to secure a debt arising from a sale of goods or services or a combined sale of goods and services and the cash price of the sale was $1000 or less, the buyer is not personally liable to the seller for the unpaid balance of the debt arising from the sale.

"(4) For the purpose of determining the unpaid balance of consolidated debts or debts pursuant to revolving charge accounts, the allocation of payments to a debt shall be determined in the same manner as provided for determining the amount of debt secured by various security interests (Section 2.409).

"(5) The buyer may be liable in damages to the seller if the buyer has wrongfully damaged the collateral or if, after default and demand, the buyer has wrongfully failed to make the collateral available to the seller.

"(6) If the seller elects to bring an action against the buyer for a debt arising from a consumer credit sale of goods or services, when under this section he would not be entitled to a deficiency judgment if he repossessed the collateral, and obtains judgment (a) he may not repossess the collateral, and (b) the collateral is not subject to levy or sale on execution or similar proceedings pursuant to the judgment.

"(7) The amounts of $1000 in subsections (2) and (3) are subject to change pursuant to the provisions on adjustment of dollar amounts (Section 1.106)."

appellants for $15,703.35 against Ronald and Jack Knutson and their wives, respondents and cross-appellants. . . .

On September 7, 1968, respondents Knutson and one Herbert Thomas entered into a contract to purchase from appellants Foster all of the outstanding stock of Hesperian Orchards, Inc., a Washington corporation engaged in fruit growing and warehousing in the Wenatchee Valley. The purchase price was $453,500 with a down payment of $131,585. As security for payment of the purchase price, the total number of shares being purchased were deposited in escrow with the Seattle-First National Bank. The down payment of $131,585, required by the sellers, was borrowed by respondents from Oneonta Trading Corporation, and respondents gave their promissory note in that amount to the lender. . . .

In the Winter of 1968-69, a disastrous freeze struck the Wenatchee Valley area destroying as much as two-thirds of the older apple trees in the valley. Hesperian Orchards, Inc. was without the financial reserves to meet a disaster of this severity. As a direct result of this freeze, the 1969 apple crop of Hesperian Orchards was severely reduced in value, and the orchard suffered extreme financial loss.

A dispute had also arisen between the parties concerning whether the annual payments called for in the contract between them included or were exclusive of interest to the date of payment. In addition to this dispute, the sellers were of the view that the contract purchasers had failed to maintain proper corporate books and records. The sellers also objected to the salaries and loans made by the corporation to the purchasers, which moneys allowed the purchasers to "bootstrap" their acquisition of the corporation. For all these reasons, sellers declared a default in the contract, obtained the pledged stock from the bank and gave notice of their intention to sell the stock.

No sale of stock, however, was consummated at that time. Instead, a new agreement was entered into on April 13, 1970 between the parties to this lawsuit, Thomas not being a party to this later agreement. In the new agreement, the effects of the 1968-69 freeze were taken into account and principal payments owing under the original agreement were deferred. Purchasers conceded in the April 13th agreement that they had "failed to keep proper books and records [and] agree[d] that the future maintenance of such books and records is paramount and that this requirement runs to the inducement for this agreement and modification."

The modification agreement of April 13th further provided that (1) "As part of the inducement given by Purchasers to Sellers for modification of this contract, the Purchasers have executed and delivered to the Sellers certain mortgages of assets, which mortgages shall be supplemental security"; (2) In the event of default sellers may "elect to declare all payments due and delinquent and bring suit to recover the same as so accelerated or may pursue any remedies provided under the Uniform Commercial Code of the State of Washington"; (3) "The Purchasers agree to provide the Sellers with balance sheets and operating statements showing the condition of the corporation at two-month intervals beginning June 1, 1970 . . ."; (4) "Purchasers shall cause the corporation to carry [adequate fire and liability] insurance . . ."; and (5) "The corporation shall at all times keep all taxes and assessments paid upon the properties."

On December 1, 1970, appellants gave notice to respondents that respondents were in default of the April 13th agreement, and that unless the defaults were cured within 30 days appellants would elect to declare the full purchase price due and seek all remedies available to them according to law and the terms of the contract as modified between the parties. Among the items of default listed by appellants were (1) respondents' failure to make a $13,000 contract payment due November 30, 1970, (2) failure to maintain adequate records sufficient to determine the financial position of the corporation, (3) failure to timely pay debts, taxes and leases of the corporation, and (4) failure to keep payment of insurance premiums current.

Respondents made their $13,000 contract payment December 24, 1970, but did not cure their defaults within the allotted 30 days. On January 6, 1971, appellants notified respondents that Hesperian Orchards corporate stock which was being purchased by respondents, and which was then held as security for payment of its full purchase price, would be disposed of at a public auction sale on February 9, 1971. Respondents made no objection to the February 9th sale. At the public auction, appellant-sellers bid for the stock against other independent private parties and ultimately purchased the stock for $120,000.

A deficiency of $115,000 plus interest was yet owing by respondents on the stock purchase contract. Sellers then went into

Superior Court seeking two remedies. They sought a deficiency judgment of $115,000 plus interest pursuant to the express terms of the April 13th agreement between the parties and as provided for in §9-504(2) and a judicial foreclosure of respondents' supplemental real estate mortgage given to appellants pursuant to the terms of the April 13th modification agreement.

The trial court found that (1) sellers held the Hesperian Orchards stock as security for payment of the purchase price of the stock; (2) the mortgage on purchasers' real estate was given to sellers as additional security for the stock purchase; (3) sellers gave purchasers adequate notice to cure defaults or sellers would accelerate the purchase obligation; (4) purchasers had actual knowledge of the public auction and sale of the stock; and (5) at the time of the public auction the purchasers were in default on their purchase agreement. The trial court also made conclusions of law that (1) the manner in which the stock was publicly auctioned, the foreclosure of the purchasers' interest in it, and the manner of giving notice of sale were reasonable; and (2) the purchasers, by their inaction prior to the stock auction, waived their right to object to the sale.

The record discloses ample evidence in support of these findings of fact.

The trial court, however, also held that "equity" would not allow sellers a deficiency judgment against respondent-purchasers on the stock purchase contract, and foreclosure of respondents' real estate mortgage was held in abeyance for 6 months. The stated grounds were:

> Because of the absence of testimony of *substantial* default, the harsh prayer for deficiency judgment will not be granted . . . To grant such a prayer on the basis of the entire evidence herein would be unjust and inequitable. [(Italics ours.)]

The trial court's error derives principally from its misapprehension of the role lawfully allocated to it in its adminstration of justice to disputing contracting parties before it. Because of the way a court exercises its powers, it cannot escape assuming a role in the litigation. Courts are constantly engaged in recognizing and defining competences and asserting managerial competences of their own. Each such decision bears a dual aspect: (1) that of defining the court's own role and, by necessary implication, that of the parties, and (2) that of playing the role which the court has assigned to itself. This is a question of allocation of competences fundamental to our state law. Although the question of competences most frequently arises when courts are called upon to resolve conflicts between levels or branches of government, the issue is no less relevant when the conflict is between private and public authority. See Jaffe, Law Making by Private Groups, 51 Harv. L. Rev. 201 (1937). Recently the United States Supreme Court addressed itself to a similar role-allocation issue in Columbia Broadcasting System, Inc. v. Democratic National Comm., 412 U.S. 94, 93 S. Ct. 2080, 36 L. Ed. 2d 772 (1973). There the Court described the question for decision as that of who shall determine what issues are to be discussed over network television by whom, and acknowledged its reponsibility for resolving that question. Thus, law may be characterized as a union of primary rules governing conduct and secondary rules designating the authoritative source of primary rules. H. Hart, The Concept of Law 77-96 (1961).

There are two questions which a court must first resolve before it may determine whether a contracting party to a dispute has breached its obligation to another. First, a court must inquire as to whether there is any basis for refusing to enforce the contract made by the parties or whether a party has asserted valid affirmative defenses to the formation of the contract. This inquiry leads the court into a consideration, among others, of whether there is before it (1) a statute of frauds problem, (2) a lack of contractual capacity, (3) an illegal contract, (4) a contract induced by fraud, mutual mistake of material fact, duress, or (5) a contract of adhesion. See text and collected cases in Williston on Contracts, §§450, 677A, 1437A, 1578A, 1602, 1617 (3d ed. W. Jaeger 1960).

When the court determines there is no basis for refusing to enforce the contract made by the parties, it must next examine the contract itself to determine what events and conduct of the parties the contracting parties intended, by their contract, to define their mutual obligations. At this stage of the inquiry, the role of a court sitting without a jury is that of a fact-finder. It must determine whether any of the events of default, specified by the parties in their contract, have occurred. Once a court has made findings of fact that events of default have occurred, as here, it must grant the non-defaulting party the remedies contracted for and permitted under our constitutions, statutory and common law. At this juncture a court is without legal power to interpose its judgment for that of the parties as to whether or not the remedies contracted for are more harsh than accord with its own sensibilities. An event of default is, within reason, what the parties have agreed in their contract that it would be and not what a court, exercising its own judgment, thinks it ought to be. See 2 G. Gilmore, Security Interests in Personal Property §43.3, at 1193 (1965).

In this case the trial court erred because it assumed a role not proper to it. The trial court substituted its judgment for that of the parties by engaging in an "interest balancing" which exceeded its power. A court's power to adjudicate the rights and duties of parties to a contract is determined by the legislative framework within which the parties have contracted, the agreement between the parties, and the common law doctrines which bear upon the parties' mutual exercise of their freedom of contract. Neither this court nor a trial court may make a new contract for the parties. Courts have the lawful power only to enforce the contract which the parties have made for themselves. Spokane Savings & Loan Soc. v. Park Vista Improvement Co., 160 Wash. 12, 294 P. 1028 (1930). Here both the legislature and the parties themselves have clearly expressed their intentions. The parties agreed that the purchasers' real estate should be mortgaged to sellers as security for the underlying stock sale contract. They also agreed that remedies allowed under the UCC would bind the parties, and that the events of default were as specified. The concern of the trial court seems to have been with the "justice" of allowing the non-defaulting sellers to both realize on their security and seek a deficiency judgment. The "justice" of the agreement could be resolved in favor of the sellers when it is understood that the orchard they sold was worth substantially less after sale than the original purchase price, as a result of freeze damage. This is an unsatisfactory way, however, to resolve the dispute.

Under §§9-501 to 9-507, a creditor may choose between two basic methods of obtaining the benefit of his bargain from a defaulting debtor. Where, as here, no purchase of consumer goods is involved, the creditor may seize the goods subject to his security interest and either keep them in satisfaction of the debt (§9-505(2)), or resell them and apply the proceeds to the debt (§9-504(1)), in which latter case the debtor is liable for any deficiency. Section 9-504(2). Alternatively, the creditor may ignore his security and obtain a judgment on the underlying obligation and proceed by execution and levy, in which case the judgment lien relates back to the date of the perfection of the security interest in the collateral. Section 9-501(5). Under pre-Code law, courts often held that a suit on the debt was inconsistent with a creditor's claim that he retain title to the goods under a conditional sales contract. 113 ALR 653 (1938).

This election of remedy issue arose first under the UCC in In re Adrian Research & Chem. Co., 269 F.2d 734 (3d Cir. 1959). There the court, under an early version of the Code, held that an execution on the debt was not inconsistent with a later claim under the security agreement. The current version of the Code expressly allows both an action on the underlying obligation and a claim against the collateral securing the debt. Section 9-501(5). Section 9-501(1) further provides that "[t]he rights and remedies referred to in this subsection are cumulative."

The meaning of §9-501(1) and (5) is clear and unambiguous. This case does not require statutory interpretation as the language is plain and admits of no more than one meaning. Krystad v. Lau, 65 Wash. 2d 827, 400 P.2d 72 (1965).

Those statutes permit the non-defaulting party to reduce his claim to judgment, foreclose, or otherwise enforce the security interest by any available judicial procedure. These rights and remedies are expressly made "cumulative.: Referring to these sections in Article 9 of the UCC, Professor Gilmore states: "If drafting can do the job, this forthright statement should put the issue to rest once and for all. Nothing the secured party may do to collect his debt through the process of the law courts will operate to destroy his security interest vis-à-vis the debtor or to impair its priority over third parties . . . It would be oversanguine to hope that §9-501 in its final version will, despite its forthrightness, put an end to the argument. The election of remedies doctrine is dear to the hearts of many lawyers and procedural reforms are always bitterly resisted. We may assume that the argument will continue to be made that the action on the debt bars a later resort to the security. It is however, hard to imagine that the argument can be successful if the provisions of §§9-501(1) and (5) are effectively presented to the court." (Footnotes omitted.) 2 G. Gilmore, Security Interests in Personal Property §43.7, at 1209-10 (1965). We agree with Professor Gilmore.

Section 9-502(2) states: "If the security agreement secures an indebtedness, the secured party must account to the debtor for any surplus, and unless otherwise agreed, the debtor is liable for any deficiency." Professor Gilmore comments, at page 1231, that "the secured party's right to claim for any deficiency is automatic unless as the draftsmen remark in an excess of caution, otherwise agreed." We agree. In an abundance of caution the security agreement before us here expressly provided for the non-defaulting secured party's right to a deficiency judgment. However, this right of the non-defaulting secured party to a deficiency judgment is subject to the limitations imposed by §9-504(3) and §9-507(1). "[E]very aspect of the disposition including the method, manner, time, place and terms must be commercially reasonable." Section 9-504(3). This requirement is mandatory and is not subject to disclaimer or limitations.

Courts have often formulated the duty of a pledgee or mortgagee who sells collateral after default in terms of a fiduciary obligation. "Equity assigns to pledgor and pledgee a trust relationship with resulting obligations of the pledgee . . . One of those obligations (on mortgagee and pledgee) is to 'use every effort to sell the estate under every possible advantage of time, place, and publicity' (Perry on Trusts and Trustees [4th ed.], §602-o;" In re Estate of Kiamie, 309 N.Y. 325, 330, 130 N.E. 2d 745 (1955). The secured party's paramount obligation under Article 9 is to act in a "commercially reasonable" manner. The last sentence of §9-507(2) provides that any disposition "shall conclusively be deemed to be commercially reasonable" if it "has been approved in any judicial proceeding . . ." In this case no judicial approval of the sale of stock was sought prior to sale as, indeed, none was required, but as noted earlier the trial court made a conclusion of law that the sale was reasonable.

A sale of collateral in which the secured party participates as a purchaser and for which there is no recognized market, as here, is "in conformity with reasonable commercial practices," §9-507(2), if certain conditions are met. The sale is valid where notice of the sale is (1) given to the defaulted debtor and to the public sufficiently in advance to allow interested bidders a reasonable opportunity to participate, (2) given to a "public" reasonably expected to have an interest in the collateral to be sold and notifying the public of the exact time of sale and place of sale, reasonably convenient to potential bidders, (3) sufficiently replete with information describing the collateral to be sold and the amount of the obligation for which it is being sold to allow potential bidders a genuine opportunity to make an informed judgment as to whether to bid at the sale and (4) published in a manner reasonably calculated to assure such publicity that the collateral will bring the best possible price from the competitive bidding of a strived-for lively concourse of bidders. If a sale is conducted under these circumstances, "[t]he fact that a better price could have been obtained by a sale at a different time or in a different method from that selected by the secured party is not of itself sufficient to establish that the sale was not made in a commercially reasonable manner." Section 9-507(2). The secured party is not required to anticipate the course a market will take. He is required to use his best efforts to sell the collateral for the highest price and to have a reasonable regard for the debtor's interest. The record before us supports the trial court's finding that the secured party's sale of collateral was "in conformity with reasonable commercial practices." Section 9-507(2).

The trial court's refusal to grant to appellants an immediate judicial foreclosure of the supplemental mortgage given by respondents as further security for the sale of stock was error. This supplemental mortgage on all of respondents' real property in the state of Washington was freely bargained for and went to the inducement of the amended purchase and security agreement between the parties. There have been instances where judicial relief, arising out of a claimed equity jurisdiction, has been granted to avoid the severe hardships to a defaulting mortgagor of a judicial foreclosure and sale of real property during a widespread staggering economic depression. Suring State Bank v. Giese, 210 Wis. 489, 246 N.W. 556 (1933). The United States Supreme Court, on the other hand, has held that a depreciation in real estate values is not sufficient reason for refusing to uphold a foreclosure and sale under a trust deed. Smith v. Black, 115 U.S. 308, 6 S. Ct. 50, 29 L. Ed. 398 (1885). These issues are not before us now. We hold on the issues presented by this case that absent such supervening events, where parties competent to contract have freely bargained for a mortgage on property as supplemental security to a secured transaction and where the mortgagor is in default of his underlying obligation, the role of the trial court is to enforce the agreement between the parties, including any supplemental mortgages. The court should not, under the facts of this case, intrude its substantive judgment as to whether or not the terms of that agreement were too severe. The trial court's order, holding foreclosure of the respondents' real estate mortgages in abeyance for 6 months contrary to the express agreement of the parties, was error.

C. THE MEANING OF "DEFAULT"

The secured party's Part 5 Article 9 rights come into being whenever there has been a *default* by the debtor. The Code, however, does not define *default*; since it does not the security agreement should do so. It is the lawyer's job to draft the security agreement so as to cover the possible exigencies with appropriate clauses. One way to do this is by a specific definition of the term *default* so that it includes not only failure to pay on time, but also failure to perform any of the terms of the agreement, as well as certain specific problems: death of the debtor, an assignment for the benefit of creditors, institution of any involvency proceeding, impairment of the collateral, etc. Some security agreements provide simply that default is the failure to observe the conditions and promises of the security agreement and then contain an acceleration clause similar to this one:

> The parties agree that if at any time the secured party deems himself insecure because in good faith he believes the prospect of payment or performance is impaired, he shall have the right to declare a default and accelerate payment of all unpaid sums or performance or, at his option, may require the debtor to furnish additional collateral.

PROBLEM 100

When Mr. and Mrs. Bankruptcy bought a mobile home from Nervous Motors, Inc., they signed a purchase money security agreement in favor of the seller that contained an acceleration clause identical to the one above. Which of the following events, in your opinion, is sufficient to trigger the proper use of the clause:

(a) a very bad financial quarter for Nervous Motors, Inc.;

(b) a serious drop in the state of the economy;

(c) knowledge that the Bankruptcy's have been talking to a lawyer;

(d) a report (which simple investigation would show to be false) that the Bankruptcy's have failed to pay their grocery bills for the last two months;

(e) an anonymous phone call that states the Bankruptcy's are getting ready to move the mobile home to Mexico;

(f) the confiscation of the mobile home and the arrest of the Bankruptcys for possessing marijuana? See Blaine v. General Motors Acceptance Corp., 370 N.Y.S.2d 323, 17 U.C.C. Rep. Serv. 641 (N.Y. Sup. Ct. 1975). Read §1-208 and its Official Comment; G. Gilmore §43.4; Annot.; What Constitutes "Good Faith" under UCC §1-208, 61 A.L.R.3d 244 (1975). The courts disagree on the *good faith* standard: compare Universal C.I.T. Credit Corp. v. Shepler, 329 N.E.2d 620, 17 U.C.C. Rep. Serv. 602 (Ind. App. 1975) (objective-reasonable person test), with Van Horn v. Van De Wol, Inc., 497 P.2d 252, 10 U.C.C. Rep. Serv. 1143 (Wash. App. 1972) (purely subjective test). An exhaustive discussion of the meaning of §1-208 is contained in the well-written opinion in Brown v. Avemco Inv. Corp., 603 F.2d 1367, 27 U.C.C. Rep. Serv. 885 (9th Cir. 1979).

The courts stretch to protect the debtor whenever the secured party's "insecurity" is unwarranted. For particularly outrageous conduct on the part of the creditor punitive damages are favored. See Annot., Punitive Damages For Wrongful Seizure of Chattel By One Claiming Security Interest, 35 A.L.R.3d 1016 (1971).

Klingbiel v. Commercial Credit Corporation

439 F.2d 1303, 8 U.C.C. Rep. Serv. 1099 (10th Cir. 1971)

Brown, J. When Vern Klingbiel (Purchaser), went outside his home in St. Louis, Missouri, on the morning of June 22, 1966 he found his brand new (1966) Ford Galaxie 500 gone. Later he was to learn that in the dark of night and with skillful stealth the car — despite its being fully locked — had been taken away, not by some modern auto rustler, but by an anonymous representative of the Automobile Recovery Bureau acting for Commercial, the installment finance company, which was described with remarkable accuracy as a "professional firm." Little did he know that with this sudden, unexplained disappearance of an automobile, which — with all its chrome and large mortgage — was still his, so much had been unleashed. First of course, was his anguish at his loss. More significant for us, time, tide, litigation, trial, victory and appeal was to instruct him in the intricacies of the fine print of the purchase mortgage contract he signed and, perhaps to his awe, the Uniform Commercial Code.

A Kansas jury, under the Judge's careful instructions, which we find to be unexceptionable, did not think much of this treatment and by its verdict awarded some small actual damages plus punitive damages in a sum almost twice the purchase price of the car.

Fleeing from this judgment as a matter of principle, if not principal, Commercial quite naturally and properly seeks a haven in the terms of the contract[2] and, as an anchor to windward, the acceleration and good faith provisions of the Kansas Uniform Commercial Code. We find the attack unavailing and affirm.

What Happened

The case was tried largely on stipulated facts. On May 26, 1966 Vern Klingbiel, a resident of St. Louis, Missouri, entered into an installment contract with Dealer for the Purchase of a new Ford Galaxie automobile. This installment contract showed a time sales price of $4,907.56. Purchaser made a down payment of $400.00, tendering to Dealer a personal check in the amount of $300.00 and a second check in the amount of $100.00, the latter being signed in his wife's name. This left a time balance of $4,504.56, to be paid in 36 equal, successive monthly installments of $125.21, the payments to commence on June 26, 1966, under the mortgage contract containing the acceleration and enforcement provisions (see Note [2] supra). Commercial shortly became the assignee, on a dealer recourse basis, for the consideration of $3,400.00.

Subsequently, but before Purchaser's first monthly installment became due, Commercial felt itself insecure, and it directed the Automobile Recovery Bureau of St. Louis, Missouri to repossess the automobile. On June 22, 1966 — four days before Purchaser's first monthly installment was due and at a time when he was not in default — the repossessing professionals, without notice, demand, communication, or correspondence with Purchaser, removed his locked automobile from the front of his house in the

2. For convenience of reference the bracketed numbers are inserted (e.g., [i] [a] [b] [c] etc.); "This Mortgage may be assigned by Seller [Dealer], and when assigned, all rights of Seller shall vest in its assignee [Commercial] and this Mortgage shall be free from any claims or defenses whatsoever which Purchaser may have against Seller. . . . [i] If Purchaser [a] defaults on any obligation or breaches any agreement or warranty under this Mortgage, or [b] if Seller should feel itself or Vehicle insecure, [c] the unpaid portion of the Time Balance and any expense (including taxes) shall without notice, at the option of Seller, become due forthwith. [ii] Purchaser agrees in any such case [a] to pay said amount to Seller, upon demand, or [b] at the election of Seller, to deliver Vehicle to Seller. [iii] This Mortgage may be foreclosed [a] in any manner provided by law, or [b] Seller may, without notice or demand for performance or legal process, except such as may be required by Law, lawfully enter any premises where Vehicle may be found, and take possession of it. [iv] Seller may retain all payments made by Purchaser as compensation for the use of the Vehicle while in Purchaser's possession. [v] Any personal property in Vehicle at the time of repossession which has not become a part thereof may be held temporarily by Seller for Purchaser, without liabilty thereof. . . . All rights and remedies hereunder are cumulative and not alternative."

dead of night, delivered it to Commercial[3] along with Purchaser's personal property. . . .

Out of the Verbal Wilderness

The skillful Trial Judge having been aware that this contract . . . was not written for those who run to read discerned its true meaning by recognizing its true sequential structure. Unlike Commercial which assumes that the right to accelerate without notice or demand is synonymous with the right to repossess without notice or demand, the Judge carefully distinguished between the two. Acceleration, he charged, was permissible without notice or demand. But upon acceleration Commercial then had to make demand or give notice to Purchaser so that the admitted failure of notice/demand . . . made Commercial's repossession an unlawful conversion.

The Court's instruction tracked the terms of the contract correctly. Though under clause [i][b] (note [2], supra) "Time Balance" might from acceleration become due at any time without notice, if Commercial felt itself insecure, the very next provision in the contract provides "[ii] Purchaser agrees in any such case [a] to pay said amount to Seller, *upon demand,* or, [b] at the election of Seller, to deliver vehicle to Seller." (Emphasis added). Clause [ii][a] [b] with its alternative stated in the disjunctive does not speak in terms of rights which Commercial has. Rather it speaks in terms of *actions* which Purchaser must take depending on the choice opted by Commercial. It could require Purchaser to pay off in full or it could require redelivery. But before Purchaser was bound to do either Commercial had first to indicate which course was required. The two words, "upon demand," are not only conspicuous, they are unavoidable.

3. Purchaser did not have the slightest idea that his car had been repossessed. He notified the police that it was missing, in the belief that it had been stolen, and it was the police who finally uncovered what had actually transpired.

Even the austere stipulation vividly portrays Commercial's conduct and presages its predicament: "On June 22, 1966, Automobile Recovery Bureau, St. Louis, Missouri, at the telephone direction and request of Commercial Credit Corporation, without notice, demand, communication or correspondence with plaintiff, some time during the night, took the locked 1966 Ford Galaxie automobile off the street in front of plaintiff's home, and delivered the car to Commercial Credit Corporation at St. Louis, Missouri. Commercial Credit Corporation had no communication either written or oral, with plaintiff prior to taking the automobile. Commercial Credit Corporation requested, ordered, authorized and directed the repossession of the 1966 Ford Galaxie 500 automobile from Vern Klingbiel because it felt itself, or vehicle, insecure."

Not yet overborne, Commercial would further have us construe the contract so as to declare that no notice was necessary prior to repossession by falling back on clause [iii][b] which provides: "[iii] This mortgage may be foreclosed [a] . . . or [b] Seller may, without notice or demand for performance or legal process, . . . lawfully enter any premises where Vehicle may be found, and take possession of it."

This is equally unavailing. At the outset, this clause follows — does not precede — but follows clause [ii] which, [a] [b] as we have held, calls for notice/demand before Purchaser is required to act upon a declared acceleration. Equally important, in the sequential structure of the contract this refers only to a *foreclosure.* This means that there must be a default on the part of the Purchaser. This can take the form of Purchaser's failure to perform as in [i][a] or an acceleration under [i][b] in effect calls for notice/demand to precipitate a default. The failure or refusal of Purchaser after such notice/demand would of course, be a [i][a] default, thus setting in train the foreclosure provisions of [iii][a] or [b], including *at that stage* even the most stealthy repossession by night riders. But this privilege is not available by skipping from [i][b] to [iii][b] over the head of [ii][a] [b]. . . .

We think there was evidence, if believed by the jury, to warrant the inference of more than simple inadvertence or a technical conversion. There was first the circumstance of the stealthy retaking without notice of any kind, although notice clearly was called for as we have held. At that time Purchaser was not in default. Further, Purchaser's own personal property was taken along with the automobile. This was never returned to him, nor did he receive recompense for it. In fact, Commercial never even contacted Purchaser to inform him of the repossession. He had to find out through his own effort and investigation. There are many other factors unnecessary to catalogue which sustain the punitive damage finding.

This leaves only the objection to the Court's instruction on actual damages. Clearly there was sufficient evidence to cover the three elements submitted by the Court for the loss of value of the automobile, purchaser's personal property, and the loss of the vehicle for an intervening period.

The objection is pointed at the term "actual value" rather than market value of the car. Assuming, but not deciding that it was error, such error was harmless. The "actual" damages awarded totalled $770.00. Of this sum $120.00 was for the loss of Purchaser's personal property, which Commercial fully concedes is correct. Purchaser's testimonial estimate of the loss from the loss of use of the car, which clearly is a permissible element of damages, was approximately $500.00. Thus, this leaves only $150.00 for the loss of value of the automobile itself. This modest recovery does not demonstrate any harm.

Affirmed.

PRACTICAL NOTE

On default the debtor's attorney should read the security agreement carefully to see if expressly or impliedly it gives the debtor a right to notice before repossession. Conversely, the secured party's attorney should make sure the security agreement avoids statements like "upon demand" which may give rise to such an implication.

Where a bank pursued its foreclosure remedy under the guise of a state attachment procedure that was clearly unconstitutional, the plaintiffs in Guzman v. Western St. Bank of Devil's Lake, 540 F.2d 948, 21 U.C.C. Rep. Serv. 332 (8th Cir. 1976), took the unusual step of suing under the Civil Rights Act, 42 U.S.C. §1983, and recovered nearly $10,000 in actual damages and $30,000 in punitive damages. The court expressly found the bank guilty of bad faith.

PROBLEM 101

Natty Birdwhistle bought a car with money borrowed from Repossession Finance Company (which perfected its interest in the car). The security agreement provided that "time was of the essence" and that the acceptance by the finance company of late payments was not a waiver of its right to repossess. Natty always paid 10-15 days late. One month Repossession Finance had had enough and it sent a man out who took the car (using a duplicate set of keys) from the parking lot of the factory where Natty worked. Has a default occurred? See Westinghouse Credit Corp. v. Shelton, 645 F.2d 869, 31 U.C.C. Rep. Serv. 410 (10th Cir. 1981); G. Gilmore §44.1, at 1214: "[C]ourts pay little attention to clauses which appear to say that meaningful acts are meaningless and that the secured party can blow hot or cold as he chooses."

D. REPOSSESSION AND RESALE

Section 9-503 authorizes the secured party to skip going through judicial processes and to repossess the collateral on the debtor's default if this can be done without a "breach of the peace." For the meaning of that elusive term see White & Summers §26-6; Census Fed. Credit Union v. Wann, 403 N.E.2d 348, 28 U.C.C. Rep. Serv. 1207 (Ind. App. 1980); Comment, 82 Dick. L. Rev. 351 (1978); Annot., What Conduct By Repossessing Chattel Mortgagee or Conditional Vendor Entails Tort Liability, 99 A.L.R.2d 358 (1965). Grant Gilmore:

> In the financing of business debtors repossession causes little trouble or dispute. In the underworld of consumer finance, however, repossession is a knock-down, drag-out battle waged on both sides with cunning guile and a complete disregard for the rules of fair play. A certain amount of trickery seems to be accepted: it is all right for the finance company to invite the defaulting buyer to drive over to its office for a friendly conference on refinancing the loan and to repossess the car as soon as he arrives. It is fairly safe for the finance company to pick up the car on the street wherever it may be parked, although there is always a danger that the buyer will later claim that he had been keeping a valuable stock of diamonds in the glove compartment. But the finance company will do well to think twice before allowing its man to break into an empty house, even though a well-drafted clause in the security agreement gives it the right to do exactly that. And if the housewife, who is invariably pregnant and subject to miscarriages, sits on the sofa, stove, washing machine or television set and refuses to move, the finance company man will make a serious mistake if he dumps the lady or carries her screaming into the front yard. Juries love to award punitive damages for that sort of thing and the verdict will often be allowed to stand.

G. Gilmore §44.1, at 1212-1213.

PROBLEM 102

Don Jose was in charge of repossession for Carmen Motors. One Monday morning the dealership told him that cars owned by four debtors (Escamillo, Micaela, Zuniga, and Morales) were to be picked up because the buyers had missed payments. Look at §9-503 and answer this question: is Carmen Motors required to give the debtors *notice* that they are in default before repossessing? Don Jose visited each of the debtors with the following results.

(a) Don Jose found Escamillo's car parked in his driveway at 2:00 A.M.; he broke a car window, hot wired it, and drove it away. Has a breach of the peace occurred? What if Escamillo heard the window break, rushed out, and began yelling? May Don Jose continue the repossession or must he quit? If he goes away, may he try again later that night? See Ford Motor Credit Co. v. Cole, 503 S.W.2d 853, 14 U.C.C. Rep. Serv. 259 (Tex. Civ. App. 1973); cf. Griffith v. Valley of the Sun Recovery & Adj. Bureau, 613 P.2d 1283, 29 U.C.C. Rep. Serv. 711 (Ariz. App. 1980) (repossessor liable in negligence for act of debtor's neighbor who used a shotgun to shoot a bystander during repossession melee).

(b) He showed up at Micaela's house accompanied by his brother (an off-duty sheriff who was wearing his sheriff's uniform). Don Jose told Micaela that he was repossessing the car, and she said nothing. Has a breach of the peace occurred? See Stone Mach. Co. v. Kessler, 1 Wash. App. 750, 463 P.2d 651, 7 U.C.C. Rep. Serv. 651 (1970) (*constructive force* also constitutes a breach of the peace); accord Walker v. Walthall, 588 P.2d 863, 25 U.C.C. Rep. Serv. 918 (Ariz. App. 1978).

(c) Don Jose broke into Zuniga's garage through the use of the services of a locksmith. The garage lock and door were uninjured. A clause in the contract provided that the secured party had the right to enter the debtor's premises to remove the property. Does the repossession comply with §9-503? See White & Summers §26-6, at 1099-1100.

(d) Don Jose phoned Morales and said that the car was being recalled becaused of an unsafe engine mount. Morales brought the car in that morning. When the time came to pick up the car, Don Jose simply smiled, said "April Fools, it's been repossessed!," and refused to return it. Is the repossession valid? Compare Cox v. Galigher Motors Sales Co., 213 S.E.2d 475, 16 U.C.C. Rep. Serv. 1390 (W. Va. 1975), with Ford Motor Credit Co. v. Byrd, 351 So. 2d 557, 22 U.C.C. Rep. Serv. 1294 (Ala. 1974), commented on in 40 Ohio St. L.J. 501 (1979).

PROBLEM 103

Octopus National Bank financed Mary Melody's purchase of a new car, in which it perfected its security interest. The loan agreement provided that on default the bank had all the rights listed in Part 5 of Article 9 of the UCC and that the parties agreed that the bank would not be liable for conversion or otherwise if there were other items in the car at the time it was repossessed. Mary missed a payment and ONB's agent took the car in the dead of night from its parking place in front of her home. She protested the next day, claiming that her golf clubs were in the trunk. ONB looked there but couldn't find the clubs. When she sued, ONB defended on the basis of the security agreement's exculpatory clause. Is it valid? See Ford Motor Credit Co. v. Cole, 503 S.W.2d 853, 14 U.C.C. Rep. Serv. 259 (Tex. Civ. App. 1973). If ONB finds the clubs and returns them promptly on her demand are they still guilty of conversion? See Thompson v. Ford Motor Credit Co., 324 F. Supp. 108, 9 U.C.C. Rep. Serv. 128 (D.S.C. 1971).

PROBLEM 104

Wonder Spa gave the Antitrust National Bank (hereinafter ANB), a security interest in its accounts receivable and chattel paper in return for a loan. When Wonder Spa missed two payments in a row, ANB notified the spa's customers that future payments should be made directly to the bank. Does the bank have this right? Read §9-502 and its Official Comments; see §9-318(3). If the spa stops opening its doors, need its former customers keep paying ANB (the spa contracts did not mention the possibility that the contracts would be assigned)? See §§9-206, 9-318; G. Gilmore, ch. 41. The ability of customers to raise defenses against the finance company is bound up in the law of negotiable instruments — see Unico v. Owen, 50 N.J. 101, 232 A.2d 405, 4 U.C.C. Rep. Serv. 542 (1967), the leading case — and special consumer protection statutes, e.g., Uniform Consumer Credit Code §3.404, and regulations like the FTC's Holder in Due Course rule, 16 C.F.R. §433 (1975); Annot., 39 A.L.R.3d 518 (1971).

After repossession the secured party may in some circumstances (§9-505, explored below) simply keep the collateral and give up further remedy (this is called *strict foreclosure*). More typically the repossessing creditor will resell the collateral, and, if the resale does not pay the debt in full, then sue the debtor for any deficiency. Section 9-504 regulates the resale. Note that in most cases the secured party must give the debtor *notice* of the time and place of the sale. The reason for this notice is twofold: on getting it the debtor may elect to use the §9-506 right of redemption (about which more later), or the debtor can attend the sale or send potential buyers who will enter real bids and, by actively competing in the bidding, bring a fair price for the collateral. The notice requirement is much litigated: what must it say, who must it go to, what happens if it is not given? These issues are raised by the problems below, which also consider another §9-504 matter: the §9-504(3) mandate that "every aspect of the disposition including the method, manner, time, place and terms must be commercially reasonable." As to the meaning of *commercially reasonable* see White & Summers §26-11; G. Gilmore §44.5.

PROBLEM 105

Mr. & Mrs. Miller decided to open a restaurant, for which purpose they needed $80,000. They went to the Apocalypse National Bank, which agreed to loan them the money if they (a) got a surety, (b) signed an agreement giving the bank a security interest in the restaurant's equipment and inventory, and (c) pledged additional collateral to the bank having a value of $20,000 or more. The Millers got Mrs. Miller's father (Mr. Stuhldreher) to sign as surety, they signed the security agreement, and they borrowed $20,000 worth of stock from Mr. Miller's cousin, Mr. Layden. The stock was registered in Layden's name at the time it was pledged to the bank, but the bank had it re-registered in the bank's name so it could be sold easily in the event of default. The restaurant became involved in an unfortunate food poisoning incident, and business fell off. The Millers (who were in the midst of a divorce) missed two payments on the loan. The bank sent its collection agent, Mr. Crowley out to the restaurant and he repossessed the assets he found there. Crowley sent a written notice to Mr. Miller (who he knew was now living in a hotel) telling him that the stock would be sold on the open market (no specific date given) and that the restaurant equipment would be sold at public auction on December 1 at the offices of the Crowley Collection Agency. Crowley phoned Mr. Stuhldreher (the surety) and told him the same thing. He sent a written notice to Mr. Layden (the stock owner), but the letter came back marked "Moved — No Forwarding Address." If asked, either Mr. or Mrs. Miller would have supplied Crowley with Layden's new address. Crowley sold the stock for $10,000 on the open market (that was its current selling price), and auctioned off the restaurant equipment on December 1 for $500 (only one bid was received — Crowley himself was the bidder; he later resold the equipment to other restaurants for $10,000). Crowley turned over the proceeds from the two sales ($10,500 total) to Apocalypse National Bank, which then brought suit against the Millers and Mr. Stuhldreher for the deficiency. Answer these questions:

(a) Is a surety entitled to a §9-504 notice? That is, is he a *debtor*? Read §9-105(1)(d) and see 5 A.L.R.4th 1291 (1981): Sachs & Belgrad, Liability of the Guarantor of Secured Indebtedness After Default and Repossession Under the UCC: A Walk on the Wild Side by the Secured Party, 5 U. Balt. L. Rev. 153, 156-166 (1976). Does the *oral* notice to Mr. Stuhldreher satisfy §9-504? See Crest Inv. Trust, Inc. v. Alatzas, 287 A.2d 261, 10 U.C.C. Rep. Serv. 482 (Md. 1972).

(b) Was Mr. Layden a *debtor* too? Read §§9-105(1)(d), 9-112; see Security Pac. Natl. Bank v. Goodman, 100 Cal. Rptr. 763, 10 U.C.C. Rep. Serv. 529 (Cal. App. 1972). Was he entitled to notice of the stock sale?

(c) Is the notice sent to Mr. Miller sufficient as to Mrs. Miller? See Tauber v. Johnson, 291 N.E.2d 180, 11 U.C.C. Rep. Serv. 1106 (Ill. App. 1972).

(d) Does §9-504 require the creditor to whom a notice is returned by the post office to take further steps to notify the debtor? See Commercial Credit Corp. v. Cutshall, 28 U.C.C. Rep. Serv. 277 (Tenn. App. 1979); In re Carter, 511 F.2d 1203, 16 U.C.C. Rep. Serv. 874 (9th Cir. 1975); In re Hardie, 17 U.C.C. Rep. Serv. 633 (Bankr., N.D. Ohio 1975); Commercial Credit Corp. v. Lloyd, 12 U.C.C. Rep. Serv. 15 (D.C. Super. 1973).

(e) If Mr. Miller denies receiving the letter what burden of proof does the bank carry and what need it prove (a recurring and frustrating problem for lawyers)? Read §1-201(38). See Leasing Assocs., Inc. v. Slaughter & Son, Inc., 450 F.2d 174, 9 U.C.C. Rep. Serv. 1292 (8th Cir. 1971) (well worth reading).

(f) Who has the burden of proof as to the commercial reasonableness of the sales? Annot., 59 A.L.R.3d 369 (1974).

(g) If Crowley had given the equipment sale no publicity, has a *public* sale occurred, and, if so, was it *commercially reasonable*? See Annot., 7 A.L.R.4th 308 (1981); In re Bishop, 482 F.2d 381, 12 U.C.C. Rep. Serv. 1256 (4th Cir. 1973); In re Webb, 17 U.C.C. Rep. Serv. 627 (Bankr., S.D. Ohio 1975); Wirth v. Hearey, 508 S.W.2d 263, 14 U.C.C. Rep. Serv. 873 (Mo. App. 1974); Miles v. N.J. Motors, Inc., 16 U.C.C. Rep. Serv. 555 (Ohio App. 1975).

(h) Does the low price alone make the equipment sale unreasonable? Read §9-507(2); see Central Budget Corp. v. Garrett, 78 Misc. 2d 485, 361 N.Y.S.2d 800, 14 U.C.C. Rep. Serv. 543 (N.Y. Sup. Ct. 1974).

(i) What would you have advised if Crowley had asked you the best procedure for compliance with §9-504? For an example of a commercially reasonable sale, see James Talcott, Inc. v. Reynolds, 529 P.2d 352, 16 U.C.C. Rep. Serv. 259 (Mont. 1974).

(j) Was Crowley required to give notice of the sale of the stock?

(k) If the court holds that the sale was not reasonable, what penalty does Apocalypse National Bank incur? See §9-507(1). Is it good policy/law to hold that failure to comply with §9-504 results in a forfeiture of the creditor's ability to sue the debtor for the deficiency? See the cases in Annot., Failure of Secured Creditor To Give Required Notice of Disposition of Collateral as to Bar Deficiency Judgment, 59 A.L.R.3d 401 (1974); White & Summers §26.15; G. Gilmore §44.9.4.

Imperial Discount Corporation v. Aiken

38 Misc. 2d 187, 238 N.Y.S.2d 269 (N.Y.C. Civ. Ct. 1963)

Composto, J. This is an action on a retail installment contract by Imperial Discount Corporation, an alleged purchaser for value of said contract. After a hearing held on this inquest, the plaintiff's complaint is dismissed.

Despite the fact that there is no appearance on behalf of the defendant, the Court deems itself duty-bound to require of the plaintiff that minimum measure of proof to sustain its cause of action. While the Court will sustain a recovery to which a plaintiff is justly and fairly entitled, it will not grant judgment where, as here, plaintiff has failed to prove to the satisfaction of the Court that it met the statutory prerequisites.

The defendant, owner of a 1955 Oldsmobile, purchased a Delco battery on credit from a retail auto store for $29.30. In order to be permitted to pay by weekly installments, he agreed to a "credit service charge of $5.70." He thus started his journey into the cavernous depths of indebtedness with his 1955 Oldsmobile, a new Delco battery and a debt of $35.00, attested to by his signature on the aforesaid retail installment contract with its inevitable fine print and legalistic verbiage.

He failed to make due and timely weekly payments, and there came a time when a summons and verified complaint of eight paragraphs was served upon him in this case. All of the allegations or charges hereinafter mentioned are made, according to the verified complaint, "pursuant to the terms of the said chattel mortgage and retail installment contract."

Paragraph third of the complaint relates to the purchase by defendant "of certain goods, wares, and merchandise (the battery), at the agreed and stated price of $35.00, no part of which has been paid, excepting the sum of $23.25, leaving a balance due and owing of $11.75."

Paragraph fourth alleges the defendant owes late charges of twenty-five cents.

Paragraph fifth alleges defendant owes plaintiff's attorney fees of $16.80.

Paragraph sixth alleges the defendant owes plaintiff repossessing charges of $45.00. The retail installment contract had a provision that "The buyer hereby mortgages the motor vehicle hereinafter described as additional security for the payment of the time balance set forth above, together with any other motor vehicle hereinafter acquired in replacement thereof." Plaintiff caused the defendant's automobile to be repossessed, and as alleged in paragraph seventh, the repossessed automobile was sold at public auction, and the defendant owes auctioneer's fees of $35.00 and storage charges of $70.00, based on a charge of $2.50 per day for 28 days.

Paragraph eighth is the only paragraph in which the defendant may find a modicum of comfort. It does not allege he owes for any item of damage — in fact, he is given credit for $50, the amount for which his repossessed automobile was sold. Then follows the allegation "That pursuant to the said chattel mortgage and installment contract, there is presently due the total of $128.80."

When the defendant's journey, which started with an indebtedness of $35.00, of which $23.25 had been paid, leaving a balance of $11.75, reached its unsought destination in this court, the defendant was sans his battery, sans his automobile, and confronted with a demand for "judgment for $128.80, together with interest, costs, and disbursements of this action." The futility of trying to free himself of the engulfing accumulation of charges must have so overwhelmed the defendant, that he failed to answer the summons and complaint, and thus this inquest.

The defendant must now have realized the import of the despairing observation that "For want of a nail, a shoe was lost; for want of a shoe, a horse was lost; for want of a horse, a kingdom was lost." For want of $11.75, this defendant lost the battery, lost his 1955 Oldsmobile, and is subject to a judgment for $128.80.

The proof offered by plaintiff failed to satisfy the Court that it complied with all the prerequisites of the applicable law; but transcending questions of proof, the conscience of the Court is shocked by the mountainous pyramiding of charges imposed on a defaulting installment buyer, which are seemingly sanctioned by the Retail Installment Sales Act (section 401 et seq. of the Personal Property Law). Apparently this is not an isolated case. The Court is of the opinion that the Legislature never contemplated such oppressive, confiscatory, and unconscionable results. If this is an example of the practical working of the aforesaid law, then clearly the need for remedial legislation is manifest.

Judgment on inquest denied, complaint dismissed.

QUESTION

Does this decision conflict with the Washington Supreme Court's decision in Foster v. Knutson, supra at 267?

PROBLEM 106

The Bunyan State Bank held a perfected security interest in the logging equipment of the Blue Ox Timber Company. When Blue Ox defaulted on its loan repayment, Bunyan repossessed the equipment. The sale was held the next day in the middle of a snowstorm. The equipment sold for very little (there was only one bidder, and he complained that it was hard to know the condition of the equipment because it was so dirty, being covered with mud from the backwoods). Bunyan sued Blue Ox for the amount still due. Answer these questions:

(a) Was the notice period too short? See DeLay First Natl. Bank & Trust Co. v. Jacobson Appliance Co., 196 Neb. 398, 243 N.W.2d 745, 19 U.C.C. Rep. Serv. 994 (1976) ("To constitute reasonable notice of a private sale, the notice should be sent in such time that the debtors would have a minimum of 3 business days to arrange to protect their interests."); Franklin St. Bank v. Parker, 136 N.J. Super. 476, 346 A.2d 632, 18 U.C.C. Rep. Serv. 632 (1975) (three days notice held too short to be "commercially reasonable").

(b) Is the secured party required to wash the collateral prior to sale? See Weiss v. Northwest Acceptance Corp., 274 Ore. 343, 546 P.2d 1065, 19 U.C.C. Rep. Serv. 348 (1976).

(c) Did it violate §9-504 to conduct the sale in the snowstorm? Liberty Natl. Bank & Trust Co. v. Acme Tool Div. of the Rucker Co., 540 F.2d 1375, 19 U.C.C. Rep. Serv. 1288 (10th Cir. 1976).

Nelson v. Monarch Investment Plan of Henderson, Inc.

452 S.W.2d 375, 7 U.C.C. Rep. Serv. 394 (Ky. 1970)

Opinion of the court by Commissioner CLAY. This is a suit to recover a balance due on a note executed by defendant appellant,

Jack Nelson, for the purchase of an automobile. The defendant counterclaimed for damages on the ground plaintiff appellee had sold the purchased vehicle for less than its market value and had failed to give defendant notice of the sale as required by §9-504. The trial judge gave plaintiff summary judgment after giving defendant proper credit, and dismissed the counterclaim.

Defendant purchased the automobile on April 20, 1965, and executed his promissory note in the amount of approximately $1400. Before the first payment was due, defendant voluntarily brought the car to plaintiff's office and directed plaintiff to sell the automobile. At that time defendant stated he did not want the car under any circumstances, and delivered to plaintiff the ignition keys and the license receipt. Not long thereafter plaintiff's representative visited defendant at his home and obtained from him a signed bill of sale and a consignment agreement, the latter authorizing plaintiff to sell the vehicle at the best price it could obtain.

Subsequently defendant took back the bill of sale and said he wanted to cancel the consignment agreement. The reason for this change of mind is not shown. Thereafter plaintiff solicited and received bids from three used-car dealers. The car was then sold at a private sale to the highest bidder for $750. No claim is made that this was not a fair price on a used-car dealer market. No notice of this particular sale was given defendant.

The principal question raised on this appeal is whether the private sale of this repossessed automobile was on a "recognized market" within the meaning of §9-504(3). That subsection provides: [the court quoted §9-504(3)].

It will be noted first that every disposition of collateral must be "commercially reasonable." The record convinces us that the method, manner, time, place and terms of this private sale were commercially reasonable. This appears as a customary business practice in disposing of repossessed automobiles. There is nothing to indicate lack of good faith, unfairness of fraud.

However, the condition above discussed does not affect the requirement of notice. Reasonable notification of the sale must be given *unless* the collateral is either (1) perishable, or (2) threatens to decline in value, or (3) is of a type customarily sold on a recognized market. The latter is the only exemption upon which plaintiff could rely in this case. The reason for exempting such transaction from the notice requirement obviously is because the price on the recognized market represents the fair market value from day to day. The purpose of notice is to permit the debtor to bid at the sale or to protect himself from an inadequate sale price. If there is an established and recognized market, theoretically the best price at any given time is the current market price. We do not have such a recognized market for repossessed automobiles as a class. They vary widely in make, style, horsepower, age and condition.

While the question is one of first impression in Kentucky, it has been passed upon in Pennsylvania and Arkansas. Alliance Discount Corp. v. Shaw, 195 Pa. Super. 601, 171 A.2d 548 (1961); Norton v. National Bank of Commerce of Pine Bluff, Ark., 398 S.W.2d 538 (1966). In the *Alliance* case it is observed (pages 550, 171 A.2d):

> . . . No other article of commerce is subject to more erratic vacillation in pricing procedures. The so-called "red book" purporting to fix prices of various makes and models of automobiles in accordance with their year of manufacture is adopted for the convenience and benefit of dealers and is not based on market prices which are arrived at in the open, based on asking prices of sellers and bids of prospective buyers. Notice, as required by the Act, should have been given.

In the *Norton* case it was said (pages 540, 398 S.W.2d):

> First, the Code dispenses with notice when the collateral to be sold "is of a type customarily sold on a recognized market." Section 9-504(3). We cannot approve the bank's contention that a used car falls in this category. Obviously the Code dispenses with notice in this situation only because the debtor would not be prejudiced by the want of notice. Thus a "recognized market" might well be a stock market or a commodity market, where sales involve many so similar that individual differences are nonexistent or immaterial, where haggling and competitive bidding are not primary factors in each sale, and where the prices paid in actual sales of comparable property are currently available by quotation. We agree with the view taken in Pennsylvania, that there is no recognized market for used cars.

We think those decisions are sound and "reasonable notification" would be required by the Commercial Code under ordinary circumstances.

It is plaintiff's contention, however, that defendant actually had "reasonable notification of the time after which any private sale . . . is to be made." It is said that since defendant delivered the automobile to plaintiff for the purpose of having it sold, the defendant was thereby on notice of the time "after which" a private sale would be made. We think this notice requirement must mean something more substantial than that. We construe this provision to mean that the debtor is entitled to notification of a specific date after which the creditor may proceed to dispose of the collateral. This would give the debtor a deadline within which to protect himself in whatever manner he saw fit. Knowledge would be brought home to him that if he failed to liquidate his indebtedness, or reach an agreement with respect to the collateral, or failed to take other appropriate action by a specified time, he would be foreclosed from attacking the subsequent sale (provided always that it was "commercially reasonable").

In the present case we do not believe defendant's knowledge that the automobile eventually would be sold to satisfy his indebtedness constituted reasonable notification of a *time* after which a private sale properly could be made. It is therefore our conclusion that plaintiff was required to give notice under §9-504 and that it failed to comply. We believe the trial court incorrectly determined that under the terms of the statute notice of a private sale to a used-car dealer was not required. However, we are convinced the summary judgment for the plaintiff was proper on the ground that the defendant had waived the notice provision of the statute.

The following facts appear. Defendant voluntarily transferred complete dominion and control of this automobile to plaintiff. He was advised in substance that he probably could obtain a better price than the plaintiff if he sold the automobile. Defendant told plaintiff that he did not want the car back under any circumstances. Defendant delivered to plaintiff the car, the car keys, the licence receipt and consignment agreement. The record indicates clearly defendant had no further interest in this automobile and did not intend to bid on it. There is no indication that any notice given him would have resulted in a higher sales price of the automobile. The evidentiary material establishes an intentional relinquishment of the right to notice. If it did not constitute a waiver, it seems clear that defendant's actions relied on by plaintiff estopped him to claim a violation of the statute.

It is true that §9-501(3)(b) provides in effect that the notice provisions of the statute under consideration may not be waived, but we construe this provision as relating to a pre-emptive waiver found in the security agreement itself. See Norton v. National Bank of Commerce of Pine Bluff, Ark., 398 S.W.2d 538 (1966). In other words, the statute prohibits an anticipatory express waiver but does not deny a party the right to invoke the principles of waiver and estoppel which may apply to the subsequent transactions of the parties.

We conclude that under the particular facts of this case the defendant either waived his right to notice or is estopped to claim damages by reason of the plaintiff's failure to give it.

The judgment is affirmed. . . .

NOTE

This case was decided under the original version of Article 9. How does it come out under the current wording of §§9-501(3) and 9-504(3)?

Liberty National Bank v. Greiner

62 Ohio App. 2d 125, 405 N.E.2d 317, 29 U.C.C. Rep. Serv. 718 (1978)

Potter, P. J. On September 7, 1973, defendants-appellants executed and delivered to plaintiff-appellee their promissory note in the amount of $56,419.56. The note was a consolidation of several business loans made by appellee to appellants and was secured by security agreements covering thirteen used trucks. Appellants defaulted on payments of both principal and interest and, with the knowledge and consent of appellant Gary Greiner, appellee took possession of eleven of the used trucks in September of 1974.[4] Appellee sold seven of the trucks at an auction and the remaining four vehicles were sold upon written bids. The amount received from the sale less certain expenses was applied to reduce appellants' indebtedness. Subsequently, appellee sought a deficiency judgment for the remaining balance of the promissory note and was granted said judgment in the amount of $39,515.20 by the Sandusky County Common Pleas Court. . . .

[The court quoted §9-504(3).]

Appellee concedes that the collateral involved herein was not

4. Appellants obtained the consent of the bank and sold two of the trucks privately before the bank repossessed the other vehicles.

such as to exempt appellee from the reasonable notice requirements of §9-504(3). Appellee also concedes that no notice of the intended sale was given by it to appellant Shirley Greiner, wife of appellant Gary Greiner and co-signor on the promissory note, who was entitled to separate notice. Cf. Modern Finance Co. v. Enmen (1970), 25 Ohio Misc. 216, 267 N.E.2d 450, a decision under R.C. 1319.07, now repealed.

Appellant Gary Greiner did receive some notice of the intended disposition of the collateral when appellee repossessed the trucks and again when appellee sent a formal notice to Gary Greiner by certified mail. Appellants contend, however, that the notice given by appellee was inadequate and failed to comply with the notice requirements in §9-504(3). Only the notice which was hand delivered to Gary Greiner when the trucks were repossessed, on or about September 9, 1974, was made part of the record. There is no contention that the notice sent by certified mail and received on October 7, 1974, differed in any respect from that which was hand delivered to appellant. In pertinent part, the notice read as follows:

> You are hereby given notice that the property secured by the financing statement or security agreement bearing the file number shown above will be sold on the tenth (10) day after receipt of this letter at Fremont, Ohio, and the minimum price for which the secured property may be sold is $4,000.

The notice also described the property, informed appellant that he would be held liable for any deficiency, and notified appellant on the last line of the notice letter that, "Any person may appear at the time and place of sale and bid on said property."

The reading of the first quoted portion of the notice would indicate that the vehicles were to be sold through a private sale. The information therein conveyed, i.e., the date after which the property would be sold, would satisfy the notice requirements of §9-504(3) for a private sale. The last line of the notice letter, however, indicates that a public sale with competitive bidding would be held. Thus, aside from any other deficiency, the notice was patently ambiguous as to what type of sale would be held. In fact, two different methods of sale were utilized by appellee. Seven of the vehicles were sold by auction on October 23, 1976. Appellee advertised this sale in several area newspapers under the caption "Public Auction." The remaining vehicles were not at the place where the auction was held and were sold upon written bids. The date of that sale was not established. . . .

Section 9-504(3) requires that the secured party send the debtor reasonable notification of the time and place of the public sale. Clearly, the written notice received by appellant did not fulfill this requirement. The notice did not specify the time of the sale and the designation of Fremont, Ohio, as the place of the sale is too broad to constitute effective notice of the location. The notice of the location of the sale provided for in §9-504 contemplates a reasonably precise designation of the place where the sale is to be held. Cf. Ohio Credit Corp. v. Harbour (1970), 24 Ohio Misc. 221, 259 N.E.2d 182, 53 Ohio Ops. 2d 38, a decision under RC 1319.07, now repealed. We find, therefore, that the written notice received by appellant Gary Greiner was insufficient to comply with the mandate of §9-504. We also find that the general advertisements of the sale placed by appellee in the classified sections of area newspapers did not constitute notice to appellants of the time, place and date of sale. See Morris Plan Co. of Bettendorf v. Johnson (1971), 133 Ill. App. 2d 717, 271 N.E.2d 404.

As previously noted, in the case of a private sale §9-504 requires only that the debtor be informed of the date after which the property will be sold. Appellee's sale of the four trucks upon written bids was a private sale. While the written notice received by appellant did contain the necessary information, when read as a whole the notice indicated that a public sale would be held. We find that the combination of the form notice for private sale with the language indicating a public sale would be held is inherently misleading and, as such, does not constitute proper notice of a private sale, pursuant to §9-504(3). See DeLay First Natl. Bank & Trust Co. v. Jacobson Appliance Co. (1976), 196 Neb. 398 N.W.2d 745. . . .

In their third assignment of error, appellants contend that a creditor who fails to comply with the notice requirements of §9-504(3) cannot obtain a deficiency judgment. The Uniform Commercial Code does not specifically address this issue and the question is one of first impression in Ohio. Decisions from other jurisdictions based on basically the same statute have not been uniform. See Annotation, 59 A.L.R.3d 401. Many courts have held that compliance with the code requirements on disposition of collateral is a condition precedent to recovery of a deficiency judgment and that the creditor's failure to give the required notice is an absolute bar to recovery of a deficiency judgment. See Skeels

v. Universal C.I.T. Credit Corp. (W.D. Pa. 1963), 222 F. Supp. 696, *modified on other grounds,* 3 Cir., 335 F.2d 846; Herman Ford-Mercury, Inc. v. Betts (Iowa 1977), 251 N.W.2d 492; Gurwitch v. Luxurest Furniture Mfg. Co. (1975), 233 Ga. 934, 214 S.E.2d 373; Bank of Gering v. Glover (1974), 192 Neb. 575, 223 N.W.2d 56; Camden National Bank v. St. Clair (Me. 1973), 309 A.2d 329; Aimonetto v. Keepes (Wyo. 1972), 501 P.2d 1017; Washington v. First National Bank of Miami (Fla. App. 1976), 332 So. 2d 644; Atlas Thrift Co. v. Horan (1972), 27 Cal. App. 3d 999, 10 Cal. Rptr. 315; Leasco Data Processing Equip. Corp. v. Atlas Shirt Co. (1971), 66 Misc. 2d 1089, 323 N.Y.S.2d 13.

In its fourth conclusion of law, the trial court in the case sub judice apparently adopted a different approach which has also been accepted in other jurisdictions. Under this approach the creditor's failure to comply with the notice provisions of §9-504(3) does not automatically bar the recovery of a deficiency judgment; however, the creditor's failure to prove compliance with code requirements raises the presumption that the value of the collateral was equal to the amount of the debt and places the burden on the creditor to prove the fair market value of the collateral by evidence other than the price obtained upon resale. If the creditor fails to overcome the presumption, no deficiency judgment is allowed. See Levers v. Rio King Land & Investment Co. (Nev. 1977), 560 P.2d 917; Walker v. V.M. Box Motor Co., Inc. (Miss. 1976), 325 So. 2d 905; Clark Leasing Corp. v. White Sands Forest Products, Inc. (1975), 87 N.M. 451, 535 P.2d 1077; Universal C.I.T. Credit Co. v. Rone (1970), 248 Ark. 665, 453 S.W.2d 37; Hodges v. Norton (1976), 29 N.C. App. 193, 223 S.E.2d 848. A related line of cases allows the creditor who failed to give proper notice to recover the deficiency subject to a credit or setoff for the loss caused by the creditor's noncompliance. The amount of damages is presumed equal to the amount of the deficiency unless the creditor proves otherwise. See Commercial Credit Corp. v. Holt (Tenn. App. 1975), 17 UCC Rpt. Serv. 316.

While there is respectable authority which supports the trial court's finding, we hold that the better and more reasonable construction of §9-504(3) requires us to adopt the view that a creditor's full compliance with the statutory notice requirements is a condition precedent to the recovery of a deficiency judgment. We hold, therefore, that the creditor's failure to prove that a proper notice of disposition was sent to the debtor operates as a complete defense in a deficiency action brought by the creditor. While UCC

§9-507 does provide certain remedies for the debtor whose creditor has not proceeded in accordance with code rules on the disposition of collateral, that provision clearly contemplates affirmative relief and has no application to defenses. Therefore, the court's traditional equitable power to deny deficiency judgments may be implemented pursuant to UCC §1-103. See Camden National Bank v. St. Clair, supra; Atlas Thrift Co. v. Horan, supra; and Leasco Data Processing Equip. Corp. v. Atlas Shirt Co., supra.

The notice provisions of §9-504(3) were intended to afford the debtor an opportunity to bid on the collateral and to solicit any available bidders in order to insure a full and fair price and minimize the possibility of a deficiency. See Herman Ford-Mercury Inc. v. Betts, supra. The code's notice provisions are minimal; requiring compliance with them before any deficiency judgment can be obtained will not impose an undue burden on creditors. See II Gilmore, Security Interests in Personal Property 1261, Section 44.9.4 (1965). We find the reasoning in Skeels v. Universal C.I.T. Credit Corp., supra persuasive. It states, in part, at 702:

> It seems to this court, however, that to permit recovery by the security holder of a loss in disposing of collateral when no notice has been given, permits a continuation of the evil which the Commercial Code sought to correct. The owner should have an opportunity to bid at the sale. It was the secret disposition of collateral by chattel mortgage owners and others which was an evil which the Code sought to correct. It is important to note in the instant case that there was no waiver of the right to notice on disposition of collateral. A security holder who disposes of collateral without notice denies to the debtor his right of redemption which is provided him in §9-506.

We find that appellee failed to prove that proper notice was sent to the debtors in accordance with the mandate of §9-504(3) and because proof of compliance with such notice requirements is a condition precedent to the recovery of a deficiency judgment, we hold that the trial court committed prejudicial error in granting appellee the deficiency judgment. Appellants' third assignment of error is, therefore, well taken.

Appellants' second assignment of error concerns the determination of the commercial reasonableness of the disposition of the collateral and raises the issue of the relationship between that determination and a finding that the creditor failed to comply with the notice provision of §9-504(3). Section 9-504(3) requires that "every aspect of the disposition including the method, manner, time, place, and terms must be commercially reasonable." The term "commercially reasonable" is not clearly defined in the code, although §9-507(2) does provide some basic rules to assist in the determination of commercial reasonableness. In pertinent part, that section provides:

> The fact that a better price could have been obtained by a sale at a different time or in a different method from that selected by the secured party is not of itself sufficient to establish that the sale was not made in a commercially reasonable manner. If the secured party either sells the collateral in the usual manner in any recognized market therefor or if he sells at the price current in such market at the time of his sale or if he has otherwise sold in conformity with reasonable commercial practices among dealers in the type of property sold, he has sold in a commercially reasonable manner.

Further, the creditor's conduct in disposing of the collateral should be evaluated in light of the obligation to act in good faith imposed by UCC §1-203. See Northern Financial Corp. v. Kesterson (1971), 31 Ohio App. 2d 256, 287 N.E.2d 923.

The code does not specifically define the relationship between the notice provisions of §9-504(3) and the requirement that the disposition of the collateral be made in a commercially reasonable manner. Some courts have held that the "commercially reasonable" requirement is general in scope and effect and is not mutually exclusive of the notice requirement. These courts consider compliance with the notice requirement as one of several elements bearing on the question of commercial reasonableness. See e.g. Mallicoat v. Volunteer Finance & Loan Corp. (1966), 57 Tenn. App. 106, 415 S.W.2d 347. Other courts have treated the issues of notice and commercial reasonableness as related but independent requirements. See e.g. Beneficial Finance Co. v. Reed (Iowa 1973), 212 N.W.2d 454. We find that the latter view best reflects the language employed by the drafters and best effectuates the purposes and policies behind the two requirements. While the issue of notice to the debtor should be considered in the determination of commercial reasonableness, that factor alone is not controlling.

In the case sub judice, appellee hired a qualified appraiser, sufficiently advertised the sale to the public, properly attempted to obtain the highest possible bids for the collateral, and selected an auctioner who conducted the sale fairly. Therefore, we find that except for the failure to give the debtors proper notice, appellee otherwise complied with its obligations of good faith and commercial reasonableness. To that extent, the second assignment of error is not well taken. However, because we have found that proper notice is an independent requirement, our determination that the sale was otherwise conducted in a commercially reasonable manner does not alter the effect of appellee's failure to send the debtors proper notice of the disposition. Where, as in the case sub judice, the creditor fails to comply with the notice provisions of §9-504(3), the creditor cannot establish a condition precedent to recovery and, therefore, cannot obtain a deficiency judgment even if the requirement of commercial reasonableness has otherwise been met.

On consideration whereof, the court finds substantial justice has not been done the parties complaining, and the judgment of the Sandusky County Common Pleas Court is reversed.

Judgment reversed.

E. REDEMPTION AND STRICT FORECLOSURE

Centuries of property law have established the right of the defaulting debtor to recover the collateral by curing the default. The courts of equity first enforced this right of *redemption,* and it has become a common maxim that the courts will not permit anything to clog the equity of redemption. See G. Gilmore §43.2; Indianapolis Morris Plan Corp. v. Karlen, 28 N.Y.2d 30, 268 N.E.2d 632, 319 N.Y.S.2d 831, 8 U.C.C. Rep. Serv. 939 (1971).

PROBLEM 107

When Paul Morphy borrowed $2000 from the Lasker State Bank in order to finance a trip to Iceland; the bank made him sign an agreement giving the bank a security interest in Paul's private yacht. He agreed to repay the loan at the rate of $200 a month. He took the trip and on his return made the first payment on time. He failed to make the second payment on the due date, and the next day the bank repossessed the yacht. Paul raced to the bank with the late payment; he had $200 in cash which he tendered. The bank refused to take the money. The bank's loan officer, a Mr. Anderssen, pointed to an acceleration clause in the security agreement that made the entire amount due if a payment were missed. Anderssen demanded the total unpaid balance. Need Paul pay off everything? See §9-506 along with its Official Comment. A leading pre-Code case on this problem (which contains a very quotable discussion of the issue) is Street v. Commercial Credit Corp., 35 Ariz. 479, 281 P. 46 (1929). For Code cases see Urdang v. Muse, 114 N.J. Super. 372, 276 A.2d 397, 8 U.C.C. Rep. Serv. 1220 (1971); Robinson v. Jefferson Credit Corp., 4 U.C.C. Rep. Serv. 15 (N.Y. Sup. Ct. 1967); Krahmer, Creditors, Consumers and Article 9 of the UCC, 5 U. Tol. L. Rev. 1, 6-10 (1973).

Strict foreclosure occurs when the creditor repossesses the collateral and simply keeps it in satisfaction of the debt. No deficiency is sought. The debtor (or other creditors having junior security interests) may not be pleased with strict foreclosure in all situations. Read §§9-505 and 9-507.

PROBLEM 108

Art Auctions, Inc. (hereinafter AAI) sold Dudley Collector a $5000 painting by Smock Pallet, a famous artist. Dudley paid $1000 down, and agreed to pay over $1000 a month thereafter. The finance charge was $151.20; the Annual Percentage Rate was 18%. The contract contained a clause saying that in the event of default, AAI could repossess the painting and keep it without reselling it, or, at its option, could resell it and sue for the deficiency. Dudley made three more payments and then missed the last one, being temporarily short of funds. AAI, without notice, sent one of its agents to Dudley's home. The maid let the agent in and he simply removed the painting from the wall and walked out, saying, "Thank you." Dudley immediately tendered $1000 to AAI and demanded the painting. AAI refused (the painting is now worth $7000). Four months later Dudley filed suit. What is the basis of his cause of action and to what relief is he entitled? See §§9-505 and 9-507; Annot., Construction and Operation of §9-505(2), 55 A.L.R.3d 651 (1974). For discussions of the consumer damages computation described in §9-507(1), see G. Gilmore §44.9.3; White & Summers §26-14, cf. In re Webb, 17 U.C.C. Rep. Serv. 627 (Bankr., S.D. Ohio 1975) (right to §9-507 damages passes to the consumer's trustee in bankruptcy).

Moran v. Holman

514 P.2d 817, 13 U.C.C. Rep. Serv. 206 (Alas. 1973)

BOOCHEVER, J. We are here confronted with the question of whether, under the provisions of the Uniform Commercial Code (UCC), a debt is discharged when the secured party, after the debtor's default in payments, repossessed a truck, used it for purposes other than its preservation, and did not initiate suit on the debt for a period of approximately four months.

In November of 1967, Rex Holman borrowed $2,050 from Jack Moran to finance the purchase of a used pickup truck. The debt was consolidated with certain prior obligations, and Holman executed a promissory note in the principal amount of $2,750, with interest at 9 percent per annum. Under the terms of this note, Holman agreed to repay the loan in monthly $100 installments commencing in February of 1968. A security agreement was also executed by Holman in favor of Moran covering the pickup truck. Holman made one $100 payment on the debt and defaulted on the subsequent installments.

On June 21, 1969, Moran appeared at Holman's residence and demanded possession of the collateral. Holman refused to surrender the truck, and Moran left. Later that same day, Holman decided to give up the truck, and so he drove it to Moran's home and left it there. He gave the keys to Moran.

On October 16, 1969, Moran sued Holman in the district court to recover on the debt secured by the pickup truck. The court found that "Moran, or persons authorized by him, used the truck for purposes not related to its preservation," and noted that Moran had waited nearly four months after repossession before initiating this action. The district court concluded that under the Alaska provisions of the UCC, Moran had retained the collateral in satisfaction of the debt; and that, moreover, the retention of the collateral amounted to an accord and satisfaction of the debt. The court also held that by taking possession of the collateral, Moran was barred from suing on the debt. On appeal, the superior court affirmed the district court's decision. Moran appeals to this court. . . .

A secured party's rights and remedies following the debtor's default are governed by Part 5 of Article 9 of the UCC as enacted in Alaska. Section 9-501(1) specifies that, except as limited by the specific provisions of §9-501(3), a secured party may enforce such rights as may be provided in the security agreement. He may also reduce his claim to judgment, foreclose, or otherwise enforce the security interest by any available judicial procedure.

Section 9-503 provides that the secured party may take possession of the collateral on default. He may sell, lease, or otherwise dispose of the chattel in accordance with provisions set forth in §9-504.

Section 9-505(2) sets forth an additional right of a secured party who, like Moran, has been paid less than 60 percent of the loan and is in possession of the collateral. He may retain the collateral in satisfaction of the debt.[5] In that event, he is required to furnish written notice to the debtor. If the debtor objects within 30 days after receipt of the notice, the secured party must dispose of the chattel by a means specified in §9-504. In the absence of such written objection, he may retain the collateral in satisfaction of the debtor's obligation.

Moran gave no such written notice to Holman nor did he attempt to sell or dispose of the property. Some four months after taking possession of the truck, during which time he used it for his own purposes, he brought against Holman for the full amount of the debt then due plus interest. The case was not tried until July 30, 1971, more than 25 months after Moran had taken possession of the vehicle. At no time did he offer to return the truck or attempt to sell it.

The facts are closely analogous to those of Bradford v. Lindsey Chevrolet Co.[6] where it was held:

> The action of the holder in legally repossessing the security under a conditional sale contract, the retention of the same without sale and without excuse for not selling, and without demand for payment of the contract, for a period of approximately 50 days before suit on the contract and for over 16 months from the time of filing suit to the time of trial, constituted a rescission and satisfaction of the contract and no recovery could be had thereon.

The requirement of notice to the debtor by a secured party proposing to retain the chattel in satisfaction of the obligation is

5. If, however, the collateral is "consumer goods," defined in §9-109(1), and 60 percent of the loan or price has been paid, then the secured creditor is precluded from retaining the collateral, and *must* sell it within 90 days after repossession. UCC §9-505(1). It does not appear, nor did the parties contend, that in this case 60 percent of the loan or price had been paid. It is unclear from the record whether the truck was "consumer goods" as defined by the code.

6. 117 Ga. App. 781, 161 S.E.2d 904 (1968).

obviously for the benefit of the debtor. A secured party who retains the chattel for an excessive period of time without disposing of it as provided for by the UCC and who uses the property as his own during that period should not be permitted to profit by his failure to furnish the requisite notice. As stated in 4 R. Anderson, Uniform Commercial Code 9-505:5, at 632 (2d ed. 1971):

> The creditor's failure to give notice of intention to retain the collateral in discharge of the debt does not prevent the debtor from showing that the collateral was in fact retained by the creditor and on the basis of such fact he may claim that he is discharged from further liability. The giving of notice protects the creditor from a subsequent claim that he should have sold the collateral. [(Footnote omitted.)]

A motor vehicle such as the truck in question is a depreciating asset. The district court found that the parties here were unsophisticated with reference to the myriad and involved provisions of the UCC. In such a situation the secured party who has retaken possession of the collateral should not be permitted to wait an inordinate period, utilizing the vehicle in the meantime, and then elect to sue for the full amount of the debt.

We are further influenced in so construing the statute by the consideration that a debtor who has defaulted on his obligation so that the collateral has been repossessed is often in a particularly disadvantageous position to sue the creditor to compel disposition of the collateral or to seek damages for its misuse. Usually, due to his poor financial position, the debtor has scant prospect of obtaining an attorney, and the amount involved is often too small to justify legal services. The possible remedies are thus illusory in most cases. On the other hand no substantial burden is imposed upon the creditor by requiring him to take action within a reasonable time and to abstain from making inconsistent use of the repossessed collateral.

Our holding does not imply that a secured party under proper circumstances may not retain possession of collateral and still sue on the obligation. When, however, he retains collateral which depreciates in value, such as a motor vehicle, for an unduly long period of time and uses the vehicle as his own, we hold that the debtor may validly claim that his obligation has been satisfied. To rule otherwise would permit overreaching and inequitable abuses by some secured parties.

In view of our holding, we do not reach the question of whether an accord and satisfaction was effected by the repossession.

Affirmed.

RABINOWITZ, C.J., with whom FITZGERALD, J., joins, dissenting.

I am unable to agree with the court's holding that if the secured party after repossession of a depreciating asset retains possession of the collateral, and uses the collateral as his own for an "unduly long" period of time, the debtor may elect to treat the debt as discharged.

On default the secured party may, unless otherwise agreed, take possession of the collateral, if he does so without breach of the peace. UCC §9-503, cf., Weaver v. O'Meara Motor Co., 452 P.2d 87 (Alaska 1969). After repossession, the secured party may exercise those remedies which are established under the default provisions of Article 9 of the Code as enacted in Alaska, and in addition may "reduce his claim to judgment, foreclose, or otherwise enforce the security interest by any available judicial procedure." UCC §9-501(1). The secured party need not make an election among these remedies, and may pursue them simultaneously.

Except when the collateral is "consumer goods," and the debtor has paid 60% of the cash price or 60% of the loan, the Code imposes no time limit upon the secured party in possession of the collateral to sell the collateral or to give the debtor written notice of his intention to retain the collateral in satisfaction of the debt. The Code, however, does require that the "method, manner, *time,* place and terms" of any disposition of the collateral by the secured party be commercially reasonable. UCC §9-504(3).

The Code does not require the secured party to sell the collateral after repossession. See, UCC §9-504(1). However, if the secured party does not elect to retain the collateral in satisfaction of the obligation, the requirement that he sell the collateral within a commercially reasonable time must apply. The commercial reasonableness of the time of the sale must be judged from the date of repossession in order for that requirement to be meaningful. Surely the secured party should not be permitted to claim that the commercial reasonableness of the time of the sale should be judged from the time he decides to dispose of the collateral rather than to retain it in satisfaction of the debt.[7]

7. The draftsmen of the Code noted in Official Comment 6, UCC §9-504 that

"... a secured party who without proceeding under Section 9-505(2) held

The debtor's remedy for the secured party's failure to comply with the default provisions of Article 9 is set out in §9-507(1). That section provides in part:

> If it is established that the secured party is not proceeding in accordance with §§782-794 of this chapter [the default provisions of Article 9], *disposition may be ordered* or restrained on appropriate terms and conditions. [(Emphasis added)]

Thus, if the secured party does not elect to retain the collateral in satisfaction of the debt, and does not dispose of the collateral within a commercially reasonable period, the debtor's remedy is to compel disposition of the collateral.

Additionally, the Code requires that the secured party use reasonable care in the custody and preservation of the collateral after repossession. UCC §9-501(2), §9-207(1). The Code provides that in the event the secured party fails to exercise reasonable care in the custody and preservation of the collateral, the secured party is liable for any resulting loss. UCC §9-207(3).

By holding that the debtor may treat the debt as discharged when the secured party fails to dispose of the collateral and uses it as his own, the majority ignores the specific remedies which the Code provides. Moran may be liable to Holman for losses caused by his failure to use reasonable care in the custody and preservation of the collateral. Holman might also have sought to compel Moran to dispose of the pickup truck if Moran failed to sell it within a commercially reasonable time. But, I find no authority in the Code for the conclusion that Holman may consider the debt discharged because Moran used the collateral in a manner inconsistent with its preservation, and did not sell the collateral during the four month period before he brought suit. Although the secured party may be liable to the debtor for failure to exercise care in the custody and preservation of the collateral, and further may be compelled to dispose of the collateral if the secured party fails to sell within a commercially reasonable period of time, the Code does not permit the debtor to treat the debt as extinguished.

A creditor may reasonably wish to defer sale of the collateral in order to secure the highest price and limit the amount of the deficiency for which the debtor will be liable. However, now that

---

collateral a long time without disposing of it, thus running up large storage charges against the debtor, where no reason existed for not making a prompt sale, might be found not to have acted in a 'commercially reasonable' manner."

the creditor may suffer extinction of the debt by waiting for a favorable market, the creditor will likely sell as quickly as possible after repossession in order to preserve his right to proceed against the debtor for a deficiency judgment. I am concerned that by creating an incentive for the quick disposition of collateral, onerous deficiency judgments will be encouraged. As Professor Gilmore has observed:

> Sad experience has taught that a power of sale, coupled with a right to a deficiency judgment, can be harder on the debtor than strict foreclosure ever was. The surplus to be returned to the debtor after sale is a glittering mirage; the deficiency judgment is a given reality. Furthermore the person who buys at the sale today, nine times out of ten, is not our hero, the good faith purchaser for value, but the holder of the security interest who pays not in cash but by a credit against the debt.[8]

Finally, since the record is devoid of any evidence which would support the district court's finding of an accord and satisfaction, and since I do not think that Moran's conduct should result in extinction of the debt, I would reverse and remand for a new trial.

NOTE

Not all courts are willing to declare a *forced* strict foreclosure where the secured party repossesses and does nothing for an unreasonable amount of time; see Jones v. Morgan, 58 Mich. App. 455, 228 N.E.2d 419, 16 U.C.C. Rep. Serv. 1450 (1975) (debtor entitled to §9-507 damages but not excused from deficiency); see also White & Summers §26-8. The delay may, however, result in a finding that §9-504 has been violated because the resale has not occurred in a "commercially reasonable" time; Harris v. Bower, 266 Md. 579, 295 A.2d 870, 11 U.C.C. Rep. Serv. 428 (1972). As a practical matter therefore, a delay in resale is a dangerous (and perhaps expensive) tactic for the creditor to adopt.

In the last case Judge Rabinowitz quotes Grant Gilmore as saying that the possibility of a surplus on resale is a "glittering mirage." That it is not always thus, see In re Ford Motor Co., 27 U.C.C. Rep. Serv. 1118 (FTC 1979), *rev'd,* 654 F.2d 599, 32 U.C.C. Rep. Serv. 1 (9th Cir. 1981).

8. Gilmore, Security Interests in Personal Property, 1191 (1965). See also, Clark, Default, Repossession, Foreclosure and Deficiency: A Journey to the Underworld and a Proposed Salvation, 51 Ore. L. Rev. 302 (1972).

Reeves v. Foutz & Tanner, Inc.

617 P.2d 149, 29 U.C.C. Rep. Serv. 1450 (N.M. 1980)

Sosa, C. J. These suits were brought as separate actions but were consolidated by the Court of Appeals because the issues were essentially the same. The trial court held for plaintiffs, the Court of Appeals reversed, and we reverse the Court of Appeals.

Plaintiffs Reeves and Begay are uneducated Navajo Indians whose ability to understand English and commercial matters are limited. Each of them pawned jewelry with the defendant whereby they received a money loan in return for a promise to repay the loan in thirty days with interest. The Indian jewelry left with defendant as collateral was worth several times the amount borrowed. The plaintiffs defaulted and defendant sent each of them a notice of intent to retain the collateral, though Reeves claimed she never received notice. The retention was not objected to by either plaintiff. Defendant then sold the jewelry in the regular course of its business.

The question we are presented with is whether a secured party who sends a notice of intent to retain collateral, in conformance with §9-505 of the Uniform Commercial Code, may sell the collateral in its regular course of business without complying with §9-504? We decide that the secured party in this case could not sell the collateral without complying with §9-504.

The Uniform Commercial Code provides a secured party in possession with two courses of action upon the default of the debtor. Section 9-504 provides generally that the secured party may sell the collateral, but if the security interest secures an indebtedness, he must account to the debtor for any surplus (and the debtor must account for any deficiency). Section 9-505(2) provides the secured party with the alternative of retaining the collateral in satisfaction of the obligation. Under this section, the secured party must give written notice to the debtor that he intends to keep the collateral in satisfaction of the debt. The debtor is then given thirty days to object to the proposed retention and require the sale of the property according to §9-504.

In the present case we will assume that defendant gave proper notice to both Reeves and Regay of its intention to retain the collateral and that neither objected within thirty days. The trial court found that the defendant, in accordance with its normal business practice, then moved the jewelry into its sale inventory where it was sold to Joe Tanner, president of defendant corporation, or to Joe Tanner, Inc., a corporation owned by Joe Tanner and engaged in the sale of Indian jewelry. There was no accounting to plaintiffs of any surplus. The trial court also found that the defendant did not act in good faith in disposing of the jewelry, taking into consideration the relative bargaining power of the parties.

The defendant argues that the trial court should be reversed because it applied §9-504. It essentially argues that once it complied with §9-505(2) and sent the notice of intent to retain, it could do as it pleased with the property once the thirty days had elapsed without objection. The debtor-creditor relationship terminates, they claim, and the creditor becomes owner of the collateral.

The plaintiffs argue that the trial court was correct in applying §9-504 to require that any surplus from the sale of collateral be returned to the debtor. They urge that the intention of the secured party should control and where he intended to sell the collateral and did sell the collateral in the normal course of business, he must comply with §9-504 which governs sales of such collateral.

Neither party to this action has cited a case which has dealt directly with the issue here, but amicus has referred us to a Federal Trade Commission case on the subject where it was stated:

> In the Draftsmen's Statement of Reasons for 1972 Changes in Official Text, the Draftsmen summarized the purpose of §9-505 as follows:
>
> "Under subsection (2) [9-505(2)] of this section the secured party may in lieu of sale give notice to the debtor and certain other persons that he proposes to retain the collateral in lieu of sale."
>
> The foregoing language strongly suggests that waiver of surplus and deficiency rights under §9-505 is appropriate only when prompt resale of repossessed collateral in the ordinary course of business is not contemplated by the creditor. . . . That being so, use of §9-505 by an automobile dealer, particularly one not disposed to pursue deficiency judgments, would appear calculated solely to extinguish surplus rights of consumers, which we do not believe was the intended purpose of §9-505.

In the Matter of Ford Motor Company, Ford Motor Credit Company, and Francis Ford Inc., 93 FTC Rep. — , 3 CCH Trade Reg. Rep. 21756, 21767 (FTC Docket No. 9073, Sept. 21, 1979). The Commission went on to say that a creditor of this type is not foreclosed from using §9-505(2) so long as he intends to retain the collateral for his own use for the immediately foreseeable future, rather than to resell the collateral in the ordinary course of business. We agree with the approach used by the Federal Trade Commission.

The Court of Appeals reasoned that once the creditor elected to retain the collateral, and followed the mechanics of §9-505, the property became his to keep or to sell. We do not find fault with this reasoning, but it misses the point. Defendant can do as he pleases with the property, but where he intends to sell the property in the regular course of his business, which is in substance selling the property as contemplated by §9-504, he must account for a surplus in conformity with §9-504.

The defendant also argues that plaintiffs could have objected to the retention, thus forcing a sale in compliance with §9-504. But because there was never any actual intent to retain under §9-505(2), the failure of plaintiffs to timely object does not foreclose their claim. Moreover, the fact that plaintiffs could have objected means nothing in this context; their objection would only have served to cause a sale of the goods, which sale was already intended by defendant.

The defendant also argues that the trial court erred in finding that it acted in bad faith. We need not reach this question because bad faith was not material to the trial court's conclusions of law and judgment, which we find to be proper.

The defendant next claims error in the fact that the trial court allowed interest on the judgment from November 1, 1974. The date is the approximate day on which the loss took place and is apparently not controverted. The amount due the plaintiffs was a sum certain once the jewelry was sold, as calculated according to the provisions of §9-504. It was not error for the court to allow prejudgment interest or to allow interest as a portion of the damages. Sundt v. Tobin Quarries, 50 N.M. 254, 265, 175 P.2d 684, 690-91 (1946).

The judgment of the trial court is affirmed.

F. THE CONSTITUTIONALITY OF SELF-HELP REPOSSESSION

In a series of cases starting with Sniadach v. Family Fin. Corp., 395 U.S. 337 (1969), the United States Supreme Court began holding unconstitutional on Fourteenth Amendment grounds state statutes that permitted judicially controlled seizure of the debtor's property, prior to trial, without a hearing (the case below tracks the Supreme Court developments). In Adams v. Egley, 338 F. Supp. 614, 10 U.C.C. Rep. Serv. 1 (S.D. Cal. 1972), a federal district court extended this idea to hold U.C.C. §§9-503 and 9-504 unconstitutional because they authorize self-help repossession without a prior judicial hearing. The *Adams* case was reversed on appeal, see Adams v. Southern Cal. First Natl. Bank, 492 F. 2d 324, U.C.C. Rep. Serv. 161 (9th Cir. 1973); the reasoning of the Ninth Circuit (and, at this writing, of all the federal appellate courts) has been that there is no significant "state action" involved with the private repossession authorized by these Code sections; Annot., 29 A.L.R. Fed. 418 (1976).

Turner v. Impala Motors

503 F.2d 607, 15 U.C.C. Rep. Serv. 533 (6th Cir. 1974)

Peck, J. Tennessee Code Annotated (TCA) §47-9-503 is the State of Tennessee's statutory implementation of the Uniform Commercial Code's §9-503 which authorizes a secured creditor to peacefully repossess collateral. The provision is generally known as the self-help repossession provision. This case presents the issue as to whether peaceful repossession under the Tennessee statute is action under the color of state law within the meaning of 42 USC §1983 and state action within the meaning of the due process clause of the Fourteenth Amendment. Upon motion of the defendant-appellee, the District Court dismissed the suit for failure to state a cause of action and this appeal followed. District Judge Garrity has characterized this issue as "one of the liveliest on the current judicial scene." Boland v. Essex County Bank, 361 F. Supp. 917 (D. Mass. 1973).

In terms of private repossession, the facts before us offer a classic example. Plaintiff-appellant Turner purchased a 1965 Buick LeSabre in June of 1972 from the defendant-appellee Impala on a conditional sales contract. Turner executed a promissory note specifying a payment schedule of twenty-five dollars per week for twelve weeks, with the remaining balance to be paid at the rate of twenty dollars per week.

The record does not indicate the circumstances of the default but the actual payments were erratic from the beginning. The contract included a provision that "in default of payment of this note, or any part of it, said payee [Impala] may take possession of said property in any manner they [sic] may elect, and dispose of same without recourse to law . . ."

Almost seven months after the purchase, Turner apparently defaulted on his note and without notice the auto was repossessed from a curbside on a public street. The incident occurred in the early afternoon on a week day after Turner parked his auto in front of his mother's house. Turner had left his five-year-old son in the auto and the keys to the auto in his pocket, but the agent of Impala was not deterred. The young child was removed therefrom and the auto sped away. The record indicates that there was no hearing to determine either contractual obligations or the rights to possession.

Turner contends that the Tennessee statute is unconstitutional and that it authorizes a deprivation of property without due process. He principally relies on Fuentes v. Shevin, 407 U.S. 67 (1972), which held that notice and a hearing are required before the execution of a pre-judgment writ of replevin. According to the appellant, the Tennessee statute allows a creditor to circumvent the requirements of notice and hearing and yet replevy his property. He contends that although the case ostensibly involves private conduct, the presence of state action is indicated by the fact that the state has intervened, authorized and encouraged repossession by secured creditors by conferring upon them special powers and exemptions from legal requirements placed on all others. Appellant also argues that the Tennessee statute, similar to the replevin statutes in *Fuentes*, deprives the debtor of his rights to notice and an opportunity to be heard. The waiver provision contained in the contract does not, appellant contends, necessarily exclude the requirements of notice and a judicial hearing on the issue of the waiver prior to the repossession. The waiver provision allows the creditor to take possession upon default.

Before we consider the constitutional dimensions of the matter before us, we must first examine the key question of jurisdictional requisites. The concept of state action as required by the Fourteenth Amendment has been found to be virtually synonymous with the "under color of state law" requirement of §1983. United States v. Price, 383 U.S. 787, 794-95 n.7 (1966); Palmer v. Columbia Gas of Ohio, Inc., 479 F.2d 153, 161 (6th Cir. 1973). But cf. Adickes v. S. H. Kress & Co., 398 U.S. 144, 211 (1970) (Brennan, J., concurring and dissenting). Appellants would have us hold that the self-help repossession which took place upon the default on a private contract providing for such repossession is an act under color of state law and thus constitutes state action within the scope of the Fourteenth Amendment. If the repossession did not constitute state action but rather only an individual invasion of individual rights, the alleged wrong cannot be remedied under the auspices of the Fourteenth Amendment. Civil Rights Cases, 109 U.S. 3, 11 (1883). The presence of state action allows the invocation of the basic procedural safeguards announced in Sniadach v. Family Finance Corp., infra, and Fuentes v. Shevin, supra.

Instances of private conduct have been found to involve sufficient state action but each such conclusion should be the product of "sifting facts and weighing circumstances . . ." Burton v. Wilmington Parking Authority, 365 U.S. 715, 722 (1961). However, a mere finding that state action is present is insufficient. The state action must rise to the level of significant involvement. Moose Lodge No. 107 v. Irvis, 407 U.S. 163, 173 (1971).

The constitutional attacks on creditors' tactics such as peaceful repossession or formal legal processes gained support with Mr. Justice Douglas' majority opinion in Sniadach v. Family Finance Corp., 395 U.S. 337 (1969). In that case a garnishment action had been instituted in a state court whose rules allowed the service of summons and complaint upon the alleged debtor's employer. The effect was to freeze the alleged debtor's wages until the merits of the case had been decided. The debtor was not required to be notified at the time of service upon the employer and there was no opportunity for the debtor to obtain a hearing or judicial scrutiny of the creditors' claims. The debtor was restricted to either showing that the suit was brought in bad faith or posting a bond in the amount of the garnishment. With Mr. Justice Black dissenting, the Supreme Court held that the Court Clerk's ex parte issuance of a summons pursuant to the state statute constituted state action and that the prejudgment wage garnishment without prior notice and opportunity for a hearing deprived the debtor of property without due process of law in violation of the Fourteenth Amendment.

Subsequently, the Supreme Court in Fuentes v. Shevin, 407 U.S. 67 (1972), speaking through Mr. Justice Stewart, held that certain state statutes providing for the summary seizure of personal property by means of a prejudgment replevin procedure involving the sheriff's execution of a writ issued by a court clerk violated the due process clause of the Fourteenth Amendment insofar as it denied a debtor the right to notice and the opportunity for a hearing prior to the loss of any possessory interest in that personal property.

However, in the recent case of Mitchell v. W.T. Grant Co., 42 U.S.L.W. 4671 (U.S., May 13, 1974), it would appear that *Fuentes* has been effectively overruled. See concurring opinion of Powell, J., id. at 4678, and the dissenting opinion of Stewart, J., id. at 4682. In *Mitchell,* judicial sequestration procedures in Louisiana, similar to the replevin statutes struck down in *Fuentes,* allowed a creditor to obtain, on an ex parte basis from a judicial authority, a writ of sequestration upon submission of an affidavit and posting of a security bond. Thereupon a public official, without providing notice and a hearing to the debtor, seized the property. Distinguishing judicial control over the process from the court clerk's control in *Fuentes,* the Supreme Court found the procedure was not invalid.

Prior to *Mitchell,* the challenge to the Commercial Code's self-help repossession provisions generated considerable litigation. However, the only federal appellate courts to have met the issue to date have failed to find significant state action present. Gibbs v. Titelman, Nos. 74-1062 to 74-1067 (3rd Cir., filed August 1, 1974); James v. Pinnix, No. 73-1866 (5th Cir., filed June 10, 1974); Nowlin v. Professional Auto Sales, Inc., No. 73-1348 (8th Cir., filed April 25, 1974), citing Bichel Optical Laboratories, Inc. v. Marquette National Bank, 487 F.2d 906 (8th Cir., 1973); Shirley v. State National Bank of Connecticut, No. 73-1783 (2d Cir., filed February 14, 1974); Adams v. Southern California First National Bank, No. 72-1484 (9th Cir., filed October 4, 1973), *revg sub nom.* Adams v. Egley, 338 F. Supp. 614 (S.D. Cal. 1972), *petition for cert. filed,* 42 U.S.L.W. 3707 (U.S. June 25, 1974).

It is the district court's opinion in *Adams* that remains the most frequently cited case finding the requisite state action. In that case, the court relied upon Reitman v. Mulkey, 387 U.S. 369 (1967), wherein the Supreme Court found that state action existed when private housing discrimination was authorized by a provision of the California constitution. Even though the California constitution did not require discrimination in the sale and rental of housing, the Court asked that the provision in question would "significantly encourage and involve the State in private discriminations" contrary to the Fourteenth Amendment. Id. at 381. Similarly, the District Court in *Adams* held that the California enactments of the UCC encouraged and involved the state in private repossession and sale, as demonstrated by their incorporation in the security agreement. Appellants here have mounted that same challenge.

On appeal, the Ninth Circuit held that there was not sufficient involvement by the State of California to constitute state action. *Adams,* supra, slip opinion at p. 7. The court distinguished *Reitman* as being a racial discrimination case having limited application to the self-help repossession cases and relied on the finding that the California statute merely codified the existing common law. The court also rejected the contention that the repossession was effectively a public function.

We are likewise persuaded that *Reitman* cannot be relied upon to justify a finding of state action here. Our opinion in *Palmer* notwithstanding, 479 F.2d 153 (6th Cir. 1973), we view *Reitman* as dealing with a state attempt to accomplish indirectly what it was prohibited from doing directly. We cannot ignore the fact that the context of onerous racial discrimination in which the case was set demanded special scrutiny. The injustices of racial discrimination cast a different shadow than that of the case now before us. See Oller v. Bank of America, 342 F. Supp. 21, 23 (N.D. Cal. 1972).

Our opinion in *Palmer* likewise responded to a different circumstance. There we considered the policies of a company with monopolistic character whose business was to provide a necessity of life and whose activities and operations were pervasively and significantly regulated by governmental and quasi-governmental regulations and statutes. We therefore conclude that the state thereby achieved a position of joint participation with the company. Id. at 165. See also Burton v. Wilmington Parking Authority, supra, at 726.

Appellant makes the principal point that the private activity before us should be viewed as encouraged by the statute and therefore a finding of state action is justified. While acknowledging that the point has a measure of merit, we do not find it persuasive.

It is clear that in this case the state did not exert any control or compulsion over the creditor's decision to repossess. The private activity was not commanded by the simply permissive statute. While mere existence of the statute might seem to suggest encouragement, we conclude that the effect of the statute is only to reduce a creditor's risk in making repossessions. As a practical matter, a creditor's decision is more likely to be principally influenced by the economics of the situation than by the presence of a permissive statute.

We fail to see where the creditor has sought to invoke any state machinery to its aid. Rather, the creditor has simply relied upon the terms of its security agreement pursuant to the private right of contract. Compare Shelley v. Kraemer, 334 U.S. 1 (1948). Assuming that the statute was non-existent, the remedy of self-help repossession could still be utilized based on its common law heritage and the private right to contract. We fail to see how the creditor is attempting to enforce any right in reliance upon a constitutional or statutory provision as in *Reitman* or is even asserting any state created right. Rather, we see a creditor privately effectuating a right which was created in advance by contract between the parties. At best, the right is one that is merely codified, but not created in the statute.

Appellant also argues that the statute authorizes an individual to perform the governmental function of seizing private property. As stated previously, the statute merely codified and did not create any right or state power. Were we to rely upon the mere fact of codification, we would in part be making available to a complex matrix of human behavior, as regulated by statutes, the scope of federal remedies. We decline to establish that precedent, particularly under the circumstance of a statute that is permissive in nature.

The decision of the district court is affirmed.

NOTE

This court's conclusion that *Fuentes* was overruled by *Mitchell* proved incorrect. See North Georgia Finishing, Inc. v. Di-Chem, Inc., 419 U.S. 601 (1975), declaring unconstitutional a Georgia statute providing for repossession on order of a court clerk with no provision for an early hearing. These constitutional attacks on §§9-503 and 9-504 have died out since the Supreme Court, in Flagg Bros., Inc. v. Brooks, 436 U.S. 149 (1978), held that §7-210 of the UCC, permitting an unpaid warehouseman to enforce the warehouseman's lien by selling the stored goods without a court proceeding, was not unconstitutional because the mere enactment of §7-210 was not sufficient "state action" to involve the government in the enforcement of the lien.

CHAPTER 10
BULK TRANSFERS

A. *INTRODUCTION*

PROBLEM 109

Because she loved birds and animals, Sacajawea decided to open a pet shop. She borrowed $20,000 from her good friend Meriwether Lewis (who, because he had no business experience in this field — he was a tour guide — failed to get a security interest in the store's inventory or equipment). Sacajawea operated the store for a year and managed to pay back only $1,750 of the money she had borrowed. When business fell off, she decided to sell out and move to Canada. At first no one wanted to buy the store's assets (she leased the space in the building), but eventually a Mr. Clark offered her $3,000, and she agreed. Without telling Lewis, she sold the store to Clark for that amount and promptly moved to Canada. Assume there is no bulk sales law in the UCC. May Lewis recover the goods from Clark? Read §§2-403(1), and 9-301(1)(c); White & Summers §19-1.

There may be a remedy for Lewis in the above problem in the law of fraudulent conveyances. If Clark did not pay a *fair consideration* for the business or if he had an actual intent to hinder, delay, or defraud Sacajawea's creditors, the injured creditors of the transferor may have the conveyance set aside or simply ignore it and levy on the goods as if they still belonged to Sacajawea. See the Uniform Fraudulent Conveyance Act, particularly sections 4, 7, and 9.

Proving lack of fair consideration and/or intent to defraud may be an impossible legal task and so the Code drafters included in the UCC a uniform *bulk transfers* statute (Article 6), to aid the transferor's creditors in protecting their interests whenever a sale is made of an existing business. As the Official Comment to §6-101 states, the central purpose of a bulk sales law is to deal with two common forms of commercial fraud:

> (a) The merchant, owing debts, who sells out his stock in trade to a friend for less than it is worth, pays his creditors less than he owes them, and hopes to come back into the business through the back door some time in the future.
> (b) The merchant, owing debts, who sells out his stock in trade to any one for any price, pockets the proceeds, and disappears leaving his creditors unpaid.

PROBLEM 110

What is a *bulk transfer?* Read §§6-102 and 6-103, and decide if Article 6 applies to the following transactions.

(a) The Little Toot Towing Service had a fleet of 12 tow trucks. The owner sold them all to a buyer but no compliance was had with Article 6. Is the buyer's attorney arguably guilty of malpractice? See §6-102 and its Official Comment; All Nite Garage, Inc. v. AAA Towing, Inc., 452 P.2d 902, 6 U.C.C. Rep. Serv. 529 (Nev. 1969).

(b) As part of a renovation program, Newman-Money, a large department store, sold *all* of the existing furnishings (display cases, wall decorations, furniture, counters, etc.) to another department store. Newman-Money then bought all new furnishings and continued its operation as before. Was the sale a *bulk transfer?*

(c) Joe Bartender, the owner of Bartender's Bar & Restaurant, comes to you for advice. He's getting ready to sell the business and retire. Should the sale comply with all the red tape Article 6 brings up? See Official Comment 2 to §6-102; cf. §2-314(1) (second sentence); compare De La Rosa v. Tropical Sandwiches, Inc., 298 So. 2d 471, 15 U.C.C. Rep. Serv. 595 (Fla. App. 1974), and Kane-Miller Corp. v. Tip Tree Corp., 303 N.Y.S.2d 273, 6 U.C.C. Rep. Serv. 721 (Sup. Ct. 1969) with Zinni v. One Township Line Corp., 36 Pa. D.&C.2d 297, 3 U.C.C. Rep. Serv. 305 (1965); Silver, Bulk Sales and the Sale of Restaurants Under UCC §6-102, 80 Com. L.J. 520 (1975).

(d) In September, Super Shoes Unlimited (a shoe store) sold 90% of its inventory at a very low price to another shoe store. The owner of Super Shoes Unlimited asks you if he needs to comply with Article 6, pointing out that the shoes sold were all summer shoes and *every* September he makes a similar disposal of unsold summer wares. Is this a sale "in the ordinary course of the transferor's business"? See §6-102(1); White & Summers §19-2, at 761; Danning v. Daylin, Inc., 488 F.2d 185, 13 U.C.C. Rep. Serv. 691 (9th Cir. 1973).

(e) Cornucopia Grocery decided to reduce the size of its operation, and sold 45% of its stock in trade to a competitor across town. Is this a *bulk transfer?* See §6-102(1); In re Albany Brick Co., 12 U.C.C. Rep. Serv. 165 (Ref. Bankr. M.D. Ga. 1972); In re Shirts "N" Slax, Inc., 4 U.C.C. Rep. Serv. 873 (Ref. Bankr. E.D. Pa. 1967) (both holding that *major part* means more than 50%). If Cornucopia Grocery sold all its inventory at this one store but kept all of its inventory at its other eight stores throughout the state, has it sold a *major part* of an *enterprise,* §6-102(4), White & Summers §19-2, and the *Albany Brick* case, supra. If Cornucopia Grocery gives Octopus National Bank an Article 9 security interest in the inventory in return for a loan, has a *bulk transfer* occurred? See §§6-103(1), 9-111. If the grocery misses a payment and the bank repossesses the inventory, is the repossession a *bulk transfer?* See §6-103(3). If Cornucopia Grocery switches from a sole proprietorship to a corporate form is that a *bulk transfer?* See §6-103(7).

(f) John Strauss ran a music store, and it was on the brink of financial disaster. Without telling his creditors he contracted to sell the business to the Vienna Woods Music Corporation, a well-known and highly successful nationwide chain, which had its headquarters in this state. Vienna Woods assumed the debts of the Strauss store and, on the date of sale, spent much money on an extensive radio advertising campaign designed to alert the general public to the switch in ownership. Does Article 6 apply? See §6-103(6) and the final sentence in §6-103; see also Official Comment 2 to that section.

B. COMPLIANCE PROCEDURE

Article 6's solution to the problem of protecting the transferor's creditors when a bulk sale occurs is to give them advance notice of the sale. If they object they can take appropriate action (threats of lawsuits, involuntary bankruptcy, injunctions, private negotiations, etc.). The first step Article 6 requires is the drawing up of a schedule of creditors (the seller's duty), and a schedule of the property involved (a duty of both the seller and the buyer). Read §6-104 carefully.

PROBLEM 111

When Big Chain Drug Stores, Inc. (hereinafter BCDS) bought out the small drug store owned by Dr. Peter Pestle, he told them that he had no creditors. Everyone, he said, had been paid in full. BCDS comes to you. They have no reason to doubt Dr. Pestle's word, but it does seem unlikely that he has *no* creditors. Does §6-104 require them to investigate his statement?

Adrian Tabin Corp. v. Climax Boutique, Inc.

34 N.Y.2d 210, 356 N.Y.S.2d 606, 313 N.E.2d 66, 14 U.C.C. Rep. Serv. 1196, 67 A.L.R.3d 1045 (N.Y. 1974)

JANSEN, J. The Plaintiff, Adrian Tabin Corporation, is a creditor of the defendant L.D.J. Dress, Inc., a New York corporation engaged in the retail sale of dresses. L.D.J. (transferor) sold its business in bulk to one Paul Warman, who in turn resold to defendant Climax Boutique, Inc. (transferee), in which he is a principal. At the closing, the transferor furnished a bill of sale, containing a schedule of the property transferred, together with an affidavit averring that the business was "free and clear of any and all liens, mortgages, security interests, levies, debts, taxes or other claims" and "that the Transferor is not indebted to anyone and has no creditors." In addition, before consummation of the sale, the transferee's attorney made a lien search which disclosed no liens, and inquired of the transferor's attorney as to creditors and was assured that there were none.

Upon learning of the sale, the plaintiff brought an action to have it declared ineffective because the transferee had failed to give notice to it as a creditor, as required by §6-105 of the Uniform Commercial Code. The trial court voided the sale holding that the transferee had a duty to inquire carefully as to the existence of creditors, intimating that a review of the seller's books and questioning of the transferor as to the source of the merchandise was required. Lacking such an inquiry, the court held that sale was ineffective. The Appellate Division, by a divided court, reversed, holding that under the Uniform Commercial Code a transferee of a bulk sale who lacks knowledge of creditors of his transferor may rely on an affidavit of no creditors and need not make a careful inquiry. The court was further of the view that, even if the careful inquiry requirement of the former law (Personal Law, §44) were superimposed on the Uniform Commercial Code, the transferee's actions were in sufficient compliance.

We affirm and hold that the transferee of a bulk sale who has no knowledge of creditors of the transferor may rely on an affidavit of no creditors furnished by the transferor and that the Uniform Commercial Code imposes no duty of careful inquiry as existed under former law.

The language of §6-104 is simple and unambiguous. In pertinent part, subdivision (1) provides that a bulk transfer is ineffective as against creditors of the transferor unless the transferee requires the transferor to furnish a list of creditors and the transferee preserves the list for six months and allows reasonable inspection thereof. Subdivision (3) places upon the transferor the responsibility for the accuracy and completeness of the list and provides that the transfer is not ineffective because of errors or omissions in the list unless the transferee had knowledge. "Knowledge," as carefully defined by the code draftsmen, means actual knowledge (Uniform Commercial Code, §1-201, subd [5]), not constructive knowledge. And as the official comment to subdivision (3) above makes clear, the sanction for the accuracy of the list of creditors is the false swearing statute of the State.

Concededly, cases interpreting the pre-Uniform Commercial Code New York Bulk Sales Act (former Personal Property Law, §44) stand for the proposition that before a transferee may rely on an affidavit of no creditors, he must make careful inquiry and otherwise have no knowledge of such creditors of the transferor. (Klein v. Schwartz, 128 N.Y.S.2d 177, Willner Butter & Egg Corp. v. Roth, 192 Misc. 970; Carl Ahlers, Inc. v. Dingott, 173 Misc. 873; Marcus v. Knitzer, 168 Misc. 9; Heilmann v. Powelson, 101 Misc. 230.) But on the face of §6-104 of the Uniform Commercial Code, there is no requirement of careful inquiry. Notwithstanding the commentary accompanying §6-104(3) that it is declarative of precode New York law (see McKinney's Cons. Laws of N.Y., Book $62\frac{1}{2}$, Uniform Commercial Code, §6-104, p. 735), in our view, the judicial gloss on the former law has not been carried over. As the report of the New York Law Revision Commission more accurately states, subdivision (3) of §6-104 is merely in "general accord" with precode law. (1955 Report of N.Y. Law Rev. Comm. [Study of the Uniform Commercial Code], p. 1747.) Although at first reading this provision may seem harsh on the transferor's creditors, a requirement of careful inquiry might, on the other hand, tend to restrain the free alienation of property. Hence, it is in this situation that the code protects the innocent transferee because "the desirability of allowing transfers to go forward outweighs the value of protecting the omitted creditor." (Hogan, The Highways and Some of the Byways in the Sales and Bulk Sales Articles of the Uniform Commercial Code, 48 Cornell L.Q., 1, 37.)

Although the Supreme Court of New Jersey has not yet passed upon the precise issue before us, we note two decisions from the intermediate appellate court of that State in accord with this analysis. In Federal Ins. Co. v. Pipeco Steel Corp. (125 N.J. Super. 563), the defendant imported three shipments of steel from Japan, each of which was subject to import duty. Federal Insurance Co. furnished bonds in favor of the United States to secure payment of the same. Ultimately, Federal was compelled to pay on the bonds. Thereafter, Pipeco made a bulk transfer omitting Federal and the United States from the list of creditors furnished to the transferee. Federal then brought an action against the transferor and the transferee seeking to recover the sums paid to the United States and alleging that the bulk sale was ineffective as to it because notice of the transfer had not been given as required by the bulk sale provisions of the New Jersey Commercial Code. (N.J.S.A. 12A:6-105). There was nothing in the record to suggest that the transferee had actual knowledge of the claim of the United States or Federal. The trial court agreed that the bulk sale was ineffective for failure to give notice and granted summary judgment for Federal. On appeal, it was urged that since Pipeco was party engaged in importing, the transferee had *constructive* knowledge that an import duty might be owing to the United States and should have inquired into that possibility. The appellate court disagreed and reversed, stating: "The statute does not render a transfer ineffective unless the transferee is shown to have had knowledge that the list of creditors was incomplete. This statutory language does not embrace the concept of constructive notice or constructive knowledge. Actual knowledge is required." (125 N.J. Super. 563.) (Accord, Silco Automatic Vending Co. v. Howells, 102 N.J. Super. 243, *aff'd* 105 N.J. Super. 511; Hansell,

Bulk Transfers Under Article 6 of the Iowa Uniform Commercial Code, 19 Drake L. Rev. 275, 284; Shkolnick, The Nebraska Uniform Commercial Code: Article 6 — Bulk Transfers, 43 Neb. L. Rev. 760, 766; White & Summers, Handbook of the Law Under The Uniform Commercial Code, §19-3, pp. 650, 651.)

This is not to say, however, that the omitted creditor is entirely without remedy. The Uniform Fraudulent Conveyance Act (Debtor and Creditor Law, §270 et seq.) was not repealed by the enactment of the Uniform Commercial Code. Under section 276 of that law, if a transferee knowingly participates in a conveyance made with actual intent to "hinder, delay, or defraud . . . present and future creditors" of the transferor, the goods may be recovered from the transferee by the transferor's creditors *notwithstanding literal compliance with the bulk transfer provisions of the Uniform Commercial Code.* (See, generally, Hawkland, Remedies of Bulk Transfer Creditors Where There Has Been Compliance with Article 6, 74 Commercial L.J. 257; 1 Glen, Fraudulent Conveyances and Preferences, §313.) Also, section 60 of the Bankruptcy Act (U.S. Code, tit. 11, §96) proscribing preferential transfers may apply in a given context. Conceivably, a preferential transfer could occur in a bulk sale triggering the filing of a petition for involuntary bankruptcy against the transferor. Upon adjudication of the transferor as a bankrupt, the transferee could be required to turn the property over to the trustee if, at the time of the conveyance, the transferee had reasonable cause to believe the transferor was insolvent.

Optional §6-106 of the official text of the Uniform Commercial Code, not yet adopted in New York and to which legislative attention is invited, provides additional protection for the omitted creditor. This section obligates the transferee to apply the proceeds of the transfer to the debts of the transferor. In practical effect, optional §6-106 Provides an additional 30 days, from the date when the notice to creditors (Uniform Commercial Code, §§6-105, 6-107) would ordinarily be given, for unlisted or omitted creditors to assert their claims. (See Hawkland, Remedies of Bulk Transfer Creditors Where There Has Been Compliance with Article 6, 74 Commercial L.J. 257, 262.) Adoption of this expedient provision would go far toward furnishing additional protection for the simple, unsecured creditor.

We recognize, as so ably stated in the dissenting opinion, that strong reasons grounded in public policy and in the equities of the situation can be raised as a basis for imposing a duty of careful inquiry upon the transferee of a bulk sale. Nevertheless, it is our view that the simple and unambiguous language of §6-104 and the precise and careful definition of knowledge as used in the Code (§1-201, subd [25]) preclude such a construction.

For the reasons stated, the order of the Appellate Division should be affirmed, with costs.

GABRIELLI, J. (dissenting). [The larger part of this dissenting opinion, joined in by one other judge, is omitted.] We are disposed to conclude that despite the inclusion of subdivision (3) of §6-104 in the New York statute the pre-existing case law regarding the duty of the buyer to investigate the seller's creditors persists. If such a case law rule is not superimposed on subdivision (3) the whole purpose of article 6 is subverted. Thus, responsibility for the accuracy of the list of creditors rests on the seller unless the buyer has actual knowledge which must be arrived at through reasonable investigation, i.e., at the very least an inspection of the seller's books together with a search for liens. In other words, the part of subdivision (3) which preserves the creditor's rights if the buyer has knowledge subsumes that the buyer has acted to acquire that knowledge. We are aided in this analysis by three factors. First, the New York Annotations state that subdivision (3) of §6-104, although new to the statute, is "but declaratory of the New York law," citing those cases which imposed the investigatory duty on the buyer. Second, an absurdity would be formulated into legal doctrine were it to be held that, as in this case, a buyer would not actually know (even without investigating) that a going mercantile establishment would have to have at least some current creditors. Third, as before stated, a decision to allow the seller to have the final word as to whether or not there are any creditors and if there are, their identities, would frustrate the express purpose of the article. His responsibility extends to furnishing a list. The buyer must verify that list through his own investigation so as to give him a basis for the acquisition of actual knowledge.

We emphasize that adherence to the position and concept adopted by the majority will permit a buyer to be entirely free of any liability despite even his own reckless disregard of the natural consequences of his failure or refusal to make any inquiry of the libability status of the business being purchased — all to the damage and loss of innocent creditors of the seller. Such a concept — permitting a buyer to completely ignore the realities of the business world and, further, to cavalierly brush aside any inquiry as to the status of the seller's business debts — destroys one of the prime aims of article 6, to wit, to safeguard creditors.

We would not rest our view for reversal, as we might, on the ground that an affidavit of no creditors is not a list contemplated under §6-104. (See the Commentary of Donald J. Rapson, McKinney's Cons. Laws of N.Y., Book 62½, Uniform Commercial Code, §6-101 p. 711.) To do this would be to postpone the inevitable question of the construction to be given subdivision (3) of §6-104 when a list is furnished which turns out to be incomplete. The proper ruling is and should be that either where a list is furnished, or where an affidavit of no creditors is furnished, the buyer must investigate, and that a reckless disregard of what might be uncovered by an investigation is tantamount to knowledge within the meaning of the statute. This is not a substitute of contructive knowledge for actual knowledge, but a recognition that willful or reckless avoidance of knowledge should be and is the equivalent of knowledge. . . .

NOTE

For critical commentaries on this case see Note, 55 B.U.L. Rev. 288 (1975), and Note, 52 N.C.L. Rev. 165 (1973).

Darby v. Ewing's Home Furnishings

278 F. Supp. 917, 5 U.C.C. Rep. Serv. 198 (W.D. Okla. 1967)

Eubanks, J. The complaint in this case alleges that plaintiff is a trustee in Bankruptcy of Trend House Furniture, Inc. It is further alleged that on or about the 5th day of December, 1966 the bankrupt transferred certain properties to the defendant in violation of the bulk transfer sections of the Oklahoma Statutes. It is specifically alleged that the transfer by the bankrupt to defendant was made without compliance with the "bulk transfer" provisions of the Oklahoma Statutes, specifically Title 12A Sections 6-104 to 6-107 of the Oklahoma Statutes, in that transferee defendant did not require the transferor bankrupt to furnish a list of his existing creditors before the sale was consummated and that transferee defendant failed to give notice to the creditors of transferor. The complaint alleges other grounds as the basis for its claim that the transfer was invalid including the claim that the transfer was made without adequate consideration and that same was made within one year prior to the filing of the petition in bankruptcy. Plaintiff seeks by this action to recover a money judgment against the defendant in the amount of $13,052.50 which is alleged to be the value of the merchandise transferred to defendant on the date of the transfer.

Defendant has filed motion to dismiss and motion for summary judgment wherein by attached affidavit, it is generally alleged that the stock of merchandise purchased by defendant from the bankrupt had a factory invoice cost of $11,270.30 and that defendant's transactions with the bankrupt was accomplished after bona fide negotiations and at an "arms-length" deal. The affidavit further states that the purchase price represented at least 70 to 75 cents on the dollar of the wholesale invoice cost which was more than a fair price considering that the defendant acquired the entire lot to be purchased including damaged merchandise, discontinued styles, odds and ends, and other items which were valued substantially less than the 70 to 75 cents of original cost which defendant paid to the transferee. Defendant makes the contention since, as shown by affidavit, a fair consideration was paid for the goods and since the plaintiff does not seek to re-claim the property or to avoid the transfer but is seeking a money judgment the plaintiff cannot prevail against the defendant who is a good faith purchaser for fair consideration. In support of this contention defendant cites Rogers' Milling Co. v. Goff, Gamble & Wright Co., 46 Okl. 339, 148 P. 1029; Johnson v. Stromon Motor Supply Co., 182 Okl. 126, 76 P.2d 373, and Whipps, Inc. v. Kling Bros. & Co., 191 Okl. 163, 127 P.2d 166. These cases hold generally to the effect that under the Oklahoma bulk sales law a plaintiff must enforce his remedy by attachment or garnishment and cannot recover individually against the vendee.

The foregoing was undoubtedly the law in Oklahoma prior to its adoption of the Uniform Commercial Code, but it is my opinion that this law was changed when, in 1961, the Oklahoma Legislature adopted the Uniform Commercial Code which became effective at midnight on December 31, 1962. Pertinent provisions of the Uniform Commercial Code now in effect in Oklahoma are:

Section 6-104 which provides in part that

> Except as provided with respect to auction sales (Section 6-108), a bulk transfer subject to this Article is ineffective against any creditor of the transferor unless: [a] The transferee requires the

> transferor to furnish a list of his existing creditors prepared as stated in this section; and [b] the parties prepare a schedule of the property transfered sufficient to identify it. . . .

Section 6-106 provides that in addition to the requirements of §6-104 and §6-105:

> (1) Upon every bulk transfer subject to this Article for which new consideration becomes payable except those made by sale at auction it is the duty of the transferee to assure that such consideration is applied so far as necessary to pay those debts of the transferor which are either shown on the list furnished by the transferor (Section 6-104) or filed in writing in the place stated in the notice (Section 6-107) within thirty days after the mailing of such notice. This duty of the transferee runs to all the holders of such debts, and may be enforced by any of them for the benefit of all.
>
> (2) If any of said debts are in dispute the necessary sum may be withheld from distribution until the dispute is settled or adjudicated.
>
> (3) If the consideration payable is not enough to pay all of the said debts in full distribution shall be made pro rata.

The 1964 edition of "Forms and Procedures Under the Uniform Commercial Code," by William F. Willier, Professor of Law, Boston College Law School, and Frederick M. Hart, Professor of Law, Boston College Law School, says in Section 61.03

> Even when Article 6 applies, the Code does not make the transfer illegal or automatically void because the parties have failed to act in accord with the provisions of the Article, and, except in those states which have adopted the optional Section 6-106, no personal liability attaches to the transferee for want of compliance. Since the results flowing from noncompliance are limited, and evaluation of the risks involved in not following the required procedure of Article 6 may be worthwhile in those situations where an otherwise profitable transaction would be rendered impractical by the delays and paper work required by Article 6. For example, the necessity of waiting ten days after giving notice of the sale before taking possession might interfere with the transferee's plans for a quick resale. If the transferee has complete confidence in the solvency of the transferor and his willingness to pay creditors, he may be satisfied that compliance is unnecessary. However, this decision should be made *cautiously as the mere failure to follow the requirements*

of Article 6 opens even an honest transfer to attack and may, where Section 6-106 has been enacted, impose personal liability on the transferee." [Italics mine — ed.]

In Section 66.02 the authors state:

> Section 6-106, makes the transferee personally liable to holders of debts owed by the transferor if there is a failure to comply with this provision. A limited degree of protection is afforded the transferee by Section 6-109 which gives the transferee credit for sums paid to creditors in good faith even though these payments were not correctly made.

From the foregoing it is abundantly clear that a "Bulk Sales" transferee who fails to comply with the sections of the Uniform Commercial Code above cited renders himself personally liable to creditors of transferor for the value of the property purchased or the amount he paid therefor.

I am of the further opinion that the suit in this case is properly brought by the Trustee.

Since defendant makes no contention of compliance with the cited provisions of the Uniform Commercial Code but only contends that he paid a fair consideration for the goods at an "arms-length" transaction, the motion for summary judgment and motion to dismiss are without merit and accordingly are overruled. Defendant will have fifteen days from the date hereof in which to answer.

Is it wise for a state legislature to adopt §6-106? In jurisdictions in which §6-106 was omitted from Article 6, is it ever wise for a seller and buyer to ignore the bulk sales laws and the red tape involved and simply let sleeping creditors lie? What risks are run? Read §6-111.

Bill Voorhees Co., Inc. v. R & S Camper Sales of Birmingham, Inc.

605 F.2d 888, 27 U.C.C. Rep. Serv. 789 (5th Cir. 1979)

Fay, J. This diversity action concerns the personal liability of a transferee under the Alabama enactment of article 6 of the Uniform Commercial Code, the Alabama Bulk Transfers Act,

Ala. Code tit. 7, §§6-101 to -111 (1975). The district court held that a transferee who fails to give notice to creditors as required under §6-105 is not personally liable to the transferor's unpaid and unnotified creditors for the value of transfer property no longer held by the transferee. From this judgment, the plaintiff-creditor appeals. We affirm.

R & S Camper Sales of Birmingham, Inc. (the Birmingham corporation) and R & S Camper Sales, Inc. (the Huntsville corporation) are separate entities. In oral argument, counsel for appellee stated that after problems arose within the original R & S corporation, the Birmingham group split off from the Huntsville corporation. The corporations share the same officers and directors, though they serve in different capacities.

Bill Voorhees Company, Inc. (Voorhees), plaintiff-appellant, sold trailers and campers to the Birmingham corporation on unsecured credit. Most of the Birmingham corporation's inventory and equipment, including that sold by Voorhees, constituted collateral under a blanket security agreement covering a debt of over $100,000 with Central Bank of Alabama. In 1976, the bank discovered that the Birmingham corporation had violated its security agreement by failing to forward proceeds to the bank after selling campers. After meeting with the bank's vice-president, the Birmingham corporation agreed to go out of businesss. Without giving notice to creditors or otherwise complying with article 6, the Birmingham corporation transferred all its inventory to the Huntsville corporation. Subsequently Huntsville sold all but eight units of the inventory to third parties at prices that approximated market value, deducted a ten percent commission, and directly paid off the bank's secured claim. Appellant does not contest the bank's superior right to this $100,000. The Huntsville corporation, however, also realized an additional $36,000 from the sales, which it turned over to the Birmingham corporation. The Birmingham corporation paid other creditors with the $36,000, leaving appellant Voorhees' claim unsatisfied. Voorhees sued, alleging violations of the Bulk Transfer Act.[1] The district court held that the Birmingham corporation owed Voorhees $31,158.40, that the

1. The district court did not find a fraudulent conveyance, and appellant did not allege one occurred in its complaint. This is not a case in which a corporation is selling its stock at substantially less than its worth nor is it a situation in which the debtor has pocketed all the proceeds and disappeared. See UCC §6-101, comments 2-4. The defendants attempted to consign the inventory but by failing to observe the formalities they conducted a bulk sale without complying with the notice provisions.

bulk sale did not comply with article 6, that Voorhees could levy upon approximately eight items still in the hands of the Huntsville corporation, and that Voorhees could recover property from any third-party purchasers who paid no value or who bought with notice of the noncompliance. Neither party contests these decisions. The district court also held, however, that the Huntsville corporation is not personally liable for the value of the trailers that it has already sold to good faith purchasers.

Appellant Voorhees argues that when a transferor and transferee do not comply with the notice provisions of article 6, the creditor should have recourse against the transferee personally for the value of the dissipated property, in addition to the creditor's right to levy on remaining property.

Under *Erie,* our duty is to determine how the Supreme Court of Alabama would rule on transferee liability. Before turning to what little law exists on the subject, it may be helpful to outline the possible bases for such liability. Theoretically, a money judgment against a transferee when bulk transfer property has been resold might take four forms: the transferee could be liable (1) on the transferor's debt, (2) for conversion, (3) for traceable funds, or (4) for the value of the dissipated property. As to the first possibility, all agree that the transferee's noncompliance with article 6 does not impose liability for the transferor's original debt. E.g., Get It Kwik of America v. First Alabama Bank, Ala App, 361 So 2d 568 (1978); Cornelius v. J & R Motor Supply Corp., 468 SW2d 781 (Ky App 1971). See J. White & R. Summers, Handbook of the Law Under the Uniform Commercial Code 655 (1972). To sue for conversion, a creditor must have a right to possession. E.G., Charles S. Martin Distributing Co. v. Indon Industries, Inc., 134 Ga App 179, 213 SE2d 900 (1975), *revd on other grounds,* 234 Ga 845, 218 SE2d 562 (1975). Voorhees was not a secured creditor and has no claim for possession, so conversion is not at issue here. The third theory can involve two types of traceable funds: the initial purchase price the transferee pays the transferor, or the receipts the transferor collects upon resale of the property to third parties. Here, for the most part, both funds are the same because the Huntsville corporation paid the Birmingham corporation only after resale to consumers. Evidently all monies paid to the Birmingham corporation have been dispensed to other creditors and are not traceable. The ten percent commission the Huntsville corporation retained is, therefore, the only fund that might be recoverable, but the record does not reflect whether these funds are actually traceable and appellant has not pursued this issue on appeal. The final theory for imposing a money judgment is, therefore, Voorhees' only possible theory for recovering a money judgment against the Huntsville corporation. The transferee would have to be held liable for the value of the property which it has resold and for which proceeds are not traceable.

Unfortunately, article 6 does not detail remedies for its breach, and the comments supply little evidence of the drafters' intentions. A noncomplying transfer is "ineffective." UCC §§6-104, -105. The Official Comments only mention actions against the property as possible remedies: levy or appointment of a receiver to take the goods under local procedures. UCC §6-104, comment 2; §6-111, comment 2. Actions against the transferee personally are conspicuous by their absence. The drafters' concern that the sections created a "trap for the unwary" and "unusual obligations" on even a good faith transferee might indicate a desire to limit the drastic remedies of article 6 to in rem actions against the property and proceeds.

Despite the lack of direction from the code, most of the few courts deciding whether to impose money judgments have held transferees liable for the value of dissipated or commingled bulk transfer property. Darby v. Ewings Home Furnishings, 278 F Supp 917 (WD Okl 1967); Moskowitz v. Michaels Artists and Engineering Supplies, Inc., 29 Colo App 44, 477 P2d 465 (1970); Cornelius v. J & R Motor Supply Corp., 468 SW2d 781 (Ky App 1971); Starman v. John Wolfe, Inc., 490 SW2d 377 (Mo App 1973). See Bomanzi of Lexington, Inc. v. Tafel, 415 SW2d 627, 631 (Ky App 1967); National Bank of Royal Oak v. Frydlewicz, 67 Mich App 417, 241 NW2d 471 (1976). See generally Commentary, Article 6: Rights of an Aggrieved Creditor of a Bulk Transferor, 10 BC Indus & Comm L Rev 281 (1969); Annot, 47 ALR3d 1114, 1142 (1973). In essence, the transferee is treated like a trustee who must account for the bulk property or be held accountable for the proceeds of its sale.

Some courts have decided to hold the transferee accountable because of the legislature's adoption of optional section 6-106. E.g., Darby v. Ewings Home Furnishings, 278 F Supp 917 (WD Okl 1967). That section directs the transferee to assure that the bulk sale proceeds are first applied to pay the transferor's debts, but it does not really address this situation, in which the parties totally failed to comply with the Act. It does, however, evidence a legislative intention to treat the transferee like a trustee for some purposes. See UCC §6-101, comment 3.

Section 6-106 was not, however, adopted in Alabama. Prior to Alabama's adoption of the Uniform Commercial Code, transferee held the proceeds of bulk transfers in trust for creditors. 1911 Ala Acts 94, 1949 Ala Acts 447 (repealed 1966). See Roberts v. Norrell, 212 F Supp 897 (ND Ala 1963).[2] A transferee of a fraudulent conveyance held the property in constructive trust and was liable to creditors for the value of disposed property. E.G., First National Bank of Birmingham v. Love, 232 Ala 327, 167 So 703 (1936); Dickinson v. National Bank of Republic, 98 Ala 546, 14 So 550 (1893). This earlier law, however, was repealed with the adoption of the Uniform Commercial Code. Ala Code tit 7, §7-10-103 (1975). We must look, therefore, to more recent Alabama case law on whether money judgments can be imposed on transferees.

Two Alabama court decisions have touched on the issue of money judgments against transferees, although neither expressly decided whether a transferee is liable for the value of dissipated bulk property. In Get It Kwik of America v. First Alabama Bank, Ala App 361 So 2d 568 (1978), the Alabama Court of Civil Appeals considered the three other theories of liability in deciding a bank's right to set off a transferee's bank account against the transferor's debt after a partially noncomplying bulk sale. The court held that a transferee is not liable on the debt, but can be liable to a secured creditor for conversion. Under its definition of "proceeds," it also held that a secured party did not have a security interest in the funds received from sale of the collateral by the transferee. It did not discuss liability under normal tracing rules, which might have governed recovery of the ten percent commission in this case. Whether a transferee was liable under article 6 for the value of property was not at issue in *Get It Kwik;* however, the court did mention the topic:

2. The question of transferee liability also arose under the original Bulk Sales Acts. The original Acts did not expressly impose liability. The uncertainty over whether transferees became receivers of the property led legislatures to enact provisions specifically making transferees trustees. See Settegast v. Second National Bank, 126 Tex 330, 87 SW2d 1070, 1072 (1935). Alabama also enacted a later amendment-imposing trusts on transferees. 1949 Ala Acts 447 (repealed 1966). It is unclear why the 1949 amendment was enacted, but its adoption may indicate that the Alabama legislature believes legislative authority is necessary before trusts are imposed on transferees.

> The court in Darby v. Ewings Home Furnishings, 5 UCC Rep 198, 278 F Supp 917 (DCWD Okl 1967), held that §6-106 of the UCC renders a transferee personally liable to creditors of the transferor for the value of the property purchased or the amount paid if there is a failure to comply with the bulk transfer provisions.
>
> However, §6-106 was not adopted by Alabama and thus has no applicability in the present case. [361 So 2d at 571.]

This statement may be evidence that the Alabama courts would not hold the Huntsville corporation liable.[3]

The second decision is by the Supreme Court of Alabama. In McKesson Robbins v. Bruno's Inc., Ala, 368 So 2d 1 (1979), the supreme court reversed, under Alabama Rule 8, the dismissal of a creditor's complaint against a transferee and another creditor. The court stated the issues as whether the complaint stated a cause of action against the transferee for participating in a scheme to hinder collection of the plaintiff's debt, and whether the creditor had "any action against the transferee" for failing to comply with article 6. On rehearing the court stressed that it was holding that the bulk sales act had been violated, but that a complaint alleging participation "'in a scheme, artifice or device to hinder or delay [a creditor] in the collection of a debt' is more than 'the bare bones of pleading.'" By its failure to grant summary judgment on the article 6 cause of action, the Alabama court did hold that article 6 grants a creditor some rights against a transferee. Just what those rights are, however, and whether those rights might be limited to in rem actions against property held by the creditor, was left unanswered.

We are in the difficult position, therefore, of deciding a state law question when the statute is almost silent, the court decisions are not definitive, and prior remedial law on point has been

3. Analogizing to the *Darby* decision, the Georgia Court of Appeals also held that Georgia's failure to adopt optional §6-106 was evidence of a legislative intent that transferees should not be personally liable. American Express Co. v. Bomar Shoe Co., 125 Ga App 408, 187 SE2d 922 (1972), *affd on rehearing,* 127 Ga App 837, 195 SE2d 479 (1973).

The court, however, was evidently holding that a transferee was not liable on the debt, as opposed to liability for the value of property, because it went on to state that the transferee held the proceeds from resale in trust and could be garnished by the transferor's creditor. For a later decision holding that article 6 does impose obligations on the transferee for breach, see Indon Industries, Inc. v. Charles S. Martin Distributing Co., Inc., 234 Ga 845, 218 SE 2d 562 (1975).

repealed. In addition, the few indications we have of what the drafters' intended and what the courts would decide seem contrary to the trend of decisions in other states. Although normally other Uniform Commercial Code decisions might be given great weight in the interests of uniformity, the remedy sections of article 6 were purposefully left open for nonuniform state provisions. See UCC §6-111, comment 2.

In light of the lack of mention of actions against transferees in the statute, the repeal of pre-existing remedial legislation, the Alabama legislature's failure to adopt §6-106, and the statements of the Alabama court in *Get It Kwik,* we agree with the trial court's *Erie* guess and conclude that under Alabama law transferees are not personally liable for the value of disposed bulk property to a creditor who does not receive notice of the bulk sale.

The decision of the district court is affirmed.

The core creditor-protection device of Article 6 is the advance notice requirement. Read §6-107; as to this latter section, subsection (1) is often said to authorize a *short form* of notice and is used only if the transferee is sure that the transferor will pay off all debts as they fall due; since the transferee is only rarely certain of this, the subsection (2) *long form* of notice seems wiser in most cases.

PROBLEM 112

George McClellan, proprietor of McClellan's Haberdashery, contracted to sell the business to Joseph Hooker. On the day the contract was signed, July 1, Hooker made a 10% downpayment. On July 2, Hooker sent out a proper §6-107 notice to the two creditors (Halleck and Meade) McClellan had listed on the schedule furnished to him. Halleck and Meade both received the notice on July 5; on July 12 Hooker took possession of the business and paid the rest of the purchase price. Answer these questions:

(a) Was the notice timely given? See §6-105; Starman v. John E. Wolfe, Inc., 490 S.W.2d 377, 12 U.C.C. Rep. Serv. 333 (Mo. App. 1973); White & Summers §19-3, at 766.

(b) If McClellan forgot to list a creditor (Burnside), what are the rights of such a creditor? See §6-104(3); Fico, Inc. v. Ghingher, 28 U.C.C. Rep. Serv. 498 (Md. App. 1980).

(c) If the parties do not comply at all with Article 6, and the sale takes place on July 12, 1983, does McClellan's bankruptcy, filed on May 8, 1984, cause any problems for Hooker? See §6-111, §544(b) of the Bankruptcy Code (supra, page 244), and Moore v. Bay, 284 U.S. 4 (1931) (discussed supra, page 243).

(d) If McClellan neglected to pay off the creditors and failed, in breach of his contract with Hooker, to give a proper bulk sales notice, may Hooker avoid (rescind) the sale? See Macy v. Oswald, 198 Pa. Super. 435, 182 A.2d 94, 1 U.C.C. Rep. Serv. 321 (1962), and remember your course on basic contract law.

(e) If Hooker promised McClellan to pay off McClellan's creditors, does this promise excuse McClellan from personal liability to his creditors? See McClain v. Laurens Glass Co., 127 Ga. App. 316, 193 S.E.2d 194, 11 U.C.C. Rep. Serv. 563 (1972).

(f) If prior to Hooker taking over but after the notice is sent McClellan's business orders new goods on credit from the Grant Corporation, is Grant a "creditor" under Article 6? See §6-109.

If a bulk sale is conducted by *auction*, the auctioneer is responsible for seeing that there is compliance with the requirements of Article 6; §6-108.

PROBLEM 113

Ignoring her unpaid creditors and the bulk sales laws, Connie sold her candle shop to Marshall on April 10. Marshall resold one third of the assets to Harold, a bona fide purchaser, and then went bankrupt himself on November 30. Connie's creditors (who were never notified of anything) want the goods back, but Harold and Marshall's bankruptcy trustee resist. Who wins? See §§6-110, 6-111, and 9-301(1)(c); White & Summers §19-6; In re Gruber Indus. Inc., 345 F. Supp. 1076, 11 U.C.C. Rep. Serv. 558 (E.D.N.Y. 1972); cf. Mayfield Dairy Farms, Inc. v. McKenney, 612 S.W.2d 154, 30 U.C.C. Rep. Serv. 1414 (Tenn. 1981).

One final point: the bulk sales laws are designed to protect *unsecured* creditors. While a technical reading of Article 6 might apply it to secured creditors, see Automatic Truck & Trailer Wash Centers, Inc. v. Eastamp, Inc., 320 So. 2d 7, 17 U.C.C. Rep. Serv. 1282 (Fla. App. 1975), only unsecured creditors need its protection: Huguelet v. M & M Assocs., Inc., 375 So. 2d 1150, 27 U.C.C. Rep. Serv. 1091 (Fla. App. 1979); In re Bulk Sale of Clement, 98 Dauph. 55, 18 U.C.C. Rep. Serv. 1280 (Pa. Ct. Com. Pl. 1976).

Article 9, particularly §9-306(2), permits the perfected secured creditor to realize on the collateral even though it is in the hands of a good faith bulk purchaser. However an unperfected secured party would lose to such a transferee per §9-301(1)(c), and a perfected secured party making advances *after* the bulk sale may have problems with §9-307(3).

Table of Cases

Italic type indicates principal cases.

Table of Statutes

Bankruptcy Reform Act of 1978
11 U.S.C. §101

Federal Priority Statute
31 U.S.C. §191

Federal Tax Lien Act of 1972
29 U.S.C. §6321

Uniform Commercial Code

Uniform Consumer Credit Code

INDEX